The Reception of German Literature
in U.S. German Texts, 1864–1918

Cover vignette of Mohonk mountain silhouette
courtesy of the Publications Office, State
University College, New Paltz, New York.

Studies in Modern German Literature

Peter D.G. Brown
General Editor

Vol. 2

PETER LANG
New York • Bern • Frankfurt am Main • Paris

John Hargrove Tatum

The Reception of German Literature in U.S. German Texts, 1864–1918

PETER LANG
New York • Bern • Frankfurt am Main • Paris

Library of Congress Cataloging-in-Publication Data

Tatum, John Hargrove
 The reception of German literature in U.S. German texts, 1864–1918 / John Hargrove Tatum.
  p. cm.—(Studies in modern German literature ; vol. 2)
 Bibliography: p.
  1. German literature—Appreciation—United States. 2. German philology—Study and teaching—United States—History—19th century. 3. German philology—Study and teaching—United States—History—20th century. 4. Textbooks—United States—History—19th century. 5. Textbooks—United States—History—20th century.
 I. Title. II. Series.
 PT63.U6T38 1989
 830'.9—dc19
 ISBN 0-8204-0420-9   88-4908
 ISSN 0888-3904   CIP

CIP-Titelaufnahme der Deutschen Bibliothek

Tatum, John Hargrove:
 The reception of German literature in U.S. German texts, 1864–1918 / John Hargrove Tatum. – New York; Bern; Frankfurt am Main; Paris: 1988.
  (Studies in Modern German Literature; Vol. 2)
  ISBN 0-8204-0420-9

NE: GT

© Peter Lang Publishing, Inc., New York 1988

All rights reserved.
Reprint or reproduction, even partially, in all forms such as microfilm, xerography, microfiche, microcard, offset strictly prohibited.

Printed by Weihert-Druck GmbH, Darmstadt, West Germany

Acknowledgements

For a number of years prior to the publication of this study, it has seemed that a work dealing with German literature in U. S. textbooks would be a valuable contribution to German studies. Consequently, this book seeks to provide insights into the *Germanistik* of an earlier day through an examination of the textbooks of the time. It is hoped that the considerable refinements which the text and appendices of this study have undergone before printing will facilitate their use.

The author is greatly indebted to Dr. Siegfried E. Mews, Dr. Christoph E. Schweitzer, and Dr. Richard H. Lawson for their generous advice, and to Dr. Ben L. Mitchell, Mr. Richard Minor, and Mr. Snider Joe of the Computer Information Systems Program at Delta State University for generating the essential printouts of statistical data. The aid offered by librarians at the Walter Royal Davis Library, Chapel Hill, North Carolina; the National Union Project, The Library of Congress, Washington, D. C.; and the William Beauregard Roberts Library, Delta State University, is likewise acknowledged. Finally, let the encouragement of Dr. O. F. White, Dr. William A. Sullivan, and Dr. Daniel T. McQuagge, but for whose interest the work might still remain unfinished, and the loving support of my wife, Carol, be gratefully recorded.

Contents

I.	Introduction	1
II.	German Texts from the Late Middle Ages through *Sturm und Drang*; Lyrics and Ballads of Goethe and Schiller	13
III.	*Klassik, Romantik, Biedermeier,* and *Junges Deutschland* as Presented in Texts of the Period	37
IV.	Texts from the Eras of Realism—Naturalism—The Early Twentieth Century	99
	Contemporaneity of Texts	99
	Realistic Drama	100
	Realistic Novels, Novellas, and Short Stories	118
	Naturalism—The Early Twentieth Century	166
V.	Conclusion	189

Sources 199

Appendices

A.	Author/Title Correspondence: *New York Times* Reviews and U.S. German Texts	207
B.	German Authors Appearing in U.S. German Texts, Reviewed in Translation, and Listed by Pochmann	209
C.	Authors of High School and College Texts Unrecognized by the *New York Times* or Pochmann	217
D.	Recommendations of the Committee of Twelve	219
E.	Recommendations on German Texts Made Before the MLA in 1917	221
F.	Texts in Chronological Order	223
G.	Texts without Main Author Listings in Chronological Order	375

Index 383

I

Introduction

Perhaps most notable among works which deal with the reception of German literature in the United States are B. Q. Morgan's *German Literature in English Translation, 1481–1927* (second edition, revised and augmented, 1965) and *German Literature in English Translation. Supplement Embracing the Years 1928–1955* (1965), W. LaMarr Kopp's *German Literature in the United States 1945–1960* (1967), Henry A. Pochmann and Arthur R. Schultz's *German Culture in America, 1600–1900: Philosophical and Literary Influences* (1957) and *Bibliography of German Culture in America to 1940* (revised edition 1982), and Arthur R. Schultz's *German-American Relations and German Culture in America: A Subject Bibliography, 1941–1980* (1984). Also among the significant reception studies are those which deal with the reception of German literature in America as exemplified by the *New York Times* and the *New York Herald Tribune*, written by Wolfgang Heinsohn, Alice Carse, Doris Auerbach, and John Gordon, and Ursula Beitter's study of the image of Germans and Germany in first-year American college texts of the 1950s and 1960s.

All these works deal to a greater or lesser extent with literature. Yet none but Beitter's, which touches upon literature only peripherally, concern themselves a great deal with what are probably the greatest purveyors of German literature in the United States: the high schools, colleges and universities. As Volkmar Sander explains,

> Unter den geschmackserhaltenden Kräften sind vor allem zwei Institutionen zu nennen: die amerikanische Germanistik und die Literaturkritik der Tages- und Monatspresse. Die völlige Einflußlosigkeit der amerikanischen (und deutschen) Hochschulgermanistik auf die literarische Aufnahme ist an der Liste der rezipierten Werke abzulesen, die keineswegs dem von der Hochschule akzeptierten und propagierten Kanon entspricht. Erfolgversprechender für die Erhellung der tatsächlichen Rezeption erscheint daher eine Untersuchung der journalistischen Kritik, die das Bild der deutschen Literatur für weite Kreise in Amerika bestimmt. (161)

Thus the insignificance of *Hochschulgermanistik* justifies its neglected state.
However, as if to counter Sander's statement, Manfred Durzak finds that

> Angesichts der Studentenzahlen, die inzwischen fast 60 Prozent der jungen Leute in den jeweiligen Altersgruppen ausmachen, kommt auch dem

akademischen Publikum durchaus beachtliche quantitative Bedeutung zu. In den zahlreichen Textbüchern, die im Literaturunterricht der Universitäten benutzt werden, sind Autoren wie Borchert, Böll, Andersch, Grass, Johnson, Gaiser häufig vertreten und entsprechend bekannt. Brecht, der von Eric Bentley, einem Professor an der Columbia University in New York, jahrelang mit geringem Erfolg propagiert wurde, war an den Universitäten längst ein vielgelesener Autor, bevor die breitere literarische Öffentlichkeit von ihm Notiz zu nehmen begann. (441)

The academic German experience, then, may be viewed as significant and as having much to do with personal and national literary experiences.

However, academic optimism, or, failing that, persistence, would seem to be on the defensive. Beyond the schools stands a segment of the population of the United States which has reached (or has been granted) a stage of demonstrable cultural advancement, inasmuch as it receives German literature through the *New York Times Book Review* and similar sources. Textbooks, meanwhile, as transmitters of German culture—especially through literature—to students of all sorts, have, in the light of what such distinguished commentators as Volkmar Sander have said, been rather disregarded.

Henry Hatfield and Joan Merrick supply another reason for a lack of attention to the schools as primary transmitters of German ideas and ideals:

A major criticism can be levelled against the teaching profession: that it failed, on the whole, to make what might have been its greatest contribution: . . . the interpretation of the German mind to a puzzled nation. This task was left, in large part, to amateurs and journalists. (354)

The textbook, as a product of Germanists, and—if one sides with the critics of *Germanistik* in the schools—therefore flawed, has been the instrument of their failure in their task.

Consequently, a German attack upon editors and publishers is evinced by Ehlert, Hoffacker and Ide, who manifest the trend in Germany today to wed sociology with literature. They descry an inadequacy in textbooks of "alle Voraussetzungen, die avantgardistische moderne Literatur adäquat zu begreifen und damit die Schüler zu bewußten und progressiv aktiven Zeitgenossen zu machen" (101). And Ursula Beitter brings the attack to the United States as she concludes: "As American editors of German textbooks are also part of *Germanistik*, their texts can be subjected to the same criticisms because their books also concentrate heavily on the established literary masters" (10). Accordingly, Beitter's study demonstrates the dependence of those who compile texts containing literature (aimed specifically at the first-year college level) upon a select few among writers, especially Goethe, Schiller, and Heine (99–104).

Questions arise after such statements. Have such conditions always prevailed in U.S. *Germanistik*? Have U.S. students always read primarily the authors whose "classical" works, for all their literary worth, do not create "progressiv aktive Zeitgenossen"—or whatever personality type a given era seeks to develop? And if, or when, students were not reading the classics, what did they read and why?

In order to answer questions such as these, this dissertation concerns itself with New High German texts edited for American high schools, colleges, and universities of the period between 1864, one year from the end of the War Between the States, and 1918, the end of World War I. This period of time is considered a cohesive half-century by John William Tebbel, who utilizes a similar division (1864–1919) in the second volume of *A History of Book Publishing in the United States*. The choice of an era further coincides roughly with the time period of Heinsohn's study.

This approximate half-century may be said to constitute a rise and fall of German studies in the United States, for the regeneration seen by such Germanists as Zeydel (317–18) had not yet come. From modest beginnings, the market for and consumption of German literature in high schools and higher education grew enormously until shortly before the outbreak of hostilities in World War I (as shown in Appendix F). We may assume that at least some of the German texts of the era did introduce and interpret "the German mind" to a large number of citizens of the United States.

As German was the leading foreign language in secondary schools, colleges and universities (Zeydel 318), many of the readers of reviews of German books in the *New York Times* from 1870 to 1918 (the time period of Heinsohn's study), as well as a number of the reviewers themselves, probably studied German. Significantly, a number of authors who appeared in textbooks from 1870 to 1918 were also reviewed in the *New York Times*; and the same works by these authors appeared a number of times in both German texts and *Times* reviews. Scholastic *Germanistik* and the world outside, if not in total harmony (which they were not), were at any rate not always at odds. (Tables supporting this statement are offered in Appendices A and B.)

Methodology

This study offers an examination of that facet of "the German mind" presented to students and teachers by the editors and publishers of literary textbooks in the United States, 1864–1918. Research expanded from a perusal of specific texts published during the period in question and of the advertisements which they contain. Verification and considerable expansion were made possible through the use of trade journals and scholarly bibliographies. The result is a general overview of the texts utilized or offered for sale in this era.

For the statistical portion of research, six catalogs were utilized. The *American Catalogue* and the *United States Catalog*, which recorded what was published in a given year for buyers of books, are similar to *Books in Print* today. The *Library of Congress Catalogue* and the *National Union Catalog* are world-wide listings of books published, primarily for research purposes. However, since only book listings turned in by other libraries to the Library of Congress appear in the *Library of Congress* and *National Union* catalogs, these could fail to list some books which appear in the trade journals. So it is that this study benefits from the "double exposure" of the commercial and scholarly points of view and from catalogs compiled in two different periods of time: the trade journals contemporary with the sale of the texts and the scholarly bibliographies compiled after the fact, showing what was actually sold. *Publishers Weekly* and the *Publishers Trade List Annual*—also trade journals—were consulted occasionally, while reference works such as the *Guide to the Study of U.S. Imprints* (Tanselle) and *The Directory of American Book Publishing* (Kurian) served to verify what was found in the catalogs.

Regarding the particulars of the study, some 458 titles, 189 authors, and 342 editors are dealt with. The publishing companies concerned number thirty-seven. The selection of certain books in German and the exclusion of others are based upon these criteria: (1) The book must be recognizable as a text, wherein such features as introduction, notes, vocabularies, exercises, and price play a significant role; editors and publishers known from other texts or from advertising as issuers of texts were a valuable guide. (2) The text must have been, if not edited, at least published in the United States.

The German-American press and publishers with affiliates outside the United States obviously offer hindrances to this simple plan for selecting a group of texts published in this country relevant to the study of German as a foreign language. It must not be forgotten that the German-language press was a powerful purveyor of the German mind to a multitude of Americans. As Carl Wittke states:

> A history of America's German-language press, from 1732 to the present, involves hundreds of publications, large and small. Some expired after a few issues; a few survived for more than a century. The German press was the most numerous, and in many respects, the best edited and most influential among all the foreign-language organs which served the many immigrant nationalist groups of America's cosmopolitan population. (v)

Yet the quite numerous German-American publications give adequate indications (publisher, title, author, price, lack of introduction, notes and vocabulary) that they are not intended for the English-speaking student of German.

However, the German-American publisher Emil Steiger's Ahn Series is included in this survey as intended for students in English-language schools. Although Steiger is regarded as having published particularly for the German-American market, advertising of the Ahn Series directed at English-language schools warrants his inclusion. Another publisher included by Tebbel in the German-American press, F. W. Christern, was affiliated in some way with Henry Holt. Thus the line cannot be clearly drawn in all cases. As to firms with foreign affiliates, texts from firms such as Macmillan, with a branch in New York and one in London, are counted only if "New York" or some other U.S. city appears on the title page or in the catalog listings.

The search for texts was facilitated by the mode of inquiry outlined above, yet it is nevertheless beyond the scope of this project to deal with all German literature texts issued during the half-century surveyed. Wittke provided rational guidelines in his study of the German-American press: "A complete tabulation of publications, even if it were possible to make one, would have little value. Instead, I have selected a number of catagories for detailed discussion" (v). Accordingly, although research has encompassed a broad spectrum of texts, a final choice was made favoring a group of texts of a type most frequently used, making works of literature easily accessible in their complete or abridged form.

The type of text addressed here is "an edited or emended copy of an original work" (Webster 913). This definition was adapted to include not only texts containing a single play, novella, short (or shortened) novel, but also texts containing several plays or short stories or collections of poetry; however, comprehensive anthologies have not been included. Such a text is approximately sextodecimo-sized, has a hard cloth cover, and usually numbers between 100 and 200 pages, though the extremes run to examples such as a retelling by Ferdinand Khull of *Meier Helmbrecht* (sixteen pages) and an edition of Joseph Viktor von Scheffel's *Ekkehard* (493 pages).

As it is ultimately impossible to attribute all the works to definite categories, there is a subjective factor involved in the criteria for selection. German literature is basically understood to be European literature in the German language, though such anomalies as Carl Schurz's autobiography or Gustav Weil's translation of *Ali Baba and the Forty Thieves* are subsumed into the general category "German" without differentiation. Similarly, literature is defined primarily as works of fiction in prose or verse; secondarily, however, the term literature has also been applied to such genres as autobiography, biography, folk tales, and history. No attempt has been made to weed out what may be regarded as *Trivialliteratur*. While the line was drawn at chrestomathies, travelogues and joke books, attention is nevertheless focused on a great deal of what was edited, printed, and, presumably, read.

Regarding completeness or perfection in the statistical portion of the study, the editor of the *American Catalogue* of 1890 may be cited:

> The editor has to make the usual apologies for the incompleteness of the work. The bibliographical machinery of the 'Publishers' Weekly,' on which this record is based, has been improved from year to year, but with every improvement, defects and omissions become the more noticeable to those charged with the responsibility of the work, and fired with the ideal, never possible of achievement, of bibliographical completeness. (*American Catalogue*, 1890)

If the catalogs upon which research is based are rendered incomplete by self-conscious editors, then some things are likely to be missed; but every effort has been made to compile data which reflects with some degree of certainty which books were available in print.

Dates listed in the appendices (primarily Appendix F) are of various types. Frequently, trade journals offer two dates under a single listing, one of which is the copyright date, the other the date of printing. Or perhaps one date is entered for a work. Whether copyright, edition, new printing (reprint) or advertisement of existing stock is uncertain. Therefore, on the best bibliographical authority, all dates found in trade journals and scholarly bibliographies have been listed. Cross-checking from catalog to catalog, from trade journals to scholarly bibliographies, gave an indication of popularity. As many librarians—including some National Union Project librarians—have stated, the more often a book is listed, the longer, in all likelihood, it was in circulation.

The purpose of the tabular research is, then, to provide a statistical basis for the frequency with which some authors were being read, the frequency with which their works were being issued. This should make evident how a large number of the 189 German authors whose works were edited as texts were received in U.S. senior high schools, colleges and universities by professors (themselves most frequently the editors of texts) and, through their intermediary services, by students. The findings are reported in the chapters which follow and may be seen in tabular form in the appendices.

Statistical Investigations

In view of the significance of the book reviews of the *New York Times* with respect to Americans' attitudes regarding German literature, it is interesting to note the correspondence between *New York Times* reviews and German textbooks of the era under consideration. Appendix A shows either (1) how many books which were, or would become, textbooks between 1864 and 1918 were reviewed (as translations) per year by the *New York Times* or (2) the number of authors read both in the schools and in translation (as indicated by the *New York Times*). Then the percentage of German authors or authors and titles reviewed in the *New York Times* which were also in textbooks is indicated. (An author reviewed several times is counted that number of times; the number of corresponding reviews is divided by the total number of reviews per year.) Only the numbers are shown in Appendix A; authors and titles (when the same) are shown in Appendix B.

It does not seem too daring to assert that the percentages shown represent a considerable part of the number of reviews devoted by the *New York Times* to German literature. In fact, the dearth of literature represented in the reviews causes the seemingly low percentage of correlation between school and public. After all, gardening manuals or visions of the Second Coming—

included in the reviews of translations—are not very adaptable to the study of German life and literature.

Further, the content of the books reviewed varies considerably from year to year, as literature vies with medical books and political tracts for the *Times* reviewers' attention. Moreover, *Unterhaltungsliteratur* is strongly represented. But if the quite varied sources of statistics are sorted somewhat, literature demonstrates a rather healthy correspondence between reviews and texts. Of about 306 book reviews which—in the broadest sense—may be categorized as dealing with literature, some 193 (approximately 63 percent) could be correlated by author or author and title to German textbooks.

However, it should be added that not all the *New York Times* reviews dealt with translations. As in the case of the translated material, the books in German reviewed present a broad spectrum of reading matter, ranging from science to literature. Of particular interest here are Hermann Grimm's *Vorlesungen* (reviewed 1877); C. A. Buchheim, editor, *Balladen und Romanzen* (reviewed 1892); Gerhart Hauptmann, *Elga* (reviewed 1905), *Die Austreibung* (reviewed 1906), *Und Pippa tanzt* (reviewed 1906), *Die Jungfern von Bischofsberg* (reviewed 1907), *Kaiser Karls Geisel* (reviewed 1908), *Griechischer Frühling* (reviewed 1909), *Griselda* (reviewed 1909), *Der Narr in Christo Emanuel Quint* (reviewed 1910); Friedrich von Schiller, *Wilhelm Tell* (reviewed 1905); Hermann Sudermann, *Stein unter Steinen* (reviewed 1906), *Das Blumenboot* (reviewed 1906), *Das hohe Lied* (reviewed 1909), *Der gute Ruf* (reviewed 1913); Gustav Frenssen, *Peter Moors Fahrt nach Südwest* (reviewed 1907); Richard Wagner, *Briefe an Minna Wagner* (reviewed 1908). Works authored or edited by the preceding appeared in textbooks, and some of their works are therefore represented in Appendices F and G. Of the titles listed here, *Balladen und Romanzen*, *Wilhelm Tell* and *Peter Moors Fahrt nach Südwest* were in the schools as texts during the period. As will be discussed later, Hauptmann was not represented in German texts in proportion to his popularity elsewhere.

In Appendix B the authors' works appeared in translations in the United States and also in textbook editions offered by U.S. publishers. The translations were reviewed in the *New York Times*, and the German originals were studied by students of German. When only authors (not particular works) are shared in common, only the author's name appears. Where both author and title correspond, the author's name and the corresponding titles are given. In the latter case, the city, publisher, and the date of the review of the translation (provided by Heinsohn, B. Q. Morgan, or the date of the paper in which the review appeared) and the first and last dates found for textbooks are indicated. In the right column, when they are applicable, appear Pochmann's figures for the number of translations of the works of the most frequently translated German authors between 1865 and 1899. Significantly, some fifty-one authors and numerous works are shared between the *New*

York Times reviews of translations and the list of textbooks published during the same period.

However, it is also requisite to the purpose of this study to learn the names of those authors whose works appear in textbooks and whose works in translation were *not* reviewed by the *New York Times*. Pochmann recognizes a number of these authors among his sixty-two most translated authors, 1865–1899:

Authors	Translations, 1865–1899
Chamisso, Adalbert	12
Fouqué, F. H. K. de LaMotte	55
Gerstäcker, Friedrich	33
Heyse, Paul	34
Kotzebue, A. F. F. von	4
Moser, Gustav von	26
Niebuhr, B. G.	5
Schiller, J. C. F. von	107
Schmid, Christoph	48
Sealsfield, Charles (Karl Postl)	11
Wildermuth, Ottilie	16

Those authors lesser-known today are Gustav von Moser (1825–1903), author of *Situationsschwänke* much enjoyed during his own time (Kummer 527); Christoph Schmid, an author of juvenile literature (Pochmann 347); and Ottilie Wildermuth, whose "kunstlos erzählte Lebenserinnerungen . . . sind von dauerndem Wert"—this last according to Wilhelm Bernhardt, himself a prolific editor of texts (71).

On the other hand, there are those authors who (sometimes suprisingly) were neither the objects of the attention of the *New York Times* nor numbered among Pochmann's sixty-seven most frequently translated authors. Several reasons for this neglect come to mind. First, certain "German" texts were actually German versions of works by foreign authors, or works written in German by foreigners. Second, the authors' period of greatest creativity lay beyond the years 1899 (Pochmann) or 1918 (Heinsohn). Then there are those whose distinction or popularity, albeit considerable, nevertheless did not acquire them a *New York Times* review; fourth come the lesser talents, some once quite popular, all now little known. And there were the authors of juvenile books, which were not directly aimed at adult translators or reviewers, and were thus less likely to be reviewed. Finally, there were authors of literary essays, histories, studies in mythology, geography and education, as well as diverse treatises and tracts of a least some literary value. All these authors are listed in their respective groups in Appendix C.

Evaluative Speculations

Utilizing these qualitative findings, the evaluative phase of this study consists of an attempt to determine why certain authors who presumably exhibited "the German mind" to American students were preferred, or gained and lost in popularity with certain editors, at given points in time. As Carse has pointed out, "What is, in fact, read will shape the image" (291). And that which is read today frequently varies from that which was read yesterday or will be read tomorrow. As Levin Schücking describes this apparently universal law,

> Selbst da . . . wo die Stellung des Künstlers anscheinend nicht bestritten ist, sogar bei einer Erscheinung wie Goethe, erkennt der schärfer Zusehende einen Vorgang ähnlich den Mondphasen, ein beständiges Abnehmen und Zunehmen der Beliebtheit. Man sieht aber auch deutlich, daß, wo die Begeisterung die gleiche ist, sie doch keineswegs den gleichen Seiten an demselben Gengenstand gilt. (9)

Of major interest here are the recommendations of the Committee of Twelve of the Modern Language Association, which appeared in 1898, for literary texts. The committee was formed to investigate the standing of modern languages (specifically, French and German) in U.S. secondary schools and to evaluate and improve upon the "methods of instruction, the training of teachers, and such other questions connected with the teaching of the modern languages in the secondary schools and the colleges" (*Report* 2).

Significant for this study is the fact that seven of the "twelve" were German teachers: Calvin Thomas, Chairman, Professor of Germanic Languages, Columbia University; E. H. Babbitt, Secretary, Instructor in Germanic Languages, Columbia University; H. C. G. Brandt, Professor of German, Hamilton College; W. H. Carruth, Professor of German, University of Kansas; S. W. Cutting, Associate Professor of German, University of Chicago; G. A. Hench, Late Professor of Germanic Languages, University of Michigan; and B. W. Wells, Professor of Modern Languages, University of the South; C. H. Grandgent, listed as Professor of Romance Languages, Harvard University (*Report* 98–99), could have given instruction in German also. All but Professor Hench published literary texts of the type under discussion for German study (by number of titles shown in Appendix F, Wells, ten; Thomas, seven; Carruth, five; Babbitt and Cutting, two each; Brandt and Grandgent, one each).

On the elementary level, the following ideas led to the committee's choice of books. The book must be:

1. Interesting to the young, wholesome, well-written, and not too difficult.
2. Lively, realistic narrative, with plenty of dialogue, is to be preferred. The German *Märchen* is apt to appear dry to American boys and girls.
3. On the other hand, teachers often complain that most of the tales furnished by conspiring editors and publishers are more or less mawkish love tales, and they sigh for vigorous stories of adventure

with the grand passion left out or made little of. This is a demand which future editors may well keep in view.
4. Meanwhile we must remember that the Germans are a more sentimental people than the Americans . . . . (*Report* 63)

Unfortunately, one can only guess at which authors, editors and publishers were written of here. That the committee members' outlook on German literature—at least in U.S. textbooks—was not entirely sanguine need scarcely be pointed out. More interesting is committee member Wells's edition of Elz's *Er ist nicht eifersüchtig*, which could be described accurately as a "mawkish love tale." Further examples of professional paltering are recorded and will be discussed in succeeding chapters; the Committee's recommendations for American students of German may be seen in Appendix D. The predominance of nineteenth-century literature makes itself quite evident here.

For purposes of comparison, a syllabus compiled by Professor Frederick W. J. Heuser in 1917—not from suggestions of a committee but from what was actually taught—is submitted in Appendix E. Heuser taught at Columbia College and was coeditor of a text of Grillparzer's *Ahnfrau* for Henry Holt in 1907. The syllabus and Heuser's accompanying recommendations were read before the Modern Language Association in 1917 and subsequently appeared in the *Modern Language Journal*.

Professor Heuser examined the "announcements" (catalogs) of some thirty "representative colleges" in order to select works typically studied as nineteenth-century German literature in German classes. Incongruently, *Aufklärung* and *Sturm und Drang* are included in the nineteenth century, but this allows Heuser's survey to cover the area inspected seventeen years before by the Committee of Twelve.

In making his findings known, Heuser assumed that the normal first-year college course would follow three to four years of high school preparation—presumably in conformance with the recommendations of the Committee of Twelve. A true comparison of the Heuser findings and the recommendations of the Committee of Twelve is impossible, as the former scheme deals for the most part only in authors, not works. However, only a glance at the two lists suffices to show that little had changed between the prescriptive syllabus of 1900 and the descriptive one of 1917.

A better perspective on what was being read in German classes, and why, can scarcely be desired: editors of textbooks, themselves professors, have judged the texts according to their pedagogical desirability or recorded what teachers and students were using in the classroom. What remains is to examine individual texts at close range.

Yet before proceeding to texts and criticism, let some general considerations concerning this reception study be repeated and expanded. Statistically and evaluatively, this study, as it broadens, seeks to answer: Who were the authors who helped to form students' opinions on Germany and the German people? Which of these authors' works were most influential, that is, dominated the book market? Who were the editors and publishers "who were the prism through which the . . . image was transmitted" (Auerbach 5)? What impression of Germany was offered by prefaces, forewords and introductions? Is "the change in the American cultural and intellectual propensity for German thought, literature, and art" apparent in the transmissions of literature via textbooks (Heinsohn 8)? Finally, according to Ulrich Weisstein: "Übrigens lassen sich auch aus dem Mangel an Rezeptivität . . . soziologisch—und indirekt—literarisch wichtige Schlüsse ziehen" (104).

All this may be said to represent an attempt at *Literatursoziologie* (Weisstein 104), which takes into account the author, the editor, the reader, and the circumstances prevailing at a given time, and poses questions which are answered primarily by reasoning from the observation of the statistical data, and of the texts themselves—their contents, the literature and the critical material. Most importantly, answers are confirmed and strengthened whenever possible by citations from contemporary literary histories whose authors were themselves frequently editors of texts or whose works appeared in texts. Among literary historians consulted might be mentioned such eminent college professors of the era as Calvin Thomas, George Madison Priest, and Benjamin W. Wells, all of whom edited texts; not to be forgotten is that indefatigable high-school teacher Wilhelm Bernhart, who probably edited more U.S. German texts than any other teacher of his day. Authors of literary histories whose literary works were used as texts included August Friedrich Christian Vilmar, whose *Die Nibelungen* was first presented to U.S. students in the later eighties, and Heinrich Kurz, whose critical essays on *Reineke Fuchs*, Wieland's *Oberon* and Lessing's *Minna von Barnhelm* were texts of the nineties. Journals and other periodicals, either current to the time period or dating from the post-World War I era, have also been consulted. With the exception of the pages devoted to the lyric poetry and ballads of Goethe and Schiller, which have been placed together near the end of chapter 2, chapters are loosely arranged in chronological order (based upon the Frenzels' *Daten deutscher Dichtung*), corresponding to generally accepted periods or movements of literary history.

The most important feature of this study is that it opens up the *Germanistik* of the nineteenth and early twentieth centuries as it saw itself and as it viewed German literature of earlier centuries; in this way the image of Germany as transmitted by edited literary texts used in high schools, colleges, and universities may be ascertained. In the process, access is provided to materials hitherto never collected in any systematic fashion.

Because differences in orthography between today's standard German and that of the era under study are quite frequent, it has seemed undesirable to acknowledge each variation with *sic*, though the more striking dissimilarities have been so indicated.

II

German Texts From the Late Middle Ages Through *Sturm und Drang*; Lyrics and Ballads of Goethe and Schiller

Statistics show that the first major cluster of authors of texts occurs in the era of *Sturm und Drang*. Yet there are major figures, albeit somewhat isolated, who precede this first major group. The literary periods involved are the late Middle Ages, the Reformation, *Spätbarock*, *Aufklärung* and *Empfindsamkeit*. Certainly, although professors probably looked upon most of these texts as "classics," a number of them are relatively vapid and did not inspire significant critical commentary.

As the earliest text from the historical point of view (not the earliest text published in the time period under examination) is a critical essay by the literary historian Heinrich Kurz (1805–1883) on the fable of *Reineke Fuchs*, with extracts from the Low German *Reinke de Vos* (1498) derived from the work of Heinrich von Alkmar, (1480), a brief overview of the animal fables utilized as German texts offers a point of departure. Published in 1895 by American Book Company, Kurz's *Reineke*, edited by Arnold Werner-Spanhoofd, credibly offered an interesting and informative preparation for the animal fables of the foremost Enlightenment figure, Lessing, and, to a lesser degree, for the more anthropocentric fables of Gellert, composed in the spirit of *Empfindsamkeit*. A collection of their fables had been published in 1887, while some of Lessing's fables were also published in a volume of his selected works in 1888. The latter volume, listed until 1893, was apparently the more popular of the two. (The texts appear in Appendix F under the years cited.)

The fables of a more prominent forerunner, Luther, had already appeared in a text before 1864 and probably received a new academic impetus in 1899 in W. H. Carruth's *Luther: Auswahl aus deutschen Schriften*. A probable selection from the fables is *Vom Raben und Fuchse*, a metaphor which connects Luther's fables with the figure of *Reineke* (Frenzel and Frenzel 1:83). As Lessing also wrote a fox fable, Alkmar's *Reinke*—or Kurz's essay—seems all the more likely to have facilitated the teaching of German *Fabeldichtung* in the U.S. Goethe's own *Reineke*, (discussed in chapter 3) though it belongs to a later period, should be mentioned here as the culmination of Alkmar's influence upon succeeding generations.

But the degree of influence of German fables upon U.S. *Germanistik*, though it must be regarded from two points of view, was not excessive. On the one hand, as will become increasingly clear as the results of this study are presented, German textbooks were to drill students in use of the language, communicate cultural information, and present wholesome situations from which moral lessons might be derived. What more suitable medium than the fable? As Heinrich Kurz himself suggested in his *Geschichte der deutschen Literatur*, in addressing himself to Gellert,

> Es ließe sich aus seinen Fabeln und Erzählungen ein vollständiger Kurs der praktischen Moral herstellen ... die einfachsten, den gewöhnlichsten Lebensverhältnissen entsprechenden Tugenden ... Rechtschaffenheit, Sittenreinheit, Treue, Bescheidenheit, Geduld, Nachsicht gegen die Fehler Anderer, Veträglichkeit, und vor Allem Klugheit. (2:567–58)

Here were works apparently ideally suited to the needs of German teachers in order to instill these virtues in their charges.

Yet on the other hand, *literature*, not didactic versifying, should be the object of academic *Germanistik*. A. F. C. Vilmar, author of *Die Nibelungen*, edited as a U.S. German text in 1888, took the side of literature over homiletics in his assessment of Gellert's fables:

> Ihrer Grundlage nach sind sie fast ohne Ausnahme, der Form nach, gottschedisch ... so sehr, daß die, zehn gegen eine zu rechen, überdeutlich, redselig, geschwätzig, platt und gewöhnlich werden; von echter Naturpoesie ist keine Spur mehr vorhanden, die Tiere, die noch auftreten, sind nicht allein *verkleidete* Menschen, sondern auch *modisch verschnörkelte* Menschen ... der Scherz hat in diesen Fabeln eine so langweilig-spaßhafte und spaßhaft-langweilige Miene, daß man eher über das Gesichterschneiden, was den Scherz begleitet, als über den Scherz selbst, lachen kann. (389)

Certainly, this is a far from uncritical point of view. Vilmar accounted for Gellert's popularity as an author as the result of his personal dignity and respectability (390). His fables were not popular as texts; this—as already pointed out—may be verified by the listings in the Appendices.

Only slightly better fared the fables of Lessing. Wilhelm Bernhardt informed students coldly that

> Lessings *Fabeln* tragen den Charakter der Fabeln des Griechen Äsopus, nur sind dieselben etwas zu doktrinär und nicht kindlich-naiv genug; er legt das Hauptgewicht seiner Fabeln nicht auf die Handlung, sondern auf die Moral am Ende derselben. (26)

Thus Lessing's fables, like Gellert's, are too didactic; nor are Alkmar, Luther or Goethe free of tutelary motives in their writings. Paradoxically, an era during which foreign language texts were to inculcate ethical values found the fable not to its liking. However, the era was also overwhelmingly that of Poetic Realism, Naturalism and *Heimatkunst*: didactic or no, what had an unrealistic genre such as the animal fable to offer such an age? Yet, at the same time, romantics such as Hauff and their imitators such as Putlitz flourished on the textbook market. The failure of the fable is therefore an anomaly within a study of trends which came to be generally predictable, unless one recalls the dictum of the Committee of Twelve which asserted that "the German *Märchen* is apt to appear dry to American boys and girls" (*Report* 63).

As time-honored as *Reineke*, though scarcely as influential upon poetic (if not academic) posterity, is Hans Friedrich von Schönberg's *Volksbuch*, *Die Schildbürger*. Frederick Betz, editor of the text, gives the reasons for his choice of the old chapbook as follows:

> Although so old a book—it was first published in 1598—the humor of it does not seem antiquated nor difficult to appreciate. It is enjoyed not only by Germans, but, though it is a purely German product, readers of every nationality are at once fascinated, amused, and set a thinking by the doings of these jolly people: for, although they lived in an age long passed by, their acts are wise and foolish enough to make us laugh about and with them. (v)

As Werner-Spanhoofd chose *Reineke*, Betz, too, turned to a much earlier period in German literature than did most editors of texts. Thus far, indeed, all the editors surveyed—Werner-Spanhoofd, Karl Hermann Breul and Horatio S. White (who edited the fables of Lessing and Gellert), Carruth and Betz—chose to bring before students fables or legends which have a timeless, universal appeal.

As a matter of fact, this sense of "no time, no place" calls into question the actual "Germanness" of such literature (Gellert's original anthropocentric fables perhaps proving the exception): the *Reineke* fable originated in Flanders (Friedrich 30), and the Schilda tradition began in classical antiquity with a city called Abdera (Betz iv). However, since these and other fables and legends came into the German-speaking area long ago, it seems fitting to record these texts as German with regard to culture as well as language, and to regard them insofar as desirable teaching aids.

Differing in convention from fable and *Volksbuch*, the product of another preclassical era, the *Spätbarock*, offered American students of German the last of a series of German versions of Defoe's *Robinson Crusoe*. Departing somewhat from Defoe's work both in content and in underlying moral intention, the pedagogue Joachim Heinrich Campe's *Robinson der Jüngere* (1779) was likewise undoubtedly meant to entertain as well as edify; for this reason, if no other, Carl Henry Ibershoff, who edited the work as a text copyrighted in 1904, stated:

> In spite of the representative list of German stories already edited for early reading, there seems to be a dearth of texts that are at once sufficiently easy and still full of action and interest. . . . If you can, through interest, bring pupils to read, of their own choice, *more* than a certain assigned portion of a foreign text, then we have at once largely solved one of the problems of pedagogy. (iii)

Yet, if only in this case, something goes awry when the end justifies the means. Should students who might be reading portions of *Dichtung und Wahrheit* be pacified with *Robinson der Jüngere*? Ibershoff justified his choice of texts as other editors, who—as will be seen—justified their choices on pragmatic rather than aesthetic grounds:

> It is hoped that the following narrative will be welcomed by teachers as a valuable aid to securing a rapid and interesting reading . . . for the theme belongs to world-literature, and has, by this time, certainly proved its perennial interest. (iii)

However, for reasons of cultural understanding and literary worth—hearkening back to the Committee of Twelve—a better choice might have been made. Consequently, *Robinson* was listed three times from 1904 to 1908; similar to all the texts discussed thus far, Campe's version of Defoe's classic had a relatively limited appeal.

Among texts chosen from literature of the *Aufklärung* period, another foreign influence in German texts was the Dane Ludvig Holberg. Sometimes called the founder of Danish literature, Holberg had influenced Johann Elias Schlegel and Gottsched with his dramas. His poem *Niels Klims Wallfahrt in die Unterwelt*, originally written in Latin as *Nicolati Klimii iter subterraneum*, and subsequently translated into Danish, German, Swedish, Dutch, English, French, Russian and Hungarian ("Ludvig Holberg") was edited by Eugene H. Babbitt as a German text which appeared in 1889 and was last listed in 1902.

From German literature of the enlightenment period, Heinrich Kurz chose to compose an essay on Wieland's *Oberon*; the essay was edited for U.S. German students in 1896 by Arnold Werner-Spanhoofd. *Oberon* itself is an ethical poem which, in the interaction between men and fairies, changes from a courtly adventure in the style of Ariosto to an acknowledgement of the humanitarian spirit. Although *Oberon* was much praised by Goethe and was said to illustrate ethical and humanitarian values (Frenzel and Frenzel 184–85), an important quality in texts of this time, Kurz's essay apparently achieved no great acclaim as a German text. It is attested to only by the date cited above, while *Oberon* itself was apparently never read by U.S. German students.

Indeed, if inferences are drawn based upon the limited appeal of the texts discussed above, it may appear that German literature (and literature in German) was a textbook editor's Siege Perilous, undoing all sitters but one enigmatically chosen tutelary. For all that, there are a number of authors whose works in textbook form have yielded quite impressive statistics in the form of editors, publishers, and dates. The first of these is Lessing.

Anyone who has studied German will find it unsurprising that from the War between the States to World War I Lessing ranks high in the statistics as compared to other German authors whose works were utilized as U.S. German texts. From 1864 to 1918, some 101 editions, reprintings, reissuings or listings show the popularity of eight Lessing texts. However, a look into Vilmar's *National-Literatur* reveals a view of Lessing which is unexpected by a present-day German major.

Lessing, the defender of Shakespeare against Aristotle, Racine and Corneille, is seen by Vilmar as a proponent of "das klassische Altertum," which was to be regarded

> nicht bloß als ein drittes, die nationalen und christlichen Elemente bereicherndes, ihnen jedoch untergeordnetes Element . . . sondern als ein Stoff, welcher sich an die Stelle der einen und der anderen oder beider zugleich zu setzen, dieselben zu verdrängen suchte. (420)

As a result, Vilmar viewed the neoclassical trend as a "Suchen und Nicht-Finden" on the part of misdirected authors, the foremost representative of whose poetic abnegation was Lessing: "Er war es, der das Suchen der Wahrheit höher stellte als den Besitz der Wahrheit, das Laufen nach dem vermeintlich niemals erreichbaren Ziel höher als das Ziel selbst" (Vilmar 421). Here one seems to hear echoes of the Lessing-Reimarus-Goeze dispute.

Thus Lessing's works, and the works of those who have followed him, do not satisfy, according to Vilmar, because the quest per se has supplanted the goal itself:

> Eben darum ist in seinen Werken, in denen die tieferen menschlichen Fragen zur Sprache kommen, eben darum ist in den übrigen nach ihm kommenden Werken gleichen Inhalts teils etwas Unruhiges, etwas Polemisches, teils etwas wirklich Unbefriedigtes und Unbefriedigendes, etwas Unabgeschloßenes [sic] und Dissonierendes, welches den höchsten poetischen Genuß nicht zu erreichen erstattet. (421)

It is safe to state that Vilmar's criticism varies somewhat from modern criticism's image of Lessing.

However, a milder, American view of Lessing's thinking, as demonstrated by a commentary on *Die Erziehung des Menschengeschlechts*, shows similar perceptions to those of Vilmar of Lessing's art. For example, it almost goes without saying that the "Education of the Human Race" is but a fragment. Thrown off, as it was, during the decay of his powers, close upon the end of his life, no work of his is perhaps more imperfect,—scarcely more than a jotting down of hints upon the greatest of topics. (Hosmer 286)

Vilmar's *Unbefriedigendes, Unabgeschlossenes* and *Dissonierendes* find an echo in Hosmer's estimation; and, not surprisingly, *Die Erziehung des Menschengeschlechts* did not appear as a text.

To turn to Lessing's more celebrated works, the dramas *Minna von Barnhelm, Emilia Galotti,* and *Nathan der Weise,* in descending order by the number of listings, were by far the most popular of his works to be utilized as texts. *Minna von Barnhelm* alone is listed fifty-six times by fifteen publishers from 1864 to 1914. The play's great popularity as a text is explained by Sylvester Primer, who edited it for D. C. Heath and Company:

> The selection of "Minna von Barnhelm" as a desirable text-book for schools and colleges is based upon two important considerations,—its fitness as reading for the young, and its value as a classical and literary work in the study of the German language and literature. Educators will recognize the difficulty of selecting unobjectionable works for the class-room in either modern or ancient languages. Few comedies in the modern languages are as suitable to be placed in the hands of the young as "Minna von Barnhelm." (iii)

Primer defends his assertion by listing the following criteria: (1) the play is "highly entertaining"; (2) almost every scene is a "masterpiece in itself"; (3) the language is "most pure and idiomatic"; and (4) "a noble spirit of honor, disinterestedness, and generosity pervades the whole piece" (iii).

Aptly, even Vilmar concurs,

> daß wir Minna von Barnhelm mit Recht als unser erstes *Nationalbühnenstück,* als ein Volksdrama, soweit dasselbe damals überhaupt noch möglich, betrachten, und es fortwährend unsern Bühnendichtern als das bedeutendste Muster der Behandlung historischer Stoffe für das Theater vorhalten müssen. (427)

Thus even those who were critical of Lessing found *Minna* to their liking.

Striking in Primer's edition of *Minna von Barnhelm,* as in so many other literary texts of the period, are the extensive notes which explain the drama, point out aesthetic elements, and relate happenings in the drama to the theories of Lessing the dramatist and critic. To do justice to all his textual scholarship, Primer cited the classics:

> I have endeavored to apply those principles of text-criticism which have long been recognized as standard in commentaries on Greek and Latin textbooks. Modern languages can never take the first place in "classic training" until the classical productions are edited with the accuracy and scholarship bestowed upon the classics of Greece and Rome. (v)

German authors were worthy of the treatment accorded Vergil and Cicero. Indeed, until the modern classics were received in a manner similar to that in which the classics of dead languages were received, the living languages must be subordinated to the dead.

Like Primer, a large number of editors felt the need for exhaustive notes after the style familiar today in editions of Latin authors' works. The keen competition between Greek and Latin and the modern languages at Primer's point in time makes itself evident in the imitation of Greek and Latin textbooks. Such notes have endured in the classics, but are more often the exception that the rule in modern languages, where introductory material and a vocabulary seem to be the most prominent aids.

Lessing's *Emilia Galotti*, second only to *Minna von Barnhelm* among Enlightenment textbooks, is similarly provided with explanatory, aesthetic and theoretical notes. After the wholesomeness of *Minna von Barnhelm*, however, *Emilia Galotti* offers something of a contrast. Thus Max Winkler stated in the preface to his edition of *Emilia* that "very few teachers would deem it wise to choose *Emilia Galotti* for high-school reading." He therefore prepared his edition for college students, particularly; but probably not, as he implies, because of the difficulty presented by Lessing's language to the high school student (iii). Otherwise, Max Poll could not have stated in the preface of his *Emilia Galotti* edition that

> the reasons for editing this particular play are obvious. It is one of Lessing's greatest works and the one from which modern German tragedy takes its rise. It holds the interest of the reader to the very end and the language is not too difficult. (iii)

It was, then, the moral exigency which rendered *Emilia Galotti* less desirable, at least in high schools. *Minna von Barnhelm*'s fifty-six listings by fifteen publishers therefore demonstrate a significant precedence over *Emilia Galotti's*—still quite considerable—twenty-one listings and six publishers.

The third of the great Lessing plays, *Nathan der Weise*, was listed fifteen times by five publishers. Why *Nathan* is statistically the least of the three is clarified by several commentators of the late 1800s. Hosmer, who calls *Nathan* Lessing's masterpiece, nonetheless interposes:

> Judged by rules of art, it is easy to find fault with it. The story is involved, the speeches of the characters often too long, the action is not always natural; it is what Lessing himself condemned,—a didactic poem. (287)

The notion that *Nathan* bored students with its length, involvement and moralizing, and thus became a source of trouble for teachers, is not difficult to conceive in view of what Hosmer has said.

Yet Wilhelm Bernhardt, who also calls *Nathan* Lessing's masterpiece, tacitly offers another explanation for its relative lack of appeal:

Lessings dramatisches Meisterwerk "Nathan der Weise" feiert die universelle Religion, welche von keiner Kirche und von keiner Konfession abhängig ist, sondern sich in der Religiosität des Herzens, in Menschenliebe und religiöser Toleranz manifestiert. (26)

It is conceivable that in many religiously conservative areas of the U.S., *Nathan der Weise* may have been little more welcome than *Die Erziehung des Menschengeschlechts*. As Vilmar has demonstrated, Lessing's philosophical writings (among which *Nathan* might reasonably be counted) were not always highly regarded by his countrymen, either.

Among Lessing's critical writings, *Laokoon* and the *Hamburgische Dramaturgie* appeared in several editions from 1892 to 1910. In Germany, Heinrich Kurz wrote of how Lessing, in the *Dramaturgie*,

> die geheimnisvollsten Kräfte der menschlichen Seele erforscht und sich dienstbar gemacht hat. Denn Lessings Größe bestand wesentlich darin, daß er durch die Kraft und freie Beweglichkeit seines Geistes die Wirkungen derjenigen Talente erzwang, die ihm die Natur versagt hatte. Aber freilich konnte er sie nur bis zu einem gewissen Grade erzwingen, und selbst in seinen besten Stücken erkennt man, wie richtig er urteilte, als er sagte, daß er noch lange kein Corneille sein würde. (2:633)

This somewhat disparaging report is echoed by Calvin Thomas in *A History of German Literature*, 1909, when he writes that

> the *Hamburg Dramaturgy* contained Lessing's famous renunciation of the name of poet. He declared that he did not feel the living spring within him, and owed solely to his critical faculty whatever success he had as a poet; wherefore it annoyed him to hear the critical faculty disparaged. (251)

A mildly critical undercurrent was, therefore, not confined to either hemisphere. As a point of view, it survives today as students study Lessing.

Laokoon fares less successfully at the hands of Thomas. Although he praises the work as "one of the most stimulating pieces of criticism ever written," he also assures his readers—presumably made up for the most part of teachers and students—that

> the argument of the *Laokoön* [sic] is vulnerable at many points. Lessing was hardly the man to be a lawgiver for the plastic arts, for of statues and paintings he had seen but little. When he wrote the *Laokoön* his eyes had never rested on a cast of the group, possibly not even on a drawing of it. He puts painting and sculpture together under the name of *Malerei*, as if they were the same thing. He writes of poetry as if its only aim were to produce a vivid mental image. Historical considerations are entirely lacking. (249)

These are picayune considerations in view of the clearly stated principal argument: that the plastic arts depict one moment in time, and that the artist or sculptor chooses the optimum moment from a continuum of action for plastic (static) representation. Literature, on the other hand, must not describe statically (*Wortmalerei*), but dynamically recount a series of particulars. One need not have seen the *Laocoon* sculpture nor must one have read Vergil's account of the fate of Laocoon to perceive—or to comment cogently upon—the differences in the plastic arts and literature. It should be pointed out that Thomas included a portion of the *Laokoon* in his highly successful *German Anthology* (as a large anthology, not surveyed by this study), in which *Laokoon* is esteemed as one of Lessing's most important works (342).

Certainly, not all commentators of the period joined in Thomas's estimation of Lessing the critic. Vilmar, for example, writes of

> Diese reinigende, nicht zerstörende, das Herkommen *vernichtende,* aber eine neue Regel schaffende, diese überall zum Mitforschen, Mitleben, Mitfortschreiten auffordernde Kritik wie sie noch niemals in Deutschland vorhanden war und seitdem nicht wieder vorhanden gewesen ist, hat Lessing zunächst in seinen *didaktischen* und *kritischen* Schriften bewiesen. . . . Gedanke folgt auf Gedanke, Zug um Zug im heitersten Spiele und dennoch mit unbegreiflicher, fast zauberhafter Gewalt auf uns eindringend. (424)

Vilmar's point of view is shared in the United States by Wilhelm Bernhardt, who states the following in his *Geschichte der deutschen Literatur* about *Laokoon*: "Dieses Meisterwerk der Kritik, welches auch in stilistischer Beziehung klassisch ist, hat für alle Zeiten und für die Kritiker aller Länder und Völker die ästhetischen Prinzipien festgesetzt, nach welchem ein Kunstwerk beurteilt werden muß" (25). And regarding the *Hamburgische Dramaturgie,* Bernhardt writes that "mit einem Worte, dieses Werk ist das Fundament und Lehrbuch der Dramatik in allen ihren Zweigen" (26).

From a modern viewpoint, the overall image of Lessing during this period is strangely blurred. Upon the place today dedicated to Germany's genial author of tolerance steps a frustrated would-be philosopher whose writings (except *Minna von Barnhelm*) are sometimes harshly judged. Certainly, Wilhelminians and Victorians studied and admired Lessing; but judging from literary histories of the period he did not stand as unimpeachably in the esteem of editors, teachers, and (therefore) students as he probably does today. On the other hand, it should not be forgotten that according to the number of textbooks copyrighted, reprinted, reissued and advertised, Lessing ranked behind only Goethe and Schiller.

Apart from Herder and the young Goethe and Schiller, the *Sturm und Drang* figures who engaged the attention of U.S. German students were Rudolph Erich Raspe, Gottfried Bürger, Heinrich Jung-Stilling and Heinrich Zschokke. In actuality, only three of these authors are conclusively "German"; emigrating from Germany to England, Raspe published some stories which he had taken from the *Vade Mecum für lustige Leute,* to which he added some material of his own to round out the stories. The book published in

English at Oxford, 1785–1786, was entitled *Baron Münchhausen's Narrative of his Marvellous Travels and Campaigns in Russia*. Raspe's work could not have become known in Germany had not Gottfried Bürger's *Rückübertragung* into German—*Wunderbare Reisen zu Wasser und zu Lande, Feldzüge und lustige Abenteuer des Freiherrn von Münchhausen*—made it famous there. The text was listed only in 1906.

Bürger's own *Leonore* was edited as a text by Arnold Werner-Spanhoofd in 1895. Unsurprisingly, this ballad is called Bürger's masterwork by Lilian Stroebe and Marian Whitney—both German professors and editors of texts—in their *Geschichte der Deutschen [sic] Literature* (iii). Indeed, no really adverse criticism meets the poem in any of the literary histories and critical works consulted. But other works by Bürger do not meet with the same approbation. As early as the 1870s Vilmar criticized Bürger the poet when he stated that "die Zahl der wirklich *guten* Gedichte Bürgers ist in der Tat nur klein . . . der zahlreichen ganz unreinen Producte [sic] nicht zu gedenken" (520); nonetheless, he praised *Leonore* "trotz einiger nicht unbedeutender Mängel" as a poem which "an Klang und Wollaut [sic] bis dahin noch nicht, selbst nicht von Schiller übertroffen worden ist, und in der Volksmäßigkeit des Ausdrucks nur die Goetheschen Gedichte über sich hat" (521).

More criticism is levelled at Bürger himself than at his poetry. For example, American students might also read of Bürger that

> in his youth he nearly made a shipwreck of his life by dissipation; the best years of his manhood were darkened by sin and sorrow and disgrace, and his end was pathetically sad. (Thomas 240)

For the most part, only *Leonore* relieves the disapprobation which is Bürger's portion:

> Bürger never afterward achieved anything quite so good as *Leonore* . . . . His average merit is high, but he was capable of dropping into repulsive vulgarity. (Thomas 240)

Only *Leonore* was edited for school use.

The case of Heinrich Jung-Stilling is, generally speaking, quite different from that of Bürger. Jung-Stilling grew up in a family of mystics and read Paracelsus and Jacob Böhme at an early age. He studied literature and philosophy, became a doctor of medicine and a professor of economics and finance, and wrote a number of books, most of them religious and mystical. The one respect in which he is similar to Bürger is that he is best known as the author of one work, in this case his autobiography: *Heinrich Jung-Stillings Lebensgeschichte*. Interestingly, Jung-Stilling was aided in his autobiographical writing by his friend Johann Wolfgang von Goethe, so that

> der erste Theil von Jungs Lebensgeschichte nicht so, wie er vorliegt, aus Jungs Feder geflossen ist . . . . [Jung-Stilling] erzählt nämlich, daß Göthe [sic], der ihn im J. 1774 in Elberfeld besuchte, die Handschrift ohne sein Vorwissen mitnahm . . . und es ergibt sich, daß böthe an die ursprüngliche Erzählung Jungs die bessernde Hand gelegt hat. (Kurz 3:553)

The fact that at least a part of the *Lebensgeschichte* had been revised by Goethe may help to account for Sigmon Martin Stern's textbook edition, which was listed in 1899 and 1912. Then, too, Jung-Stilling's life of religion, education and striving was certain to strike many U.S. educators and many of the religious as sound instructional material.

Apart from Goethe and Schiller, the *Sturm und Drang* figure whose works are most cataloged was Johann Heinrich Daniel Zschokke. Zschokke is remembered today for *Aballino der große Bandit* (1794), a *Ritter- und Räuberroman* influenced by Schiller's *Räuber* and Goethe's *Götz von Berlichingen*. It is probable that *Aballino* was deemed strong fare for the classroom; at any rate, it was apparently not published as a textbook.

Actually a gentle, intellectual schoolmaster, Zschokke afterward repented writing the novel. Later in life he began to write what the editor of *Das Wirtshaus zu Cransac* and *Der zerbrochene Krug*, Edward Southey Joynes, terms

> works of fiction . . . written with the like object, the education or improvement of the people. Such "novels with a purpose" are usually dry reading; but many of Zschokke's are redeemed by keen insight of character, a lively style, and often a playful humor. (*Wirthshaus* x)

Joynes then offers other teachers the foremost advantage of Zschokke's moralistic stories: "Zschokke's plots and portraits are always pure. Nothing unclean soils his pages. His treatment of women and of love is always delicate and tender" (*Wirtshaus* x). Books both clean and humorous were sure to attract a following.

As a narrative, the *Wirtshaus zu Cransac* meanders from person to person and place to place. Only the central figure, the Colonel, is constant. Much of the story is dull, full of clichés and too sentimental for modern tastes: "Ich fürchtete, jener zarte Engel, zu schön, zu gut für diese Welt, sei in eine bessere hinübergeeilt" (40). As Joynes himself has said, Zschokke preaches in his prose. Thus it is not surprising that Zschokke is remembered for the *Sturm und Drang* of *Aballino*, and not for his later works. Finally, in view of the introduction to German culture so strongly endorsed by the Committee of Twelve, it seems somewhat arbitrary that Joynes offers German students a story which takes place in France. It has not been forgotten that such plays as *Nathan der Weise*, *Maria Stuart* and *Iphigenie auf Tauris* also take place in parts of the world other than the German-speaking area of Europe. Yet those, and even *Sinbad the Sailor*, have a historical, mythological or cosmopolitan character not shared by a prosaic short story about a German colonel in nineteenth century France.

From sentimental moralizing, students could turn to Herder; but to only one volume, *Laokoon*, which was shared with Lessing and Goethe. Notably, Zschokke received twenty-nine catalog listings as compared to one for Herder. Aside from the title, sources stated only that the text contains "selections" edited by William Guild Howard. It may seem peculiar today that Herder was bested by authors who are now outside the standard literary canon. Yet cases such as Herder's could be used to indicate the consistency of the experiences of students of German and readers of translations in the United States. Herder's works were not reviewed by the *Times*, nor was he one of Pochmann's most frequently translated German authors. Zschokke, on the other hand, was reviewed by the *Times* and was translated twenty-five times from 1865 to 1899 as shown in Appendix B. Students in high schools, colleges and universities and the reader at large were receiving the same author, even if the exclusion of *Aballino* from the schools must be taken into consideration.

A more positive sharing between academics and those not engaged in programs of study focuses around Johann Wolfgang von Goethe. Goethe is number one among Pochmann's most translated authors, was reviewed seventeen times by the *Times*, and editions, reprints, reissues, or listings of his works catalogued as textbooks number 156, the largest number of texts by any German author except Schiller. In this chapter some textbook editions of Goethe's earlier works will be discussed.

Götz von Berlichingen chronologically headed the list of Goethe's works studied by U.S. German students. However, with but five catalog listings relating to only two texts, the play lies far behind many of Goethe's works as far as its dissemination among U.S. students is concerned. As was the case with Zschokke's novel *Aballino*, this play's popularity in the classroom did not conform to the popularity it enjoyed outside. In writing of critical notes on Goethe's works in journal volumes from 1885 to 1889, Pochmann states that

> *Faust* was the single work most frequently discussed, and *Meister*, the lyric poems, *Werther*, *Goetz*, *Hermann und Dorothea*, *Iphigenie* and *Tasso*, the *Wahlverwandtschaften*, *Dichtung und Wahrheit*, *Egmont*, and *Reineke Fuchs* ranked next in frequency in the order named. (*German Culture* 337)

As far as textbook statistics are concerned, the works listed above outnumber *Götz* with the exception of *Wilhelm Meister*, *Werther*, *Reineke Fuchs*—and *Die Wahlverwandtschaften*, which is not listed.

Calvin Thomas states that *Götz* "caused a great and a very wholesome sensation" when it first appeared in Germany in 1773 (273). However, it is conceivable that for many teachers, *Götz* was too strong for the classroom. As Thomas himself states:

> The subject-matter of the play was revolutionary. *Götz* was not presented as a pestilent robber knight, warring against the forces that were making for public order, but as the champion of a good cause—the cause of individual freedom and self-reliance . . . while the empire and church were made to play a rather shabby role of intrigue and oppression. *Götz* was thus in a double sense a manifesto of freedom, and it proved that Germany was all ready for just such a declaration of independence. (274–75)

The U.S. reading public read *Götz* in translation; but were the schools ready to support individualistic manifestos of freedom at the expense of church and state? When the discipline, patriotism and religious communion which characterized most U.S. public and private schools until the mid-twentieth century is considered, the vast lead in editions of *Hermann und Dorothea*—full of peace-loving, contented and obedient characters—over the defiant recklessness of *Götz von Berlichingen* is not difficult to understand.

One edition of *Götz*, edited by Karl August Hildner for Ginn in 1911, was printed together with one of Goethe's critical works, *Zu Shakespeares Namenstag* (originally *Zum Shäkspears Tag*). A speech honoring Shakespeare, the work was the result of Goethe's Strasbourg experience under the tutelage of Herder. It originally appeared in 1771, the year of the *Urgötz* drama, which prompted Herder's famous remark, "Shakespeare hat Euch ganz verdorben" (Krell and Fiedler 165). With regard to the success of Goethe's revised *Götz* and his Shakespeare essay in U.S. German texts, the following must be conceded: when compared with the longer listings for *Egmont*, *Iphigenie*, *Tasso*, and *Faust* (to mention only the dramatic works), *Götz*'s comparatively weak showing seems to demonstrate a certain regard for Herder's famous criticism among many of those who chose German texts for schools and colleges.

In 1774 appeared another of Goethe's most popular works, which fared even worse than *Götz* as a textbook: *Werther*. About *Werther*, the chairman of the Committee of Twelve stated:

> From the point of common-sense, which happens to coincide in this case with that of science, *Werther* is a morbid book. The suicide of a young man because of a disappointment in love is not a subject on which a healthy imagination likes to dwell. Nevertheless, the melancholia of adolescence, as psychologists now call it, is a human fact (Thomas 275).

Further, although he calls *Werther* "of all the sentimental novels of the eighteenth century . . . easily the best," Thomas describes the effect of the book in the classroom as a failure. Goethe's hyper-aesthetic, weak-willed, and toward the end rather maudlin hero no longer draws tears from mankind, because the modern reader is rarely able or willing to receive the pathetic tale naively and to suppress, for the time being, his sense of humor. (275–76)

In this case, Thomas has apparently spoken for the majority of teachers (as perhaps he did not in praising *Götz*); only one textbook edition of *Werther*—edited by Ernst Feise in 1914—appeared from 1864 to 1918. A similar pedagogical opinion on Werther had already been voiced by Hosmer in 1879; firstly, "the circumstances are singular, almost repulsive" (369), and then "there is enough in the book which will seem to any modern reader absurd" (371). It should be mentioned that Thomas and Hosmer praised Goethe's genius in the writing of *Werther*—it is the plot which offends. Finally, it seems relevant to mention that from 1885 to 1887 *Werther* outranked all Goethe's works except *Faust*, the lyric poems, and *Wilhelm Meister* in the number of critical articles published in U.S. journals (Pochmann, *German Culture* 337). Here again, students and readers outside academe are at variance.

Egmont, which may be considered essentially a *Sturm und Drang* drama (Friedrich 85), was much more successful as a textbook; however, the play (with six texts, twelve listings) led only *Reineke Fuchs* out of a field of twelve of Goethe's works as far as journal articles in Pochmann's survey are concerned (*German Culture* 337). Teachers preferred *Egmont* to *Götz* and *Werther* because

"*Egmont*" versetzt uns in die von der Tyrannei der Spanier leidenden Niederlande, macht uns zu Augenzeugen der Hinrichtung des Grafen Egmont, des Führers der nationalen Partei des Landes, durch General Alba (1568) und motiviert mit dieser Bluthat den Abfall der Niederlande von Spanien. In die politische Geschichte der Zeit ist ein ungemein zartes Liebesverhältnis eingeflochten, welches den Grafen Egmont als Menschen und Geliebten Klärchens, eines einfachen, frischen und lebenslustigen Bürgermädchens, einführt. Die beiden Hauptcharaktere, Klärchen und Egmont, sind mit unaussprechlicher Anmut gezeichnet und nehmen unsere vollste Sympathie in Anspruch. (Bernhardt 42)

Unlike the rebellious *Kraftkerl Götz*, who dies because he cannot live in a country ruled by law, Egmont dies for the sake of his country, executed by the forces of an invading tyrant. Unlike Werther, whose self-centered whimperings end with his suicide, the national hero Egmont, in both his patriotic self-sacrifice and his happy love relationship with Klärchen, is a sanguine and appealing character. Neither a rebel nor a suicide, Egmont was doubtless considered a more wholesome example for the young.

Nonetheless, Egmont must have his tragic flaw as well as his attractiveness:

> A strange fascination goes out from him on account of his amiable personality. But the buoyancy of temper which trusts and laughs and declines to worry, blinds him to the obvious dangers which other men can see; thus it becomes the tragic weakness that carries him to his doom. . . . Egmont is done to death by the . . . power of his happy-go-lucky temperament. (Thomas 280)

Thomas thus offers a characterization of Egmont reminiscent of Wagner's Siegfried: an innocent person who dies for sheer lack of guile. This was a relatively innocuous tragic flaw for a student's consideration.

Less numerous were texts specifically devoted to Goethe's lyric poetry and ballads; only three are listed a total of ten times in the statistics (though a number of anthologies of poetry which doubtless contained Goethe's poetry are found in Appendix G). With regard to Goethe's poetry, there was considerable controversy among Germanists as to which lyric poetry and ballads were greatest. For example, Vilmar sharply contrasts Goethe's *Sturm und Drang* poetry with that of his later years, written under the influence of Greece and the Orient; implicit in his words are praise of the former period and apology and some distaste for the latter:

> Daß Goethe in einer Lebenszeit [dem Alter] in welcher die, wenn auch gesundeste, physische und geistige Natur sich der Ruhe and dem heiteren Spiele zuneigt, sich dieser Dichtungsart zuwandte, darf nicht befremden: noch weniger, wenn wir erwägen, daß die unruhige und freilich auch in mancher Beziehung inhalts- und ziellose dichterische Begeisterung der Freiheitskriege dem Greise, der sich zur französischen Revolution, also auch zu deren Bekämpfung durch deutschen Sinn und deutsche Kraft nicht zu stellen wußte, und der das Stürmen und Drängen im Leben wie in der Dichtung längst hinter sich liegen hatte, in dreifacher Beziehung unangenehm sein mußte, so daß er sich in seinem Alter gewissermaßen in den Orient hinein *rettete*. Das alles können wir in Goethe entschuldigen . . . daß aber die Epigonen, statt sich an den Vulkanen der goetheschen Jugend zu erwärmen, zu dem Kaminfeuer des Greises eilten, das wird für alle Zeiten gerechte, und zum Teil unwillige Verwunderung erregen. (Vilmar 485)

Vilmar "excuses" Goethe for works such as the *Trilogie der Leidenschaft*, *Pandora* and *Der westöstliche Divan*, while condemning Grillparzer, Platen and Immermann for their admiration for and emulation of such works "of an old man."

Kurz stands opposed to Vilmar's point of view. All Goethe's poetry is full of beauty and truth; this art evinces the master's hand which has made nature its own. Certainly, this is seen not only in the early works:

> Daher sind aber auch die Gedichte, welche er in den reiferen Mannesjahren schuf, noch ganz von der Frische durchdrungen, welche sonst nur dem jugendlichen Alter eigen ist. . . . Und wie er in seinen ersten Schöpfungen schon als der größte Dichter seiner Zeit hervorgetreten war, so wurde er in seinen spätern zugleich auch der größte Künstler, in welchem sich Natur und

> Kunst so glücklich durchdringen, daß es nicht möglich ist, zu bestimmen, wo die eine aufhört und die andere beginnt. Und so ist eine hervorragende Eigenthümlichkeit seiner Dichtungen, die wunderbare Mäßigung, die ihn nie über die Gränzen [sic] des Schönen und Wahren hinausgehen läßt . . . wir erkennen diese Mäßigung selbst in den ausgelassensten und muthwilligsten Erzeugnissen seiner Jugend, wenn sie auch nicht in der göttlichen Milde erscheint, die seine späteren Werke erfüllt. (Kurz 3:99)

The "fiery volcanoes" of "Prometheus," so highly recommended by Vilmar, are abandoned by Kurz for a harmonious blending of art and nature characterized by *Mäßigung* and *Milde*.

Concerning the varying evaluations of Goethe's poetry, one interesting feature of the American teachers' attitudes toward Goethe's poetry is what seems to have been the relative scarcity of the great hymns of the Storm and Stress in the classroom. For example, Wilhelm Bernhardt mentioned the following poetry by Goethe in his literary history of Germany "for school and home":

> Aus der großen Zahl seiner herrlichen lyrischen Gedichte . . . sind zu nennen: "Heidenröslein" (1775), "Der Fischer" (1778), "Erlkönig" (1781), "Mignon" (1782), "Der Sänger" (1778), "Schäfers Klagelied" (1802), "Trost in Thränen" (1803), sowie die lyrischen Partieen in "Wilhelm Meister," in "Egmont"und "Faust." Zu den bekanntesten Balladen Goethes gehören "Der Zauberlehrling" (1797), "Die Braut von Korinth" (1797), "Johanna Sebus" (1809), "Der getreue Eckart" (1813) u.a. (38–39)

Within the boundaries of the *Sturm und Drang* era fall "Heidenröslein," "Der Fischer," "Erlkönig," "Mignon," and "Der Sänger"; yet, with the possible exception of "Erlkönig," none of these works actually "storms." "Wanderers Sturmlied" (though it is indeed contained in a text of the period edited by Goebel) and "Prometheus," as well as the less tempestuous hymns such as "Mahomets Gesang" or "An Schwager Kronos," are lacking.

Calvin Thomas provides students after the turn of the century with a reason for the apparent dearth of the great hymns in literary texts:

> The animating spirit of the "Storm and Stress" was the spirit of passionate revolt against the conventional standards of life and of literature. The battle-cries were freedom, genius, power, nature; genius meaning lawlessness, and nature being conceived in the spirit of Rousseau as the antithesis of civilised [sic] convention. Shakespeare was ignorantly worshipped as the archetypal genius. There was a disposition to attack social arrangements, or at least to put them on trial before the tribunal of feeling. . . . Feeling, instinct and passion were regarded as the only noble elements of human nature. . . . As for style, the worst of shortcomings was tameness, the greatest of merits an unbridled energy of expression. Hence an appetence for hyperbolic dictions, wild comparisons, repetitions, broken sentences, perfervid exclamations. (281–82)

If Professor Thomas may be taken as a representative of other teachers and editors of texts (and, as chairman of the Committee of Twelve, he should be), it would not be surprising to learn that the *Kraftkerl* Prometheus, like Götz von Berlichingen, was relatively infrequently heard of in the classroom. Convention, standards and civilization came before freedom, power and nature.

Thomas's recommendations of Goethe's poetry for students would doubtless include those poems dealt with in his history: "May Festival," "Welcome and Parting," "On the Lake," "New Love, New Life," "Restless Love," "Comfort in Tears," "To the Moon," "The King in Thule," and "Über allen Gipfeln ist Ruh" (270–71). In contrast to Bernhardt, therefore, Thomas chooses Goethe's earlier poetry over that written after the trip to Italy (1786):

> The songs which were written by Goethe during the next few years of his life [after 1770], after he had . . . found himself as a poet, opened a new era in German lyricism. . . . It is no doubt a simple art; compared with the wonderful wordcraft of Keats or the imaginative splendours of Shelley, it seems almost tame. But in its simplicity power resides. It is based on absolute fidelity to the truth: nowhere is there anything scintillant or exaggerated. In these songs the love of woman seems to blend with a deep joy in the visible forms of the outer world, and a suggestion of feeling too deep for words is conveyed by means of descriptive touches that are copied exactly from nature. (Thomas 271)

Thomas centers the students' attention on poetry from the Sesenheim and early Weimar days; Bernhardt concentrates on Weimar to a greater extent. Kurz praises Goethe's later, neoclassically and orientally influenced poetry. Only Vilmar defends the great hymns of *Sturm und Drang*—a type of poetry either disapproved of or neglected by the others in their writings on Goethe's verse.

The Committee of Twelve, including Thomas, recommended lyric in the German class to this extent: no lyric poetry by any German author was recommended for the elementary (or first-year) course; lyric poetry by Heine, Schiller and Uhland was intended for the intermediate level (although Goethe was represented by the epic poem *Hermann und Dorothea* and the drama *Iphigenie*); no lyric poetry was recommended on the advanced level, where Goethe was represented by "dramas (except *Faust*) and prose writings (say extracts from *Werther* and *Dichtung und Wahrheit*)" (Report 63–73). After the praise of Goethe's lyric poetry on both sides of the Atlantic, the lack of interest shown by the recommendations of the Committee of Twelve is surprising. As it happens, the underplaying of Goethe the lyricist took place for the following reason:

> Now poetry, as the language of emotion, is a more or less artificial—often a highly artificial—form of expression, and it is better that the natural become lodged in the mind first. The beginner who has learned to recite "Sah ein Knab

ein Röslein stehn, Röslein auf der Heiden," is hardly in a better, but rather in a worse, position for learning how a German would ordinarily express that idea. (Report 54)

With regard to the texts themselves, three texts, edited by Schütze, Goebel, and Harris, respectively, were listed a total of ten times (slightly behind *Egmont*'s twelve, far ahead of *Götz*'s five). Fortuitously, the texts edited by Goebel and Schütze were compared and contrasted in a review for *The Modern Language Journal* in 1917. John Scholte Nollen, himself a German professor at Lake Forest College and an editor of Kleist's *Prinz Friedrich von Homburg* and Schiller's *Maria Stuart* and *Poems*, reviewed Schütze's edition by comparing it with Goebel's:

> There is a striking difference in selection between the two collections. . . . Though considerable individual variation was to be expected, in choosing from so extensive a body of lyric verse as Goethe's, yet it is surprising to find that fully half of the poems and epigrams in G[oebel] are missing from S[chütze], and that just two-thirds of the selections in S[chütze] are not found in G[oebel]. . . . Thus G[oebel] alone includes *Aussöhnung, Dauer im Wechsel, Wanderers Sturmlied, Bei Betrachtung von Schillers Schädel, An das Schicksal, Künstlerlied, Wenn im Unendlichen*, and several of the more familiar Roman Elegies. S[chütze]'s anthology] has to its advantage such poems as *Bergschloss* [sic], *Rastlose Liebe, Gesang der Geister über den Wassern, Der Liebende schreibt*, Klärchen's and Gretchen's songs, the watchman's song from *Faust, Mailied, Nähe des Geliebten* (one of the "twelve greatest songs," according to S[chütze]), and *Diner zu Koblenz*. The balance here inclines to the side of S[chütze]; both collections contain much that would not be missed to make room for the poems lacking from this list. And both lack some of Goethe's best—e.g., the wonderful *Zueignung* to *Faust*, one of the poet's finest "confessions." (Nollen 320–21)

Nollen concludes that Schütze's text is superior to Goebel's only after vigorously finding fault with the former text. As might be expected because the contents of the texts are so diverse, the article ends with a compromise: "Neither of these two editions makes the other dispensable, and the teacher at least will find it advisable to use both" (Nollen 322). The Schütze text (in different editions) is prominent at the beginning and end of the period surveyed, the Goebel text during the first decade of this century.

Schiller's lyric poetry fared better than Goethe's during the fifty-four years under consideration. Eight texts with some twenty-five listings place Schiller's poetry far beyond that of Goethe (three texts, ten listings) in popularity among editors, teachers and, presumably, also students. Thus it is interesting to remember at this point that Schiller's works in English translation were not reviewed by the *New York Times* from 1870–1918, while Goethe's works were frequently reviewed. Both authors rank outstandingly in Pochmann's list of the most translated German authors: Goethe was first; Richard Wagner was second; Schiller was third, 1865–1899 (346). In the course of exploring why students read Schiller, certain reasons for his being neglected by the *Times* may be established.

Schiller's *Sturm und Drang* lyric poetry, like most of Goethe's *große Hymnen*, was, as far as can be established from the data assembled, more or less ignored. Yet this early poetry, including the odes *Der Triumph der Liebe, Die Kindsmörderin, Gruppe aus dem Tartarus* and *Die Freundschaft*, was very popular during the early part of the time period, as attested to by Vilmar:

> Nicht ohne Grund ist Hektors Abschied, nicht ohne Grund ist Amalia (aus den Räubern), ist Minna, ist sogar die Kindsmörderin und sind noch andere so lange Zeit die gesungensten und beliebtesten Lieder der jüngeren Welt gewesen, und freilich muß behauptet werden, daß das Leidenschaftliche, das Uebergährende und Excentrische [sic] mancher dieser Lieder ihnen nicht wenig von dieser großen Gunst des Publikums zuwendete. (501)

It seems safe to conclude that poems such as *Die Kindsmörderin* were not considered optimum classrooms projects by American editors.

Much more popular as texts were works dating from Schiller's classical or second period, although Vilmar, to the contrary, speaks "von dieser großen Gunst des Publikums . . . die eben nicht dadurch gesteigert wurde, daß der zu künstlerischem Bewußtsein gelangte Dichter das 'wütende Entzücken' in ein 'paradiesisch Fühlen' verwandelte" (501). Happy about it or not, scholars were to be treated to *An die Freude* instead of *Die Gruppe aus dem Tartarus*.

And, while a literary history after the turn of the century extolls "die rednerische Sprache Schillers mit ihren glänzenden Bildern und den glitzernden Weisheitssprüchen . . . die wie Christbaumschmuck äußerlich an Stamm und Zweigen der Dichtung hingen," the same source does not hesitate to note that, in the 1880s, "in den Kreisen gelehrter Germanisten war der Schillerhaß üblich, und Nietzsche nannte Schiller den Mordtrompeter von Säckingen" (Kummer 42–43). Elucidation of Nietzsche's remark is offered indirectly in a following chapter, in which Josef Viktor von Scheffel's *Trompeter von Säkkingen* is discussed. Perhaps Schiller's idealism has been scoffed at more derisively only once—in Brecht's *Die heilige Johanna der Schlachthöfe*.

Yet in America in 1879, the assessment of Schiller was quite opposite that apparently prevailing in Germany; and on this continent, too, Schiller's role as *Moraltrompeter* was being assessed:

> For nobility of soul Schiller is supreme, and his nobleness is of a German type. Göthe [sic], for the questionable passages of his life, has found warm defenders who undertake to make all square with the highest standards; few have ever presumed to speak of Schiller as needing defenders; to prove his virtue would be like proving sunshine to be light. (Hosmer 420–21)

Thus it was that Schiller, not Goethe, was considered, by at least some scholars, to be "the representative German poet." Though Goethe was superior in a "cosmic" sense, Schiller mirrored "the German soul" (Hosmer 421)—a true revelation of "the German mind" to students of the era.

Yet such praise is, after all, somewhat weak; Schiller is not the greatest poet, he is representative and virtuous. And other assessments of Schiller's ballads and lyrics by U.S. professors are outspokenly negative. Shortly after the turn of the century, Schiller was viewed almost as an imitator of Goethe. Concerning Schiller's ballads, it was taught—in a chapter called "Schiller on the Height"—that

> These ballads, as a whole, are good in proportion as they approximate the depth and intensity of passion that make Goethe supreme in this field. Schiller's best work has in it invariably an essential element of Goethe, so that we feel that it could not be as it is without him. (Wells 257)

Certainly, perhaps most especially during the *Balladenjahr*, 1797, Goethe and Schiller worked closely with one another. Even so, this assessment of Schiller's gifts as a poet seems rather harsh.

Bernhardt offered a considerably more sympathetic estimation, informing students that

> Es mag sein, daß, wie die Kritiker sagen, Schiller nicht so groß ist wie Goethe, und daß er in der Weltliteratur nur mit Dichtern wie Virgil, Tasso, Corneille, Spenser und Lord Byron auf gleiche Stufe gestellt werden kann—aber die größe Maße des deutschen Volkes verehrt ihn doch als ihren ersten und größten Dichter. . . . *Schiller hat unendlich viel für die Litteratur gethan* [sic]. (35)

However, others continued their criticism of Schiller. According to Calvin Thomas, "Schiller had some difficulty in effecting a return from philosophy to poetry. . . . As for the ballad, he had never cared greatly for the folksong, and in any case its style was not at his command. . . . Under the influence of Goethe he tried to school himself . . ." (313–314). Ultimately, two camps may be described as having more or less committed themselves to or having discarded the idealism, morality and philosophical speculation which are inherent in Schiller's ballads and lyric poetry. Idealism, morality and philosophical speculation are qualities in a work of art which—at least from the viewpoint of some teachers then as well as now—lend themselves well to teaching a language; the students study the language, are exposed to art, and become inculcated with the idealistic, moral and philosophical truths contained in the work. Perhaps for this reason Schiller was more popular among professors than Goethe, not only in the realm of lyric poetry. On the other hand, Schiller is disparaged by others for exactly these qualities—idealism, moralizing and abstraction. If, therefore, the *New York Times* neglected Schiller (who was, after all, one of the "most translated"), its editors had a critical leg to stand on; yet it should not be forgotten that for Hosmer, and probably for Bernhardt, Schiller was an especially important revealer of "the German mind."

Among the individual poems listed as text titles, the earliest stem from 1797, the *Balladenjahr* Schiller shared with Goethe. *Der Taucher*, according to Wilhelm Bernhardt, "zeigt den für Liebe und Ehre begeisterten Menschen im Kampfe mit der rohen Naturgewalt" (33). Wells praises the ballad as "one of the most remarkable instances of the power of poetic imagination. The nearest approach to a whirlpool that Schiller had ever seen was a mill-race by the Saale, but he has given here a picture of one that is classic in the literatures of the world" (257). Having awarded this wry compliment, Wells proceeds (as quoted above) to offer Goethe the laurels.

The other ballad by Schiller found as a text which is most frequently cited in literary histories of the period reviewed is *Die Kraniche von Ibykus*. This ballad demonstrates "daß der Dichter unter dem direkten Schutze der Götter steht, die seinen Tod an den Mördern rächen; die Macht des bösen Gewissens ist drastisch gezeichnet" (Bernhardt 33). Here are idealism and moralizing, but perhaps abstraction is somewhat palliated.

That significant example of *Gedankenlyrik*, *Das Lied von der Glocke*, outpaced the ballads discussed above to stand in first place in number of listings with regard to Schiller's poetry (eight listings, four publishers). Not to be overlooked is the fact that *Das Lied von der Glocke* stands alone in the universal approbation of all the American professors who comment upon it; for example, "to express his ideals of culture in language of emotional warmth and rhythmic distinction . . . is what he undertook in his philosophic poems—most happily in . . . *The Song of the Bell*" (Thomas 313). While Thomas describes the process of composition, Wells points out the great popularity of Schiller's poem—"perhaps the most prized of his lyrics in Germany, and certainly the best known abroad" (258). And Bernhardt elevates both execution and content to sublimity: " 'Das Lied von der Glocke,' eins der vollendetsten Gedichte aller Zeiten und Völker, enthält die herrlichsten Gedanken über das häusliche und öffentliche Leben" (33). Apparently much read in the U.S., *Das Lied von der Glocke*—a poem to bourgeois life, in which culture and nature are harmoniously united—contributed substantially to the U.S. students' *Deutschlandbild*.

Even so, Schiller's drama far surpassed his lyric poetry and ballads as far as texts were concerned. As Kurz had stated:

> Schillers poetisches Talent war zwar keineswegs auf eine oder die andere Gattung beschränkt, vielmehr haben wir gesehen, daß er im Lyrischen wie im Epischen höchst Bedeutendes leistete, ja die beiden Gattungen in eigenthümlicher [sic] Weise erweiterte, aber es ist doch unverkennbar, daß sein Talent für das Drama geschaffen war. (3:445)

And the Americans agreed. Professor Thomas states, for example, that

> the best energies of Schiller were devoted to playwriting, and it was he who first gave the German drama its European prestige. It is largely due to his influence that, throughout the nineteenth century, there was a continuous current of creditable production in the line of poetic tragedy, and that to this day nearly every German poet regards success in that genre as the highest kind of success. (288–89)

It seems certain that more of Schiller's plays than Goethe's plays were read by U.S. students; it should not be forgotten that Schiller led in the survey in total number of listings—and most listings relate to his plays.

The earliest of Schiller's dramas used as a text is *Kabale und Liebe*; indeed, it is his only *Sturm und Drang* play edited as a text. Vilmar provides some essential information not only about *Kabale und Liebe*, but also about *Die Räuber* and *Die Verschwörung des Fiesco von Genua*:

> Die Räuber bleiben auf einem ganz und gar erdichteten Boden, so zu sagen im Ueberall [sic] und Nirgendslande stehen . . . ; Fiesco spielt in einem wirklich republikanischen Staate; Kabale und Liebe rückt nun in die deutsche Wirklichkeit ein und repräsentiert uns auf das Deutlichste, welche Gesinnungen man damals *gegen*, und welche Vorstellungen man *von* der Hofwelt, der französierten, in Frivolität und Niedrigkeit allerdings tief versunkenen Hofwelt hatte. (492)

All three plays deal with a fight against oppression; what then, set *Kabale und Liebe* apart, making it alone suitable for a text? *Die Räuber* centers upon the outraged Karl Moor's attacks on society and ends with his repentance for his crimes; *Fiesco* is the story of a successful Genoese revolutionary who, when he seizes power, becomes a worse tyrant than the former, aristocratic oppressors. Certainly, these plots, for all their *Sturm und Drang*, contain morals of which students do well to be aware: personal wrongs are no cause for an attack upon society; absolute power corrupts absolutely.

Why, then, was *Kabale und Liebe*, in which a corrupt, aristocratic society brings about a double suicide (the play then bearing the message: aristocratic society is corrupt and kills), preferred? Vilmar has probably answered the question in stating:

> Alle Scheußlichkeiten, die man sich irgend denken mochte, wurden in diese Region [die Hofwelt] verlegt, ihr ein gedrückter, verachteter, mishandelter Bürgerstand gegenübergestellt, und aus dieser Gegeneinanderstellung ein Kampf entwickelt, welcher zunächst einen sittlichen Widerwillen gegen jene Regionen wie zum Grunde so auch zum Zwecke hatte. (492)

Corrupt aristocracy and despised, downtrodden middle class—this is the old world which the founding fathers fled in order to fight aristocratic tyrants.

Here is a cause more wholesome than attempted anarchy (*Die Räuber*) and personal tyranny (*Fiesco*), be the action itself ever so distasteful. Thus it was, perhaps, that *Kabale und Liebe* (the name which Iffland gave Schiller's play) was chosen for students of German as a foreign language over *Die Räuber* and *Fiesco*.

Although Bernhardt merely lists *Kabale und Liebe* together with the other early plays, not commenting upon it, he does mention—when discussing *Die Räuber*—that "die darin ausgesprochenen Freiheitsideen machten einen tiefen Eindruck auf die durch die Unabhängigkeits-Erklärung der nordamerikanischen Kolonieen . . . enthusiastisch erregten Zeitgenossen" (31). Certainly, the effects of the Declaration of Independence were also present in *Fiesco* and *Kabale und Liebe*; concerning the latter, Calvin Thomas writes that

> *Cabal and Love* is much more vitally related than either of its predecessors to German life . . . a drastic comment on class feeling as a factor in the social order, and on the infamies that might flourish, and often did flourish, beneath the glamor of court life in the eighteenth century. . . . The play lives, on the boards and as literature, by virtue of its fearless and virile treatment of the relations existing between the plain people and the so-called nobility. Like the *Robbers*, it belongs emphatically to the literature of revolt, but its criticism of the social order is much more temperate than in the earlier play. This time Schiller had his eye on the facts, and not on a madman's dream. (286–87)

Clearly, of the three earliest dramas *Kabale und Liebe* was—if not a wholesome play—the staunchest advocate of a democratic society. As such, it alone was chosen for publication as a text.

III

Klassik—Romantik—Biedermeier—Junges Deutschland

The fact that Goethe and Schiller represented German Classicism in American German texts between 1864 and 1918 is not a surprising revelation. Additionally, August Friedrich von Kotzebue and Johann Gottfried Seume offered students a different view of German culture in a classical vein.

Goethe's classical works were, to be sure, originally "mit einer an Gleichgültigkeit gränzenden [sic] Kühle aufgenommen worden." However, according to Heinrich Kurz, in time the German people became aware that these new, classical creations were

> doch von entschieden deutschem Geiste beseelt; bei aller antiken Form hatten Iphigenie, sowie Hermann und Dorothea in Sprache, Gesinnung, poetischer Auffassung doch nur von einem deutschen Dichter geschaffen werden können, und sie waren eben deshalb so großartig, weil sich in ihnen zeigte, wie es möglich sei, sich die vollendete Form der Griechen anzueignen, ohne weder Sprache noch volksthümliche Eigenthümlichkeit aufzugeben. (3:96)

Goethe's classical works were regarded, therefore, as the end result of a sort of Hegelian dialectic; classical form and German content were perfectly adapted to one another and blended together.

Calvin Thomas in his assessment of *Iphigenie* seems to follow Kurz's thoughts on Goethe's Classicism directly:

> The German public, expecting something like *Götz von Berlichingen* received it [*Iphigenie*] indifferently. . . . it was like the Greek *Iphigenie* in threatening a tragic conclusion and then avoiding it. But here, for the seeing eye, the resemblance to anything Greek ended. . . . In short, it was a poetic drama of the soul. (297)

Dating from 1787, *Iphigenie* was utilized as a text for U.S. German students practically from the beginning of the era under consideration, its initially mediocre reception in Germany notwithstanding.

Yet a defense of *Iphigenie* also presented itself to Thomas—who also apologized for *Götz*—as a necessity:

To be sure its "action" is not the kind to captivate Philistia. But given actors and an audience equal to its demand on their culture as well as their intelligence, and Goethe's *Iphigenie* is a fascinating play, as well as a beautiful poem. (297)

According to findings in Appendix F, *Iphigenie* far exceeded *Götz* in number of listings, for, as has been stated elsewhere, the rebellious *Kraftkerl* was rejected by academe in favor of harmony and order.

Less in demand than *Iphigenie* was *Torquato Tasso*, the play which "sprang from the same soil" (Thomas 298). Perhaps the strongest point of the play to editors and professors was that "die Entwicklung von Tassos Charakter bekundet Goethes große psychologische Einsicht" (Bernhardt 41). On the other hand, though, it was also asserted that the

> subjective element had been written into the play with such fulness of detail as to render its representation on the stage virtually impossible. And, indeed, it can hardly be denied that much of *Tasso* is occupied with feelings a little too refined and delicate for human nature's daily food, or for the purposes of the acted drama. (Thomas 300)

But too great refinement, which could become tedious, was rivaled in undesirability by the equation of Weimar with Ferrara. It is commonly supposed that the conflict between Goethe the poet and Goethe the government minister is represented in the friction between Tasso and Antonio. The relationship of Tasso and the Princess Leonore, it is postulated, shows Goethe's frustrated love for Frau von Stein—a subject which may have rendered *Tasso* as unwholesome to some as *Götz* or *Werther*, at least for less mature students. Certainly, Iphigenie's chastity surpassed Tasso's fall in number of editions, reprints, reissues or catalog listings.

More positive was the scholars' response to *Reineke Fuchs*, though only one edition of the text appeared. The fable, composed in hexameters (finished in 1793), is a "satirische Tierfabel" in which Goethe caricatures "die Politik und die streitenden Parteien" in the Germany of his days (Bernhardt 37). Though Goethe's version is based upon the Low German rendering of Alkmar's *Reinke de Vos*, Goethe's work is more than a translation. As Heinrich Kurz, whose critical essay on the Low German version is briefly considered in chapter 2, states:

> *Reineke Fuchs* ist keineswegs eine Uebersetzung im gewöhnlichen Sinne des Wortes, nicht einmal in dem Sinne einer Herder'schen Uebersetzung; denn Göthe [sic] hat das ursprüngliche Gedicht schon formell umgestaltet, indem er die mittelalterliche Darstellungsweise mit ihren kurzen Reimpaaren mit der antiken epischen Form vertauscht und dem Gedicht dadurch schon nicht bloß ein mehr künstlerisches, sondern auch das Gepräge größerer Allgemeinheit gegeben hat. Und eben dadurch war es ihm auch möglich, die Beziehung auf seine Zeit mehr im Auge zu behalten. (3:322)

Thus Goethe poured medieval content into a classical form and made the *Tierepos* into a political satire.

If there be a question as to why *Reineke* was not more popular as a text, an answer is provided by a prominent editor. After Goethe and Christiane lived as a couple, fewer people took an interest in Goethe's literary endeavors; therefore,

> he turned his attention to botany and other scientific studies, and for several years he wrote nothing of more than third-rate literary importance. Two or three prose plays . . . and a hexameter version of the old poem of *Reynard the Fox* . . . were the most notable. (Thomas 311)

In the textbook market, the "third-rate" *Tierepos* simply could not compete successfully with *Faust, Hermann und Dorothea*, and other, greater works of Goethe.

A similar fate was shared by *Das Märchen*, listed once during the years surveyed and all but entirely neglected by literary histories of the era. One professor, for example, mentions only Goethe's "cryptic symbolism in his Märchen" (Thomas 317). Another quotes Matthew Arnold:

> The 'Mährchen [sic],' woven throughout of symbol, hieroglyphic, mystification, is therefore a piece of solemn inanity, on which a man of Göthe's [sic] powers could never have wasted his time, but for his lot having been cast in a nation which has never lived. (Hosmer 404)

In view of comments such as the preceding, the dearth of editors for Goethe's *Märchen* is easily comprehensible.

Less understandable to certain individuals of the later twentieth century is the enormous popularity earlier enjoyed by *Hermann und Dorothea*, Goethe's "bourgeois epic." Leading Goethe's other works by a considerable margin in the statistics, *Hermann und Dorothea* likewise received only accolades from authors, professors and editors. Vilmar, for example, near the end of his treatment of Goethe, states that

> Neben den bisher aufgezählten Werken Goethes steht endlich noch eins *von gleichem*, und sogar, Faust ausgenommen, *höherem* Range: *Hermann und Dorothea*, in welchem der Dichter das theoretisch fast für unlösbar zu haltende Problem auf bewundernswerte Weise gelöst hat, Begebenheiten der Gegenwart, und zwar der Gegenwart des häuslichen und bürgerlichen Lebens im reinsten epischen Stile zu schildern—mithin ein bürgerliches Epos zu schaffen. (479)

Moreover, Heinrich Kurz echoes Vilmar's praise as follows:

> Der Dichter hat die Personen nicht durch Schilderung ihrer äußern oder innern Eigenthümlichkeiten [sic] gezeichnet, sondern durch ihre Handlungen und Reden charakterisiert; aber er versteht dies so meisterhaft, daß sich jedem Leser

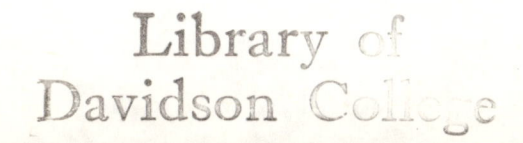

ein vollständiges, lebenswarmes Bild der einzelnen Personen entfaltet. . . . Es ist unmöglich, alles Vortreffliche in der schönen Dichtung auch nur anzudeuten; wir begnügen uns, noch darauf aufmerksam zu machen, daß kein Vorgang, keine Begebenheit eintritt, ohne daß sie vorher, manchmal schon lange voraus, motiviert worden wäre. (3:320–21)

The elevation of the middle class to the epic was certainly a popular feat.

In the United States the reception in some quarters was scarcely less enthusiastic. Wilhelm Bernhardt told students that Goethe's "idyllisches Epos 'Hermann und Dorothea' (1797) ist ein Meisterwerk ersten Ranges; mit der großen Zeit der französischen Revolution im Hintergrund entwirft es ein treues Bild echt deutschen Familienlebens" (39). Professor Thomas delivered more interesting, if less positive remarks:

In the young Hermann and his parents one quickly recognizes the young Goethe and *his* parents; while in the wise judge who discourses so ably of the Revolution we hear the maturer Goethe, who had come to look with aversion on the course of events in France. . . . And . . . all the characters . . . reel off their philosophy of life in stately hexameters, with many a reminiscence of Homeric phrase. . . . the common reality is invested with a stylistic veil that idealizes everything. (317)

It is difficult to decide whether the reeling off of hexameters under an idealizing stylistic veil is considered by Thomas to be one of the highest manifestations of poetic expression or not.

Editions of *Hermann und Dorothea* were quite numerous in the years surveyed (14), and professors could be selective in the adoption of a text. For example, in a review of Ernst Feise's edition of *Hermann und Dorothea* (1917), Bert John Vos (himself a textbook editor) discussed Feise's omission— necessitated by space—of discourses upon Homeric epic and the Salzburg refugees:

The Salzburg story, while of interest, is in no way vital to a proper understanding of the poem, a view that can hardly be maintained as regards the dependence of Goethe upon Homer in the matter of style and diction. . . . the "Vorbemerkung" (p. xiv), that gives in ten or twelve lines an account of the scansion of the hexameter . . . was doubtless an afterthought. (182)

Whatever the critical material accompanying it, *Hermann und Dorothea* was apparently the most popular Goethe text of the era. It raised the middle class to epic splendor; it dealt with reasonable people—not rebels (except for the French in the background); feelings were not too refined—there were no breakdowns or suicides. It was wholesome.

Warren Austin Adams, who edited the poem as a text for Heath, makes his readers aware of the tranquil aura of the work:

The poem always afforded its author a peculiar pleasure. As it called up no unpleasant memories, he was able, he tells us, to read it all his life with delight. Few readers would pass other judgement. In it Goethe has given us not a grand but a *most* charming poem. It has simplicity, dignity, and tranquility, qualities that seldom fail to work their charm; the character drawing is clear and life-like, the love story attractive. (xii)

Plainly, the age which thought little of *Götz* and less of *Werther* rallied to the cause of the "bourgeois epic."

Not as popular as *Herman und Dorothea* and *Iphigenie* was *Faust*, both parts of which were edited as texts. The lag in *Faust* editions was probably due to the essence of *Sturm und Drang* which lingered about the work, although the first part was completed in 1806, the second part in 1831. A list of the forbidding goings on (to name only a few: fornication, infanticide, the fiery end of Baucis and Philemon) seems unnecessary here; however, in view of some editors' and literary historians' views of other Goethean works, particularly those of the *Sturm und Drang*, the content of *Faust I* and *II* must have played a part in putting *Faust* in third place after the two classical works mentioned above. Indeed, when the lesser offenses of *Götz* and *Werther* are considered, it is interesting that *Faust* so far outdistanced them as a text.

Vilmar views *Faust* as a Storm and Stress product, but simultaneously calls it more:

Dieser Stoff [war] der Dichterzeit der siebziger Jahre überhaupt ganz nahe gelegt. . . . und es wird das Drama niemals vollständig begriffen werden, wenn es nicht in dem genauen Verhältnis begriffen wird, in welchem es zu der Zeit stehet [sic], in der es seinen Ursprung fand. Aber freilich würde es eine beschränkte Auffaßung sein . . . es würde dieß [sic] gerade die besten Elemente der Dichtung zerstören, und dieselbe im besten Falle mit Werthers Leiden auf eine Stufe stellen heißen; es wäre dann ein *Zeitbild* . . . aber bei weitem keine Dichtung ersten Ranges, kein *Weltbild*, was alle großen Dichtungen gewesen sind. (475)

Thus, as a German text, *Faust* outdistanced *Werther* and *Götz*; the latter two works must ever remain *Sturm und Drang* (not an era favored by professors of the epoch), while *Faust*, though conceived in the same period, transcends time as it becomes a *Weltbild*.

Less cosmic and more personal is Hosmer, who urges the student to pity Faust—maintaining that he is not "precisely vicious"—prior to an enumeration of his crimes (396). In this interpretation, Faust is seen as a kind of everyman:

We do not execrate him; we pity him. The strong, thoughtful, passionate man, who has passed onward through the inevitable mortal course of sin, suffering, doubt, repentance, beholds in the career of Faust a typical rendering of the tragedy of his own life, of power almost superhuman. (Hosmer 397)

To the microcosm of the beholder, then, Faust represents a sort of macrocosm—he is everyman magnified.

Somewhat more ominous is Benjamin Wells's assessment of the impression produced by *Faust*:

> We have lived to see the real exalted above the ideal, action above thought, perhaps in undue measure. Hence the general popular comprehension of "Faust" as a whole in this period more than ever before, because more than ever before it reflects the popular mind to which, as to Faust, the "logos" is neither "word," nor "thought," nor "power," but "action." The dangers of such a philosophy of life are obvious: some of them are already realized in the luxury of our hedonists and the socialism and nihilism of our proletariat. (217–18)

Wells's statement was made in 1895. The dangers of action considered above thought bore fruit in two world wars; Hitler was considered by some to be a Faust-figure. Faust's striving has been regarded negatively by some in the post-Hitler era.

However, Wells concludes his teachings on *Faust* with a requiescat:

> "Faust" if rightly apprehended, offers two poisons, each an antidote of the other, which joined together help and strengthen [each other]. Neither Euphorion's idealism that will not touch earth, nor Mephistopheles' realism that will not rise above it, but that just mean that idealizes the real and realizes the ideal,—that is the world-wisdom of Faust. (218)

Unbeknown to Wells, the extremes of Euphorion and Mephisto could call to mind the dark idealism and cynical realism of the Third Reich. It is to be hoped that the western world has finally hit Wells's golden mean.

Along similar lines, Bernhardt also centers on action. Faust finds no contentment in knowledge, aesthetics, magic, or sensuality

> bis er endlich in der *That, im praktischen Leben,* in der industriellen und commerciellen [sic] Arbeit für das Wohl der Menschheit . . . die lang ersehnte Ruhe des Herzens und die Vergebung des Himmels für die Irrungen seiner Jugend findet. (42)

Faust hits the mean between knowledge and magic (attempts to know and to control) and sensuality and aesthetics (aimed at enjoyment, physical and mental) in practical life, work for the good of humanity. As Wells stated above, each of the "poisons" acts as an antidote to the other; all blend, giving peace of soul and divine forgiveness.

Calvin Thomas first edited *Faust I* for D. C. Heath in 1892. Though Thomas is sometimes abrasive in his *History of German Literature*, his introduction to *Faust* is exceedingly bland; he follows the lead of established sources, among them other editors of U.S. German texts, Starr Willard Cutting and Julius

Goebel, and playwright Adolf Wilbrandt (three of whose works appeared as texts):

> I have of course endeavored to profit by the labors of preceding editors, critics and expounders. . . . In dealing with a subject like *Faust*, about which such mountains of literature exist, it is, in general, possible to attain originality only at the expense of either truth, usefulness or importance; and my aim has been to be useful rather than to seem acute or learned. (iii)

Certainly, Thomas's voluminous notes are useful, in that they are informative. A vast rehash of what "everyone" knows about *Faust* is offered the student; for example,

> If a man means well and "strives," he will not be lost for following the impulses of his nature whereof God is the author. He may go wrong, but his wrong-doing will be a mistake, and God pardons mistakes. (xxxvii)

Such ideas are surely useful to the student if he is to understand *Faust*; and Thomas's accentuation of striving runs parallel to the ascertainments of other editors consulted.

Thomas's *Literary History*, like his *Faust* edition, is uncharacteristically bland:

> It is clear that from the first Goethe thought of the old magician who had sold his soul for a mess of pottage as a man better than his reputation; as a titanic truthseeker, in whose nature there were the very largest potentialities of good as well as of evil. (278)

To those familiar with *Faust* this is a more or less self-evident, if not acute or learned, truth. It should be recalled at this point that Thomas abhorred "Prometheus" and *Werther*, but nurtured a predilection for *Götz*. Perhaps his ambivalence toward *Sturm und Drang* manifested itself again in the case of *Faust I*, which, despite its date of completion, is at least to some extent a product of that era. (Or might one speculate upon whether the editor's mild approach to the work could have been at all affected by the economics of textbook publishing?)

Only slightly behind *Faust* in listings were various editions of all or part of *Dichtung und Wahrheit*. Vilmar gave a most positive assessment of the autobiography, descrying "ein in seinem innersten Kerne *gesundes* Leben in dem ihm zusagenden Gewande." This wholesomeness is furthered, according to the same critic, by an atmosphere reminiscent of the *Abglanz* found in *Faust II*:

> Die kunstvolle Bewältigung des Stoffes, den uns der Dichter nicht in seiner rohen Unmittelbarkeit, sondern aus der Ferne, im Spiegel und Bilde, sehen läßt, ist es, welche dem Werke seinen Namen "Dichtung" als das vollste Recht

zueignet. . . . Denn es fehlen ja alle Angaben über Abstammung und Herkunft seiner Familie, über die Namen und Verhältnisse seiner Geliebten (Gretchen, Friederike, Lilli), denen man in der neuesten Zeit mit wahrer Spürerei, oft auf kindische ja auf unehrenhafte Weise, nachgegangen ist. (483)

Dichtung und Wahrheit, then, was a popular source of text material because life was regarded at a distance, transfigured and purified.

Five years later (1879), an American regarded the autobiography with less reverence, yet noted—in opposition to Vilmar—its clarity as well as its distancing. Of Goethe's historical and biographical activity he stated, therefore, that

> nothing is so interesting as the "Poetry and Truth". . . . It was written in age, and in telling the stories of his childhood more in adulation than perspicatiousness, perhaps, the old man is often garrulous; but it is the most graphic and picturesque detail possible of a splendid development. (Hosmer 369)

Bernhardt states flatly that " '*Dichtung und Wahrheit*' ist ein Meisterstück der Biographie nach Inhalt und Form," and adds that "eine teilweise Fortsetzung der Erzählung seines Lebens findet sich in der 'italienischen Reise' " (Bernhardt 42).

This last was anticipated by Vilmar, who saw *Dichtung und Wahrheit*, the *Italienische Reise* and the *Campagne in Frankreich* as parts of one work, and, in what seems an echo of Goethe's "Mahomets Gesang," described these "fragments of a great confession" as follows:

> Es ist der milde, klare, durchsichtige Strom, der ruhig seiner eigenen Natur folgend hinabfließt durch die Gefilde, die Bäche in sich aufnimmt und ihre Trübe in seinem hellen Spiegel abklärt, Blumen, Gebüsch und wildes Gestrüpp des Ufers, heitere Auen und kahle Hügel, an denen er vobeiströmt, in gleicher Wahrheit und mit gleicher Ruhe wiederspiegelt [sic], und der nur zuweilen durch dumpfes Brausen aus der Tiefe zu erkennen gibt, daß er dort unten über Felsenrisse geströmt ist und diese Klippen überwunden hat; nur leise Wirbel und leichte Schaumkreiße [sic], die wie im anmutigen Tanze auf den Wellen auf und nieder schweben, geben auf der Oberfläche Kunde von den in der Tiefe überstandenen Kämpfen. (482–83)

This amazing metaphor demonstrates not only profound admiration for Goethe's autobiographical works, which has possibly waned somewhat in the present time (it seems safe to say that fewer undergraduate students now read all or portions of *Dichtung und Wahrheit*), but is also notable as a demonstration of criticism at a time when there were more often poetic statements about poetics.

Who other than Schiller stands as the first in the struggle to unite art and criticism? Yet, according to commercial and scholarly catalogs, students did not read all or sections of works such as *Über naive und sentimentalische*

Dichtung or *Über Anmut und Würde* (some parts of which do find their way into some classes of today) in texts of the type surveyed. Rather, it was Schiller's dramas, his most important contributions to German literature, which were, judging statistically, quite probably responsible for the greatest German textbook sales in U.S. history to 1918 and for some years thereafter. Schiller led all other German authors in catalog listings—it is established that his works in textbook form were advertised more frequently for sale and could be found in greater volume in libraries than the works of Goethe or any other German author.

To continue with the discussion of Schiller begun in chapter 2: Schiller's classical period began with *Don Carlos*, a drama which was first conceived in the spirit of *Sturm und Drang*. This may account for the fact that only one German textbook edition of the play appeared, 1864–1918. Academe had, on the whole, little liking for *Sturm und Drang*, as has been shown in the case of Goethe, as well as of Schiller:

> *Don Carlos* wurde von Schiller noch entworfen ganz mit dem dunkeln, leidenschaftlichen Interesse für die vulgären Zeitgedanken, aus welchen die drei ersten Stücke hervorgegangen waren. (Vilmar 493)

Then came the change to classicism, from Don Carlos to Marquis Posa, and an "objektivere Darstellung" (Vilmar 493). Still, Vilmar taught that the last two acts could not undo the offenses of the first three.

Indeed, as Kurz reports,

> So erkannte Schiller doch, daß er in diesem Stück künstlerisch auf Abwege gerathen war, er erkannte, daß es ihm an gründlicher ästhetischer Bildung und vor Allem an richtiger und klarer Anschauung des Lebens fehle, ohne welche ein dramatisches Kunstwerk unmöglich sei. Er wendete sich dem Studium der Geschichte und der Philosophie zu. (3:433)

Schiller the classicist—the Schiller critics admired—had not yet ascended to the ultimate height which he would reach.

In the United States, reception of the drama among academics was similarly negative. Bernhardt grants *Don Carlos* only one sentence, in which he says that Schiller's study of historical sources for *Don Carlos* awakened his interest in history (31). Calvin Thomas, on the other hand, writes at length on *Don Carlos*; interestingly, his assessment of the play runs counter to that of the German critics, who favor the last two acts, though there is agreement otherwise:

> Toward the end the intrigue becomes so very complicated that the spectator, or even the reader, can hardly keep track of it. The play lacks the simplicity and the concentration that are necessary to a harmonious tragic effect. There is material in it for two tragedies, and they interfere with each other. (304)

Thus *Don Carlos* scarcely fared better than *Kabale und Liebe*. Both were tainted with the *vulgären Zeitgedanken* of *Sturm und Drang*.

Der Geisterseher, an uncompleted novel which has been called Germany's first artistic *Kriminalroman* (Krell and Fiedler 184), follows *Don Carlos* chronologically, and was also represented by one edition (although this was re-edited, reprinted, reissued or listed under five different dates). Among all the secondary sources consulted, only Hosmer's literary history offers a terse piece of information about the work: "That he [Schiller] might have become a skillful writer of romances is indicated by the incomplete story of the 'Ghostseer' " (426). Few conclusions may be drawn, therefore, except that the book was not a very popular text, and as such excited little attention. Schiller's more significant classical works, especially his dramas, were far too important to allow *Der Geisterseher* a larger share of the student market.

Not dramas, to be sure, but classical and of greater significance were Schiller's historical studies, *Der Abfall der Niederlande* (1788) and *Die Geschichte des dreißigjährigen Kriegs* (1802). Parts of these works were edited as texts under four different titles, as shown in Appendix F. However, it is of interest that during the earlier decades of the years under consideration the histories were either neglected by commentators or described as necessities for Schiller's growth as a dramatist. After *Don Carlos*, therefore, Schiller had turned to the study of history and philosophy, and

> erst als er durch die erste eine tiefere Einsicht in die Welt- und Menschenverhältnisse gewonnen hatte . . . regte sich der Drang zu dramatischer Production. . . . Schon während er an der 'Geschichte des dreißigjährigen Kriegs' arbeitete, entstand der Gedanke in ihm, den größten Helden dieser Zeit, den Wallenstein, dramatisch zu bearbeiten. (Kurz 3:433)

The historical study was necessary for Schiller's composition of *Wallenstein*—and this in Kurz's estimation is its primary justification.

In the United States, the historical works were likewise a side issue:

> His labors in this field, though important, were transitory. . . . The books show no deep investigation, and have therefore sometimes been lightly prized. His discrimination was, however, excellent; what materials he had he used to good purpose. He wrote with enthusiasm, showed constant improvement, and might have become great. (Hosmer 426)

Schiller might have become a great historian had he not gone back to writing plays. Yet it should not be forgotten that "auf Grund dieses Geschichtswerkes wurde er durch die Empfehlung des weimarischen Staatsrats Goethe als Professor der Geschichte an die Universität Jena berufen" (Bernhardt 32). Perhaps, if one considers Goethe's esteem of the historical works, it is only because Schiller's dramas are so much greater than his historical works that the latter are praised only faintly by these relatively early commentators.

But with a change of emphasis in the later part of the Wilhelminian period, the historical writings took on luster of their own: "Rather hastily written, with but little examination of the sources . . . their eloquent dignity of style, their philosophic temper, and their vivid portraiture of scenes and persons set upon them the stamp of literary classics" (Thomas 311). Viewed as literature rather than history, the works are freed from the onus of superficiality. All things considered, this is probably the fairest approach to *Der Abfall der Niederlande* and *Die Geschichte des Dreißigjährigen Kriegs*.

In contrast to the historical works, the *Wallenstein* trilogy, which sprang from them, received for the most part only praise. The greatest exception was the action between Max Piccolomini and Thekla, Wallenstein's daughter. For example:

> Das älteste [Trauerspiel] und nicht allein dem Umfang, sondern auch dem Stoff und der Behandlung nach größte, ist die Trilogie Wallenstein. . . . Die Wahl dieses Stoffes ist die glücklichste, welche Schiller in allen seinen Dramen getroffen hat. . . . Diese Momente von Schillers glücklicher Wahl werden allen künftigen Tragödiendichtern als unabweichliche Richtschnur dienen müßen [sic]. . . . Nur . . . daß gerade die Partie im Wallenstein, an welcher Schiller die größte Freude hatte, und die ihm für sein Stück das größte Publikum gewann, völlig verfehlt ist und die Wirkung des Dramas zum Teil geradezu zerstört: Max und Thekla. (Vilmar 496–97)

In fact, Vilmar goes on to relate that many readers skip over or try to ignore the offending portions, "um das Uebrige desto reiner genießen zu können" (497). However, Vilmar is almost effusive in his praise of the drama excepting the Max and Thekla action.

Heinrich Kurz is very similar in his estimations of *Wallenstein*: "Mit dem 'Wallenstein' betrat Schiller die Bahn des historischen Dramas, in welchem er so Großes leisten, ja unübertroffen bleiben sollte." And about Wallenstein's tragic flaw Kurz states:

> [So] gelang es dem Dichter, auch höhere Theilnahme für seinen Helden zu erregen, ja den Wunsch zu erwecken, es möchte dessen Unternehmen gelingen. Allein so hoch die Idee der Liebe für das gesammte Vaterland . . . so war sie doch von einer noch höheren überwogen, der nämlich . . . daß das Gute auf diesem Wege nicht erreicht werden darf. Und so muß Wallenstein fallen, weil er das höchste Sittengesetz verletzt. (3:435)

Wallenstein is motivated by a love for Germany and a desire to rescue it from imperial *Pfaffenherrschaft*, as well as by his own ambition. Thus he calls forth sympathy as well as censure.

In America, if there was agreement with regard to Wallenstein's character, a quite different view of Max Piccolomini and Thekla prevailed:

> Precisely where Wallenstein is wanting, on the moral side, are Max and Thekla strong. Max is aghast at the very mention by his father of Wallenstein's mediated treason, and heart-broken at its confirmation. The incomparable Thekla, at the moment of crisis, flings to the winds his happiness and her own, while she bids him be faithful and abandon her father and herself. There is in them fidelity to the highest duty. (Hosmer 456)

Far from agreeing with Vilmar that readers should ignore or skip over the Max and Thekla scenes, Hosmer praises them, although he adds that the two characters are "supernal beings, of a purity more than mortal—not flesh and blood types" (457). Could it be that, like *Werther* and *Kabale und Liebe*, the Max and Thekla portions of *Wallenstein* were rated by the U.S. critic upon their moral purity or wholesomeness? If the former two works were not prominent as texts due to the characters' defects and iniquities, perhaps the latter succeeded due to their virtue.

Indeed, in another literary history students are told that Max, "der Geliebte von Wallensteins Tochter Thekla, eine ideale, über jeden Tadel erhabene Persönlichkeit ist" (Bernhardt 34). Wells devotes the greater part of his discussion of the play to the lovers, and favors above all the role of Thekla:

> What is left for Max? Of himself he might waver, but Thekla, with a woman's more idealized sense of duty and readiness of sacrifice, sees that the tragic end is the only noble one. With his devoted soldiers Max falls, resisting the advance of the Swedes, and Wallenstein's world-embracing plans are dashed in pieces on the simple uprightness of his daughter. (266)

Thus Max and Thekla become a major part of the drama through the "readiness of sacrifice" and "simple uprightness" of Thekla. The Max and Thekla episodes of *Wallenstein* were—in Wells's opinion—anything but extrinsic frills best overlooked by the reader.

Calvin Thomas viewed Wallenstein as an "unheroic hero" exhibiting "repellent passions" who suffers a "miserable fate." However,

> by contriving that the spectator see him through the partial yet searching eyes of the young idealist, Max Piccolomini,—Schiller makes his hero's taking off appear like the tragic nemesis of a great man's error. (321–22)

Max is once again made a vital part of the action; in this case, it is Max who predominates in critical esteem over Thekla.

Held unworthy of the theatre by Vilmar, the young couple assumed a considerably more important role in America, where *Wallenstein* was loved for its virtues, not its vices. In this case, moral parts of the text were stressed over the story of Wallenstein's transgression; and, as in other cases, the moral issue had an effect on the textbook market.

Wallenstein was followed chronologically by *Der Neffe als Onkel* (1797), an adaptation of a comedy by the French playwright Picard. Schiller translated the play literally, "ohne sich jedoch diejenigen Abweichungen zu versagen, welche ihm für die Durchführung der Charaktere nothwendig [sic] schienen." Kurz praises Schiller's choice of Picard's play, for he finds it "lebendig und frisch," and perceives that it has "viel komische Kraft" (3:444). As a text, *Der Neffe als Onkel* went through at least six editions and nineteen listings; perhaps because it was only a translation, it excited little or no critical attention among the American literary historians, German professors and editors consulted.

Much more significant was *Maria Stuart*, although, according to Vilmar, this play shares the weaknesses of those which preceded it:

> Schiller hatte, wie er sagt, die Helden einmal an dem Wallenstein herzlich satt, und sehnte sich nach einer Darstellung menschlicher Leiden, bei denen er menschlich mitfühlen konnte; gerade dieß [sic] aber war die Klippe, an welcher er in seinen vier früheren Dramen, an welcher er auch auf der höheren Stufe, zu der er jetzt emporgestiegen war, scheiterte. (498)

Vilmar, as matters stand, is not alone in his negative view of *Maria Stuart*.

Consider, however, the opposing viewpoint offered by Kurz:

> Obleich "Maria Stuart" unmittelbar nach dem "Wallenstein" begonnen wurde, so zeigt dieselbe doch einen außerordentlichen Fortschritt des Dichters; er konnte nun die tiefere Einsicht in das Drama, die er sich mit unsäglicher Mühe im "Wallenstein" erworben hatte, mit der größten Freiheit wirken lassen, und so durfte er auch zu Stoffen und Charakteren, zu denen er nicht bloß künstlerische Liebe fühlte, übergehen, ohne befürchten zu dürfen, in die rein idealistische Manier der frühern Jahre zu verfallen, und die objektive Anschauung des Gegenstandes zu verlieren. (3:436)

Thus Schiller's personal involvement with his characters was either a great strength, as seen by Kurz, or a painful weakness as shown in Vilmar's estimation.

U.S. Germanists, siding with Vilmar, perceived asthenia in *Maria Stuart*. Bernhardt has no real praise for the play and seems to echo Vilmar's assessment almost literally. Maria Stuart

> erscheint im Stücke nur als das leidende Weib, der wir unser Mitleid nicht versagen können. Ihr Charakter ist ein wunderliches Gemisch von Schuld und Unschuld, Hoheit und Demut, Heroismus und Schwäche. (34)

The accents seem to fall on *leidend* and *wunderlich*, and Bernhardt's feelings toward the Queen's character seem a *Gemisch* of admiration and perplexity. Professor Wells writes in a similar vein:

> Nowhere had Schiller yet shown such power of theatrical pomp, nowhere had he arranged his materials so artistically. . . . But on the other hand, the

> conception leaves much to be desired. . . . Neither Mary nor Elizabeth have Wallenstein's tragic depth; we do not feel that these are people to move the world, and shape the destinies of men. . . . taken as a whole, "Maria Stuart" is inferior to "Wallensteins Tod," while it marks an advance on it in metrical skill and narrative composition. (269, 271)

What Schiller had gained in technical skill was counterbalanced, in Wells's estimation, by the loss of either the desire or the capability to create characters with depth.

Given the historical data, Schiller could have written a Catholic/Protestant drama—a play with a world view. This, presumably, would have given Mary and Elizabeth depth; they would be not only historical characters, but would represent opposing viewpoints in the Christian faith, and, as such, would necessarily represent the politics prevailing on either side. However,

> Schiller wished to make a human drama. . . . The great difficulty was that, if the action was to end with her [Mary's] death, her long-past misdeeds could not be represented, but only narrated. Thus she would appear all along as a doomed prisoner awaiting her fate—a pathetic rather than a tragic situation. (Thomas 323)

Once again, *Maria Stuart* is viewed primarily as purveyor of *Leiden*, awakener of *Mitleid*—not as a truly dramatic event.

Interestingly, listings for the *Wallenstein* trilogy and its separate parts (thirty-nine listings) surpassed *Maria Stuart* (thirty-seven listings) by only two. It is significant, too, that this is a contest of "four to one"—*Wallenstein*, having been edited both in toto and in parts, could be ordered four different ways. Although U.S. literary historians consulted—most of whom were also textbook editors—favored *Wallenstein* greatly over *Maria Stuart*, the two plays are virtually tied in number of publishers (sixteen, *Wallenstein*; fourteen, *Maria Stuart*). *Maria Stuart*, therefore, despite adverse criticism, was a significant part of the U.S. German textbook mélange. Perhaps the play's popularity was due to students' familiarity with the story of Mary, Queen of Scots. Although both plays were recommended by the Committee of Twelve, only *Wallenstein* was edited by a committee member, William H. Carruth. Of the two plays, *Wallenstein*, which deals with things German, was probably considered more compatible with the committee's stress on German life as well as German literature.

Of greater significance than either of the preceding plays was *Die Jungfrau von Orleans* (forty-six listings, second only to *Wilhelm Tell*). Yet, as in the case of *Maria Stuart*, critical opinion is not always favorable. Vilmar once again criticizes Schiller's wish to portray *Leiden*—"noch weniger gelungen, noch stärker zerschellt an derselben Klippe ist *Die Jungfrau von Orleans*." However, in this case, the portrayal of a historical character was distorted not only through suffering, but also through Schiller's vagueness with regard to religion:

> Schiller ergriff diese kirchlichen Motive, ohne derselben mächtig zu sein noch mächtig zu werden; eben das ist allerdings einer der schwersten Fehler der Tragödie, daß die religiöse Begeisterung der Jungfrau durch das ganze Stück nicht viel mehr ist als Phrase und der nächste aus diesem unmittelbar herfließende ist der, daß Johanna im Kampf zwischen himmlischer Begeisterung und irdischer Liebe der letztern unterliegt, während . . . es fast unvermeidlich war, . . . daß sie hingerissen von weltlicher Ehre ihren ursprünglichen himmlischen Beruf *überschreitet*. (Vilmar 498)

In Vilmar's view, Schiller's lack of understanding of religious tradition yielded a pious fraud: the worldly was brought too closely before a saint—who capitulated before love, not honor. The history professor had been too wanton with "historical" facts.

As in the case of *Maria Stuart*, Kurz offers a refutation of Vilmar's views. With regard to religion, it is stated that

> Dieser Glaube, der sich ihrer mit unwiderstehlicher Kraft bemächtigt hatte, hatte ihre ganze Natur verändert. . . . Dies Alles hat der Dichter eben so klar als meisterhaft dargestellt; er entwickelt diesen Charakter der Jungfrau so glücklich und wahr, daß selbst der Zuschauer unwillkürlich zu dem Glauben an ihre göttliche Sendung hingerissen wird. (3:438)

Everyone is carried away with Johanna's religious experiences—and no less so by her love life:

> Eben so tief psychologisch ist das spätere Verhalten der Jungfrau motiviert. Sie wird von plötzlicher Liebe ergriffen, von Liebe zu einem Feinde ihres Volkes . . . und die Leidenschaft bemächtigt sich ihrer mit solcher Gewalt, daß sie dem Geliebten gegenüber wieder zum schwachen Weibe wird, daß die schwärmerische Begeisterung, die sie bis dahin über ihr Geschlecht hinaus gehoben hatte, wie mit Einem [sic] Schlage verschwindet. (Kurz 3:438)

In contrast to Vilmar, Kurz finds it plausible that Johanna's love for Lionel wins out against her supposedly supernatural powers.

In the U.S., Bernhardt merely reports the plot, taking neither side as to Schiller's stagecraft (34–35); Wells, however, is more outspoken:

> Unnatural idealism is the fundamental fault of the "Maid of Orleans." There is more of true tragedy in the story of Joan of Arc than in Schiller's artificial heroine. . . . he does not always perceive the narrow bound that separates the childlike from the childish. . . . The realists of the play, Talbot and Thibaut, are caricatures. Joan's love for the English Lionel is a gratuitous humiliation of the single-minded purity of the historic Maid. (273–75)

Wells, like Vilmar, has little liking for the play. He shares the latter's dislike for the love element, and, if "childish" is Wells's assessment of Schiller's handling of the religious element, the two share the same opinion here, also.

More positive, though not totally so, is Professor Thomas's assessment of the play. In detailing Schiller's approach to Saint Joan, Thomas states that Schiller

> threw himself boldly on the Catholic tradition, even adding to it some dubious supernaturalism of his own invention, and called his play a "romantic tragedy." In his hands the rustic maid became a divine amazon . . . but all the while invincible, under the terms of her mandate from the Holy Virgin, only on condition of resisting all earthly love. . . . at last, her expiation completed, she receives back her supernatural power and dies in glory. (325)

Though more positive in his approach, Thomas calls forth the points of view shared by Vilmar and Wells as he writes of Schiller's "dubious supernaturalism" and the romantic tragedy of the divine amazon.

Perhaps the critical dualism with regard to *Die Jungfrau von Orleans* can be no better shown than through citing two opinions as to the popularity of the play. Firstly,

> the play is replete with Schiller's finest dramatic effects. Anyone not constitutionally hostile to his methods will come away from a good performance . . . saying: It is magnificent, even if it is not Jeanne d'Arc. (Thomas 325)

Secondly, however:

> That it should be still a favorite with the great mass of German theatre-goers is due partly to the real merits of the individual scenes, partly to the humiliating fact that the theatre-going public is neither aesthetically trained nor critically cultured. (Wells 275)

Whom one believes depends, ultimately, upon how one judges the play. Undoubtedly, it is well to repeat that, among Schiller's plays, *Die Jungfrau von Orleans* was second only to *Wilhelm Tell* in listings, and thus, presumably, in popularity.

As in the case of *Maria Stuart*, one possibility for the play's wide circulation lies in the fact that U.S. students were familiar with the historical Saint Joan and were therefore more prepared for this play than, for example, for *Don Carlos* or *Die Braut von Messina*. Then, too, the legend of a saint, even of one who falls from grace, was more wholesome fare for the young than, say, *Kabale und Liebe*—at least in the days of *in loco parentis*. Most interesting is the fact that one editor of *Die Jungfrau von Orleans* (for a Heath text listed 1888–1909) was the U.S. literary historian and professor who, among those consulted, was least predisposed toward the work: Benjamin Willis Wells. Why Professor Wells chose to edit the play in 1888 and to criticize it so severely in 1895 in his *Modern German Literature* is an interesting question. Perhaps he had come to disparage the play through editing it.

Die Braut von Messina fared better in literary histories than *Die Jungfrau von Orleans*, although hardly so well with regard to editions and listings (there were two editions and two listings of *Die Braut von Messina*). After laying the blame for the *Schicksalstragödien* of Werner, Müllner and Grillparzer at Schiller's feet, because "*Die Braut von Messina* ist bekanntlich die Quelle der späteren unsinnigen Schicksalstragödien," Vilmar praises Schiller's play:

> Dagegen ist dieses Stück unter allen Werken Schillers dasjenige, welches den *vollesten* Glanz und die *ganze* Pracht der Schillerschen Diction, und somit allen Glanz und alle Pracht unserer modernen Sprache überhaupt, entfaltet, und in so fern wahrhaft bewundernswürdig ist. (499)

If the plot of the fate tragedy is somewhat distasteful (as it deals with incest and fraternal hatred), Vilmar can at least praise the language.

Another critical objection to *Die Braut von Messina* is Schiller's use of the chorus. Kurz shows himself at first ambivalent in his evaluation, citing Schiller's letter to Körner of March 10, 1803. Here Schiller states that the chorus has two functions: (1) to represent humanity in general in reflective moments; and (2) to represent individual persons acting in moments of passion. Kurz then finds fault as follows:

> Da aber nur die erste Eigenschaft, die er seinem Chor beilegt, das Wesen des antiken Chors ist, so wird dieses durch die zweite verletzt, und der Chor hört in der That auf, ein wirklicher Chor zu sein. . . . Und da die zweite Eigenschaft ihrer Natur nach auffallender ist, so wird diese als die eigentliche, wesentliche aufgefaßt werden. Noch mehr: Schiller trennt den Chor noch in zwei Theile, indem die eine Hälfte aus den Anhängern Don Manuels, die andere aus denen Don Cäsars besteht. Schon dadurch hat er ihnen wieder die Allgemeinheit genommen, die das Wesen des griechischen Chors bildete. (3:439)

The effect on the stage, then, was in Kurz's estimation not what Schiller had reckoned it would be.

However, as with Vilmar, so here; the saving grace is the language:

> Betrachten wir den Chor dagegen an sich, ohne Rücksicht auf die dramatische Verknüpfung, so finden wir in demselben die herrlichsten lyrischen Ergüsse, die sich dem Trefflichsten anreihen, was Schiller je gedichtet. (Kurz 3:440)

Both European commentators find weaknesses in the play but laud it for its poetry.

In the United States, *Die Braut von Messina* was not a popular text. If previous experience prove true in this case, Professor Bernhardt provides an explanation. In his literary history, he offers students the following information—but no praise of the play:

Am Abend desselben Tages ermordet Don Cesar seinen Bruder aus Eifersucht, da er seine Geliebte, die in einem benachbarten Kloster lebende Beatrice, in den Armen seines Bruders findet. Unmittelbar nach der Katastrophe stellt sich heraus, daß Beatrice die totgeglaubte Schwester der beiden Prinzen ist, und nun tötet Don Cesar sich. (35)

Here are echoes of *Wilhelm Meister* (only excerpts chosen as textbook material) as well as of Klinger's *Die Zwillinge*. In the period of time under consideration, with so many other texts to choose from (e.g., Baumbach's *Die Nonna*, Wilhelmi's *Einer muß heiraten*), *Die Braut von Messina* was rather strong fare.

Professor Priest's comments on the play are terse, but he does mention the chorus—criticized yet praised by the Europeans:

In order to give his drama a classical tone and to increase its tragic effect, Schiller introduced the antique chorus; it gave the poet opportunity to express many beautiful lyric reflections, but it proved itself unsuitable for the modern stage here. (239)

The chorus, which at best aroused ambivalent feelings in *Germanisten*, nonetheless fared better in Germany and in the U.S. than the rest of the play.

Perhaps Calvin Thomas summarizes the case against *Die Braut von Messina* most succinctly:

Schiller's lofty poetic diction is at its very best in the *Bride of Messina*, but his innovation in the matter of the chorus met with little favour. On the other hand, his use of the curse-idea . . . was a seed dropped on fertile soil. The *Bride of Messina*, an experiment in pseudo-Hellenism, is the least available for the stage among Schiller's plays. It was followed by *William Tell*, the most popular of them all, and the only one which is not a tragedy. (326)

Turning now to *Wilhelm Tell*, a beginning will be made with a *Germanist* who runs counter to the majority, a critic who considers *Wallenstein* Schiller's greatest drama:

Wilhelm Tell endlich erscheint noch immer den Meisten als die Krone aller Dramen Schillers. . . . Ich gestehe, daß ich mich zu dieser Ansicht nicht bekennen kann; so wenig ich für die Mängel Wallensteins blind und für die Schönheiten des Tell unempfänglich bin. . . . [trotzdem] ist es nicht zu bestreiten: die *Idee*, welche unklar und leidenschaftlich in den Räubern, Fiesco, Kabale und Liebe, gereinigter in Don Carlos erscheint, ist künstlerisch vollendet, fast ganz rein aus der Befangenheit und leidenschaftlichen Teilnahme des dichtenden Subjects herausgelöst, im Tell dargestellt, und von dieser Seite betrachtet, muß allerdings Tell für das vollendetste Schauspiel Schillers gelten. (Vilmar 499–500)

The idea was the fight of those who would be free against tyranny, of *Republikaner* against *Hofwelt*. The German audiences saw themselves as Tell fighting tyranny of the Napoleonic forces; ironically, however—as Vilmar is quick to point out—Tell represented the Swiss fighting their Imperial (German and Austrian) oppressors. "Napoleon war damals der einzige, welcher dieß [sic] einsah und seine Verwunderung aussprach, daß Deutsche dieses so ganz antideutsche Stück als ein das deutsche Vaterland verherrlichendes Drama preisen könnten" (500).

Diametrically opposed to Vilmar's choice as to Schiller's best drama, as in many other cases, is Kurz:

> Einige Dramen Schillers mögen einzelne Vorzüge vor dem "Wilhelm Tell" haben, so z.B. die "Jungfrau von Orleans" in der Anlage, die "Braut von Messina" in der Ideenfülle, aber doch ist "Wilhelm Tell" ohne Zweifel, wie das letzte, so auch das trefflichste Werk, das Schiller gedichtet. In diesem hat er das, wornach er unablässig strebte . . . in größter Vollendung erreicht, nämlich die rein objektive Auffassung seines Gegenstandes, was ihm gelungen ist, ohne daß er seine eigene große Natur verläugnet [sic] oder in den Hintergrund zurückgedrängt hätte; vielmehr hat er diese mit seinem Stoff zur schönsten Einheit verschmolzen. (3:441)

Notably, the two critics agree on Tell's strong point, its objective yet still idealistic conception, which renders the play superior to Schiller's others. Interestingly, while Vilmar concedes some of *Wallenstein*'s glory to *Wilhelm Tell*, Kurz, who was formerly favorable toward *Wallenstein*, makes no mention of it as a possible rival to *Tell*, choosing *Die Jungfrau von Orleans* and *Die Braut von Messina* as alternates.

Hosmer, in the U.S., joins forces with Vilmar: "Some dramas of Schiller may have particular advantages over 'Wilhelm Tell.' For my own part I am more impressed by 'Wallenstein.'" Yet, again like his German predecessor, he concedes that

> "Wilhelm Tell" is the best known and most popular, and perhaps it is right to say it is artistically the most perfect. In this Schiller reached more nearly than elsewhere that after which he had striven . . . namely a good objective presentment, in which he succeeded without denying his own great nature or pushing it into the background. (457)

Thus far, European and U.S. critics agree that *Tell* may be Schiller's best drama due to Schiller's successful blending of his own nature with objectivity. Such agreement has thus far shown itself to be a relative rarity in the world of teachers and texts.

Bernhardt, for whom *Wallenstein* was Schiller's masterpiece, has little to teach about *Tell*, upon which he lavishes faint praise, if any:

> Schillers letztes und populärstes dramatisches Werk ist ein objektiv-historisches Schauspiel voll reger Handlung. Der Dichter schildert darin eine große Zeit, nämlich die Befreiung der Schweiz von der Tyrannei des Hauses Österreich im

Jahre 1308, und entwirft zugleich ein treues Bild von dem Leben, dem Land und den Leuten in der Schweiz. (35)

Any student who had read the editor's excursus upon "Schiller's dramatisches Meisterwerk"—*Wallenstein*—which Bernhardt compares to Shakespeare's *Henry VI* (35), would probably find that play easier to enjoy than *Wilhelm Tell*.

Wells presents his students with a synthesis of opinions in regard to *Tell*. More than other commentators, he remains ambivalent with regard to the play's merits. First, he praises the play:

> "Tell" is sharply differentiated from all the plays of the Weimar epoch. Its differentiation from the earlier dramas is as sharp, but yet of another character. The confidence in mankind and its destiny shown in "Fiesco" and the "Robbers" was a rebellious, anarchical confidence, born of wild notions of equality, fraternity, and a millennium to be won by destruction of the existing social order. But in "Tell," age and the French revolution have ripened his experience, the visionary, idealistic reformer has become a practical realist, taking society and mankind as he finds them. . . . So "Tell" stands apart and marks an advancing serenity . . . we feel, too, that there is growth. . . . Never had he caught so perfectly the *genius loci*, as here. (285–286)

The facts that *Tell* is not a tragedy, and that it shows Schiller's ripening beyond all *Sturm und Drang* to achieve a serenity of sorts, sets this play apart.

These general ideas or impressions are vaguely good. However, Wells also offers quite concrete criticisms; among them, that *Tell*

> conceded too much to popular and literary prejudice. It would be artistically better for the omission of the generous, but rather romantic love of Bertha and Rudenz. The killing of Gessler, too, is made less important to the liberation of the people. . . . No one was likely to take Tell's deed as an indirect argument for regicide, and one resents the suggestion of such a possibility by the introduction of John of Austria . . . as a contrasted figure to the executioner of Gessler. (287)

Nonetheless, the greater part of these faults fades away if one but equate the Swiss with the Germans and the Austrians with Napoleon (Wells 287), Napoleon's amazement notwithstanding.

Priest postulates three plots (Tell versus Gessler, the Swiss versus Austria, and Bertha and Rudenz versus Austria), but finds little fault with the play:

> This division into three sets of actions makes *Tell* far looser in construction than any other of Schiller's plays, but we overlook this defect in the enjoyment of the play's perennial freshness of feeling and under the spell of many wonderfully dramatic scenes. (240)

Professors Kurz and Priest may be said to represent the positive, almost totally uncritical pole of opinion regarding *Wilhelm Tell*.

Finally, Calvin Thomas answers the unbelieving, who would find fault with Schiller's last drama:

> One must suppose that the critics who have sometimes taxed it—the play as a whole—with a lack of unity and concentration, can never have seen a German audience hang on it with delight from first to last, without ever becoming aware of any such defects. . . . The theme is the liberation of a people by their own efforts. All the scenes converge, all the characters contribute, to that end. (327)

Suffice it to say that *Wilhelm Tell* not only led Schiller's other dramas in the number of textbook listings recorded, but also made an unusually strong showing among German professors. These last, in books aimed generally at students, indulged in uncharacteristic praise or demonstrated only a mild preference for another work—usually *Wallenstein*. Perhaps only *Hermann und Dorothea* (forty-three listings) approached *Wilhelm Tell* (sixty-five listings) in popularity as a German text.

Carl Schlenker, in his edition of *Wilhelm Tell* (Allyn and Bacon 1913), characterizes Schiller for U.S. German students as a "Poet of Liberty" (76). In this connection, the people's fight for liberty and Tell's upright independence were probably seen as a parallel to the American Revolution, and Schiller was thus seen as a glorifier of America's role in that struggle; most importantly, perhaps, there were no immoral goings-on as in the early plays or *Die Braut von Messina*. To Schiller and *Wilhelm Tell*, then, belong the laurels of Classicism in U.S. German texts.

Another Weimar playwright during the classical period was August von Kotzebue, whose *Die deutschen Kleinstädter* was listed as a text in 1903 and 1912. Although Kotzebue and Iffland had outdone Goethe and Schiller on the German stage with their specious drama, Iffland's work was not represented in U.S. texts, and Kotzebue could claim but one text. In all probability, by the time the German textbook market began to increase, their reputations had preceded them to the U.S. For example, as Vilmar wrote about Kotzebue:

> Alles, was in den bisherigen Richtungen im Einzelnen Tadelnswertes lag, die nüchterne Darstellung der nüchternen Wirklichkeit, das Weinerlich-Rührende, das Bombastisch-Aufgeschwellte und Unwahre, die bürgerliche Plattheit, die sentimentale Zimperlichkeit und den ritterlichen Humpenspuk, zusammenzufassen war *August von Kotzebue* berufen. (533)

There seems almost a personal animosity on Vilmar's part against Kotzebue—in actual fact almost an impossibility chronologically.

More interesting is Vilmar's theory as to *why* Kotzebue aspired to be an author:

> Es ist oft gesagt worden, es sei eigentlich nur kindischer *Neid* des geborenen Weimaraners gegen die großen Geister gewesen, welche sich in seiner Vaterstadt angesiedelt, Neid gegen Goethe und später gegen Schiller, der den

talentvollen, aber eitlen und leeren Kotzebue getrieben habe, Dinge zu produciren, mit denen er über Goethe und Schiller siegen könne. (533)

And the generally more sanguine Kurz is equally vehement against Kotzebue. From his history, the student learned that

> Kotzebue kannte die Menschen; er wußte, daß sie auch etwas Neues haben wollten, er wußte, daß man sie am sichersten gewinnen konnte, wenn man ihre Fehler und Gebrechen, sogar ihre Laster als verzeihlich, ja selbst als liebenswürdig darstellt. So lockerte er das Gefühl für Anstand und Sittlichkeit und reizte sogar zur Unmoralität. (3:456)

Kotzebue is said to have exerted an unwholesome influence, beyond mere pettiness, on German society. Some of the charges brought against him are that he made fun of Goethe in *Incognito*; he laughed at Kant in *Besuch oder die Sucht zu glänzen*; he ridiculed the Schlegels in *Der hyperboreische Esel*, and so on (Kurz 3:456).

About Kotzebue's play which became a U.S. German text, Kurz states:

> Wie die Entwickelung seiner Dramen vorzüglich auf Ueberhäufung effectvoller Situationen beruht, so beruht auch seine Charakterzeichnung auf Ueberladung; er trägt immer die grellsten Farben auf, wodurch er freilich das ungebildete Publikum am leichtesten gewinnen konnte.... Diesen Charakter der Ueberladung tragen namentlich seine Possen, wo sie freilich am rechten Orte ist. Berühmt sind unter diesen die "Deutschen Kleinstädter," "Die Zerstreuten," "Die Pagenstreiche". (3:457)

Possen are not entirely unlike cabaret performances; both share *Revuestil*, poke fun at prominent figures, and at least occasionally are somewhat coarse. If Kotzebue was not a great dramatist, perhaps he was a cabarettist before his time. At any rate, considering the dark view of Kotzebue taken by critics, it is no wonder that *Die deutschen Kleinstädter* was not a great success. The day of theatrical bluntness had not yet come, at least to academe.

A similarly negative reception awaited Gottfried Seume. Perhaps his greatest fault lay in the fact that

> er alle seine Darstellungen an das eigene Ich anknüpft und dieß [sic] in den Vordergrund stellt; dieses Ich ist aber nichts weniger als geistig-reich, liebenswürdig und poetisch, im Gegenteil gar arm und trocken, und nun pocht und trotzt es noch auf diese Armut und Trockenheit; sein Humor ist mehr Verbißenheit [sic] und Ingrimm. (Vilmar 543)

Does Seume deserve such scathing criticism?

Certainly, Priest is more positive in his approach. He equates Seume's unhappy youth with Schiller's, and does not find fault with his *Ich*-centered style:

Like Schiller during his young manhood, Johann Gottfried Seume (1763–1810) suffered many hardships from the political oppressions of his time; *Mein Sommer, 1805* (1806) contains a graphic account of Napoleonic tyrannies. From a purely literary standpoint, however, Seume's best work is his *Spaziergang nach Syrakus* (1803) which, like *Mein Sommer*, is autobiographical and in prose. (Priest 243)

Yet neither of these works was edited for German classes; rather, Seume's autobiography, *Mein Leben*—which was completed after his death by Clodius—was selected for pedagogical purposes. The autobiography was probably chosen because, through the trickery of brutal recruiters, Seume was shipped to Canada as a Hessian soldier. In this way there was a connection—albeit unsympathetic—to U.S. students.

Priest is not alone in his more positive approach to Seume. In 1909, the year Priest's *Brief History of German Literature* was published, Kummer's *Deutsche Literaturgeschichte* also appeared. With regard to Seume, Kummer states that he was in some ways similar to the more genial Ernst Moritz Arndt:

> Hier sei auch *Gottfried Seumes* gedacht, einer höchst charakteristischen, Arndt in mancher Hinsicht verwandten Persönlichkeit der Zeit *vor* den Befreiungskriegen. Seume war einseitiger, eingeengter, hölzerner als der feurige Arndt, aber sehr wacker und mannhaft, als Mensch und Dichter ein reiner Charakter von kraftvoller Tüchtigkeit. (153–54)

The correspondence between the U.S. and German literary histories is of interest not only concerning the reception of Seume's works, but also because it shows the close correspondence of American and German *Germanistik* which often makes itself felt during this era.

The close relationship of Seume to Arndt and his work brings this study to the War of Liberation and the era of Romanticism. Now Germany would put behind her any inclination to intellectual *Französelei*, and *Vater Rhein* and *Spiegelbilder* would be more characteristic of German literature than the classical hexameter's *Springquell*. It is most appropriate, therefore, to continue from Seume to Arndt and other poets of the War of Liberation.

Vilmar becomes sanguine in his assessment of Arndt and his poetry:

> An die Spitze dieser Vaterlandsdichter stellt sich der Sängerheld von der Insel Rügen, der alte *Arndt*, dessen kräftige Lieder zu ihrer Zeit alle Herzen erhoben und entflammten, und hoffentlich auch noch in der Zukunft manches deutsche Herz erheben und entzünden werden. . . . ihr unsterbliches Verdienst ist das, daß sie die beste Stimmung der Zeit in voller Wahrheit, ohne Uebertreibung und Phrase, poetisch aussprachen. (564–65)

Indeed, it may be that some literati hoped that the *Vaterlandsdichtung* of the era of the War of Liberation would inspire a later age to daring deeds, for Vilmar writes (in 1850 in the preface originally composed for an early edition of his *Geschichte der deutschen National-Literature*) of the life of his people "in dem Stolze seiner angeborenen Weltherrschaft," and sees it as his people's task "ein Hüter zu sein unter den Völkern für Zucht und Sitte" (iv). Vilmar apparently saw Arndt's poetry as supportive of such thoughts.

But not all commentators were quick to award Arndt the laurels, though these scholars, too, ended by offering more praise than blame:

> Arndt war kein großer Dichter; andere übertreffen ihn an Gedankenreichtum, an sprachlicher und künstlerischer Schönheit, aber er war weitaus der wichtigste und größte unserer Dichter aus den Befreiungskriegen, und zwar beruhte Arndts Größe in seinem Charakter. Er war ein frommer Christ, ein schlichter kraftvoller Mann aus dem Volke, von glühender Vaterlandsliebe. (Kummer 152)

Even his enemies, according to Kummer, had to admit that "dieser Mann ein Gefäß sei, das stets mit dem lautersten Inhalt gefüllt war" (152). Arndt's character rather than his art—what he said rather than how he said it—contributed greatly to his popularity. Love of God and country taught by a man of the people made his work less warlike for Kummer.

In the United States, Hosmer took care to characterize Arndt's prose and poetry for Americans as something quite apart from the concurrent school of Romanticism (although others do not agree). Arndt's songs, for example, were

> most energetic, not a breath of vapory vagueness, not a whisper of allusion to any far-away time, they speak right to the German's heart with patriotism the deepest, with ardor that becomes sometimes ferocity. Such is the tone of Arndt's fierce thanksgiving to the God that made iron grow, so that there might be weapons. (500)

Hosmer's approach is more cautious, less enthusiastic. Ferocity and fierce thanksgiving to the war god are not generally features of American patriotism.

Bernhardt, on the other hand, recommended Arndt's poems to all patriots as "jene kraftvollen Vaterlandslieder, die noch heute das Herz eines jeden Patrioten erwärmen" (44). However, the single American Arndt textbook did not center on poetry. It was Arndt's remembrance of time in service to Reichsfreiherr von Stein: as a freedom fighter he had traveled to St. Petersburg to help organize the final effort against Napoleon. It is not altogether surprising that Arndt's prose was chosen over his poetry. Firstly, there are those who believe that "mehr jedoch als in den Liedern ist Arndts Bedeutung in seinen patriotischen Prosaschriften zu suchen" (Kummer 153). Secondly, the story of the trip to Russia may have been preferred because, when the text was published in 1909, German war hymns may already have become distasteful to many Americans. *German Patriots in Russia* was thought more appealing than *Der Gott, der Eisen wachsen ließ*. Even so, the text was listed only once.

More propitious is the case of liberation poet Theodor Körner, though his patriotic poetry makes a showing equally as weak as Arndt's. In Körner's case, a patriotic, tragic drama, *Zriny*, carries the liberation message to the people. However, *Zriny* was not received only with critical accolades:

> Von Körners Dramen können wir schweigen, da sie nichts mehr sind, als Copien von Schiller, doch nicht unglaubliche Copien, die im Gegenteil, wie Zriny, trotz aller Uebertreibungen wenigstens den großartigen erhebenden historischen Hintergrund besitzen, welcher für eine Tragödie unerlaßlich [sic] ist, woher es denn kommt, daß der fremdländische und geschichtlich nicht einmal tadelfreie Nicolaus Zriny uns fast zu einem vaterländischen Helden geworden ist. (Vilmar 565)

Somewhat as in the case of Wilhelm Tell, a foreigner has become a national hero. Not only this, but also the historical background calls Schiller to mind. Another assessment states more negatively that Körner "ist fast überall von fremden Vorbildern abhängig. Literarische Bedeutung kommt unter seinen Werken nur den Kriegsliedern zu" (Kummer 155).

Zriny, however, was listed five times from 1866 to 1902 (more times than *Götz von Berlichingen*, for example). If the play is heavily dependent on Schiller, this may well have been a plus rather than a minus in the market for German textbooks. However, much is made of Körner's poetry in the literary histories consulted, while little is said about *Zriny*. For example, "Körner's tragedy *Zriny*, an imitation of Schiller, has maintained some favor by its central theme, love of freedom and native land" (Priest 261). Only Thomas ventures a brief analysis:

> *Zriny*, while too ethereal and monochromatic for a good drama—all the characters being doomed to certain death from the first, and having nothing to do but to express their emotions and sell their lives as dearly as possible—is instinct with the stern joy and the blessed hope of dying for the fatherland. (346)

The play apparently succeeded to some degree as a text because it was regarded as an imitation of *Wallenstein, Wilhelm Tell* or the *Jungfrau von Orleans*. Idealism made the copy marketable.

A similar case was Uhland's drama *Ernst von Schwaben*. The play's strong points are a "größtenteils gute deutsche Färbung, insbesondere aber die Treue," which the play demonstrates with dramatic vividness. Like *Zriny*, however, *Ernst von Schwaben* is said to be monochromatic and lacking in motivation: "In Individualisierung der übrigen Charaktere, an gehöriger Motivierung der Begebenheiten und selbst an Handlung fehlt es—die Reden haben ein merkliches Uebergewicht" (Vilmar 562). However, this assessment from the year 1874 contrasts interestingly with an American viewpoint of 1879:

> His popularity was unbounded. . . . Perhaps his genius was at its best when he considered some mediaeval subject, catching the spirit of the old minstrels, whose songs he so much loved. Of that kind is his famous drama, "Ernst von Schwaben," and many a sounding ballad. (Hosmer 502–503)

Uhland's popularity is similarly reflected by Bernhardt's literary history in 1892: "Ludwig Uhland ist nächst Schiller der populärste Dichter Deutschlands" (54); as regards *Ernst von Schwaben*, students read in 1909 that it "is a touching glorification of the loyalty of a friend and is still popular among Germans" (Priest 264). Somewhat like *Zriny*, then, *Ernst von Schwaben* offered an idealized concept of a cardinal virtue.

In that same year, a German literary history records: "*Ernst, Herzog von Schwaben* . . . ist mehr eine in dramatische Form gebrachte Märe, als ein Drama. . . . Die dramatische Entwicklung ist bereits mit dem Schluß des ersten Aktes zu Ende, alles weitere ist nur Folge" (Kummer 132). Thus it seems that after his own time Uhland the dramatist was perhaps better loved in America than in his homeland.

Regarding Uhland's poetry, all commentators share a similar point of view—with the exception of Vilmar, who perceives Uhland only as a dramatist. Uhland's verses do not rank with the greatest of lyric poetry, but they convey the simple voice of the heart:

> [Uhland] felt no enthusiasm for the old empire; the intense subjectivity of Romanticism he forsook, and gave to the outer world due respect. Once more appeared in German literature the simplicity, truth, and unaffected grace of the volks-lied. His subjects are for the most part simple, and near to our sympathies; his lyrics sometimes pensive, but generally cheerful, abounding in love of nature, and sometimes humorous. (Hosmer 502)

Professorial respect for Uhland and his poetry—especially the ballads—was very much the rule in resource books used by teachers and students of the era. An edition of Uhland's poetry was listed four times between 1896 and 1912.

If Arndt, Körner and Uhland opposed the romantic trends of their day, Jean Paul Richter pleased the romantically inclined *Lesewelt* "für die der rauschende Flug des Goetheschen und Schillerschen Genius etwas Ueberwältigendes und Beängstigendes hatte, und die es darum vorzog, sich in die weichen silbernen Fäden des individuellen Gefühls einzuspinnen" (Vilmar 539). Subjectivity was certainly characteristic for this forerunner of Romanticism; perhaps this was portrayed for scholars nowhere so graphically as in Hosmer: "In his romances he has brought into the world genuine poetic figures, but they all drag about a foolishly long umbilical cord, entangling and strangling themselves with it" (487).

Aside from his subjective orientation, Jean Paul brought another striking hallmark to literature of his age—he brought back humor. As Bernhardt states:

> Seit *Johann Fischart* und *Sebastian Brandt* . . . war kein Humorist von Bedeutung in der deutschen Literatur aufgetreten. Bei den Klassikern fand sich der Humor nicht repräsentiert, außer vielleicht in einigen Jugenddichtungen Goethes sowie Schillers "Wallensteins Lager." Diese Lücke auszufüllen erschien . . . "Jean Paul" . . . der größte humoristische Schriftsteller Deutschlands. (43)

Indeed, subjectivity and humor are necessarily blended in a humorist:

> Ueberhaupt ist an ihm das zu bemerken, was freilich bei einem eigentlichen Humoristen nicht anders sein kann, daß er keine Entwickelungsphasen seines poetischen Daseins gehabt hat—hätte ein Humorist diese, dränge er zur vollen Klarheit und künstlerischen Vollendung durch, er würde eben aufhören ein Humorist zu sein. (Vilmar 539)

If a writer should rise to full clarity and artistic completeness (objectivity and high seriousness?), he cannot be a humorist. Thus Jean Paul is vindicated by Vilmar; he likewise won more praise than censure in the relatively early U.S. literary histories surveyed.

Later, in 1909, a German work offered students and professors the following estimation of Jean Paul:

> Am liebsten gestaltete Jean Paul seelenvolle, grundgute, aber etwas beschränkte und närrische Leute, so arme Schullehrer und Landgeistliche. . . . ja, er hat das Verdienst, daß von ihm die Armen und Mühseligen zum ersten Male in unserer Literatur dichterisch behandelt worden sind. Die Werke Jean Pauls in fremde Sprachen zu übersetzen ist unmöglich. Auch den Spätergeborenen und den heutigen Menschen ist Jean Paul nur durch geschichtliche Betrachtung verständlich und genießbar. (Kummer 76)

Jean Paul brought the poor and downtrodden into the popular consciousness. Yet it must be remembered that Jean Paul's poor are contented with their simple, idyllic lot.

In the U.S. in 1909, Calvin Thomas painted a considerably darker *Jean-Paul-Bild*:

> When he died Ludwig Börne said of him . . . "He has not lived for all men, but the time will come when he will be born for all. . . . He stands patiently at the gate of the twentieth century, waiting with a smile for his crawling countrymen to come up with him." The prediction has not been fulfilled, and only illustrates the difficulty that besets the vocation of prophet. To-day [sic] Richter is hardly

read at all. In an age of revivals there is no sign of reviving interest in him. The neglect of him may be ascribed first and foremost to his style. (329)

Important to this study is the fact that Jean Paul rose and fell almost simultaneously on the textbook market and declined steadily in academic esteem.

Students were offered one text of Jean Paul in 1898, composed for the most part of *Kleinere Idyllen,* the most famous of which is probably the *Leben des vergnügten Schulmeisterleins Maria Wuz*:

> Dem trotz seiner Armut vergnügten Schulmeisterlein Maria Wuz in Auenthal ist so voll, so warm, so satt in seiner kleinlichen Häuslichkeit, wo er zu den Titeln der Bücher, die ihm der Meßkatalog meldet, sich selbst die Werke schreibt. Er besitzt die beneidenswerte Kunst, stets fröhlich zu sein. Den Gipfel der Seligkeit erreicht Wuz durch seine Hochzeit mit Justine. So vergehen viele Jahre, bis Wuz als glücklicher Greis in einer Maiennacht entschlummert. (Kummer 74)

Although the style cannot be assessed from such a summary, some of the criticisms ring true: the silvery threads of subjectivity, with which an individual strangles himself; no urge for clarity or artistic completeness; limited, silly people. Yet later ages should not be so quick to judge: one of the more delightful characters to be found in nineteenth-century U.S. German texts seems to emerge from the mold which cast Maria Wuz—Heinrich Seidel's Leberecht Hühnchen (discussed in the following chapter).

Like Jean Paul, another author who may almost be counted as one of the romantics is Hans Christian Andersen—a Dane who himself wrote excellent German and some of whose works also appeared in German. As Bernhardt noted, Andersen "schrieb seine 'Märchen,' mehrere Romane, sowie sein farbenprächtiges 'Bilderbuch ohne Bilder,' eine Reihe interessanter Skizzen von dem, 'was der Mond erzählte', im elegantesten Hochdeutsch" (57). Andersen's works are listed some thirty-one times in commercial and scholarly catalogs and the *Märchen* and *Bilderbuch ohne Bilder* were recommended for the elementary level by the Committee of Twelve. However, only Bernhardt discusses Andersen even briefly—not even Calvin Thomas, chairman of the Committee of Twelve, deigned to mention him. Nonetheless, in view of his strong showing in commercial and scholarly catalogs, Andersen was quite popular in German class.

Proportionally far less published for the classroom were the works of Heinrich von Kleist. *Michael Kohlhaas, Prinz Friedrich von Homburg* and *Die Verlobung in Santo Domingo* appeared in three separate texts with six listings among them. Reasons for Kleist's lack of popularity in post-Civil War academe are provided by professors and editors. In 1874, it seems that the tide had no yet turned in favor of Kleist: "Kleists Käthchen von Heilbronn und Prinz von Homburg sind auf unsern Bühnen bekannt—sie zeugen von einem trefflichen, aber auch von einem noch völlig unausgebildeten, seiner selbst noch nicht gewissen Talent" (Vilmar 562). *Bekannt* is not *beliebt*; and an excellent talent which seems uncultivated and unsure of itself deserves less scholarly attention than the works of more assuming geniuses—or so Vilmar seems to have believed.

Concerning the *Prinz von Homburg*, Kurz declared that the play "verbindet die höchsten Schönheiten mit den auffallendsten Mängeln." Among the flaws, which included the fact that an audience could feel no sympathy for a somnambulist, that the scenes were poorly joined, and that an unwholesome *Charakterzug* of Kleist (cowardice) was even less appealing in the Prince,

> da er die Heldengröße desselben vollständig vernichtet, und ihn lächerlich, beinahe verächtlich macht. Zwar findet er sich später wieder, aber der Makel, der auf ihm liegt, kann dadurch nicht ausgelöscht werden. So macht das Stück oft eine widrige Wirkung, und wenn wir auch eben so oft durch die vortrefflichsten Stellen überrascht werden, so ist der Gesamteindruck doch keineswegs erfreulich. (Kurz 3:466)

Thus the prejudice of the nobles, particularly the descendants of the Prince of Homburg, continued to assert itself against the play.

In the U.S., Wilhelm Bernhardt was, if not negative, more than characteristically terse, characterizing Kleist as "der bedeutendste Dramatiker der romantischen Schule . . . bekannt durch sein Lustspiel 'Der zerbrochene Krug' sowie durch sein Ritterschauspiel 'Das Käthchen von Heilbronn' " (47). The three works published as texts do not rate even a mention.

By 1909, however, it seems that attitudes had changed in Germany and America. In Kummer's words, "im Allgemeinen ist die frühere Gleichgültigkeit gegen Kleist einem tiefen Verständnis, ja einer glühenden Bewunderung gewichen" (96). Priest goes even further in his praise of Kleist: "With more balance of character and in a more favorable time, Kleist might have become that which nature, it seems, intended him to be, the German Shakespeare" (256). Calvin Thomas, too, is not without praise for the "finest dramatic genius thus far vouchsafed to any Prussian" (351–52). Kleist is transformed from a tragically flawed poet to a tragically misunderstood genius.

Concerning the three works which appeared as texts, the later literary histories contained the following assessments about *Michael Kohlhaas*: "Es ist die machtvollste Novelle im ganzen Bereich der deutschen Literatur" (Kummer 105); "the best of Kleist's stories is *Michael Kohlhaas*, a tragedy in the form of a short story" (Priest 257); "*Michael Kohlhaas* . . . is one of the best novelettes in the German language" (Thomas 351). *Die Verlobung in Santo Domingo* was not commented upon. Regarding *Prinz Friedrich von Homburg*, Kummer terms it "das letzte und reifste seiner Dramen . . . . Dies edelste preußische Stück, das von höchster Geschlossenheit war, ist denoch zu des Dichters Lebzeiten nicht auf die Bühne gekommen" (106–07). Priest, similarly, terms the play "Kleist's last and most beautiful work." And further:

"Various figures, especially those of the Prince, old Colonel Kottwitz, and the Great Elector . . . are among the truest and most real in German drama" (257). Finally, Thomas calls the play "a masterpiece of such fine and satisfying texture as to suggest almost limitless possibilities for the young dramatist who wrote it at the age of thirty-two" (351).

Thus Kleist has passed from an eccentric playwright to a true dramatic genius. All this notwithstanding, three texts and six listings do not show Kleist to be one of the most-read authors in German courses of the era under investigation; in fact, his first textbook edition appeared only in 1895. In view of the uphill fight of the author and his works for understanding, it is unsurprising that these works were not prominent as texts during the years under consideration.

Considerably more popular were the *Märchen* of Jakob and Wilhelm Grimm. Although the tales, having been collected and recorded in folkloristic style, were not considered pure literature, the brothers—especially Jakob—were nonetheless considered an important part of the literary tradition. An interesting illustration is provided by Kurz as he concludes his remarks on the Grimms:

> Wir haben daher nur noch die Bemerkung hinzuzufügen, daß sie, besonders in den Märchen, die Ueberlieferungen keineswegs in der unvollkommenen Form wiedergeben, in der sie ihnen aus dem Munde des Volkes mitgetheilt wurden, sondern daß sie, ohne am Wesen und der Eigenthümlichkeit des Erzählten das Geringste zu ändern, indem sie vielmehr in dieser Hinsicht die zarteste Scheu an den Tag legten, die volksmäßige Darstellung zur künstlerischen Schönheit entfalteten. Die Sprache in den Märchen ist bei aller schlichten Einfalt, die sie auf das Getreueste bewahrt haben, doch würdig und von der hinreißendsten Anmuth. Noch mehr tritt die künstlerische Begabung der Bearbeiter darin hervor, daß sie oft fragmentarische Mittheilungen einzelner Märchen durch glückliche Benutzung anderer unvollständiger Ueberlieferungen des nämlichen Stoffs auf das Trefflichste ergänzt haben. (3:608)

Whether the Grimms, as folklorists, would have approved of Kurz's assessment of their craft seems somewhat questionable, though Kurz intends to pay critical tribute in speaking of the development of *volksmäßige Darstellung* to *künstlerische Schönheit*.

Hosmer deals more with theory than form, praising the Grimms' research while standing somewhat in awe of the results:

> The brothers Grimm . . . study and compare . . . each circumstance and feature, every whiff of aroma and line of tinting in the Märchen, all with scientific purpose. As a first result the Grimms dared to propound the striking theory that the genuine Märchen were nothing more or less than the remains of the great legends of the old religious faiths, softened down, but still living in the souls of the people. (552)

Hosmer goes on to state that the Grimms asserted that "phantoms of the . . . Norse gods" haunt the modern "Teutonic stock" in the form of *Märchen* (552).

The student is provided by Bernhardt only with a list of the Grimms' greatest works, including the *Märchen* (50); Priest comments briefly but admiringly:

> The place of honor which the Grimms occupy in German literature is . . . based on the *Deutsche Kinder- und Hausmärchen* (1812–15), which they collected and retold. In this priceless treasure of childhood they struck the tone of the people with wonderful precision and established a universal standard in the telling of fairy tales. (253)

Once again, "retold" is somewhat questionable when viewed from the standpoint of folklore, though the overall positive approach is clear. More in conformance with the view of the Grimms as scholarly collectors is the following statement from the chairman of the Committee of Twelve, who in speaking of the *Märchen*, stated that "these now world-famous tales, taken down from the lips of story-tellers who had received them from an age-long tradition, are an interesting by-product of the new romanticism" (Thomas 341). Thomas also finds the *Märchen* "well adapted for the earliest experiments" in sight reading (Report 69). Certainly, the positive attitude demonstrated in the histories was reflected in the use of the *Märchen* in the schools. From 1881 to 1909 some twenty-one scholarly and commercial listings indicate the popularity of the tales as texts.

Following the lead of the Grimms, Ludwig Bechstein produced his *Thüringische Volksmärchen*, which appeared in 1823. Like the Grimms, Bechstein was a true gatherer of *Volksmärchen*. However, professors of German were apparently little taken with the folklorist, as he was not dealt with in any of a number of German and U.S. literary histories consulted published during the time period concerned. Even so, three of his stories appeared in Bierwirth and Herrick's *Ährenlese*, which appeared in 1918: *Der Fuchs und der Krebs*, *Gevatter Tod* and *Der Schmied von Jüterbog*. The editors of the anthology claim only to present "indigenous fruits of the good old German soil and not the product of our own cultivation" (Bierwirth and Herrick iii); though the text basically consists of short pieces of fiction, Bechstein the folklorist could conceivably have been pleased by the text description had be seen it.

To return once again to *Märchen*, Ludwig Tieck's *Volksmärchen* are misleadingly named; actually they are *Kunstmärchen*. During the time period under consideration, seven listings appear for one volume: *Zwei Märchennovellen: Das Rothkäppchen, Die Elfen*. It is surprising, firstly, that Tieck appeared in only one U.S. German text, and secondly, that what readers of the later twentieth century regard as his more famous works, such as *Der blonde Eckbert* and *Der gestiefelte Kater*, are not represented. Explanations should be provided by the professors.

Vilmar offers the initial explanation. After mentioning various "greater" works, he states that

> Von kaum geringerem Werte und vielleicht beliebter als Alles geworden, was Tieck geschrieben hat, sind die Sagen und Märchen im Phantasus, in welchem er in der zartesten und geschicktesten Einkleidung die trefflichsten alten Volkssagen von der Magelone, vom getreuen Eckart, vom Rotkäppchen und andere erzählt. (553)

Das Rothkäppchen and *Die Elfen* were chosen because of their popularity; the possibly negative aspects in the classroom of *Der gestiefelte Kater* and *Der blonde Eckbert* need not have been weighed in the editor's mind.

Hosmer brushes past Tieck's *Märchen* remarking only that Tieck "dealt indefatigably with fairy tales" (494). More voluminous are the teachings of Kurz, who offers some works, such as *Der gestiefelte Kater*, very faint praise while ignoring other modern-day notables. But—like Vilmar—Kurz has the most praise, though it is not unqualified, for Tieck's *Märchen*:

> In den Märchen selbst ist die schlichte, volkstümliche Auffassung im Ganzen trefflich gelungen, doch auch durch unklare mystische Anklänge, diese Erbsünde der Romantik, verunstaltet. Die gelungensten sind wohl "Der getreue Eckart," "Die Elfen" und "Der Pokal." (3:589)

If Kurz's praise is limited, certainly these are among his kindest remarks regarding Tieck.

Quite superficial are the comments of a U.S. professor in 1892: "Ludwig Tieck hat sich durch seine Romane sowie seine Fortsetzung der von Wilhelm Schlegel begonnenen Übersetzung Shakespeares einen Namen gemacht" (Bernhardt 47). No mention is made of the *Märchen*. Nearer the end of the era, Kummer stated that "diese Märchendichtungen waren etwas neues und doch angeweht von Goetheschem Hauche; sie waren aus der Bewunderung der alten volkstümlichen Märchen und Sagen hervorgegangen, erfüllt von einer überquellenden Sehnsuchtsstimmung nach dem Geheimnisvollen und Wunderbaren" (113). However, Tieck "erkannte, daß eine weitere Entwicklung in *dieser* Richtung nicht mehr möglich sei. . . . Mit dem Phantasus nahm Tieck von der Romantik Abschied" (Kummer 116). Although *Die Elfen* and *Das Rothkäppchen* are not named, the collection of which they were a part is regarded as Tieck's farewell to Romanticism. Kummer's contemporaries in the United States, Priest and Thomas, offered students no information on the two Tieck stories published as a German text.

The text was first listed in 1864 and for the last time in 1912. Of those who dealt with the *Märchen*, the earlier works were most complimentary; the *Märchen* were largely ignored toward the end of the time period—supplanted by works such as *Der gestiefelte Kater* and *Der blonde Eckbert*. Since the latter two works could be the best-known of Tieck's works among students today, a shift in taste is clear—away from "Little Red Ridinghood" toward social, political and artistic satire and the romance of the forest coupled with madness stemming from incest. As in the case of other authors, notably Goethe and Schiller, a more permissive academic environment and a different moral outlook have changed the nation's taste in texts.

Finally, it should be noted that Tieck received much more acclaim from the German commentators than from their U.S. colleagues. As Hosmer stated in 1879, Tieck "was for a time greatly overestimated" (493). But not, as it would seem, in the United States.

Tieck's interest in folklore and the medieval past was shared by Karl Simrock, who

> like the early Romanticists, revived Old German poems; he translated several into modern German and began his version of the Dietrich saga, *Das Amelungenlied*, with a poem, *Wieland der Schmied* (1835), that is permeated with the true epic spirit. (Priest 289-90)

Wieland der Schmied appeared as a U.S. text, in an adaptation by A. E. Wilson, in 1912; two shorter works were anthologized in 1918. Although Middle High German is not dealt with in this investigation, artistic adaptations such as Simrock's are considered worthy of a place among more original New High German works. Notably, however, the adapted verses did not thrive as a text.

Much more significant was Fouqué's *Undine*, listed twelve times. Yet not all literati held favorable opinions of Fouqué. Vilmar, in consequence, took the author's defense upon himself:

> Den Geist des alten Rittertums in edleren Gestalten als die ungeschickten Verfaßer [sic] der früheren Ritterromane darzustellen, versuchte *Friedrich Baron Fouque* [sic], auf welchen zu schimpfen heut zu Tage Mode geworden ist. Ich kann in diesen Ton nicht nur nicht einstimmen, sondern muß im Widerspruch mit demselben behaupten, daß es außer Fouque noch Niemanden gelungen ist, eine wenn auch hin und wieder allerdings phantastische, zuweilen sogar formlose, aber im Ganzen doch vollkommen *getreue* poetische Wiedergeburt der alten heitern Ritter und Sängerzeiten . . . zu bewerkstelligen. (554-55)

Certainly, this is not faint praise; among the many who would recall the glorious past, only Fouqué manages to do so.

As frequently, Kurz represents the opposing argument:

> Freilich ist seine Auffassung des Mittelalters durchaus verfehlt; er schöpfte seine Darstellungen des Ritterthums nicht aus der Geschichte, sondern theils aus den nordischen Sagen, theils aus den Rittergedichten des Mittelalters, und zudem

weht durch seine Dichtungen ein moderner Geist der Sentimentalität, der jener Zeit . . . gänzlich unbekannt war. (3:605)

However, Kurz also sees redeeming features in a piece such as *Undine*: "Glücklicher ist er ohne Zweifel in seiner Auffassung des Wunderbaren, weil er sich das Reich des Märchen nicht willkürlich bildete, wie es die andern Romantiker thaten, sondern hiebei der volksthümlichen Anschauung folgte" (3:605). In following the popular point of view with regard to the supernatural—rather than by subjectively evolving such a magical atmosphere—Fouqué surpassed his works flawed by an entangled conception of the actual medieval past.

An uncritical view of Fouque as a romantic figure, a point of view which corresponds somewhat to that of Vilmar, was offered U.S. students by Hosmer: "Fouque, the . . . author of 'Undine,' is a Romanticist through the enthusiasm he felt for mediaeval subjects; in still others, the bond of connection is some tinge of mysticism" (500). *Undine* is the only work mentioned in Hosmer's evaluation. This is a further indication that, as Kurz indicated, the supernatural outlived the knightly. Bernhardt concurs, offering only the information that "Fouqué ist der Dichter der lieblichen Märchennovelle 'Undine ' " (47).

Priest, on the other hand, does not limit Fouqué's effect on posterity only to *Undine*. In addition, "various songs by Fouqué, such as *Frisch auf zum fröhlichen Jagen* . . . are still great favorites" (254). However, Calvin Thomas does not concur:

> Of all the immense mass of Fouqué's writings in prose and verse, only *Undine* (1811) can be said to have survived. . . . there is certainly something of the savour of geniune romantic folklore. But even *Undine* has been overpraised. It is not free from literary sophistication. At best it was a thing for the very young. (364)

Among the sources consulted, Thomas offers academe what seems the most reasonable and fair estimate of Fouqué's art:

> Had he been granted a modicum of humor, a keener historical sense, and a livelier feeling for the plain, homely fact, he might have become the German Walter Scott. As it was, his creations were so very supernal and unlifelike, and so mixed up with futile irrationality, that the public soon tired of them, even as it tired of the dissimilar unrealities of Jean Paul. (363–64)

Comparison with Sir Walter Scott and Jean Paul is hardly a humiliation, the "could have" and the unrealities notwithstanding. And *Undine*, unlike some other literature then popular, continues to be read today.

In the introduction to his edition of *Undine*, J. Henry Senger impressed upon students that Fouqué was a true disciple of the German Romantic School, which laid more stress on a world of wonders than on the wonderful world; a school which, with the means furnished by modern culture itself, combated modern culture, modern life,—in short, the modern soul; a school which raised the importance of the individual to such a degree as to make him the irresponsible arbiter of the visible and invisible world.

Though the romantic school meets with Senger's disapproval, he nonetheless says nothing against *Undine*. Instead, the student is informed that

From the time of its publication Undine has succeeded in retaining its hold and promises to do so as long as there shall be readers able to distinguish real pathos from mere rhetoric. As the fairy tale will never cease charming the children of men, whether young or old, Undine has merely claimed its rightful place among the fairy stories of the world with its ever true and touching recital of the love of a woman who has a soul and deems herself happy in its possession despite all the suffering that the divine gift entails (9–10).

As Senger indicates, Undine seems to have taken her place among the touching characters of German literature.

Another previously more highly regarded literary figure who lingers in academe (as shown by recent textbook catalogs) is Wilhelm Hauff. As Bernhardt states,

Das schwäbische Herz mit seiner Wärme und Innigkeit des Gefühls besitzt... Wilhelm Hauff (1802–1827), der leider allzu früh verstorbene Lyriker, Märchenerzähler und Novellist. Einige seiner Lieder sind im wahrsten Sinne des Wortes Volkslieder geworden.... Als Novellist ist Hauff am erfolgreichsten gewesen in seinem historischen Roman "Lichtenstein," in welchem er, im Sinne Walter Scotts, eine Periode aus der Geschichte seiner Heimat Schwaben... poetisch fixiert hat. (55–56)

With eight listings from 1901 to 1914, Lichtenstein proved itself a popular text near the end of the era.

However, due to his dependence on Scott, Hauff was not always highly respected by critics in Germany:

Die Merkmale des Modedichters trug... Wilhelm Hauff an sich.... Es liegt nahe, daß derjenige, der Hauffs Vorbilder nicht kennt, ihn überschätzt. Er war, wie er selbst gesteht, in der romantischen Sage Lichtenstein von Walter Scott abhängig, und bei seiner beliebten Novelle, dem Mann im Mond, ist es wenigstens wahrscheinlich, daß sie ursprünglich eine Nachahmung... Claurens sein sollte.... Ähnlich wie Amadeus Hoffmann war auch Hauff ein geborener Erzähler. Dennoch war Hauffs Schaffen so gut wie niemals selbständig, vielmehr war es ein geschicktes Ausbeuten erfolgreicher Vorgänger. (Kummer 170–71)

Like Fouqué, then, Hauff was considered another would-be Walter Scott; about *Lichtenstein*, Thomas remarked that it "envinces no great original power, but it is pleasantly written and shows . . . that its author read Scott to advantage" (367). But does being "pleasantly written" justify the survival of an author's works when they are imitations?

The fact is that Hauff's more original works, his *Märchen*, far exceeded the imitative *Lichtenstein* in editions and listings. As Neil C. Brooks, who edited *Das kalte Herz* for Henry Holt in 1912, stated:

> In such a short life as was granted to Hauff there can be little literary development. All his works show the same natural gifts, a fertile imagination, a good style, and a fine sense for what is entertaining. . . . he still lives in the affections of the German people, while many of his famous contemporaries live only in histories of literature. (iv)

Certainly, this assessment is more favorable than those concerned with *Lichtenstein*. And justification is made for some of Hauff's shortcomings as an author: he simply did not have time to ripen.

One of the most original of Hauff's *Märchen* is surely *Der Zwerg Nase*, which first appeared as a U.S. German text in 1888. As critics have maintained, the story is interesting and well told, though somewhat superficial when compared to the works of other romantics. However, Otto R. Patzwald and Charles W. Robson, who edited *Der Zwerg Nase* in 1913, regard this simplicity as a point in favor of Hauff's work:

> With Hauff there is none of the morbid mysticism, none of the obscurity and vagueness which is generally so characteristic of the Romantic School. On the contrary, Hauff's works are wholesome, sparkling with delightful humor, full of life and interest, of freshness and originality, and his style is a model of clearness and precision. (vi)

Teachers of the era could ask for little more in a textbook if they desired what such a book has to offer—and quite a number of them wanted just that. Hauff's *Märchen* are not great literature (this being, according to his editors, a plus); they are somewhat childish; but they are wholesome and entertaining and, indeed, continue to be used as texts today, although presumably less often than formerly.

Far surpassed by Hauff in the period's pedagogy was an author much better known today, Ernst Theodor Amadeus Hoffmann. Indeed, Hoffmann's fame is far more a matter of the present than of the past, if Vilmar be given credence:

> Daß nicht manche seiner Darstellungen gelungen seien, wie namentlich in den Phantasiestücken und in den Serapionsbrüdern, kann und soll nicht geleugnet, daß aber seine Werke noch weit weniger als Jean Pauls Werke künstlerischen Genuß gewähren und den Ruhm künstlerischer Vollendung errungen haben,

muß auf das Nachdrücklichste behauptet werden. Wer seinem Kater Murr, seinen Teufelselixieren, seinem Nußknacker und Mäusekönig Geschmack abgewinnen kann, für den ist schwerlich Schiller und Goethe noch vorhanden, geschweige denn ein Nibelungenlied oder ein Homer. (542–43)

Hoffman is declared inferior to Jean Paul, his works appeal to minds incapable of appreciating Classicism, and somehow his romantic tales are weighed in the balance with Greek and Middle High German epic poetry, whereby the former literature clearly hits the beam.

Hosmer, who grants a number of pages to discussion of Jean Paul and commits a whole chapter of his book to Heine, refers to Hoffmann only as "the writer of weird romances, whose counterpart is Poe" (501–02). But Kurz presents an opposing viewpoint:

> Sein dichterisches Talent war sehr bedeutend. Mit einer reichen und stets geschäftigen Phantasie begabt, die ihm das Reich des wunderbaren und Märchenhaften eben so lebendig eröffnete, als das der Wirklichkeit, mit einem stets heitern Humor, und einem unerschöpflichen Witz begabt, verband er damit eine seltene Klarheit des Geistes . . . seine Sprache ist reich tiefpoetisch, von großer Anschaulichkeit. . . . Was er auch schildern will. Alles gelingt ihm. (3:610–11)

About the two works which appeared as U.S. German texts, Kurz wrote:

> Wir erinnern namentlich an *"Meister Martin der Küfner und seine Gesellen,"* worin er das altreichsstädtische Leben mit seiner Kunst und seinem Gewerbe mit großer Wahrheit und Natürlichkeit zeichnet, und nur hie und da romantisch affectirt [sic] wird. . . . Eine seiner trefflichsten Schöpfungen ist das *"Fräulein von Scudéry,"* eine Erzählung, welche durch ihre glückliche Verwickelung das höchste, immer steigende Interesse gewährt, und in welcher der Dichter seine Kunst, Furcht und Grauen zu erregen, zwar in hohem Grade entfaltet, ohne jedoch dabei die Grenzen der poetischen, ja selbst die historischen Wahrheit zu überschreiten. (3:611)

Special praise is accorded to the two works used in texts because of their historical truthfulness (realism), and because they only occasionally slip over into Romanticism.

Bernhardt makes no mention of Hoffmann. Priest, however, praises Hoffman's art, and particularly

> the best illustration of Hoffmann's genius in the short story . . . a pretty romance of old Nuremberg, *Meister Martin der Küfner und seine Gesellen*, and Hoffmann's most artistic story, *Das Fräulein von Scuderi*. (259)

Once again, the two works edited as texts are singled out for special praise. In seeking an answer for the popularity of the two, one finds these lines by Calvin Thomas: "And all this haunting uncanniness he was able to make vividly real by mixing it with realistic narrative and description" (366). These are almost Kurz's words; the special mixture of phantasy and realism found in the two stories was particularly appealing to the tastes of literary historians of the era under investigation. And, if Vilmar, Hosmer and the listings of German texts are consulted, the taste for Hoffman apparently took some time to arrive in academe; the texts appeared in 1907 and 1908.

Robert Herndon Fife, Jr., editor of *Meister Martin der Küfner*, described the reasons for his choice of that particular story as follows:

> *Meister Martin* has been selected as one of the best of Hoffmann's *Novellen*, a sunny story, unmarked by any of the grewsome [sic] elements found in some of the author's best work. Of importance for the study of German literature and culture is the charming background of Old Nuremberg. ... The lasting human interest of the story and the charms of the old city ... have already made *Meister Martin* a school classic in France and England. (iii)

The story may be sunny and free from gruesome elements, but the attempt to de-Hoffmannize Hoffmann cannot be called an unqualified success. *Das Fräulein von Scuderi*, perhaps more typical of Hoffmann, was listed only once, while *Meister Martin der Küfner* was listed but two times.

Quite different is the case of Joseph von Eichendorff, whose *Aus dem Leben eines Taugenichts* was listed twenty times from 1864 to 1911. This work was popular for the same reasons which brought critical praise to Hoffmann's *Meister Martin der Küfner* and *Das Fräulein von Scuderi*:

> Sein bestes Erzeugnis ist die Novelle "Aus dem Leben eines Taugenichts" .... Hier verschwindet das Phantastische und Willkürliche ganz; wir hören zwar fortwährend romantische Klänge, aber sie tönen uns freundlich und gemüthlich entgegen .... Wir haben ... gesagt, daß er sich nicht in allgemeine poetische Abstractionen verliert, sondern sich aus der Vergangenheit wirkliche Gestalten hervorholt, die er mit seinen Empfindungen, seiner Sehnsucht und seiner Poesie beseelt. (Kurz 3:616)

Once again, there is a preference for the concrete and realistic. Romanticism in Eichendorff's novella soughs a soothing lullaby as a background for real characters and situations summoned from memory.

Among Eichendorff's prose works, Bernhardt mentions only *Aus dem Leben eines Taugenichts*, "die jugendfrische Erzählung ... welche zu den besten Originalproduktionen der romantischen Schule gehört" (48). Less laconically, Kummer delivers an excursus on *Taugenichts* in which appear the following lines:

> Das ist das Schönste nach Eichendorffs poetischer Schilderung, frühmorgens herauszutreten—hoch oben ziehen die Zugvögel fort—und noch gar nicht zu wissen, welcher Schornstein für einen raucht, noch gar zu ahnen, was einem bis zum Abend für ein besonderes Glück beggnen könne. Die Darstellung, wie in

den anderen Novellen durchaus lyrisch, war von auserwählter Anmut, Feinheit und liebenswürdigem Humor. Überhaupt ist Eichendorff einer unserer feinsten Stilisten. (124)

Again, the desire to escape from it all is a real human feeling, not a dream of the *Waldweib* or birds which lay eggs containing pearls.

Yet not all commentators stress the tempering of Romanticism with realism in Eichendorff which has been noted up to this point. Priest writes of "A captivating Romantic spirit in his poems and stories" (253), and Thomas likewise ascertains "the purest essence of romanticism" in *Aus dem Leben eines Taugenichts* (358). However, for Thomas or for Priest, the "purest essence" of Romanticism or a "captivating romantic spirit" may include a dose of realism and a considerably reduced amount of mysticism. One need only peruse Thomas's assessments of Fouqué and Hoffmann to become aware of this possibility.

From a text of the story, George M. Howe's 1906 edition, comes what is perhaps the best explanation of the blend of Romanticism and realism in *Taugenichts*, an insight into Eichendorff's own life and character, and into the times for which the U.S. text was prepared:

> A review of Eichendorff's life will convince the student that the idle existence of the *Taugenichts* is not Eichendorff's ideal of life. The Romanticist wrote, not to show life as it was or should be, but to speak to the spirit of man. The *Taugenichts* was from the pen of a man who fretted in the musty atmosphere of somewhat distasteful surroundings. It was what is nowadays the city banker's dream of his boyhood days on the old farm. Though the free life, its songs and joys, are past, there is still strength and refreshment in dreaming of them. And as long as men love hills and woods, songs and dreams, so long will the *Taugenichts* find a place in their hearts. (viii)

Eichendorff's own life experience seems to parallel that of an urban American in 1906. Both found solace in romantic dreams of bucolic rambles—laced with a dose of realism for reality's sake. Of all the romantics read in the schools, Eichendorff must have been the favorite.

Another late romantic author of considerable popularity was Adelbert von Chamisso, represented in U.S. texts by a story with a moral: *Peter Schlemihls wundersame Geschichte*. Schlemihl sells his shadow, is driven from human society, and eventually finds peace in nature. Three *Schlemihl* texts were listed a total of eighteen times from 1888 to the teens of this century, rendering the misfortunes of Schlemihl a commercial success.

According to Kurz, who reflects at some length about the plot, the shadow symbolizes the outward signs of honor:

> Der Mensch in der gesellschaftlichen Welt. . . . muß sich in der Gesellschaft bewegen können, der Mode huldigen, einen Orden, einen Titel haben, sich in

Nichts von den andern Menschenkindern unterscheiden, mit einem Worte im hergebrachten Gleise leben. (3:614)

Giving up the shadow pulled Schlemihl out of society.

One year later (1892), Bernhardt curtly characterizes the Schlemihl story as *mysteriös* and *märchenhaft*, but also offers students one of his comparatively rare plot summaries—a possible result of Chamisso's effect on lower-level German classes. *Märchenhaft* the story may be, but it also verges on the realistic:

> Das eigentümlich Bannende der Darstellung liegt in dem Realismus, mit dem das Wunderbare, nicht in ahnungsvoller Dämmerung oder in dunkler Nacht, sondern am hellichten Tage vorgeführt wird. (Kummer 228)

Like Hoffmann, Chamisso presented students with a blend of the real and the supernatural; however, in Chamisso's works the real, if it does not outbalance the supernatural, is at least equal to it. As Priest taught, the story "is both Romantic and popularly realistic" (267). For this reason, perhaps, the teachers of the era of Realism (and Naturalism) probably preferred Chamisso to Hoffman.

Thomas, however, seems at first to make no differentiation between the techniques of Chamisso and Hoffmann:

> The charm of Chamisso's little masterpiece lies in his easy and natural approach to the impossible. And it is just this plausible realism of detail, gradually leading up to and at last inextricably blent with the spooky, chimerical and gruesome, that constitutes the literary knack of *Ernst Theodor Amadeus Hoffmann*. (365–66)

Yet, if reading between the lines is allowed, Thomas's remarks seem to convey a considerable difference in intensity between Chamisso's "natural approach to the impossible" and the "chimerical and gruesome," between Peter Schlemihl and, for example, Rat Krespel. Presumably, this difference of degree made Chamisso more palatable to teachers than Hoffmann.

Not a sophisticated aristocrat like Chamisso, but, like him, a romantic who wrote stories with morals, was the *Volksschriftsteller* Johann Peter Hebel. Hebel's *Schatzkästlein des rheinischen Hausfreundes* was listed as a text by Menco von Stern in 1913—perhaps too late to be reissued, reprinted or listed again due to the outbreak of World War I. Hebel's impact on the U.S. German text market, therefore, is by no means representative of his standing as a writer. Vilmar, for example, states that

> Die Erzählungen des rheinischen Hausfreundes, von denen die besten in dem "Schatzkästlein" gesammelt sind, sind an Laune, an tiefem und wahrem Gefühl, an Lebhaftigkeit der Darstellung vollkommen unübertrefflich und wiegen ein ganzes Fuder von Romanen auf. Zu diesen anspruchslosen Erzählungen, ja sogar zu den eigens didaktischen Stücken kehren wir, wehet

nur noch ein Hauch echten deutschen Volkslebens in uns, unzählige Mal im Leben mit neuem Vergnügen zurück. . . . Uebrigens darf es nicht unbemerkt bleiben, daß die meisten Hebelschen Erzählungen dem Stoffe nach alt, und aus den seiner Zeit erwähnten volksmäßigen Scherz- und Anekdotenbüchern des 16. Jahrhunderts entlehnt sind. (527)

Popular stories from *Volksbücher* recycled by a writer of the people—if Lessing could make use of Boccaccio's ring parable, if Goethe could borrow *Iphigenie* from Euripides, perhaps no fault should be found with Hebel for his reliance on others' writings.

Further proof of Hebel's popularity in Wilhelminian Germany is offered by Kurz, whose remarks—as only rarely—harmonize with those of Vilmar. Kurz asserts that

was Jakob Grimm irgend wo [sic] so wahr und treffend von Hans Sachs sagt, daß er Alles dichtet und doch Nichts erdichtet, läßt sich auch im vollsten Sinne auf Hebel anwenden. Man vergleiche nur die ursprüngliche Gestalt dieser Stoffe mit dem, was er daraus gemacht hat, und man wird sich bald überzeugen, daß er sie als wahrer Dichter behandelt, daß er den in ihnen liegenden Keim zur schönsten Frucht entwickelt hat. (603)

Hebel transfigured simple stories into true works of art, although "es sieht so natürlich aus, als ob jeder auch so schreiben könnte, und doch . . . wem ist es gelungen?" (Kurz 602)

In the U.S. in 1892, Bernhardt esteemed the *Schatzkästlein* as "eine Sammlung prächtiger volkstümlicher Erzählungen" (57). By 1909, Hebel's reputation had grown greater:

The witty anecdote, which had long since fallen into vulgar coarseness, Hebel revived and molded into a classic form in his *Schatzkästlein*. . . . The idea of a popular writer which the youthful Herder had imagined, was realized in the poetry and personality of Hebel. (Priest 241)

This speaks for Hebel's *Schatzkästlein* as wholesome textbook fare—which it became only four years later. In the same year (1909), another commentator told students that "Hebel ist frisch, natürlich, gesund, anschaulich, von bäuerlicher Einfalt und Schlauheit, dabei doch von schalkhafter Lehrhaftigkeit wie ein alter Sternseher und Kalendermacher" (Kummer 168). Certainly Hebel's writing is made to sound fascinating and genial. It may have had everything to give it success as a text—except time to circulate through the schools and colleges of the land. World War I and a decline in enrollment in German programs probably made the *Schatzkästlein* a casualty of war.

With the close of the War of Liberation came the Congress of Vienna, reactionary government policies and strong censorship. This atmosphere, in which domesticity and obedience replaced political fervor, would later be termed *Biedermeier*. Among *Biedermeier* authors, perhaps no other portrays the triumph of order over self-assertion as distinctively as Franz Grillparzer. Vilmar mentions Grillparzer only in connection with his early *Schicksalstragödie, Die Ahnfrau,* which he calls "das Widerspiel aller Poesie" (563). More favorable are the remarks of Bernhardt, who called Grillparzer

> Der größte Dramatiker Östrrichs [sic] . . . dessen Dramen ("Die Ahnfrau," "Medea," "Sappho," "Das goldene Vlies," "König Ottokars Glück und Ende") sich durch Jugendfrische und meisterhafte Charakteristik auszeichnen, während seine Tragödie "Des Meeres und der Liebe Wellen," welche die Sage von *Hero und Leander* behandelt, ein würdiges Seitenstück zu Shakespeares "Romeo and Julia" bildet. (57–58)

Like the earlier historians, Wells, too, writes only of the Grillparzer "whose significant work had been done . . . chiefly from 1819 to 1830" (388). Once again, *Sappho, Ottokar* and *Das goldene Vlies* are mentioned, along with *Ein treuer Diener seines Herrn*. The later, "posthumous" plays and *Der arme Spielmann* are omitted.

Indeed, these later works are neglected until nearer the end of the era under consideration, probably due in part to Grillparzer's declining to stage his dramas after the public's scorn of *Weh dem, der lügt*—though, as Kummer asserts, there may have been two reasons:

> Grillparzer schrieb fortan nur für sich, nicht mehr für die Welt. Doch ist es ein Irrtum zu glauben, daß er durch die Niederlage von Weh dem, der lügt so verbittert worden sei, daß er nur noch wenig produziert habe: Grillparzer hörte zu schaffen auf, weil seine Schaffenskraft allmählich versiegte. (Kummer 148)

Not only were Grillparzer's later works less in circulation because they were published later; they were also inferior to the earlier works—if one sides with Kummer—due to the author's waning creative powers.

However, in the U.S. near the time of World War I, among the literary historians surveyed, only Calvin Thomas neglected to acquaint students with *Der arme Spielmann* and the later plays (368–372). In a tone of discovery, Professor Priest told students about Grillparzer that

> several tragedies were found among his literary remains which are thoroughly worthy of their author, *Ein Bruderzwist in Habsburg, Die Jüdin von Toledo,* and *Libussa,* Grillparzer's most thoughtful work. Besides his dramas, Grillparzer also wrote a short story, *Der arme Spielmann,* a masterpiece in psychology. (280)

Certainly, taste was changing with regard to Grillparzer's later creations. In 1912, Professors Stroebe and Whitney turned the subject completely around:

> Wenn wir in seinem ersten Drama den Einfluß der Romantiker, in seinem zweiten die antikisierende Tendenz der deutschen Klassiker deutlich erkennen,

so kommt er in seinen späteren Dramen dem realistischen und individualisierenden Streben der Neuzeit immer näher und sein letztes, großes Werk, *Libussa*, ist ein symbolisches Drama großen Stils, das erst im zwanzigsten Jahrhundert Verständnis und Würdigung gefunden hat. (203)

The change in Grillparzer's style, then, was not due to bitterness or dearth of creativity. He was emerging from the *Biedermeier* to Poetic Realism.

As interesting as these alternations in taste may be, the fact is that *Sappho* and *Des Meeres und der Liebe Wellen*, both dealing with the *Antike*, were edited more than twice as many times for students as *Der arme Spielmann* and *Libussa*. All editions, reprints, reissues or listings but the first two editions of *Sappho* were published in the twentieth century. Taking the leader, *Sappho* (three editions, five listings from 1898 to 1916), as an example, let us examine the reasons for this classical preference.

In twentieth-century Germany, Kummer waxed lukewarm on the subject of the play:

Tasso und Iphigenie sind für die Ausführung bedeutend gewesen. Zum Thema erhob der Dichter den Gedanken von Schillers Teilung der Erde, daß Kunst und Leben unvereinbar sind. . . . Das Drama ist reif; es enthält in seinen Grundgedanken, daß Leid das Schicksal des Poeten sei, auch ein Stück schmerzlich errungener Lebenswahrheit; doch mangeln dem Drama Kraft und Ursprünglichkeit; alle Personen sprechen dieselbe Sprache; bei aller Einfachheit der Motive und dem edlen Fluß der Jamben liegt doch eine gewollte künstliche Klassizität in dem Stück. (141–42)

Here are no real justifications for the play's academic popularity, unless the dependence on Goethe and Schiller enhanced the play as a pedagogical tool. Then, too, the fact that all the characters speak the same language would make comprehension or translation all the easier.

Even if not their equal, then, *Sappho* would certainly be suitable as a follow-up to *Iphigenie* or *Tasso*. As Priest stated: "the discord between life and art, which wrecked Sappho's happiness, as it had that of Goethe's Tasso, Grillparzer had himself experienced" (279). But Priest, as has already been pointed out, saved his best compliments for the later plays. Neither Thomas nor Stroebe and Whitney give the play more than desultory remarks. It appears that the play's classical style and its connection with Goethe and Schiller afforded it first place among Grillparzer's works used as German texts.

Another epigone was Friedrich Halm (Eligius Franz Joseph, Freiherr von Münch-Bellinghausen), whose play *Griseldis*, which received much praise at the *Burgtheater* in 1835, became a U.S. German text in 1894. However, the play did not receive much praise from critics and professors; Vilmar, for example, writes of dem verderblichen Opern und Decorationsgeschmack . . . den allermassenhaftesten Rühr- und Spektakelstücken der älteren längst überwundenen Zeit . . . wie z.B. die nicht allein unpoetische, sondern antipoetische Griseldis des Herrn von Münch-Bellinghausen. (563)

One cannot help but be reminded of Tieck's poking fun at just such offenses in *Der gestiefelte Kater*.

As so frequently, Heinrich Kurz supports the antithesis of Vilmar's statements—yet Kurz, too, finds some fault with the *Rühr- und Spektakelstück* as he compares Halm's work with the original in Boccaccio:

Während Boccaccio über dieses Motiv in Zweifel läßt, wird Percival bei Halm durch eine Wette veranlaßt, die Treue und Hingebung seiner Gattin auf die unwürdigste und eine wahrhaft barbarische Weise zu prüfen. Dies ist zwar bei dem Italiener auch der Fall, aber was bei dem Erzähler Mitleid erregt, erregt bei dem Dramatiker Abscheu, da uns die Seelenfoltern, denen der grausame Gatte sein Weib unterwirft, in der lebendigsten Anschaulichkeit vor die Augen gerückt werden, ja selbst der Dichter erscheint grausam. (4:555)

Yet Kurz excuses the author on the following grounds:

Das Unnatürliche in Halms Dramen ist durch die Stoffe bedingt, die er aus Vorliebe wählt, so wie auch die übrigen Mängel, die allzu große Weichheit und Sentimentalität, das vorherrschende lyrische Element, die rhetorische Breite eine nothwendige Folge dieser Stoffe sind, die beinahe sämmtlich mit der Absicht gewählt sind, außerordentliche psychologische Erscheinungen zur Anschauung zu bringen. Dieß [sic] tritt schon in "Griseldis" (1833) hervor. (4:555)

Because the story lines themselves are unnatural or sentimental, it is hardly fair to expect a realistic drama. In return, one sees extraordinary psychological phenomena.

Perhaps a happy solution to the problem of how these works were to be regarded was offered to the student by Professor Wells, who grouped Halm with less literary "purveyors of mild dramatic sensation": "Meanwhile melodrama was being successfully cultivated by Münch-Bellinghausen (1806–1871), better known as Friedrich Halm" (390). As to the esteem in which he and his works were held, Priest witnesses as follows: "The dramatist Friedrich Halm . . . seems to use romantic elements chiefly for the sake of artistic effect. His plays . . . are more spectacular than true, but for a time they eclipsed the masterpieces of Grillparzer in general popularity" (291). Although Halm's plays may have been more popular than Grillparzer's in theatres, it is to the credit of U.S. German professors that they did not surpass Grillparzer's works as German texts.

It is best to part from Halm with the words of Stroebe and Whitney, who offer a summary assessment of the author and others like him:

> Die Nachahmer Schillers bemächtigten sich während dieser Zeit des Gebiets des idealisierenden Dramas und versuchten die Sehnsucht nach dem Hohen und Edlen in der Dichtung dadurch zu befriedigen, daß sie historische oder sagenhafte Stoffe in fünffüßigen Jamben für das Theater bearbeiteten. Leider fehlte es ihnen an Kraft, große Konflikte und Leidenschaften darzustellen, und sie brachten nur hohle Sentimentalität und leeres Pathos hervor. So galten eine Zeitlang Theaterdichter wie . . . *Friedrich Halm* . . . für große Tragiker, und sie ernteten den Beifall, der wirklich großen Dichtern wie Kleist und Grillparzer versagt wurde. (209)

Griseldis is listed only in 1894.

However, vastly more popular than Kleist or Grillparzer during the era under consideration was Roderich Benedix. With some seventy-one listings, Benedix trails behind only a small group of authors with regard to texts edited, re-edited, reissued and listed in commercial and scholarly catalogs. Heinrich Kurz indicates the reason for Benedix's popularity—in the world at large as well as in the schools—when he calls Benedix a poet whose plays

> auf allen großen und kleinen Bühnen Deutschlands gegeben und vorzugsweise in gesellschaftlichen Kreisen gespielt werden, [er] würde selbst dann noch Beachtung verdienen, wenn seine Dramen nur auf die vorübergehende Unterhaltung des Publikums berechnet wären, da sie wenigstens den Bildungszustand einer ganzen Generation bezeichnen würden; um so mehr aber verdient er Anerkennung, wenn diese Dramen in Form und Gestalt zu den besseren Erscheinungen der Zeit gehören. (4:548)

Kurz then outlines what were considered the strengths and weaknesses of Benedix's art:

> Benedix ist nicht eigentlich reich an Erfindungen, aber in denselben beinahe immer äußerst glücklich; er ist eben so wenig reich an neuen Motiven . . . aber er ist unerschöpflich an komischen Einfällen, die er zu höchst effektvollen Situationen zu entfalten und den Charakteren auf das Glücklichste anzupassen weiß, die er überhaupt mit Sicherheit und Schärfe zeichnet. . . . Der Dialog ist lebendig und schlagfertig, und immer anziehend, ohne eben tief und geistvoll zu sein, wie ihm auch der feinere Compositionston nicht zu Gebote steht. (4:549)

One is reminded of Scribe's *la pièce bien faite*: there is little originality, but the materials of the play are used to their best advantage.

These ideas are echoed in the U.S. in Wells's literary history:

> The lighter vein of farce is represented by the prolific Roderich Benedix . . . whose extraordinary success, both in Germany and in foreign adaptations, is due in part to intimate technical knowledge of the stage, in part

to lively humor and never failing action. "Dr. Wasp," "The Love-letter," "The Lawsuit," "The Sunday Hunters" may be named as typical of his healthy tone, simple, lively wit, burly humor descending frequently to the burlesque, and mastery of stage technic hardly excelled in Germany. (390)

Wells was himself an editor of Benedix's *Der Prozeß* and *Günstige Vorzeichen*. Perhaps the keys to Benedix's success (as far as texts are concerned) lie in the words "healthy tone, simple, lively wit."

Kummer brings together several ideas already stated when he calls Benedix "ein wohlerfahrener Theaterhandwerker," who "besaß große Situationskomik und schilderte, ein zweiter Iffland, das engbürgerliche Familienleben . . . immer wie ein rechter Spießbürger. Sein Streben ging auf Natürlichkeit, der Dialog war breitspurig, die Handlung klar, aber dünn, mit zahlreichen Episoden" (437). Only three years later, any pretensions to literary greatness were denied Benedix by Stroebe and Whitney: "Die anderen Lustspieldichter der Zeit, wie Roderich Benedix . . . sind ohne jede literarische Bedeutung und bemühen sich nur, das Publikum zu unterhalten" (209).

What Benedix's farces are actually like may be appreciated from the following sketch. In *Der Prozeß*, two farmers engaged in a lawsuit against each other over a fish pond wind up in the same jail cell in a large city. Farmer Lehmann got lost, could not find his way to his hotel (he had forgotten the name of it) and was arrested for vagrancy; Farmer Schulze, arriving late in the evening, tried to waken the hotel personnel, during which attempt he broke a window glass and was arrested for burglary while attempting to climb into the foyer. In the jail cell the two men at first carry on their feud. But Lehmann has ordered a dinner while Schulze has lost his wallet; Schulze, however, has pipe tobacco coveted by Lehmann. The two eventually agree to share with one another. Then they compare a series of legal documents which each has had drawn up for the trial, ending with the lawyers' fees. Both farmers realize that they are being taken advantage of by city lawyers and resolve to share the pond. Advocate Lohmeier, summoned by Schulze to effect his (and now Lehmann's) release from prison, laments that the two have shared the cell.

The play plainly pits the country against the city, to the advantage of the former:

Lehmann: "Mein Advocat sagte immer: ich müsse mein Recht durchsetzen."
Schulze: "Und der Doktor Lohmeier riet mir, nicht ein Titelchen von meinem Recht aufzugeben."
Lehmann: "Was werden die ins Fäustchen gelacht haben!"
Schulze: "Und uns für dumme Bauerntölpel gehalten!"
Lehmann: "Wenn sie unsere schönen Thaler einstrichen!"
Schulze: "Und Schinken, Butter und Eier in die Küche bekamen."
Lehmann: "Nachbar!"
. . . .
Schulze: "Wir bauen die Mühle zusammen!"
(Benedix, *Der Prozeß*, 64)

As if in a sort of reprise, Doktor Lohmeier says at the end of the play:

> Wenn die beiden Töpel nicht zusammenkamen, konnte der fette Prozeß noch sieben Jahre dauern. Die verdammte Mündlichkeit richtet uns Advokaten noch zu Grunde. Und ich gutmütiger Esel beeile mich noch so, die Kerle frei zu machen. (67)

Thus Benedix's sympathies are clearly on the side of the farmers.

As editor Wells states in his introduction to *Der Prozeß*, strangely placing Benedix among the Young Germans, Benedix's plays

> picture phases of the social condition of Germany after the rise of the agitation for national unity, political reform and social progress that in literature is connected with the movement known as "Jungdeutschland." (iii–iv)

It was apparently Benedix's intent to record in his *bürgerliche Rührstücke und Lustspiele* (Frenzel and Frenzel 355) various aspects of the social climate in Germany after the War of Liberation.

Significantly less received were the works of the poet Otto Roquette: only one text containing one of his lesser-known works was listed in 1887 and 1899. Roquette's fame in Germany and the United States was based upon his epic poem *Waldmeisters Brautfahrt*. In Bernhardt's assessment, "Roquette (geboren 1824) hat sich durch sein reizendes humoristisch-idyllisches Rhein-, Wein- und Wandermärchen 'Waldmeisters Brautfahrt' (1851) vorteilhaft in die poetische Litteratur eingeführt" (62). More expansive was Heinrich Kurz: "Das ganze Gedicht ist von einer jugendlichen Heiterkeit beseelt, die den Leser unwiderstehlich hinreißt und ihn über Mängel hinwegsehen läßt, als deren größter der zu bezeichnen ist, daß man nicht recht weiß, ob der Dichter die Kräuter und Weine Personificiert hat oder nicht" (4:425). If one reads no later commentaries, Roquette's popularity appears established.

But after the turn of the century, professional opinion is quite different: "An idle singer of an empty day. . . is Otto Roquette . . . whose 'Waldmeister's Bridel Trip' . . . swam into favor with the reactionary political tide, and gives the keynote to his later, not very significant work" (Wells 387). To which Professor Priest adds: "This 'tale of travel, of the Rhine and wine,' Roquette's only successful literary venture, was extremely popular in its day" (296–297). Kummer praises the *Brautfahrt*, and at the same time explains the negative effect the poem had on Roquette's later works: "Der Erfolg der Dichtung war groß, aber verhängnisvoll insofern, als Roquettes spätere Werke . . . nicht die gleiche Anerkennung erringen konnten" (335). Perhaps this is what happened to *Der gefrorene Kuß*—the only one of Roquette's works used as a U.S. German text and totally neglected by all of the literary histories consulted. "Waldmeisters Brautfahrt," as it seems, would have been a more auspicious choice on the part of the editor and publisher of the Roquette text.

It remained for the indifferent epic poetry of Joseph Viktor von Scheffel to take Germany and the United States—at least *Germanisten* and students—by

84 *Klassik—Romantik—Biedermeier—Junges Deutschland*

storm. Famous not only as a lyric and epic poet, but also as the author of the novel *Ekkehard*, Scheffel was probably best known to students as the poet of *Der Trompeter von Säkkingen*. Bernhardt offered students an effusion of praise for Scheffel and *Trompeter* such as he scarcely offered Goethe and Schiller:

> Einer der originellsten Dichter der neuesten Zeit ist Joseph Viktor Scheffel (1826–1886), der erklärte Liebling Deutschlands, besonders der akademischen Jugend, deren freies und frohes Studentenleben er nach jeder Richtung hin besungen hat. Deutsch sind die Stoffe in allen Dichtungen Scheffels, deutsch sind seine Männer und Frauen in ihrer Einfachheit, Wahrheit und Treue, mit ihrem fühlenden Herzen und tiefem Verständnis für das Leben der Natur; deutsch ist vor allem der Dichter selbst mit seiner Sehnsucht nach Italien, mit seinem gutmütigen Humor und seinen Sympathieen für das burschikose Studentenleben. . . . Das populärste deutsche Gedicht der Gegenwart ist Scheffels Epos "*Der Trompeter von Säkkingen*" [sic], in welchem er frisch und "lerchenfröhlich" Scenen aus dem deutschen und italienischen Volksleben des 17. Jahrhunderts vor unsern Augen entrollt. (62)

Such praise is only infrequently encountered in literary histories (especially Bernhardt's) and does much to show how academic tastes change with time.

However, if Bernhardt has nothing but praise for the poem, Kurz allows himself at least some measure of disquisition. He criticizes Scheffel for ignoring certain epic conventions:

> Wenn wir oben gesagt haben, daß "der Trompeter" sich wesentlich von andern epischen Gedichten unterscheidet, so darf doch nicht verschwiegen werden, daß auch er [Scheffel] der herrschenden Mode nicht ganz entgehen konnte, den epischen Gang durch lyrische Einschiebungen zu unterbrechen. . . . Nicht zu billigen sind ferner manche Allegorien, die Personification des Rheins, der [sic] Tiber, des Obelisken . . . die . . . der epischen Haltung widerstreben. Endlich ist auch der Schluß zu schnell herbeigeführt. (4:447)

All these critical remarks notwithstanding, Kurz concludes as he began, in praise of Scheffel: "Bei allen diesen Mängeln nimmt, wie schon bemerkt 'der Trompeter von Säkkingen' einen hervorragenden Rang unter den neuen epischen Gedichten ein" (4:447).

In the early twentieth century, professional opinion was largely unchanged. Scheffel's " 'Trumpeter of Säkkingen' . . . is the most popular of modern German epics, and has, indeed, been twice translated into English. It has uncommon verve and bubbling humor" (Wells 386). Kummer wrote of "eine gesunde, klare Dichtung von nicht unbedeutender Eigenart" (341), and Priest called the poem "the most spontaneous and pleasing of all the romantic stories in verse" (297). Only Calvin Thomas foresaw the eclipse of Scheffel's popularity: "His *Trumpeter of Säkkingen*, probably the most widely read narrative poem of the century, was built on familiar romantic lines . . . the story told in slovenly, easy-going verse" which left the reader "satisfied, if not edified. This is the secret of his immense popularity" (385).

In his *Trompeter*, Scheffel seems to offer a veiled apology for his verse as the *Freiherr* offers Werner the position of *Schloßtrompeter*:

> Seht, mein junger Freund, so lang die
> Welt steht, wird's auch Menschen geben,
> Die auf Steckenpferden reiten;
> Der liebt Mystik und Askesis,
> Jener altes Kirschenwasser,
> Ein'ge suchen Altertümer,
> Andere essen Maikäfer,
> Dritte machen schlechte Verse.
> 's ist ein eigner Spaß, daß jeder
> Das am liebsten treibt, wozu er
> Just am wenigsten Beruf hat.
> Und so reit' auch ich mein Rößlein. . . .
> (58)

Whether or not these lines are a confession by Scheffel, why his verse has been called slovenly is clear.

Even Carla Wenckebach, who edited *Der Trompeter von Säkkingen* as a text for D. C. Heath, states that "as regards the form of Scheffel's verse, it must be admitted that he occasionally permits himself, in Heine's own fashion, to drop into commonplace expression, or to indulge in careless and slipshod rhyme." Yet Wenckebach, as all others consulted except Thomas, ends her criticism on a laudatory note: "But the reader is compensated for these defects by the general excellence of the verse, and by the poet's naïve diction." Indeed, she terms *Trompeter* a work "of high and lasting worth among the enduring landmarks of German literature," citing its "wholesomeness of tone." And, seemingly presupposing the dicta of the Committee of Twelve, which would be published five years later, the editor informs the student that "in its accurate reflection of the German nature, German customs and habits of thought, the poem deserves an honorable place beside Goethe's 'Hermann und Dorothea'" (xv–xvi). Probably there are few Germanists of the 1980s who would agree with Professor Wenckebach on any point save "wholesomeness of tone."

Quite opposite is the case of Annette von Droste-Hülshoff. She was little known to students of the era under discussion—a single edition of *Die Judenbuche* was listed once in 1910—but ranks at present as one of German literature's major figures and is relatively frequently studied by U.S. students. Vilmar, though he characterizes Droste-Hülshoff's work as belonging "weitaus zu dem besten, was die neueste Zeit erzeugt hat," also proffers a reason why her work was not a prominent choice for German instruction:

> In der Form nicht überall den Stoff bewältigend, vielleicht nicht überall hinreichend klar. . . . Wenigen zugänglich im Leben, ist sie bis dahin auch durch ihre Gedichte nur einer kleineren Anzahl von Lesern zugänglich, vielleicht verständlich gewesen. (560)

Although *Die Judenbuche* (the Droste-Hülshoff text, listed only in 1910) is not specifically mentioned, much of what is said could apply to the novella.

Bernhardt mentions only Droste-Hülshoff's poetry (69), as does Kurz, who states that as a person in poor health, Annette was often alone: "In dieser Einsamkeit beschäftigte sie sich hauptsächlich mit der Poesie und den Wissenschaften" (4:140). To *Poesie* and *Wissenschaft*, Kummer (1909) adds *Prosa*: "Zu den Meisternovellen der deutschen Literatur ist *Die Judenbuche* zu rechnen. Es bleibt zu beklagen, daß Annette nicht mehr Novellen geschaffen hat" (270). *Die Judenbuche* is cursorily mentioned by Priest as "permanently enriching" German literature "by the sympathetic delineation of character" (276). Professor Thomas makes no mention of Droste-Hülshoff.

It seems that the era was not too much taken with the author, and was particularly slow to expend praises on *Die Judenbuche*. Possibly, the same mechanism which operated against *Götz von Berlichingen* and *Die Räuber* was in operation here; lawlessness, instinct and passion, and revolt against conventional standards made *Die Judenbuche* strong fare for the classroom. If Droste-Hülshoff was widely known to U.S. students from 1864 to 1918, it was because some of her poetry was printed in anthologies.

On the other hand, as in the case of *Torquato Tasso*, which has not always enjoyed the popularity of other works by Goethe, certain works have developed and retained over the years a relatively smaller yet frequently enthusiastic audience. One such work is Mörike's *Mozart auf der Reise nach Prag*. The usual sources—sources consulted by students of that day—mention Mörike less often than other authors of the period, and less favorably as well:

> Beinahe alle Kritiker und Literarhistoriker erklären Mörike für einen höchst bedeutenden Dichter. . . . Wir müssen gestehen, daß wir diese Ansicht in keiner Weise theilen und Mörike's Dichtungen weder in Form noch in Gehalt für so bedeutend halten können. (Kurz 4:158)

However Mörike was regarded, by Kurz he was considered a poet, not a writer of *Novellen*—the *Novellen* are not even mentioned in his discussion.

The other side of the argument is expressed a few years later. While Mörike's greatness as a poet is stressed, his prose writings, particularly *Mozart auf der Reise nach Prag*, are also taken into account:

> Ein echter Dichter war Mörike auch in Prosa. Seine schönsten novellistischen Werke sind: Lucie Gelmeroth, Das Stuttgarter Hutzelmännlein und Mozart auf der Reise nach Prag. Die letztgenannte Erzählung gehört zu dem Lieblichsten,

> was die deutsche Erzählungsliteratur hervorgebracht hat. Sie ist frei erfunden, aber sie ist das Muster einer geschichtlich gefärbten Novelle. (Kummer 266)

Not only are Mörike's novellas classics; one of them is the pattern of a novella with historical overtones. This was *Mozart*, and it may be presumed that the novella (two editions, each listed once) was read by a relatively small group of U.S. German students whose teachers' tastes were almost a century ahead of their times.

Professor Thomas, for example, writes only of Mörike's poetry and his one novel, which he terms "a book . . . rather badly composed," adding that Mörike's "fame rests on his poetry" (384). Having called Mörike a great poet, Priest goes on to mention several novellas, including *Mozart*; however, he concludes by saying that "Mörike's distinction. . . . rests upon his collected poems" (290).

In 1904 even William Guild Howard, who edited *Mozart auf der Reise nach Prag* for D. C. Heath, told students that "Mörike is greatest as a lyric poet" (vi). However, he proceeds to point out that

> Mörike's prose is no less artistic than his verse, and in respect to subject and treatment, his prose writings form a worthy counterpart to his poetry. . . . *Mozart auf der Reise nach Prag* (1855) is Mörike's ripest work and at the same time his last considerable product, his most successful effort in pure narration. . . . It is as if the soul of music took human shape, and harmony and melody acquired a new significance through the endowment of articulate speech. (ix–x)

Although he agrees with the literary historians of his day that Mörike's poetry is his greatest contribution to literature, his praise of *Mozart auf der Reise nach Prag* foretells the future popularity of the novella.

A writer apparently somewhat better known to U.S. students of the era investigated, and, possibly, better known to students of the later twentieth century is Adalbert Stifter. As in the case of Mörike, it is surprising to find but two American literary histories among those surveyed which deal with Stifter (in this respect, it is well to remember that Benedix led all other *Biedermeier* authors in listings for texts, if not in critical esteem). Bernhardt, for his part, dealt briefly with Stifter as follows:

> Prächtige idyllische Landschaftsbilder aus seiner böhmischen Heimat entwirft Adalbert *Stifter* . . . in seiner Novellensammlung "Studien"; obschon arm an Handlung wirken dieselben doch bezaubernd durch frischen Natursinn und feine Psychologie. (59)

Two years later (1894), a similar, yet profounder assessment of Stifter's art was current:

> Der Hauptreiz seiner Schilderungen liegt in der Naivität, die Alles sieht, Alles merkwürdig findet, Alles mit Liebe, mit großer Treue und Frische beschreibt.

Dieses liebevolle und wohlbegründete Eingehen in die kleinsten Einzelheiten des Naturlebens hat ihn aber verleitet, in eben derselben Weise bei Darstellung seiner Personen zu verfahren. (Kurz 4:785)

Stifter's greatest charm, then, is his manner of description—yet this also may be a disadvantage when he describes his characters at too great length.

Kurz goes on to discuss the success of Stifter's *Studien* as follows:

Dieser Erfolg war um so überraschender, als er in seinen "Studien" . . . der herrschenden Vorliebe für das Spannende und Aufregende nicht entgegenkam. . . . Die einzelnen Stücke der "Studien" sind meist ohne bedeutende Handlung; es scheint oft, als ob die darin auftretenden Personen nur um des Schauplatzes willen, den er beschreibt, eingeführt wären; doch weiß er für dieselben immer Interesse zu erregen. (4:785)

Stifter's stories became popular despite a dearth of tension, vigor and plot. Nature, psychology and description were the keys to success for the *Studien*, in which *Brigitta* and *Das Heidedorf*—the two U.S. Stifter texts—first appeared.

Kummer offered students similar information to that presented by Bernhardt and Kurz, but he added politics:

Gerade in den vierziger Jahren, als der politische Sturm und Drang in Deutschland seine Höhe erreicht hatte, erschienen jene zarten duftigen leidenschaftsscheuen "Studien" Stifters, in dem er aus dem Lärm des Tages in die Waldstille flüchtete . . . . Ruhesüchtig waren seine Werke, und sein Stil, obschon fein, farbenreich und von großer Klarheit, war süß und weich. (329)

Once again a lack of poetic vigor, or engagement, is coupled with great beauty. As the preceding quotation demonstrates, changing sources merely gives an echo of what has been written before; nonetheless, let Professor Priest be heard:

Stifter . . . remained untouched by the political currents of his age. The isolated life of his native province is the subject of his best work, *Studien* (1844–50) and *Bunte Steine*, collections of short stories which include several gems of descriptive art such as *Das Heidedorf*. . . . Stifter's tales are uneven in value, but all of them are expressions of a poetic soul who overcame intense passion by simple piety. (291)

Das Heidedorf is cited as a "gem." However, only two editions were listed a total of four times; yet this is considerably more than the other text, *Brigitta* (listed once).

Of the two stories, *Brigitta* is probably read by more students today. Frenzel and Frenzel term *Das Heidedorf* the story of "junge, edle und zurückhaltende Menschen in zarten Beziehungen zueinander, die leicht durch ein Zuviel an Stolz, Eigensinn, Leidenschaft und Eifersucht zerstört werden," while *Brigitta* demonstrates the antithesis to the preceding: "Glaube an Reifen und Bändigung des Gefühls" (2:375). Would this last not be more in keeping with the ideals under study?

Robert Warner Crowell, who edited *Brigitta* for Oxford University Press, American Branch, stated affirmatively that

> the Major and Brigitta herself are real persons, they are characters that live. For its landscape painting, too, *Brigitta* is admirable. . . . Perhaps it may not be out of place in this day of realism to commend also the elevated tone of this simple story. Its characters aspire and struggle; they win our love and command our respect. (iv)

Most probably, Crowell's text disappeared as a victim of World War I, as it appeared in 1914.

A greater success in schools than Stifter, Mörike, or Droste-Hülshoff was Marie Nathusius, whose *Tagebuch eines armen Fräuleins* represented "den christlichen Familienroman" (Bernhardt 71). If one may judge from the literary histories (of then and now) which include Nathusius, her Christian family novel is not legitimately within the literary canon of the era under examination or that of our own time. Presumably the vanished *Tagebuch* was more Sunday school lesson than literature—only the high school teacher, Bernhardt, mentions it. It is not a heartening view of academic textbook choices that from 1864 to 1910 more students were apparently reading Nathusius (or Scheffel, or Benedix) than Stifter, Mörike or Dröste-Hülshoff. However, for the teaching of *Sitte und Moral*, Nathusius probably carried the day; and, as so often, this was a prime consideration in the era's textbook selection.

From the *Biedermeier* as it was experienced by teachers (editors) and students of the period surveyed, the focus changes to *das Junge Deutschland*. The most famous poet of the movement was actually a transitional figure representing both Romanticism and Young Germany—Heinrich Heine:

> Ausgegangen von der romantischen Schule ist endlich auch *Heinrich Heine*, der indes bald ganz neue, aber für die Poesie nichts weniger als heilbringende Töne anschlug. Eine ungemein tiefe dichterische Anschauung neben der oberflächlichsten Frivolität, ein dem Gegenstand sich zwanglos und oft mit der anmutigsten Bequemlichkeit anschließender Ausdruck neben nachläßigen nur zu oft schlottrigen und unschönen Formen charakterisierten ihn von seinem ersten Auftreten an . . . . im Ganzen wird das unerbittliche Urteil der Nachwelt kein anders sein, als das, welches sie über Bürger gefällt hat . . . ein vortreffliches Talent, vielleicht sogar ein schöpferisches Dichteringenium, welches sich durch Maßlosigkeit zerrüttete. (Vilmar 561)

According to Vilmar, then, as a victim of romantic *Zerrissenheit*, the genius proved his own undoing, in accomplishment of which he managed to leave at least some deep poetic insights and beautiful phrases.

Even less charitable were the teachings of Professor Hosmer in the United States. He illustrates his remarks by citing Heine's "Song of Praise in Honor of King Ludwig," which "few translators would care to present to English readers. . . . [since] its audacity and acrid malice can scarcely be paralleled." As Ludwig kneels before the Blessed Virgin, she addresses the infant Christ as follows:

> Es ist ein Glück dass [sic] ich auf dem Arm
> Dich trage, und nicht mehr im Bauche;
> Ein Glück dass ich vor dem Versehn
> Mich nicht mehr zu fürchten brauche.
> Hätte ich in meiner Schwangerschaft
> Erblickt den hässlichen Thoren,
> Ich hätte gewiss einen Wechselbalg
> Statt eines Gottes geboren.

And Hosmer concludes that

> The brilliant wit and poet must be judged with severity, however beneficial the scourging may sometimes have been which he administered. No further illustration is necessary that his wit was often distorted to cynicism, his frivolity to insolence and vulgarity. It is hard to believe that he was earnest about anything. (536–37)

Even in the later twentieth century poetry such as the above could be considered too strong for use in many a classroom. In Hosmer's day such verse amounted to—in Hosmer's words—"blasphemy" (536). Yet Heine was obviously a choice of many professors, according to the number of listings to be found in both trade and scholarly catalogs.

Some of these academics lamented the fact that Heine's works must be censored in German studies. In *The Modern Language Journal* of 1918, for example, Professor P. R. Kolbe—who himself had edited *Die Harzreise* for U.S. German students—reviewed a new *Harzreise* edition by Robert Porter Keep as follows: "If any criticism of the selections is to be made it is the obvious one, applying equally to all Heine editions, that one can present at best but a milk-and-water Heine in school editions" (180). Thus scholastic Heine enthusiasts might have been puritan or worldly.

One reason for Heine's popularity to both groups is provided by another commentator, who writes of Heine and Börne together:

> Der Publizist Ludwig *Börne* . . . und der Lyriker Heinrich *Heine* . . . beide Meister der Satire und der vernichtenden Ironie, sprachen mit Überzeugung und Entschiedenheit ihre demokratischen Ansichten aus, jener durch seine "Briefe aus Paris," dieser durch seine die Herzen der deutschen Jugend entflammende Revolutionslyrik. (Bernhardt 51)

Heine could, therefore, be regarded as a freedom fighter against the forces of tyranny and oppression, not a purveyor of blasphemous poetry. This is the most favorable assessment concerning Heine found among the materials consulted.

The *Reisebilder*, excerpts from which constitute the greater part of the Heine texts, are mentioned by but one source as follows:

> Für uns sind die Reisebilder heute fast ganz verblüht; sie sind von einer Geschraubtheit, Überheblichkeit, komödiantischen Ziererei und Unwahrheit, daß sie nur sehr schwer heute noch Leser finden. (Kummer 240)

Further, with regard to the two parts of the *Reisebilder* which constitute most of the U.S. prose texts, the following verdict fell:

> Die Harzreise ist, obwohl der beste Abschnitt der Reisebilder überhaupt, in einem frivol romantisierenden Stil geschrieben. . . . Der Charakter des Werkes *soll* poetisch sein; gelungen sind nur einzelne Abschnitte. . . . Das Buch Legrand . . . besteht aus einer unorganischen Anhäufung der verschiedensten Sachen. (Kummer 240)

Concerning Heine's lyrics as well as his prose, "in der Gegenwart kann und darf uns weder der Lyriker noch der Prosaiker Heine ein Führer mehr sein. Nur einige der besten Gedichte werden von ihm fortleben" (Kummer 239). It is surprising, in view of so much negative opinion, that numbers of U.S. students were reading Heine's prose and poetry during the time investigated.

Calvin Thomas sums up the general disapprobation as he discusses the German view of Heine:

> What wonder is it if the Germans of to-day decline, on the whole, to concede to him that towering importance commonly ascribed to him in English books: He was a great lyric poet, they say, but what else? . . . But the verse of Heine remains a precious possession, however it may fall short of proving that talent can dispense with character. (379–380)

Both Germans and Americans, regardless of their feelings toward Heine's work, place his poetry far above his prose. Why, then, did German students in the United States read parts of the *Reisebilder* more than his poetry?

Robert Porter Keep's edition of *Die Harzreise* (1916) offers little insight into this circumstance. On the one hand, students are told that "he could thrill the heart with his lyrics, which are probably his best productions and have often been proclaimed superior to Goethe's" (xix). And on the other hand, "the charm of Heine's *Harzreise* is universally acknowledged. Many of his other works, however, possess equal charm" (v). Thus, in seeking a reason why, as in the cases of Goethe and Schiller, texts devoted to poetry apparently did not find as wide a reception as the prose texts, one must recall the advice of the Committee of Twelve that "poetry, as the language of emotion, is a more or less artificial—often a highly artificial—form of expression," and its recommendation that the "natural" form of expression become lodged in the mind first (Report 54).

The second great representative of Young Germany known to U.S. German students was Karl Gutzkow. Vilmar refuses to mention Gutzkow by name; rather, he chastises him along with the totality of "das jüngere Geschlecht unserer Theaterdichter," and is especially critical of the fact

> daß manche Personen dieser Dramen, aus denen sich wirkliche dramatische Figuren hätten bilden laßen [sic], durch einen seltsamen Misgriff [sic] der Dichter zu Zerrbildern verunstaltet sind, wie z.B. König Friedrich Wilhelm I. in "Zopf und Schwert." (564)

Despite this criticism, Gutzkow's comedy *Zopf und Schwert* was one of his most popular plays; significantly, it became popular as a U.S. German text.

Dealing more with Young Germany than with individual literary works, Bernhardt paired Gutzkow with Heinrich Laube; the two were considered followers of Börne and Heine:

> Diesen Führern schlossen sich jüngere Talente, vor allen die Dramatiker Karl *Gutzkow* . . . und Heinrich *Laube* . . . an und kämpften als "das junge Deutschland" energisch für die Freiheit des Individuums, für allgemeine Humanität und Emanzipation aller Geknechteten, besonders der Frauen und der Juden. (51–52)

No mention is made of any plays written by either Gutzkow or Laube.

Kurz offers a lengthy discourse on Gutzkow's life and art, in which the most interesting feature is a comparison of Lessing and Gutzkow. Lessing

> verstand es im höchsten Grade zu verbergen, daß seine Dramen Ergebnisse der kältesten Berechnung waren; bei Gutzkow wird es sogleich klar, daß der berechnende Verstand bei der Bildung seiner Dramen thätig gewesen ist. Daher erwärmen sie nicht, sie lassen kalt. (4:536)

Gutzkow's dramas are based in Kurz's estimation upon cold reasoning which seeks to create theatrical effects at the expense of the truly dramatic.

An example of this technique is offered by *Uriel Acosta* (edited as a text for U.S. German students) as Kurz continues:

> Obgleich in dieser Tragödie das Didaktische vorherrscht, so macht sie doch durch die geistvolle Ausführung eine nicht geringe Wirkung, und manche Situationen sind von echt tragischem Geist durchdrungen. Die Charaktere tragen alle den Stempel lebensvoller Individualität . . . mit einem Wort alle geben Zeugniß [sic] von dem Gestaltungstalent des Dichters. Aber dem Ganzen fehlt doch die poetische Wärme, die allein bleibenden Eindruck hinterlassen kann. (4:537–538)

Whatever "poetic warmth" in Kurz's concept may be, the textbook market apparently felt the lack thereof. *Uriel Acosta* was listed once in 1910. Far better fared *Zopf und Schwert*, listed nine times from 1881 to 1910,

> weil es einen nationalen Stoff behandelt. Friedrich Wilhelm I. ist bei den merkwürdigen Widersprüchen in seinem Charakter eine höchst interessante Erscheinung, und es ist dem Dichter gelungen, dessen patriarchalischen Despotismus, seine gemüthliche Roheit, seine vaterländische Gesinnung . . . auf das Anschaulichste darzustellen. (Kurz 538)

In short, Kurz has nothing but praise for *Zopf und Schwert*, and his taste is again reflected on the textbook market. The comedy was apparently considered better suited for the classroom than the tragic *Uriel Acosta*, and there was more to be learned about German history and culture from *Zopf und Schwert* than among Dutch Jews in Amsterdam.

In 1901, however, Professor Wells recommended *Uriel Acosta* to U.S. students as Gutzkow's best play (366). Professor Priest termed *Acosta* "a plea for freedom of thought and Gutzkow's best dramatic work" (286). And Calvin Thomas taught that of all Gutzkow's plays, *Uriel Acosta* is "the best of them." However, he also noted that "some of Gutzkow's lighter prose plays, notably *Queue and Sword*, and the *Original of Tartuffe*, have also proved to have vital stuff in them" (394–395).

In Germany, Kummer continued the praise of *Uriel Acosta*:

> Von Gutzkows Tragödien ragt durch den poetischen Adel, den reinen und hohen Stil, durch tragische Wirkung *Uriel Acosta* bedeutsam hervor. Es ist Gutzkows reifstes und edelstes Werk, das einzige, das aus der Zahl der jungdeutschen Dichtungen dauernden Bestand besitzt. (252)

Priest, Thomas and Kummer published their literary histories in 1909. It seems almost more than happenchance that Starr Willard Cutting published his textbook edition of *Uriel Acosta* in 1910. The scholars left no doubt as to Gutzkow's best play.

But Kummer also wrote of *Zopf und Schwert*, although in a considerably less enthusiastic tone than that which he used in evaluating *Uriel Acosta*:

> *Zopf und Schwert* . . . war dramatisch allerdings . . . ziemlich schwach motiviert; nach Art des Scribeschen Intrigenlustspiels wird mit den geschichtlichen Ereignissen in unverantwortlicher Weise Fangball gespielt, aber das Leben und Treiben am Hofe Friedrich Wilhelms des Ersten . . . ergeben ein frisches und heiteres Gesamtbild. (251)

The eventual victory of *Uriel Acosta* over *Zopf und Schwert* in academic America seems certain, though the comedy was listed over the tragedy nine to one in the era surveyed; neither play was listed after 1910.

In their literary history, however, which was published from 1912 through the 1920s, Stroebe and Whitney mention only one play by Gutzkow: "*Gutzkow* hat einige wirkungsvolle Dramen geschrieben, unter denen das historische Lustspiel *Zopf und Schwert* sich noch heute auf dem Theater behauptet" (208). Thus *Zopf und Schwert* held the stage as well as teachers and students of German before 1918 more successfully than *Uriel Acosta*.

Somewhat similar to Gutzkow politically was the Austrian Moritz Hartmann, called by Bernhardt a "demokratisch-politischer Lyriker" (60). Of considerable significance to Hartmann's development was Georg Herwegh, who, after an active role in the movement of 1848

> was not pleased with his own creation, and spent his later years in retirement. The work that he had inaugurated was taken up by Moritz Hartmann . . . a Bohemian Jew of cosmopolitan inspiration, who also took an active part in the political movement of 1848, and afterward lived chiefly in exile. Noteworthy among his poems is the political satire, "The Rhymed Chronicle of Pastor Maurizius" (1849). (Wells 383)

Thus Hartmann was successor to a poet considered today one of the most important poets of *Vormärz* (Frenzel and Frenzel 2:391). Hartmann was known to what was certainly a relatively small number of U.S. students through his novel *Die Ausgestoßenen*, listed only in 1886. Few of the sources consulted—of the period or of the present time—mention Hartmann.

Slightly better received in American academe was Droste-Hülshoff's sometime companion, Levin Schücking. His tale *Die drei Freier* was listed in 1903 and 1904 (possibly the copyright date and date of actual printing). His style was assessed in 1892 for U.S. students as follows:

> In einfacher, verniger Sprache schildert Levin *Schücking* (1814–1883), Land und Leute seiner westphälischen [sic] Heimat. Seine zahlreichen Romane . . . sind von einem gesunden Realismus erfüllt und zeigen einen kräftigen Patriotismus. Durch frischen Humor und philosophische Betrachtungen weiß er das Interesse des Lesers immer von neuem zu beleben und zugleich seinen Stoffen ein tieferes Fundament zu geben. (Bernhardt 66)

Although this description seems to give Schücking's work almost a *Biedermeier* flavor, it is well to bear in mind that—to Droste-Hülshoff's disillusionment—he became a participator in Young Germany and was acquainted with Gutzkow.

Indeed, as Kurz quotes Schücking on his writing:

> "Der Grundgedanke meiner Schriften," schreibt Schücking, "ist Emancipation des Menschen im Allgemeinen und der Frau insbesondere von den Fesseln jener Anschauungen und Lebensverhältnisse, die das Individuum in seinem Bestimmungsrecht beschränken und es hindern, sich seiner Natur gemäß zu echtem Menschenthum zu entwickeln." (4:771)

However, Kurz thereupon takes care to assure the student that Schücking is more than a mere crusading journalist. Commenting upon Schücking's statement, he remarks that

> Es ist Dieß [sic] ganz richtig, aber man würde es ganz mißverstehen, wenn man daraus den Schluß ziehen wollte, daß dieser Grundgedanke sich übermäßig vordränge und den Romanen eine vorzugsweise didaktische Färbung gebe. Schücking hat ein zu entschiedenes poetisches Talent, als daß er in diesen Fehler verfallen könnte. (4:771)

In the light of the reception of some of the other authors considered, Schücking might have been more popular as textbook fare—if less successful as a literary talent—had he preached. As it was, his fame was fleeting both in and outside academe.

This last is attested to by Professor Wells in 1901:

> Another historical novelist . . . and of transitory popularity, was Levin Schücking (1814–1883). His "Son of the People" (1849) and "The Peasants' Prince" (1851) suggest by their titles and dates their character. (374)

Wells's remarks are borne out by the fact that none of the four literary histories consulted published in or after 1909 mentions Schücking. Moreover, none of the sources mentioning Schücking commented on *Die drei Freier*, which was apparently not a popular text.

Nor can the popular as well as significant work of Charles Sealsfield (Karl Postl), *Die Prärie am Jacinto*, be accorded success in U.S. classrooms of the era, though Professor Bernhardt taught that Sealsfield was one of the two *Hauptrepräsentanten* of the *Reise- und Seeroman*, stressing his "Erzählungen farbenprächtige[r] und lebendig[er] Szenen aus dem nordamerikanischen Leben." Further, U.S. German students were told that

> *Sealsfield* . . . "der deutsche James Fenimore Cooper," verbindet in seinen Romanen . . . eine gründliche psychologische Kenntnis der menschlichen Natur mit einem geistvollen dramatischen Dialog und einem seltenen Beschreibungstalent. (Bernhardt 67)

Certainly, so much praise and the lack of faultfinding indicate a warm reception of Sealsfield's art on the part of Wilhelm Bernhardt.

Kurz, too, is quite positive; for example, Sealsfield surpasses other novelists such as Gerstäcker, who followed in his footsteps, "durch die Tiefe und Wahrheit der Auffassung, durch die echt poetische Gestaltung seiner Personen, durch die bewundernswürdige Größe seiner Schilderungen." Only one criticism is made: "Besonders unangenehm wirkt der häufige Gebrauch fremder Wörter." Yet this fault—as Sealsfield himself protested— is a minor infraction when a German-speaking author writes from personal experiences in the United States and Mexico (Kurz 4:715–716).

Concerning the work edited as a text, "'Die Prairie [sic] am Jacintho' gehört zu dem Vortrefflichsten, was Sealsfield geschrieben; sie übertrifft beinahe alle übrigen Romane in der Composition, die eben wegen ihrer Einfachheit das Detail ruhig genießen läßt" (Kurz 4:717). Offered as an example by Kurz is the episode in which Colonel Morse, lost on the prairie, follows the tracks made a short time before by his own horse, circling in the same area for several days. The splendor of nature is seen in connection with the changes in Morse's moods. But Kurz broaches a more compelling topic in the warfare which would result in the acquisition of Texas from Mexico,

> der umso bedeutender erscheint, als er zu gleicher Zeit ein Kampf der Germanischen Nationalität gegen die Romanische, als ein Kampf des freien Christenthums gegen das Römische Pfaffenthum erscheint, dessen unheilbrütendes Treiben in kurzen, aber aus dem Leben gegriffenen Zügen auf das Anschaulichste dargestellt wird. (4:717)

Perhaps such an interpretation seems farfetched at first glance, but it must be remembered that Sealsfield was a Catholic priest of the Austrian order of *Kreuzherren vom roten Stern* until 1822, when he fled Austria and the order, coming via Switzerland to the United States. Surely, if this interpretation became current in academe before or after 1905 (the year *Die Prärie am Jacinto* appeared as a text), it did not promote Sealsfield's work in Catholic parochial schools.

By 1909 esteem for Sealsfield in the sources consulted had fallen considerably. In Germany, students were taught that "er wollte nicht bloß unterhalten, sondern auf seine Zeit erziehend wirken und die Kulturzusammenhänge zwischen der alten und neuen Welt darlegen. Einen künstlerischen Eindruck machen seine Schriften nicht. Von 1848 an nahm seine Beliebtheit ab" (Kummer 284). And in the United States, Priest said of Sealsfield that "he practised his remarkable descriptive powers exclusively on foreign conditions, often in a very careless style" (284), and it would seem that foreign conditions as well as careless style are faulted here.

On the subject of foreign conditions the *Report of the Committee of Twelve* was most outspoken:

> The first and greatest value of the study of the modern languages must be looked for, then, in the introduction of the learner to the life and literature of the ... great peoples who ... have made ... important contributions to European civilization. (11)

Because Sealsfield wrote about Americans and America, "wo er sich das Bürgerrecht erwarb" (Kurz 4:714), giving Priest's indictment of foreign conditions a reversal of sorts, reading works such as *Die Prärie am Jacinto* cannot introduce the student to life in Germany.

As Kurz stated, Sealsfield

wollte Europa und namentlich Deutschland mit Amerika, mit den Vereinigten Staaten bekannt machen, er wollte seinen Landsleuten begreiflich machen, was Freiheit sei, er wollte sie für dieselbe empfänglich machen. (4:715)

Had *Die Prärie am Jacinto* really succeeded as a text, students in the United States might have learned something about their own heritage as they saw their country and countrymen through the eyes of an arrival from Austria. Significantly, Sealsfield is read by some U.S. German students of today.

A follower of Sealsfield whose works were considerably more successful as texts was Theodor Mügge. Paradoxically, he was not included in the U.S. literary histories consulted, though the German commentators show themselves satisfied enough with his writing and his social consciousness:

> Man kann von Mügge nicht sagen, daß er genial sei, aber er besitzt ein sehr bedeutendes Talent. . . . Er zeigt sich nämlich in seinen Dichtungen stets als einen begeisterten Freund der Unterdrückten. . . . und es sind diejenigen seiner Romane auch ohne Vergleich die gelungensten, in denen er die Sache der Humanität gegen rohe Unterdrückung oder diplomatische Falschheit vertritt. (Kurz 4:732)

Works of this type serve a double purpose when used as pedagogical tools. As students increase their facility in German, they likewise absorb a disquisition on humanity's struggle against raw repression and diplomatic treachery. (Brecht in today's classroom comes to mind.)

In addition, Mügge was "der erste, der Dänemark, Schweden und Norwegen in deutschen Romanen darstellte" (Kummer 285–86), not only in novels, but also in novellas. One group of novellas titled *Leben und Lieben in Norwegen* was praised by Kurz as "vier meisterhafte Erzählungen, in welchen das Leben in Norwegen mit der ganzen Kraft und Frische seines Talents zur lebendigen Anschauung gebracht wird" (4:734). Called in textbook advertising "graphic Norwegian tales," *Riukan-Voss* and *Signa die Seterin* are published separately. As U.S. German texts, the two novellas were listed seven times collectively from 1869 to 1910.

As a contemporary of Sealsfield, and because he followed him in his liberalism as well as his exoticism, Mügge has been considered the last representative of Young Germany in U.S. German texts of the era surveyed. Upon the basis of present-day literature texts and literary histories, it can be said that Mügge is all but forgotten in Germany as well as in the United States.

IV

Texts from the Eras of Realism—Naturalism—the Early Twentieth Century

Contemporaneity of Texts

With the onset of Poetic Realism (1850) comes the era in which German studies and German texts from all periods from the Reformation through Realism spread across the land. The study which professors and students dedicated to earlier literary periods, as indicated by textbooks edited and utilized, has been investigated in Chapters II and III. This chapter, in contrast, deals with literature which was roughly contemporary to the teachers and students who studied it. In dealing with the concept of contemporaneity, the speed with which literary works appeared as texts in the United States after their publication in Germany is an important consideration. Shown in the listing below are authors and works selected from Appendix F; dates shown are the date of the first German publication of the work and the date of the earliest listed U.S. German text containing the work. Dates ending in a hyphen were listed as shown in commercial or scholarly catalogs.

Author	Text	Work	Text
Baumbach, R.	Frau Holde	1881	1894
Dahn, F. L. S.	Ein Kampf um Rom	1876	1900
Eckstein, E.	Der Besuch im Karzer	1875	189-
Fontane, T.	Vor dem Sturm	1878	1899
François, L. v.	Phosphorus Hollunder	1881	1887
Freytag, G.	Die verlorene Handschrift	1864	1898
Fulda, L.	Der Talisman	1892	1902
Hauptmann, G.	Die versunkene Glocke	1896	1900
Heyse, P.	Kolberg	1868	1894
Jensen, W.	Die braune Erica	1868	1869
Keller, G.	Das Fähnlein der sieben Aufrechten	1878	1907
Meyer, C. F.	Gustav Adolfs Page	1883	1893

Author	Text	Work	Text
Moser, G. v.	*Der Bibliothekar*	1878	1887
Rosegger, P. K.	*Waldheimat*	1873	1895
Saar, F. v.	*Die Steinklopfer*	1876	1906
Seidel, H.	*Leberecht Hühnchen*	1882	188-
Storm, T.	*Der Schimmelreiter*	1888	1908
Sudermann, H.	*Der Katzensteg*	1889	1890
Wilbrandt, A.	*Der Meister von Palmyra*	1889	1900
Wildenbruch, E. v.	*Das edle Blut*	1892	1892

Based upon this random selection, the average variation between the publication of a work in Germany and its utilization as a U.S. German text is approximately fifteen years. At the present time, when students may read the works of contemporary authors such as Dürrenmatt, Frisch, Lenz, Grass, and Böll, many of whose works appeared in the fifties and sixties, the contemporaneity of texts is scarcely better. And in this day of second-year anthologies, a glance through the U.S. publishers' catalogs from which teachers ordinarily select their materials may indeed suggest the idea that today's teacher (if he contents himself with U.S. publishers) has fewer choices in contemporary literature than his counterpart of a century ago.

Realistic Drama

To return to the textbooks of 1864–1918, it is not surprising, when the comparative dearth of great drama during the era of Poetic Realism in Germany is borne in mind, that texts of plays were less numerous than texts of novels, novellas and short stories. From the point of view of the present, the greatest authors whose works appeared in drama texts were Hebbel, Ludwig, and Wagner. Few of their works were edited as texts, and these few appeared relatively late in the time period.

It is a commonplace that Hebbel's work formerly attracted admirers with a force only slightly stronger than the power with which it repelled detractors (characteristics shared by the works of Wagner and, to some extent, by those of Ludwig). Some significance may therefore be placed upon the fact that Hosmer and Bernhardt did not mention Hebbel. But Hebbel's genius did not go unrecognized in the other professors' estimations; for example

> Friedrich Hebbel ist der originellste und genialste dramatische Dichter unserer Tage, ein Dichter, von dem man trotz der Absonderlichkeiten seiner Werke sagen kann und sagen muß, daß jeder Zoll . . . ein Dichter ist. . . . Er verliert sich niemals in schwatzhafte Phrasenhaftigkeit, noch sucht er durch hochtrabenden, nichtssagenden, den Mangel an innerem Gehalt durch Dunkelheit verbergenden Ausdruck zu täuschen, vielmehr sind die Gedanken

immer mit der größten Klarheit und doch stets in echt poetischer Sprache dargestellt. (Kurz 4:563)

However, with praise came also such descriptions as "extravagant . . . grotesque or gruesome" (Wells 389).

Wells applied these negative descriptions in the main to *Judith* or *Maria Magdalena*, which were not listed as texts—like Schiller's *Räuber* or Kleist's *Käthchen von Heilbronn*, they were too unconventional for use in the schools of this era. Yet only somewhat more palatable were *Herodes und Mariamne* (listed once) and *Agnes Bernauer* (listed twice). Thus the fate of *Agnes Bernauer* at the hands of the literary historians and professors consulted bears investigation.

In Kurz's estimation, a major weakness of the play is the conclusion. At this point, Albrecht, once filled with a desire for vengeance on Agnes's murderers, shows what Kurz sees as a contemptible weakness, inasmuch as "er sich beruhigen läßt, weil nunmehr Agnes als seine rechtmäßige Gemahlin anerkannt wird und ihm sein Vater die Herrschaft auf ein Jahr abtritt." He has let himself be bought, in that literary historian's opinion, by those who killed his wife—something out of character for the Albrecht seen in the rest of the play. Very good, however, is the characterization: "Die Fürsten, die Ritter, die Patrizier, die Bürger, alle sind mit der größten Wahrheit geschildert, und in Agnes hat er eine Gestalt geschaffen, die des größten Dichters würdig ist" (Kurz 4:564).

Yet there is disagreement as to the real truth of the conclusion. Far from bringing forth a major weakness in the play, as Kurz saw them, the actions of Herzog Ernst are regarded by others as a conception ranking among Hebbel's greatest:

> Der Held der Tragödie—dies muß hervorgehoben werden—ist Herzog Ernst, der bereit ist, seinen eignen Sohn zu opfern um den Staat zu retten. Er fühlt menschlich mit Agnes, der Unglücklichen, die er dem Tode weihen muß. . . . Das Einzelwesen, so groß und herrlich, so edel und schön es sei, es muß sich der Gesellschaft, dem Staat, der Allgemeinheit beugen oder daran zu Grunde gehen. (Kummer 379)

Herzog Ernst is not, therefore, a corrupt aristocrat who sought to bribe his son, but becomes in this interpretation a character who represents the principle of *der notwendige Gang des Ganzen*; this in contrast to Agnes and Albrecht, who will not assume their proper roles in society. This view of *Agnes Bernauer* is shared by Kummer, Priest, Stroebe and Whitney. It endures to the present day as "eine bittere Lehre" for a democratic world, from which Hebbel could expect no thanks (Frenzel and Frenzel 2:428).

Indeed, as is shown by Hebbel's absence from earlier literary histories, as well as the fact that no Hebbel texts were listed before 1905, "der wahrhaft große Dramatiker Hebbel konnte nicht hoffen, in dieser Zeit [the 1800s] verstanden und gewürdigt zu werden" (Stroebe and Whitney 210). At least, his admirers in academe (as shown by the small number of texts edited) were fewer during the era of Realism. One pedagogical reason for this small group's choice of *Agnes Bernauer* over Hebbel's other dramas is that he "introduces more of the native, popular elements than in any other of his dramas" (Priest 300). If it is taken into consideration that the major goal of German studies of the period was described as the "introduction of the learner to the life and literature" of Germany (*Report* 11), then it is clear that the advantage of the realistically created milieu of *Agnes* (albeit antiquated) was preferred to the exotic scenes of dramas such as *Herodes und Mariamne* or *Gyges und sein Ring*.

Hebbel's relative latency in U.S. *Germanistik* of the era under consideration was closely matched by that of Otto Ludwig, who is likewise missing from earlier literary histories. In 1901, students were told only that Ludwig's *Der Erbförster* and *Die Makkabäer* exhibited "great but ill-regulated genius," and that he was a dramatist "now interesting chiefly as preparing the way for the development of historical drama in the succeeding period" (Wells 389-90). The historical drama of the succeeding period, the Second Empire, was represented mainly by Heyse, Wilbrandt, Wildenbruch and Greif (Wells 414-16).

Ludwig's drama *Der Erbförster* appeared as a text in 1910, and although the play had been a great success on the stage, the student was offered widely varying assessments thereof. Kurz, after labeling Ludwig one of those great talents which "entweder zu Grunde gehen, oder in ihren Bestrebungen irren oder wenigstens nicht zu der Entwickelung [sic] gelangen, die man unter glücklicheren Umständen von ihnen zu erwarten berechtigt gewesen wäre," proceeds to point out at length all the improbabilities which mar the play. For example, the basic argument between *Erbförster* Ulrich and his employer, Stein, is decided altogether in Stein's favor, despite the nature of his orders:

> Sein Freund und Dienstherr Stein hat ihn nämlich entlassen, weil er dessen Befehl, den Wald zu "durchforsten" nicht ausführen wollte. Dieser Befehl war allerdings unsinnig, weil das "Durchforsten" nur dem Wald und somit dem Besitzer zum Schaden gereichen müßte. Und weil der Befehl unsinnig war, bildete sich Ulrich ein, daß Stein nicht das Recht habe, ihn zu entlassen; er erklärt daher, daß er weder die Entlassung noch den ihm gegebenen Nachfolger anerkenne. (Kurz 4:626–28)

Just how certain Stein's position in this situation is depends upon one's point of view. As far as Ulrich is concerned, he, as "hereditary forester" holds the title to his position; he is saving the forest while waiting for his friend to realize the error of cutting down his trees.

Professor Thomas regards the play and the quarrel in another light:

> It is a prose tragedy of family life, illustrating the peril of a choleric temperament. Two men who are good friends quarrel over a trifle, each insists on having his own way, and increasing exasperation leads to murderous madness. (397)

Thus the quarrel does not seem so improbable, as such incidents appear only too often in newspaper reports. Significant is the fact that the play is viewed positively in 1909, the year before the text was published.

In Germany in 1909, however, after considerable praise for the psychological truth, the characterization, the realism and the variety of scenes, ranging from the comic to the tragic, Kummer nonetheless reflects

> daß der Förster Ulrich in seiner Eisenköpfigkeit so absolut nicht einsehen will, daß der neue Besitzer des Waldes mit dem Walde machen kann, was er will, und daß am Schluß sich Mißverständnisse und Zufälle häufen, die sich . . . nimmer in . . . dramatischer Behandlung ertragen lassen. (353)

These two aspects of the play were only two among many in Kurz's list of inanities. Thus, on both sides of the Atlantic, Ludwig appears to gain in stature with the passage of time.

In confirmation thereof, Professor Priest (1909) termed *Der Erbförster* "one of the most impressive products of German realism" (302), while Stroebe and Whitney (1913) not only impressed upon students the fact that *Der Erbförster* is Ludwig's only drama truly to master the stage; they were also the first to justify Ludwig's creation of *Förster* Ulrich as an "iron-headed" character:

> Es ist ein realistisches Milieudrama, denn nur aus dem einsamen Leben, das der alte Förster mitten im grünen Walde führt, erklärt sich die Unkenntnis der Welt und der Menschen, die ihn ins Verderben stürzt. (215)

The forester's environment is responsible for his attitude and actions. Thus some literary historians' first and foremost criticism of the play—that people do unwise things for no apparent reason—is refuted.

Morton C. Stewart, editor of the U.S. *Erbförster* text, offered another solution to the problem of the *Förster*'s character—the character of Ludwig's own father, Ernst Friedrich Ludwig, city treasurer of Eisfeld:

> Ludwig . . . described his father as a man of rugged honesty, firm even to the point of obstinacy, but at heart tender and loving—traits which are reflected in the chief character of the *Erbförster*. The father made enemies . . . through his arrogance and headstrong will and must have furnished his opponents with great cause for dislike . . . it seemed as if he would be forced by public opinion to resign. (iii)

There are further parallels between Ludwig's father and *Erbförster* Ulrich, and Stewart's justification of the *Erbförster*'s character is at least as convincing as the theory advanced by Stroebe and Whitney.

Perhaps World War One terminated Ludwig's commencing attraction in academe (*Zwischen Himmel und Erde* was also a text). As Stewart stated in his preface to *Der Erbförster*, "Otto Ludwig should be better known by American students, and it is hoped that this edition of his great tragedy will serve to awaken an interest in his works" (iii). However, the texts do not appear to have awakened a great deal of interest.

Far more widely known today than Hebbel or Ludwig, but their equal in the field of German textbooks during the era under study, is Richard Wagner. In the nineteenth and early twentieth centuries a controversy existed as to whether or not the texts of Wagner's music dramas are to be considered—and studied in German classes as—literature. Although complimentary toward Wagner in other respects, one German commentator assured the student that

> Wäre bei ihnen [den Musikdramen] die Musik nur ein Mittel, so müßten sie auch ohne musikalische Begleitung auf der Bühne dargestellt werden können und bleibende Wirkung hervorbringen, was aber selbst der Dichter nicht wird behaupten wollen. (Kurz 4:586)

However, if one but calls the disputed dramas libretti, all controversy vanishes, because "als Operntexte betrachtet [verdienen sie] das höchste Lob" (Kurz 4:586). On the other hand, one professor assures his reader that Wagner's dramas "would rank high as poems even without the tone-dramas they illustrate" (Wells 387). Thus the use of *Das Rheingold* and *Die Meistersinger* as German textbooks.

In the 1900s, while Kummer writes "daß kein Wagnersches Drama dazu bestimmt ist, bloß gelesen zu werden" (365), and Priest celebrates Wagner's "surpassing dramatic art in the librettos" (297) of his music dramas, Stroebe and Whitney resolve the question of libretto versus drama for the student as they state "daß Dichtung und Musik dabei gleiche Bedeutung hatten" (215). Hence it is said that no composer's music suffers more from being excerpted to provide instrumental selections for symphony concerts or phonograph records than Wagner's.

And the same thing happens when the words are extracted, according to Calvin Thomas:

> Nor is it possible to separate the poet from the musician, and treat of the former only. For Wagner without his music is simply not Wagner at all. Read as literature, the great mass of his verse would have, for the public at large, but little interest. At any rate, it is not as literature that his works have won the popularity they enjoy. (399)

Reading a Wagner drama to study the text may offer interesting subject matter for a class in German drama; however, the fact that the class may be getting less than half the picture should be clearly understood. Students of the early 1900s were apparently reading *Das Rheingold* and *Die Meistersinger*— but, as it seems, only to the small extent to which they seem to have studied Hebbel or Ludwig.

Far more popular was Gustav Freytag, whose most popular text was *Die Journalisten* (thirty-two listings). Near the beginning of the era Hosmer placed

Freytag in the ranks of "figures not great, though often respectable" (549). However, Bernhardt, though he preferred to number Freytag among the authors of historical novels, nonetheless taught that *Die Journalisten* belonged among "den besten Produktionen der neueren deutschen Komödie" (65). And Kurz has little but praise to offer Freytag:

> Vor Allem besitzt Freytag eine große dramatische Fertigkeit, seine Compositionen sind meist vortrefflich, seine Sprache gebildet und natürlich; der Dialog geistreich und im Ton der guten Gesellschaft, und endlich weiß er auch bei den kräftigsten Ausbrüchen der Leidenschaft eine weise Mäßigung zu bewahren. (4:577)

In contrast to some of the characters of Ludwig or Hebbel, Freytag's characters are fit for genteel society—and for U.S. German students, who have more positive things to learn about German culture from *Die Journalisten* than from *Der Erbförster* or *Agnes Bernauer*.

In his consideration of the play itself, accordingly, Kurz determined that "die Handlung ist reich, aber verliert niemals die strengste Uebersichtlichkeit; die Verwickelungen sind geschickt erfunden und mit Takt durchgeführt und gelöst." The characters, further, are described as "ein fester, seines Strebens sich bewußter Geist, keck, humoristisch, von scharfem Verstand" or "seine Jugendfreundin . . . die ihm mit ihrer Sicherheit und ihrem weiblichen Uebermuth, der jedoch nie die Grenzen des Anstandes überschreitet, würdig zur Seite steht." In short, "so sind nun auch alle andern Personen . . . aufgefaßt" (Kurz 4:578). Little need be added to convince anyone that the play is nothing if not wholesome.

In 1901, American students were taught that *Die Journalisten* is "on the whole perhaps the most artistically perfect of modern German comedies" (Wells 390). By 1908, Professor Priest declared *Die Journalisten* to be "the finest comedy on contemporary life since *Minna von Barnhelm*" (303). Yet already the idol's feet of clay had begun to show beneath critical sand; Kummer waxes almost vociferous as he considers the adulation hitherto lavished upon the play:

> Mit erheblicher Übertreibung hat man das Stück das beste Lustspiel des 19. Jahrhunderts genannt und es neben Lessings Minna von Barnhelm gestellt. Je mehr man beide Stücke vergleicht, desto weniger wird man die Behauptung billigen. Schon der Charakteristik haftet bei Freytag viel Schablonenhaftes an (Oldendorf, Oberst Berg), Bolz ist der echte Lustspielheld, der alles kann und der mit allen spielt. Adelheid wird mehr direkt als indirekt charakterisiert; nur Einzelszenen können heut noch gefallen. . . . Es findet sich viel Mittelmäßiges und Plattes darin, und der Humor grenzt oft bedenklich an Kalauerspaß. (389)

Professor Thomas also seems to take a somewhat negative view of the play, for he mentions *Die Journalisten* only in passing as "very successful" (392). Stroebe and Whitney, too, reinforce Kummer's assessment of *Schablonenhaftigkeit* by linking Freytag to Scribe's *la pièce bien faite*; yet all is not negative:

"das Leben der Journalisten wird uns in einer Fülle von interessanten Charakteren, in lustigen Situationen und witzigen Dialogen vor Augen geführt" (208–09). Indeed, today's estimates of Freytag and *Die Journalisten* seem to seek the middle path struck by Stroebe and Whitney.

Why the text was a popular one is easily perceived. For the students there were social conflict and comment, the aura of the journalistic milieu, two love stories, witty banter and troubling perplexities. Further, as Walter Dallam Toy, Professor of Germanic Languages at The University of North Carolina, wrote in the introduction to his edition of *Die Journalisten*:

> An important feature of the play is its natural setting. All the persons introduced stand out clearly before us as real men and women, actuated by familiar motives and perplexed by problems which easily occur in life. The tone of the sentiment expressed is healthy and the conclusion is a triumph of common-sense. The style is vigorous, idiomatic and vivacious: a model of conversational German. (vi)

For the teacher, then, there were a number of advantages to the text: the "real" situations would probably interest more students than the symbolism of *Das Rheingold*; it was more wholesome than *Agnes Bernauer*; it would teach more about German culture than *Herodes und Mariamne*; and—in opposition to *Der Erbförster*—the language was a model of conversational German.

Then, too, journalism and politics were shown—or concealed—to good advantage:

> The happy end is indicative of Freytag's tendency to deemphasize the candidates' ideological concepts and to stress the importance of their personal integrity. In fact, nowhere in the play is the reader or spectator fully informed as to which political platform the two candidates represent. (Mews 9)

This text was edited more times than—and apparently outsold—many others. Because the play was so popular outside academe, it would seem that "the German mind" of the day—at least on one particular level—was definitely communicated to the students.

In a different way, the same can be said of the plays of Gustav von Moser, which were popular entertainment in Germany and popular texts in the United States. They are not great art, and their fame was relatively ephemeral. However, as Wells evaluated Moser, after mentioning insignificant writers such as Blumenthal, Lindau and L'Arronge:

> Better than any of these and more characteristically German is Gustav von Moser (b. 1825), who began a career of almost unbroken success . . . in 1861. The most noteworthy of his comedies, "Foundation Day" (Stiftungsfest, 1873), "Ultimo" (1873), "The Violet Eater" (1876), "The Private Secretary" (1878), "War in Peace" (1880), and "Köpnickerstrasse 120" (1884) . . . promise to hold their place in popular favor well into the coming century. . . . none has caught so

well in its comic aspects the spirit of Germany in the decade that followed the French war. (415)

Three of the comedies listed by Wells, as well as three other Moser comedies, were U.S. German texts.

In 1909, Moser's popularity continued in Kummer's writings:

> Der beliebteste deutsche Vertreter des Situationsschwankes *Gustav von Moser.* . . . war Offizier und Landwirt gewesen, ehe er Schriftsteller wurde. Der liebenswürdige, heitere Mann hat Tausende unterhalten. (527)

Yet Kummer is careful to place Moser among the *Unterhaltungsschriftsteller.* The composition of Moser's works is described as quite simple:

> Die stehenden Figuren (Professor, Leutnant, Kommerzienrat, Backfisch, Erzieherin, Schwiegermutter, schüchterner Liebhaber) waren in der alten deutschen Lustspielposse überliefert; nur das Zuständliche, den äußern Anstrich des Lebens . . . entnahm Moser der Zeit nach 1870 . . . . nie ging er auf das Gemeine, Unanständige und Pikante. (527–28)

Stock characters, the neutrally objective outer coating of contemporary life, and nothing common, improper or racy—such a combination satisfied the German theatre-going public of the age, and, precisely because of these characteristics, was in the eyes of many educators ideally suited for American German texts.

Nevertheless, not all educators were agreed as to the pedagogical worth of Moser's comedies. Priest taught, for example, that

> The most successful plays of these years were those on the manners of contemporary society written partly in imitation of the French by Gustav von Moser . . . and others. . . . The dramas of these men have always, however, lacked any aim other than that of passing entertainment, and they are devoid of literary merit. (311–12)

This negative view—which might be interpreted positively as a desire for good literature in the classroom—was repeated as follows in 1913: "Die anderen Lustspieldichter der Zeit, wie . . . Gustav von Moser, sind ohne jede literarische Bedeutung und bemühen sich nur, das Publikum zu unterhalten" (Stroebe and Whitney 209). Notwithstanding, Moser's plays apparently sold as texts from 1887 to 1917. The "good clean fun" of the comedies must surely have been a strong point in their favor.

One point against the leading Moser text, *Der Bibliothekar,* in the eyes of the Committee of Twelve should have been the fact that the play is set in England, where *English* manners and customs are rendered comical. For all that, Professor Wells (himself a member of the Committee of Twelve), who edited the play as a text in 1897, insists in his introduction that "all this is external, and as far as the essence of the play is concerned the scene might as well have been laid in Moser's own house at Görliz or in Thomas More's Utopia" (iv). Wells defended his edition of *Der Bibliothekar* partially on the grounds that Moser's plays "are excellently fitted to make a foreigner's early steps in German pleasant as well as profitable" (Moser iii). For the times concerned, at least, perhaps Wells's statement stands, but his choice of texts is questionable from the point of view of today.

A contemporary of Moser, who also wrote comedies of manners somewhat after the French fashion, was Oskar Blumenthal. His *Paulas Geheimnis* was listed three times from 1885 to 1917, thus besting some of the classics thus far surveyed. Professor Wells, so enthusiastic about Moser, had little to offer concerning Blumenthal:

> In the comedy of modern life the great mass of production for the daily needs of the commercial stage is French in technic, often in spirit. The humor of . . . Blumenthal . . . is seldom free from a touch of that biting irony which the French call *blague*. (415)

Not only were the comedies a bitter variety of *Französelei*, they were also the result of a very mechanical composition process.

Indeed, according to another literary historian, Blumenthal's plays were only *dramatische Scheinwerke*:

> Es war ein erfreuliches Zeichen für den Wandel des Geschmackes, daß *Oskar Blumenthal*, geboren 1852 in Berlin, der von 1883 bis 1889 als vollgültiger Zeitdramatiker angesehen wurde, in den neunziger Jahren die Scheindramatik fallen lassen mußte und sich nur noch als Schwankfabrikant und reimgewandter Versspieldichter zu behaupten vermochte. . . . Blumenthal ward unerträglich, wo er ernst sein wollte . . . allein oder mit Geschäftsteilhabern . . . begann er nun eine Schwankfabrikation. Lustig blühte die Firma Blumenthal . . . bis über die Jahrhundertwende hinaus. (529)

As Kummer indicates, Blumenthal had no true claim to greatness.

In the same year, Priest taught that Blumenthal's "dramas . . . lacked any aim other than that of passing entertainment, and they are devoid of literary merit" (312). Yet students were apparently reading *Paulas Geheimnis* during World War I, probably for the same reasons they read the plays of Moser: easy reading placed in modern times, featuring amusing plots—although the humor tends toward the ironic.

Far more obscure was Alexander Elz, another comic playwright whose work *Er ist nicht eifersüchtig* was—like *Der Bibliothekar*—also edited by Professor Wells. Wells's preface to his edition of the former text (1900) informed the student that

> This little comedy has been a favorite in American schools for thirty years, and is recommended for early reading by the Committee of Twelve of the Modern

Language Association in the report adopted at the session of 1899. That imprimatur relieves an editor of the necessity of discussing its fitness, ethical, artistic or linguistic for school use. To apply to such a trifle the canons of serious criticism would be uncritical. Characters and situations are not natural, but they are not meant to be. On the other hand the language of the little play, which most concerns the pupil, is simplicity itself, and it has been found possible to put all necessary explanations in the vocabulary. With regard to the author, Alexander Elz, the usual bibliographical sources of information are silent. He himself figures in the catalogue of the British Museum only as the author of a story in Polish. This play was first printed in Bloch's Dilletanten-Bühne No. 13, which must have appeared in 1858 or 1859. (iii)

This trifling situation dramatized by an unknown author cannot be said to fulfill entirely the oft-cited requirement for making the student acquainted with the "life and literature" of Germany. Wells himself apologizes for the plot, declares the play non-literature, and takes care to point out Elz's obscurity. Indeed, he does not even mention Elz in his *Modern German Literature*. His entire defense of the play rests upon its recommendation by the Committee of Twelve, of which he was a member, in 1899—the year before his edition of *Er ist nicht eifersüchtig* appeared. As a matter of fact, this popular text (eleven listings from 1870 to the teens of the 1900s) does little to fulfill the Committee's expectations, except, perhaps, for language which is "simplicity itself."

Two inducements to examine the text are to experience the language which apparently popularized it and to see if the play is as bad as Wells' comments and Elz's inconspicuousness indicate. Cäcilie Hohendorf is upset because her husband, Dr. August Hohendorf, is not jealous concerning her. As Cäcilie's Uncle Baumann ponders the situation,

> Nun ja, das fehlte mir noch—(Lacht) Ha, ha, ha, was so ein junges Ding für Schrullen im Kopfe hat! Aber es ist fast natürlich, daß es—da sitzt so ein armes Wesen fast den ganzen Tag mutterseelenallein, fängt Grillen, liest dazu einen verschrobenen neuen französischen Roman, in dem alles auf die Spitze gestellt ist und was kommt heraus? Narrenspossen! (Mit Lachen Cäcilie kopierend) "Er ist nicht eifersüchtig!" Das nennt sie ein Unglück und lamentiert darüber.—Ich möchte wohl wissen, ob es viele Frauen gibt, die sich darüber grämen! (20)

These lines might be called the center of the play—which afterward decomposes into broad farce.

Perhaps Elz is making a serious comment on the role of women in the nineteenth century, sitting alone, reading novels and daydreaming; however, this is by no means certain. Then there is the moral of the play: how many women really want jealous husbands? (Implied answer: only silly women, who could later regret it if their husbands did become jealous.) The laughter of the audience when Cäcilie's uncle imitates her is practically audible from reading the lines—yet is this the literature wished for by those who wanted to reform high school and college German programs? Wells, it seems, would answer affirmatively—in any case, his assessment of simple-to-read German is correct. Whether or not such a work reveals "the German mind" or instills an appreciation for German literature is uncertain at best.

Another author whose work was edited by Professor Wells was Alexander Wilhelmi (Alexander Viktor Zechmeister), whose comedy *Einer muß heiraten* accrued some eighteen listings from 1865 to 1911 (Wells's edition was listed from 1897 to 1911). Once again the author is unrecognized in literary histories by all commentators consulted—including Wells himself. However, some information on the author, as well as his reasons for the choice of this play as a German text, are stated by Wells in the preface to his edition of the play as follows:

> *Einer muß heiraten* . . . is by Alexander Viktor Zechmeister, who took for the stage and literature the name of Alexander Wilhelmi. He was born in 1817, educated in Vienna, and attempted a business career. This he abandoned in 1842 for the stage. For seven years he acted in various parts of Germany but was engaged, in 1849, by the court theatre in Dresden where he remained till 1876. He died the next year at Meran. His dramatic work is in the main insignificant, but this little play has been a favorite from the first, in Germany, while its literary associations, its graceful humor and its simple style have commended it abroad. (Benedix and Wilhelmi iv)

The literary associations in the play consist primarily of the two main characters, Jakob and Wilhelm Zorn: "Zorn, an obvious synonym of Grimm. The given names of the Grimm Brothers are taken without any attempt at disguise. The women are, so far as I [Wells] can learn, freely invented" (Benedix and Wilhelmi, *Lustspiele* iv). The source of the humor is primarily the plot. The Zorns' rich aunt Gertrude insists that in accordance with their father's dying words, "einer muß heiraten." If neither Jakob nor Wilhelm consents to marry, then Gertrude, her fortune and her housekeeping will depart. Straws are drawn, and Jakob must marry his pretty niece, Luise. The latter, however, prefers Wilhelm. In attempting to teach the shy Jakob how to court Luise, Wilhelm becomes carried away and proposes to Luise himself. Aunt Gertrude blesses the couple (the fortune is saved) and once more attempts to interest Jakob in marriage; the latter demurs. In the lines ending the play, the "graceful humor" as well as the simplicity of style cited by Wells may be met with:

> Gertrude (zu Jakob). "Nur sich nicht gleich abschrecken lassen. Versuche es nur bei einer anderen; jetzt wird es schon besser gehen."
> Jakob. "Daß mich der Himmel bewahre! Einmal und nicht wieder. Es ist ganz gut so. Ich lasse mich nicht mehr verleiten, bleibe ledig und bei meinen Büchern. Der Vater sagte auch nur: 'Einer muß heiraten.' " (Benedix and Wilhelmi 98)

Perhaps the play amused classes of adolescents; the style is indeed simple. A recurring pattern presents itself in the selection of this and similar plays as texts by Wells and others.

Another example is provided by the work of a part-time litterateur, Ernst Wichert. George T. Flom, editor of the textbook containing the comedy *Als Verlobte empfehlen sich—*, one of three works by Wichert to be listed once between 1895 and 1911, proudly touted Wichert's successful career as a jurist and government official in his introduction:

> Ernst Wichert, since 1888 Counsellor of the Exchequer in Berlin, and well known as an author, was born in Prussian Lithuania in the city of Insterburg in 1831. He was educated for the bar in Königsberg and began practice in that city in 1853. In 1863 he was appointed Municipal Judge, and in 1879 promoted to "Oberlandsgerichtsrat."

Whether Wichert was actually well known as an author is questionable, as none of the sources consulted contained information on him. Yet, as Flom proceeds,

> Wichert is best known as a writer of comedies. . . . Among the best may be mentioned . . . *An der Majorsecke*, 1873 . . . besides *Als Verlobte empfehlen sich—*, 1866, which has perhaps been the most popular. Of Wichert's historical plays, *Aus eigenem Recht*, 1893, enjoyed the greatest popularity on the stage. . . . On the occasion of the opening performance . . . the Emperor William conferred upon the author the Prussian order of the Red Eagle. (Wichert iii–iv)

It seems strange that the author of more than twenty comedies, several historical plays and other dramatic works, an author decorated by the Emperor, should have been so entirely ignored by the literary historians of his time—who showed at least some interest in Moser, Blumenthal and other indifferent talents.

Yet a glance at *Als Verlobte empfehlen sich—* offers insight into Wichert's failure to arouse the interest of critics. Plot: Franz and Malwine are cousins in love and want to marry. Two impediments to their marriage are that Malwine's governess wants to keep her position by keeping Malwine unwed, and that if Malwine marries, her mother, Frau von Grumbach, must turn over her estate to Malwine's husband (which she is loath to do). Franz has a bogus newspaper printed, in which the fraudulent report of the governess's engagement to Andreas Langerhans, overseer of Frau von Grumbach's estate, appears. As the governess vapors, horrified over the announcement, Franz prepares Langerhans to tell the governess he (Langerhans) loves her. Overseer and governess fall in love and plan a new life. Frau von Grumbach declares Franz her new overseer, since he will soon be her son-in-law—but only after his exams. The plot is to some extent a simplified version of Moser's *Der Bibliothekar*; two couples work their way through confusions and frustrations to a happy end. All the action occurs on the surface; there is no deeper meaning.

As for the humor of the play, a trite, hyperbolic idiom and grammatical errors are the natural order of things. The manner of expression can be sampled in the lines in which Adelaide, the governess, reads the bogus advertisement:

Frau von Grumbach.	Aber Sie leben ja noch.
Adelaide.	Nur noch wenige Minuten. Die Augenblicke meines Daseins sind gezählt—schon rührt des Sensenmannes Sichel an mein Herz.
Frau von Grumbach.	Es scheint in der Tat nicht ganz richtig—
Adelaide.	O! eine ungeheure Schmach ist mir angethan! Ich bin das unglückliche Opfer einer höllischen Intrigue. (19)

Such a mode of expression seems more appropriate for Kunigunde von Thurneck than for Adelaide. Of course, the unnaturalness itself was part of the humor.

Grammatical errors are the other big source of humor:

Adelaide.	Mein Herr, es würde unedel sein—
Langerhans.	Fürchten Sie nichts, mein Fräulein; denn warum? (Schmerzlich.) Ich existiere für Ihnen gar nicht.
Adelaide.	Sie nehmen meine Worte vielleicht zu schwer; in Gegenwart der gnädigen Frau freilich—(Bei Seite.) Wenn er nur nicht wieder den abscheulichen Fehler gemacht hätte! (26)

Whether there is danger in a text which exposes students to "für Ihnen" is arguable.

Flom defended teaching such works as he stated that "the colloquial style of a text of this sort makes it very well adapted to early reading. It is full of idiomatic expressions and possesses the peculiar flavor of the language in the highest degree" (iv). As a further recommendation of Wichert's style, his *An der Majorsecke* was one of the six plays recommended for early reading by the Committee of Twelve in 1899. (Flom's edition of *Als Verlobte empfehlen sich—* had not yet appeared.) Finally, to have students read a passage and identify mistakes or *Volksmund* could have a positive effect on their mastery of grammar and syntax.

All these things aside, however, it is difficult to perceive *Als Verlobte empfehlen sich—* as more than broad farce. An unrealistic plot, dialog featuring hyperbole and bad grammar (both meant to be laughed at), and stock characters (rich mother/aunt, young lovers, spinster and bachelor) do much to confirm the fact that writing *Unterhaltungsdrama* was merely Judge

Wichert's avocation. It is not surprising, after all, that the literary historians and professors left his work unevaluated.

The Committee of Twelve recommended for the elementary level only plays by Benedix (discussed in Chapter III), Elz, Wichert and Wilhelmi—primarily because "five act plays are too long" (Report 64). Of the six plays recommended in 1899 (Benedix's *Der Prozeß, Der Weiberfeind,* and *Günstige Vorzeichen;* Elz's *Er ist nicht eifersüchtig;* Wichert's *An der Majorsecke;* Wilhelmi's *Einer muß heiraten*), four appeared in Wells's editions. Three of these editions had already appeared in 1897, one separately and all in *Drei kleine Lustspiele;* the fourth appeared in 1900. Thus it is difficult not to wonder whether the recommendations for the elementary level were not made without some self-interest on the part of members of the Committee of Twelve, until other one-act plays are sought. They are relatively scarce, and at least some of them the age would probably have found unsuitable. Given these conditions, less may be said against the Committee's choices and the members' self-interest; rather, it seems untoward that three-, four-, or five-act plays were found to "require more time than it is advisable to devote to any one text" (Report 64) —at least on the lower levels prescribed by the Committee. The time saved by reading plays which make little or no pretense of being literature seems to conflict with the Committee's by now familiar aims.

A case in point is offered by the drama of Wolfgang Müller von Königswinter, who, if judged upon the basis of scholarly reception, was another little-known author justly forgotten today. An acquaintance of Simrock, Eichendorff, Heine and Freiligrath, Müller was a successful physician who wrote verse—particularly about the Rhine and its environs:

> Wie Müllers lyrische Dichtungen, so sind auch beinahe seine sämmtlichen epischen Gedichte, die größeren, wie die kleineren, dem Rhein und der Verherrlichung desselben gewidmet. . . . Er ist überhaupt nicht schöpferisch, aber er besitzt das Talent, den Stoff, wenn er sich nicht von irgend einem Vorbild beherrschen läßt, gewandt und anschaulich zu entfalten. (Kurz 4:394–95)

It seems, then, that Müller was a dilettante. As such, he is mentioned by none of the U.S. literary histories consulted and by only one German source. Interesting is the fact that he is called by Kurz a lyric and epic poet; no drama is mentioned. The text that bears Müller's name, however, is a comedy: *Sie hat ihr Herz entdeckt.* It was listed three successive years, 1883–1885, and subsequently disappeared.

A better dramatist, who was also ignored to some extent by literary historians, was Adolf Wilbrandt. Wells briefly mentions Wilbrandt's historical drama *Kriemhild* (414) and his novel *Hermann Ifinger,* stating about the latter that

> there is a healthy atmosphere about this book that is peculiarly refreshing, and true to the best that is in German character,—a strong, clear vision of duty, and an unswervingly hopeful will. (404)

This evaluation could also have been applied to Wilbrandt's masterpiece, *Der Meister von Palmyra* (1889), strangely absent from Wells' remarks.

Yet as late as 1909, Calvin Thomas made no mention of Wilbrandt, and Priest mentioned tersely only that "the novel *Die Osterinsel* (1895) and the poetic drama *Der Meister von Palmyra* (1889), by Adolf Wilbrandt (born 1837), present questions of the time and metaphysical ideas" (316). At the same time, Kummer wrote of Wilbrandt that his "dichterisches Talent war nicht sehr groß oder ursprünglich; aber es war höchst wandlungsfähig und elastisch" (496). He was able to write harmless comedies in the manner of Gustav von Putlitz, to write novellas using poetic motives as Heyse did, and he also created "Dramen von nervenaufregender, fast krankhafter Üppgkeit" (Kummer 496). It may be that this last description is aimed at *Der Meister von Palmyra*, although Kummer calls it elsewhere "poetisch am wertvollsten . . . unter den Dramen" (498).

By 1913, students were taught that "die Versdramen von *Adolf Wilbrandt* (1837–1911) haben trotz mancher Schönheit der Form und des Gedankens keine tiefere dramatische Wirkung ausgeübt" (Stroebe and Whitney 217). Eclipsed by the dawn of Naturalism, the drama based on beauty of form and ideas had begun to vanish from the stage. It seems almost more than mere chance that *Der Meister von Palmyra* and *Vor Sonnenaufgang* appeared in the same year; it is as if the muses staged "Willkommen und Abschied," and a greater contrast than that between the departing classical and arriving naturalistic plays is scarcely imaginable.

Théodor Henckels, in his edition of *Der Meister von Palmyra* which appeared in 1900, praised Wilbrandt in stating that

> If not the greatest, *Der Meister von Palmyra* is undoubtedly one of the few real masterpieces of modern German literature. The literary form of the work is in keeping with the atmosphere that pervades it, which is pure, generous, even as the atmosphere of the high mountains' peaks. Its poetic parts are of a very high order . . . the language . . . refined and chaste; of provincialisms and colloquialisms we find but a few. (5)

Why, then, was such a work so soon forgotten in academe?

In answer, Henckels informed students that

> It is not by chance that Wilbrandt's activity, which has exerted such deep effect upon the intellectual movement of Germany, has found no suitable recognition in the literary world. This rare genius, reaching out in so many directions, continually surprising the world with renewed activity in the intellectual arena, grappling with the ancients and superior to the moderns, seems . . . to bid defiance to superficial examination. (8)

Yet the editor of *Der Meister von Palmyra* has said that certain circles concerned themselves with Wilbrandt and his work; for example, here are the words of Mark Twain:

> I have just been witnessing a remarkable play here at the Burg Theatre in Vienna. I do not know of any play that much resembles it. . . . it is in any case a great and stately metaphysical poem, and deeply fascinating. . . . for the audience sat four hours and five minutes without thrice breaking into applause, except at the close of each act; sat rapt and silent—fascinated. This piece is "The Master of Palmyra". . . . whenever it is put on the stage it packs the house. . . . I know people who have seen it ten times. (143)

Near the end of the article, the reader is firmly enjoined three times to "Send for 'The Master of Palmyra' " (150). Twain ends his remarks lamenting that New York theatres at that time offer only light comedies—no tonics for the soul like Wilbrandt's drama.

In view of such adulation, a small excerpt from the drama is offered for the reader's consideration. Pausanias ("deliver from pain," the deity or personification of death) has come to take the old, sick mother of Meister Apelles, whom the gods have granted immortality. Apelles forces Pausanias away from his mother; thus it occurs that Apelles's mistress, who, on her way to Rome with a new lover, looked Pausanias in the eye, will die instead of Apelles's mother. Apelles knows that he has traded the life of his mistress for that of his mother. (Pausanias is visible only to Apelles or persons near death. Longinus is a friend of Apelles.)

> (Apelles hebt langsam den Kopf; blickt auf den unbeweglich dastehenden Pausanias.)
>
> Apelles: Fragt mich dein steinernes Auge, blasser Geist,
> Ob diese wunde Brust nun noch begehrt,
> Endlos zu atmen und den Tag zu schaun?—
> Ja; deinem Auge trotz' ich. Denke nicht,
> Ich könnte wanken, zagen! Dir ins Antlitz
> Ruf' ich das *Leben* wieder, halt' es fest—
> Und wie Antäos an der Mutter Erde
> Richt' ich mich stärkend auf an seiner Brust.
> Ja, ringen, schaffen will ich, Schweiss [sic] im Antlitz
> Und Sieg im Herzen, und des Mannes Wert,
> Des Lebens Wert bezeugen und behaupten!
>
> Longinus (der bewundert horchte):
> Wohl dir; doch wen beschwörst du so? Was rufst du
> So feierlich ihn an? Den Arzt—
>
> Apelles (fasst [sic] sich. Lächelnd.)   Mein Geist
> Ging irre, scheint es. Schreck und Weh . . . Nun
>   wach' ich.
>
> (Wilbrandt, *Meister* 110)

Here are the "strong clean vision of duty, and . . . unswervingly hopeful will" described by Wells (404), as well as at least a trace of *nervenaufregender Üppigkeit* (Kummer 496).

One final thought is offered on *Der Meister von Palmyra*'s relative insignificance as a high school and college text. The central thought of the play is metempsychosis; the *Meister*, with his eternal life, withdraws himself from the cycle of reincarnation until, having seen the truth of things, he wills his own death (and consequent rebirth). In present-day America there are certain educators and administrators to whom the drama would be distasteful in the classroom because the "religious ideas" carried by the action and inherent in the underlying philosophy are not in conformance with biblical revelation. That such thoughts ran in the minds of yesterday's educators is clear—one need but reflect on the negative view of Lessing's *Erziehung des Menschengeschlechts* taken by literary historians of the era. Caught between naturalistic drama on the one hand and religious fundamentalism on the other, Wilbrandt's *Meister von Palmyra* could not attract a U.S. following in academe to match the European enthusiasts.

A variegated career running parallel to that of Wilbrandt, though—as far as it was reflected in the U.S. textbook trade—more successful, was enjoyed by Ludwig Fulda. Fulda's earliest plays are to some extent naturalistic. Indeed, while writing on Hauptmann and Sudermann, Professor Wells briefly mentioned Fulda to students as follows:

> Nor were these alone in their assertion of dramatic realism in its extremer form. It is worth while [sic] to record that these years witnessed also the first performance of naturalistic dramas that challenged critical attention by . . . Fulda (The Female Slave, The Lost Paradise).(417)

This view of the author is somewhat distorted. Fulda was actually much under the influence of Paul Heyse, to whom he wrote: "Ich wählte dich zum Führer ohne Schwanken" (*Talisman* iii).

It therefore appears that Priest was more exact in his assessment of Fulda's initial phase as semi-naturalistic; further, writing some eight years after Wells, he presented a fuller view of the artist, albeit negative:

> Ludwig Fulda (born 1862) first made a reputation for himself with *Das verlorene Paradies* (1890) and *Die Sklavin* (1891). He was afterward still more successful when he turned from his former semi-naturalism and wrote the symbolical drama *Der Talisman* (1892); but . . . Fulda is chiefly an artist in technic, and his plays are ephemeral in content and aim. (327)

As Wilbrandt experimented in many types of drama, but was known for his symbolical drama *Der Meister von Palmyra*, so Fulda went "vom harmlosen Charakterlustspiel zum sozialen Drama und von da zum bunten Märchenstück und zur Tragödie und zum dramatischen Versspiel" (Kummer 513). However, he is best known for his dramatized fairy tale in verse, *Der Talisman*.

In 1913, Stroebe and Whitney taught that Fulda

hat der deutschen Bühne viele leichte und anmutige Dramen gegeben. Er ist ein vorzüglicher Verskünstler und ein Meister der dramatischen Technik. Seinen dauerndsten Erfolg hat ihm das schöne und heitere Märchendrama *Der Talisman* gebracht. (74)

The praise which rings through the professors' lines reflects the rather enthusiastic reception of Fulda's works, especially *Der Talisman*, in U.S. German programs. Indeed, as Professor C. W. Prettyman, who edited the *Talisman* text for Heath, took care to point out in his introduction, "*Der Talisman* was recommended for school use in the 'Report of the Committee of Twelve of Modern Language Association.' It was in response to this suggestion that the present edition was undertaken" (ix). That those who set the prevailing tone in U.S. *Germanistik* chose Fulda's work should lead to some conclusion about that choice.

The plot is a combination of Andersen's "The Emperor's New Clothes," Lessing's "Ring Parable," the fairy tale of "The Fisherman and His Wife" and many other sources. Astolf, King of Cypress, is an arrogant monarch misled by his retinue after banishing Gandolin, the only man who always told him the truth. The king attempts to force himself upon a noble lady, who resists his advances with the help of Diomed, a nobleman. For their effrontery, Astolf condemns the two to change places with a father and daughter in a nearby fisherman's hut; in turn, the fisherman and his daughter assume the roles of the two banished from the palace.

At this point, Omar enters, having come from afar to offer Astolf the only thing he lacks:

> Die Kraft die Wahrheit von dem Schein,
> Unwert von Wert und falsch von echt zu trennen
> (Fulda 29)

This power comes from a talisman given Omar by his father (none other than the banished Gandolin). With the aid of the talisman, Omar will weave Astolf a magic cloak:

> Und allen Treuen, Klugen und Gerechten
> Erscheint es hoheitvoll und farbenklar;
> Dagegen ist es völlig unsichtbar
> Für jeden Dummen oder Schlechten.
> (Fulda 29)

The king wears the "robes" to the parade celebrating the anniversary of his coronation. All "see" the garment until the newly elevated fisherman's daughter cries out the truth. Pandemonium ensues; the King condemns Omar and the fisherman's daughter to death. But with the help of Omar's talisman, *der Mut der Wahrheit*, Astolf realizes that belief based upon illusion is unsatisfactory. Omar has given the king what he promised, the only thing the king lacked—freedom from illusions. The banished nobles return to the palace; the fisherman and his daughter return to their hut—to be joined by Omar.

Iambic pentameter and frequent end-rhymes evince the epigonal conception of the work. As stated above, the plot is obviously taken from many sources. The popularity the play enjoyed on the stage in Germany and as a text in the U.S. would seem to stem from its exalted style of diction, both for its beauty and for its lack of dialect, as well as from its moral essence. It was conceived as an uplifting experience. Thus a play which conflicted with no conventional mores, stressed a moral positively, and was written in classically clear style was the choice of U.S. German teachers.

In summary, it has been shown that three groups of dramatists manifested themselves within the period of Realism for students of German: the leading talents (Hebbel, Ludwig, Wagner, Freytag), the epigones (Wilbrandt, Fulda) and those of little consequence (Blumenthal, Elz, Müller von Königswinter, Moser, Wichert and Wilhelmi). For reasons suggested in the course of this chapter, the greatest number of textbook listings falls to Gustav Freytag. The others, taken in groups, descend from the dramatists of little consequence to the epigones, and thence to Hebbel, Ludwig and Wagner. This does not make the texts featuring German drama contemporary to the period under consideration first-rate when judged from the standpoint of today; viewed positively, the contemporary drama offerings probably strengthened the preference shown in the statistics for short stories, novellas and short novels among teachers of the era.

Realistic Novels, Novellas, and Short Stories

One of the earlier and more significant manifestations of the school of Realism in epic genres was Berthold Auerbach's *Schwarzwälder Dorfgeschichten*. Auerbach, as an American professor said in 1879, was "not great, though . . . respectable" (Hosmer 549). By the 1880s, however, Auerbach and his *Dorfgeschichten* had reached their peak of popularity. As Bernhardt informed students, Auerbach offered

> ein treues Bild von dem Land, dem Leben und den Leuten im Schwarzwald; namentlich zeigt er in diesen originell und fesselnd geschriebenen Erzählungen seine Meisterschaft in der Schilderung von Gemütszuständen und psychologisch interessanten Charakteren. Die Dorfgeschichten fanden allgemeinen und verdienten Beifall und wurden in fast alle europäischen Sprachen übersetzt. (56)

What Bernhardt terms a *true* picture of the land, life and people of the Black Forest earned Auerbach what Bernhardt describes as universal and well-deserved praise, as well as popularity in translation in other countries. And in Auerbach's case there is an indication of popularity in the classroom (five texts, thirteen listings 1886–1918) as well as outside.

Indeed, at this point in time, at least some literary historians preferred Auerbach to Jeremias Gotthelf, considered today to be the true master of the *Dorfgeschichte*:

> Wie bei Jeremias Gotthelf tritt uns Alles in lebensvoller Wahrheit entgegen, aber [Auerbach] schildert uns nicht die gemeine Wirklichkeit wie Jener, vielmehr erscheint Alles veredelt in idealer Gestaltung. . . . Mit eben so großer Kunst versetzt er sich in alle Bildungsstufen . . . ohne je den feinsten Geschmack zu beleidigen. (Kurz 4:764)

Here is a triumph of refinement over realism. Why should Gotthelf's works, with their actuality, prevail over "good taste"—above all in academe? Moreover, Kurz, like Bernhardt, stresses the international recognition of the excellence of the *Dorfgeschichten*:

> Die "Dorfgeschichten" fanden wegen ihrer Vortrefflichkeit nicht bloß in Deutschland die allgemeinste Anerkennung; daß auch die Ausländer sie zu schätzen wußten, beweisen die zahlreichen Übersetzungen. (4:765)

Yet by the turn of the century, the literati had begun to turn from Auerbach.

A small indication thereof is offered by Professor Wells. Teachers and students were told that "Auerbach . . . was himself a native of the Black Forest, of which his 'Village Tales' deal gracefully, though his peasants are apt to be rural Spinozas" (378–79). The artificiality hinted at when Auerbach's good taste and genteel rendering of reality are praised in the 1880s has become a negative feature by 1901. Exactly why Auerbach's characters were created as they were was explained by Calvin Thomas: "Auerbach's people were somewhat sophisticated by his own local patriotism . . . his very genial temperament, and his speculative bias. In his later works, his didactic bent became so strong as to make him a special pleader" (388–89). The peasants were made to transcend reality by virtue of where they lived, because Auerbach was kindly disposed toward them, and due to Auerbach's own mental tendencies.

Therefore, Auerbach never succeeded in creating "wirklich echte Bauern und naturwahre ländliche Zustände. . . . Seine Gestalten waren frisiert, parfümiert, stilisiert" (Kummer 328). Priest termed the *Dorfgeschichten* "highly colored and untrue" and praised instead Gotthelf's "thoroughly wholesome popular stories" (284). Stroebe and Whitney mention both authors only in passing (233). The rise and fall of Auerbach's *Dorfgeschichten* would seem to have run its course; Gotthelf's stories, apparently never used as texts during the period surveyed, are read in academe today, while Auerbach's are not so well known.

At the risk of redundancy, it remains to sum up why Auerbach's tales were once so popular as texts, even after certain professors had become critical of them:

> Auerbach hatte eine stark moralisierende und lehrhafte Art zu erzählen. . . . Überall streute Auerbach bis zum Übermaß eigene Betrachtungen ein. In den Erzählungen bildete Auerbach das Leben wohl nach, aber nur mit vorsichtiger Auswahl ihm geeignet erscheinender Momente, seine Bauern waren alle stark idealisiert. (Kummer 329)

The reason for their popularity is that the *Dorfgeschichten* were wholesome and didactic, full of idealized characters in contrived situations.

A lesser-known author whose work is said to show similarities to that of Auerbach is Gustav Henrich Gans, Edler, Herr zu Putlitz. He was included in only one of the literary histories by American German professors, that by Benjamin Wells:

> Most nearly related to Auerbach in the short story is Putlitz, who is more worthy to be remembered for "What the Forest Tells," "Forget-me-not," and "The Alpine Bride," . . . than for the trifling farces usually associated in America with his name. In him there is a saving salt of realism. (379)

In the United States, then, the one commentator to record Putlitz's achievements praises his *Märchen*.

Kurz, on the contrary, stresses Putlitz's efforts in the drama:

> Putlitz hat zwar meist nur kleinere Stüke geschrieben, in denen sich begreiflich entwickeltere Verhältnisse, spannende Intriguen und breit angelegte Charaktere nicht darstellen lassen; aber et hat auch in dem beschränkten Raum . . . sehr Bedeutendes geleistet. (4:597)

As a sample of Putlitz's plays, the one-act comedy *Das Herz vergessen* (six listings as a text from the 1860s to the 1880s) is offered. Oswald Born, a rich merry, bold young man makes an exorbitant list of the good qualities and talents which his wife-to-be must possess. A young woman who is married pretends to be single, "develops" all the desired qualities, and "läßt ihn erkennen, daß er bei seinen Forderungen das Beste, das Herz vergessen habe." She recommends that Oswald marry his guardian's niece Eveline, who has all the characteristics which can make a marriage happy (Kurz 4:597).

From today's point of view there is little that is praiseworthy in *Das Herz vergessen*. In 1894, however, it seems that there was something good in academe about nearly any didactic play. Further, two upper-middle-class characters are having an amusing, wholesome conversation: the sensibilities are not offended by bad language or undue ideas such as *Seelenwanderung*.

Putlitz's popularity is discussed in an enlightening manner by Kummer, who addresses himself in the main to the *Blumen-* and *Elfenmärchen* so popular in the 1850s:

> Sein Jugendwerk Was sich der Wald erzählt 1850 [sic] war eine Sammlung süßlicher Prosamärchen von Blumen, Käfern und Elfen. Das kleine Werk war hold, aber unbedeutend, gleichwohl versetzte diese Spielerei die Leute in den Jahren der Reaktion in Entzücken. Außerdem schrieb Putlitz gefällige Lustspiele und Schwänke, z.B. . . . Spielt nicht mit dem Feuer, Badekuren, in denen er Kotzebue und Scribe verschmolz. (334)

Insignificant fairly tales and plays after the manner of Kotzebue and Scribe rendered Putlitz an ephemerally famous author, yet his works were read by U.S. German students from 1864 to the 1890's.

The U.S. texts by Putlitz were *Badekuren, Was sich der Wald erzählt, Das Herz vergessen* and *Vergißmeinnicht: Arabeske. Vergißmeinnicht*, a flower-bug-and-elf story of the type derided more in the 1980s than in the 1880s, does indeed prove—as Professor Wells suggested—that Putlitz should be remembered for his tales more than for his plays. *Vergißmeinnicht* deals in teleology and *Chiffrenschrift*; a disbelieving dwarf who is resident gnome of a printing office argues with an elf who reads nature from leaves and flowers. (Here one might mention the polarities nature/art, concrete/abstract, romantic/enlightened—so dear to the romantic *Kunstmärchen*.) The elf picks a forget-me-not and proceeds to read the stories on each of the five petals; elf and dwarf now serve to frame the inner story. All the petals save one are fragments of a love affair which runs from two lovers' childhoods through the young girl's days as a grandmother. In each of these five episodes, the two are in some way united or reminded of one another by forget-me-nots: the boy and girl feel the first pangs of love while picking forget-me-nots; the boy, on a camping trip, sees some forget-me-nots and thinks of the girl; the bitter young man offers the young lady—who is marrying someone else—a corsage of forget-me-nots; a young officer, wearing a forget-me-not over his heart, seeks and finds a soldier's grave out of unrequited love; the young lady, now a grandmother, adamantly opposes her granddaughter's choice of a husband until the unhappy young man gives the granddaughter a forget-me-not, whereupon the grandmother assures her granddaughter that she may marry the young man she has chosen. All the leaves have now been read. The elf and the dwarf part company, the latter a believer in the teleological *Chiffrenschrift* in nature.

The story is too sentimental for modern tastes, but it is not terribly difficult to understand the charm of some of Putlitz's writings in his more sentimental age. Since Professor Wells asserted the superiority of Putlitz's stories over his plays—so reiminiscent of Benedix, Elz, Wichert and Wilhelmi—it is surprising that the Committee of Twelve (on which Wells served) failed to recommend the tales of Putlitz for U.S. classrooms.

One of the most successful blends of art and reality in U.S. German texts is met with in the novellas of Paul Heyse. To be sure, Heyse was considered "not great, though often respectable" by Hosmer in 1879 (549), but this assessment was improved upon by a number of the other literary historians consulted; for example,

> Der kunstreichste Meister unter den jetzt lebenden Novellisten Deutschlands ist Paul Heyse . . . der Jugendfreund . . . Scheffels. Seine Romane sowohl . . . wie auch ganz besonders seine zahlreichen Novellen ("L'Arrabbiata," "Marion," "Anfang und Ende" u.a.) sind in Charakterzeichnung, Entwicklung der Handlung sowie in Lösung psychologischer Probleme Kunstwerke ersten Ranges. (Bernhardt 64)

Most interesting, perhaps, is the fact that Bernhardt names the nearly forgotten Scheffel as if in enhancement of Heyse's talent.

Kurz continued the praise in 1894. Among his remarks appeared: "Er hat das Wesen der Novelle rein und sicher aufgefaßt und kaum ist ihm in dieser Beziehung ein andrer Dichter gleich zu stellen" (4:831). Here reference is most probably made to Heyse's *Falkentheorie* and the *starke Silhouette*—quite simply, those things which differentiate one novella from any other. Accordingly, in 1901, it was taught that Heyse "produces masterpieces of form. The little stories are cameos cut with a firm hand, leaving an impression on the mind in which every line tells" (Wells 404).

The highest acclaim from a literary historian surveyed was probably received in 1909, when Kummer wrote that

> Einer der seltenen Fälle seit Goethe, daß scheinbar das Schicksal selbst den jugendlichen Werdegang eines Dichters überwacht hat, bietet das Leben Heyses dar. In weit höherem Grad als Scheffel, Keller, Otto Ludwig oder Hebbel war Heyse die Gabe verliehen, glückliche, anmutvolle Werke hervorzubringen. (399)

A comparison with Goethe, and, at least in some ways, superior to Keller, Ludwig and Hebbel (as well as Scheffel): Heyse could scarcely have hoped for more critical acclaim.

The high point reached, however, implied criticism follows:

> Heyse hat sich eine eigene Form für die Novella geschaffen und den dafür geeigneten Stil aufs feinste ausgebildet. Die Zahl seiner Novellen ist sehr groß, aber eigentlich besitzt Heyse nur einen kleinen Kreis von Charakteren, die er zu schildern versteht. Mit Vorliebe schilderte der Dichter einen Mann und zwei Frauen in seinen Novellen dar, in denen er den Mann in der Liebe zwischen beiden schwanken läßt. (Kummer 402)

This is reminiscent of Scribe and *la pièce bien faite*; one takes a familiar pattern, adds some new twists, and writes a perfect novella.

Likewise seemingly uncritical is the judgment of Professor Priest, who enlightened the student with the thought that

> Many of Heyse's short stories . . . are little models of storytelling. . . . The theme of these stories is usually an interesting psychological problem. The scene is frequently laid in Italy; Heyse knows the Italian people through and through, and he describes their lives with great art. (295)

Little models, the theme usually a psychological problem, frequently laid in Italy: once again there is a sense of sameness, of mechanical putting together which renders these bland comments slightly negative.

As if in contradiction, Calvin Thomas states that "the great distinction of Paul Heyse . . . perhaps the most versatile German writer of his century, is to have created a new standard of style and artistic finish for the novellette," a feat which Thomas terms "epoch-making" (393). Yet once again strict limitations to Heyse's greatness are dictated:

> In the fashioning of . . . literary pastels, especially of Italian life . . . Heyse has remained without a peer. But his very cosmopolitanism seems to have unfitted him to be a portrayer of German life in its humbler phases. (393-94)

Literary pastels of Italian life, it seems, can go only so far toward bringing a German author true greatness (as well as toward bringing the "life of Germany" to the classroom). Stroebe and Whitney seem to echo Thomas's statements in a comparison of Heyse and Storm: "Weniger tief und packend, aber auch künstlerisch wertvoll sind die Novellen von *Paul Heyse*. Er ist einer der fruchtbarsten und geistreichsten der deutschen Novellisten" (235-36). The usual remarks about cheerful pictures of sunny Italy and psychological problems follow.

Thus opinions of Heyse were somewhat mixed in academe. Professor Edward Southey Joynes, for example, who edited *Niels mit der offenen Hand*, praised Heyse effusively only to grow captious:

> It is to be regretted that neither the situation nor the sentiment is always in accord with the requirements of a scrupulous morality—not to say religion. Some of Heyse's pieces are by no means "void of offense." (vi)

Whether Joynes inveighed against any of the novellas edited as U.S. German texts is uncertain. However, if one judges Heyse by his popularity (despite the involvement of "the grand passion" spurned by the Committee of Twelve [63]) his offenses were relatively slight.

Regarding the most popular Heyse text, a general consensus of sources consulted confirms the indication of the listings: "L'Arrabbiata" was read by more students than any other work by Heyse. As the novella continues to be read today, suffice it to say that Lauretta, called L'Arrabbiata ("the angry one"), her would-be suitor Antonio and a priest sail from Sorrento to Capri in the interest of financial gain or churchly duties. Lauretta and Antonio sail back to Sorrento alone. Antonio attempts to force his affections on Lauretta, who bites him on the hand, jumps into the sea, and is only with difficulty persuaded to return to the boat. When she sees the blood and wounded hand, she releases her long suppressed love for Antonio. That night there is a mutual declaration of love. The *Falke* of this novella is then, the blood and wounded hand. It is not unreasonable to suspect that blood and wound are a symbol of Lauretta's spiritual defloration—through which she is transformed from a termigant to a loving, marriageable girl.

Max Lentz, who edited *L'Arrabbiata* for the American Book Company in 1899, defended Heyse's apparent narrowness in conception and design by praising his underlying poetical idea:

> The greatest charm of these novels consists neither in the accurate description of Italian scenery nor in the peculiarities of Italian life; all of them receive their stamp as true works of art from the underlying poetical idea, which idealizes even such episodes from common everyday life as Heyse has chosen for his little story *L'Arrabbiata*. (4–5)

The popularity of *L'Arrabbiata* among the general public and as a text cannot, as in so many cases, be based upon moral preachments or middle-class mores. Artistic finish and Italian settings must certainly have played a role, although, as already stated, the latter would scarcely fulfill the Committee of Twelve's desire that the life of Germany be introduced through literature. Other criteria cited were:

> Die Handlung ist . . . sehr einfach, sie ist auch einfach erzählt, aber gerade dadurch von der größten Wirkung. Die Schilderung der Leidenschaft ist meisterhaft, und wirkt um so mächtiger, als sie in natürlichen und unverdorbenen Gemüthern dargestellt wird. Vortrefflich ist die Zeichnung des Mädchens, wie dem Dichter überhaupt die Darstellung trotziger selbstständiger [sic] Charaktere vorzüglich gelingt. (Kurz 4:832)

For students, a simple yet moving plot told in simple language—*la belle passion* between natural unspoiled characters—is delicately handled. Lauretta herself is created from the pattern of one of Heyse's most admired character types. All these things taken together with Heyse's outstanding reputation made *L'Arrabbiata* a great success. Some of the reasons cited could, presumably, apply to the teachers' choice of the other Heyse texts also.

Fascinating yet simple plots expressed in simple language were a trademark of Heyse's friend Theodor Storm, whose works are more celebrated today than those of Heyse. By 1892 in U.S. *Germanistik*, Storm had acquired "den Namen eines ganz bedeutenden . . . Novellisten . . . durch seine . . . zahlreichen Prosa-Erzählungen, von welchen die reizende Novelette 'Immensee' unbestritten das zarteste Produkt seiner Feder ist" (Bernhardt 57). *Immensee* was the most popular of Storm's works used in texts, and runs like a leitmotif through students' histories of literature—not only in the time period surveyed, but also in more recent times.

Because *Immensee* was generally admired, Professor Wells's views on Storm and his writings are rather exceptional:

> In Theodor Storm . . . the tone is . . . frankly romantic; but his little story of "Immensee," though mawkish in sentiment, has been one of the most popular novels of that or this generation. There are admirable bits of local color here, as indeed there are also in his "Aquis Submersus" and "Der Schimmelreiter," though here, too, sentiment inclines to sentimentality. (379)

Though the three works of Storm most often praised by U.S. professors consulted are brought together here, the negative viewpoint is unusual for the time. However, in the 1940s even a devotee of *Immensee* writes: "The majority of students reading *Immensee* will put up with it as a sweet sentimental story of unreality" (Schulz-Behrend 162). Putting up with sentimental unreality cannot be said to constitute active (or even passive) enjoyment of a classic work of fiction. Perhaps Professor Wells wrote prophetically.

Yet David Brett-Evans was to write in 1970 that

> As might be expected, the tremendous vogue that *Immensee* enjoyed among German readers during the nineteenth century carried over into the curricula of North American schools and universities, and when Dr. Wilhelm Bernhardt, an energetic high school teacher in Washington, D.C., brought out a little edition of this work, he was also creating one of the earliest—and certainly one of the most successful—pedagogical aids to the study of German literature. By 1910 this college edition had been reprinted, with minor revisions, for the fourth time. (184)

Brett-Evans goes on to note the decline of *Immensee* as a U.S. text since the late forties (185). Yet it is clear that, if Wells was finally correct in his negative assessment of *Immensee*, he was correct only as a prophet.

Priest, for example, has a more ambivalent attitude: he sees *Immensee* as "a romantic story of wistful resignation, with scenes of warm, sympathetic coloring." Yet he praises other stories such as *In St. Jürgen* as being "more vigorous," having a "more substantial content," and being "not less sincere" than *Immensee*. Among the stories called Storm's best work are *Aquis Submersus* and *Der Schimmelreiter* (Priest 305). The same ideas are expressed by Kummer (398), Thomas (402), and Stroebe and Whitney (235) in one of the rather infrequent cases of their agreement: *Immensee* is a very good story, but it is not Storm's best.

Nevertheless, Bernhardt, in the introduction to his edition of the story, sought to refute such ambivalence as he remarked that

> The romance *Immensee*, by many considered the most charming idyl that has emanated from the pen of Theodor Storm, and by which alone he will probably

be known to coming generations, has always been a great favorite with the German people. . . . No doubt, in his later creations Storm to a great extent abandoned the romanticism of his earlier days for a healthy realism . . . but for all that *Immensee* . . . will always be taken as a good specimen of his talent as a poetical romancer. The author himself shared this belief. (viii–ix)

If the number of editions and listings is considered, it seems certain that Bernhardt spoke for a number of teachers. The importance attached to *Immensee* as a textbook lasted some seventy-five years. Then Wells's opinion came into its own and a slow decline began.

The answers as to why so many students read *Immensee* for such a long time are said to be the "brevity of the story and easiness of vocabulary and style, the attractiveness or charm of tradition, and . . . the combination of pureness, goodness and unhappiness" (Schulz-Behrend 159–61). *Aquis Submersus*, never edited as a text during the years considered, was probably considered *contra bonos mores* and too morbid for the classroom; *Der Schimmelreiter*, which was listed only in 1909, was too long and sometimes provocative; of the three works by Storm most often discussed by the professors consulted, only *Immensee*, first in a field of nine Storm texts and listed thirty-four times from 1864 to 1917, was an outstanding text.

Less popular as classroom fare were the works of Gottfried Keller; the most popular selection was apparently *Romeo und Julia auf dem Dorfe*, from the collection *Die Leute von Seldwyla*. In 1892, this particular collection was recommended to German students as consisting of "geradezu ideale Dorfgeschichten" (Bernhardt 56). This idea was echoed by Heinrich Kurz, although he began his Keller commentary with a stunning censure: "Wenn die Neigung, sich in Reflexionen und Phantasiegebilde zu verlieren, jemals einem großen Talente zum Nachteile gereichte, so ist Dieß [sic] bei Gottfried Keller der Fall" (4:822). However, the *Seldwyla* stories had fared better than other works by Keller, especially *Der grüne Heinrich*:

> Von größerem künstlerischem Werthe sind die Erzählungen, die unter dem Titel *Die Leute von Seldwyla* erscheinen; sie sind meist abgerundet, in sich abgeschlossen, und ob sie gleich nicht weniger von feinem psychologischem Blick, von tiefer Beobachtung des äußeren und des Seelenlebens zeugen, als "Der grüne Heinrich," so erscheinen die Reflexionen nicht als Reflexionen des Dichters, sondern ergeben sich aus den Handlungen und Reden der Personen. (Kurz 4:822)

Die Leute von Seldwyla is considered by Kurz to be Keller's best collection of novellas, and the best novella of the collection, in his estimation, is *Romeo und Julia auf dem Dorfe* (4:822).

Wells terms Keller a romantic "whose extravagant humor and mock pathos suggest at times the inferior work of Jean Paul Richter." Wells does note Keller's keen observation of detail; if he may be said to favor one Keller creation it is, in opposition to Kurz, *Der grüne Heinrich*: "Most noteworthy of his books, in spite of its mystical maunderings, is 'The Green Henry' . . . which has still its small circle of ardent admirers" (379). However, Calvin Thomas terms Keller "the Wizard story-teller of Zürich, whose books are on the whole the very best reading to be found in the whole range of nineteenth-century German fiction. . . . he is universally considered a fixed star of high magnitude." Professor Thomas does not single out one work as best, but compares Keller to Goethe, and applies the term "romantic realist"—as Keller is a man "with the soul of a poet, the eye of a man of science, and the temperament of an artist" (389-90).

Likewise applying the term romantic realist to Keller, Kummer sets out to prove the applicability of the term:

> In Romeo und Julia auf dem Dorfe zum Beispiel ist das Pflügen und die sittliche Verwilderung der alten Bauern ganz realistisch geschildert, romantisch dagegen ist der Charakter von Sali und Vreni, die in dieser krassen Verwilderung rein wie Kinder bleiben; romantisch ist auch der Tod der beiden Liebenden geschildert. (343)

Although Kummer calls *Das Fähnlein der sieben Aufrechten* Keller's finest novella, he writes considerably more about *Romeo und Julia auf dem Dorfe*, and terms the latter work one of the three best novellas in the *Seldwyla* collection (346-47).

Die Leute von Seldwyla, according to Priest, is Keller's masterpiece. He directs students' attention in particular to two novellas in the collection, *Romeo und Julia auf dem Dorfe* and *Die drei gerechten Kammacher*, and balances poetry and truth in the now familiar way: "Keller . . . depicted contemporary life, especially that of his native country, with absolute truth, and yet he gave his pictures the glamour of pure Romanticism" (306). This subject is not broached by Stroebe and Whitney; they number *Die Leute von Seldwyla* among Keller's finest works—though they subordinate Keller to C. F. Meyer (237).

The overall expression made by the pronouncements of these literary historians and professors is easily summarized. Keller was regarded as half romantic, half realist. Among his best works was the collection of novellas *Die Leute von Seldwyla*; the best novella in the collection was probably *Romeo und Julia auf dem Dorfe*, a blend of romance and reality.

If Keller could arouse so much admiration among German professors (Wells excepted), why was *Romeo und Julia auf dem Dorfe*, the most prominent Keller text, listed only from 1900 to 1914 in only two editions (five listings)? Firstly, the double suicide was objectionable. Then too, the touches of irony and skepticism were probably not widely appreciated. Further, the fact that Sali and Vreni run away from home, exchange rings, pretend to be a married couple, and are tempted to join *der schwarze Geiger* and his vagabonds may have rendered the text less than welcome in some quarters.

Warren Austin Adams, in his edition of *Romeo und Julia auf dem Dorfe* for Heath in 1900, brought up two more considerations which may have slowed the sales of various Keller texts:

> Some critics claim—and justly—that Keller's characters lack depth. It is true that, generally speaking, they do not stir our deepest emotions. This criticism, however, could never apply to *Romeo und Julia auf dem Dorfe*. Here love and hate rule in all their intensity. (x)

The emotions of U.S. students are not sufficiently stimulated by the patriotic element of *Das Fähnlein der sieben Aufrechten* (as opposed to what was probably the usual classroom interpretation of Schiller's *Wilhelm Tell*), but emotions could possibly become overstimulated through a reading of *Romeo und Julia auf dem Dorfe*. Thus, perhaps, because of too little or too much appeal to the emotions, Keller's works were only moderately successful as texts.

Unexpected from the point of view of today is the quite considerable popularity of Wilhelm Henrich Riehl in U.S. German studies during the period under investigation. Like Keller, Riehl was classified a "romantic realist" with regard to his works of fiction (Kummer 426). However, perhaps he was better known during most of the era for his historical writings:

> Creditable work in historical fiction was done also by Wilhelm Heinrich Riehl ... who as an historian had contributed to the political evolution of the epoch "A Natural History of the People as the Foundation of National Policy" ... and also wrote a considerable number of short stories based on his studies of German life during and after the period of the Reformation. (Wells 374–75)

Though Professor Wells writes of Riehl as the author of short stories, he actually praises Riehl the historian, naming a historical work while mentioning the novellas only in passing.

Kurz likewise stresses Riehl's activities as a historian:

> "Wie ich durch mein lustiges Wanderleben erst ins Bücherschreiben hineingewandert bin," sagt er im Vorwort zur zweiten Auflage von "Land und Leute," "so sollen auch meine Bücher allerwege lustig zu lesen sein." Und das sind sie in der That, aber nicht bloß durch den sie belebenden Humor, durch die witzigen Einfälle, oder geistreichen Bemerkungen, sondern vorzüglich dadurch, daß sie eine immer frische und anregende Unterhaltung gewähren. (Kurz 4:907)

It should be pointed out that "Land und Leute" is the first part of Riehl's *Naturgeschichte des deutschen Volkes*. To set out to write a work of this nature with the intent of always being *lustig* is a departure from what is usually expected of a dedicated scholar. Also peculiar is the fact that Kurz calls such scholarship merry, indeed, because it is so entertaining.

The dearth of information offered the student concerning Riehl's fiction was due to the fact that "Riehls bleibende Bedeutung liegt übrigens nicht in den Novellen, sondern in seinem dreibändigen kulturgeschichtlichen Werk Die Naturgeschichte des deutschen Volkes" (Kummer 426). Priest is the first—and the last—to write of the novellas as a major contribution to the literature of the nineteenth century:

> Riehl . . . embodied in his stories, *Kulturgeschichtliche Novellen* (1856) and others, not only the poetic results of a scholar's investigations—he was a professor of history at the university in Munich—but also true human portraits of lasting value. (307-08)

How lasting the value of Riehl's fiction may be is called into question by Calvin Thomas, who granted Riehl but one sentence; however, he mentioned only the fiction in writing of "Riehl, whose historical novelettes enjoyed great favor during the third quarter of the century" (387). From Thomas's statement, it would seem that Riehl's popularity had begun to decline after 1875.

Yet Riehl's novellas were in demand as U.S. German texts from 1884 to at least 1916—the year Garrett W. Thompson's edition of *Burg Neideck* was prefaced with the following words:

> No edition of *Burg Neideck* could fail to carry with it the sincere hope of the editor that the works of Wilhelm Heinrich Riehl may come to be more and more widely read, and therefore better known, by American students. The value of his ideas, the inspiration of his ideals, the moral purity of his stories wherever matters of character are at stake appear as a refreshing offset to the less stable, more morbid and sensational tendencies which are always present in literature. (3)

Thus *Burg Neideck*, and Riehl's stories in the main, were preferred textual material for the ideas, ideals, and moral purity which they convey. However, in one point, according to Thompson, Riehl's writings differed from those usually used as texts:

> Riehl's style is less clear to the average student than is generally supposed. His love of antithesis, his terseness, which often falls little short of being blunt, naturally affect his types of sentence structure and tax the reader's reason more than his imagination. (3)

Thompson proposed to alleviate these difficulties by increasing annotation beyond the usual limits.

But language or style caused difficulties on another level, as Julius Sachs demonstrated in 1918:

> Of a certain German tale, Riehl's *Burg Neideck*, there exist at least half a dozen different editions; evidently the story appeals to many teachers and is largely used by them. To forestall criticism, I may state that personally I find the work exceedingly amusing, but that is not the issue. Will it so impress our pupils? It is conceived in a vein of gentle satire, intelligible in its curious conceits only if

you have saturated yourself with the grotesque contrast that the author has in mind between actuality and a fancifully exaggerated sentimentalism. Read it as the story runs on, with the attention of the pupils riveted on the literal interpretation of the language, and not a glimmer of its underlying spirit is apt to reach their minds. . . . Does it serve any purpose to annotate with elaborate suggestions the various incongruous situations? . . . It is my contention that a work . . . involving elaborate apparatus to make it at all palatable, is not wisely chosen. (144)

So Thompson's plan is challenged: elaborate notes cannot render the satire intelligible to students attempting to comprehend the words of a text at face value. A text which is clearly serious or obviously funny, and which requires few grammatical and content footnotes is, if Sachs's suggestions are followed, the best choice. However, as *Burg Neideck* first appeared as a U.S. text in 1886 and was still on hand in several editions in 1918—a survivor of the World War—this demonstrates the popularity of the text as a part of U.S. German programs.

However, Riehl's most popular text was *Der Fluch der Schönheit*, a tale of the Thirty Years' War and of Amos Haselborn, who bore the curse of too much beauty. Too handsome and too vain to get along with people or to keep employment, Amos undergoes a series of war experiences through which he loses his outward beauty but gains an inner beauty. The story is actually a treatise on *praesumptio* structured around a shallow reprise of *Simplizissimus*. That the narrative is used to point a moral—a popular feature of German texts of the era—is seldom absent from the reader's mind.

Arthur N. Leonard, who edited *Der Fluch der Schönheit* for Ginn in 1908, told of the profits to the student from Riehl's discourse on beauty and pride:

In the experience of the editor, *Der Fluch der Schönheit* has proved to be an interesting textbook for the college student as well as for the pupil in the preparatory school. It is seldom that a reader fails to become interested in the development of the hero's internal beauty, if we may use the expression, as the hero himself realizes the departure of his external beauty. (vi)

The difficulties pointed out by Julius Sachs with regard to *Burg Neideck* are largely absent from *Der Fluch der Schönheit*. The story may be said to speak plainly, and if the student grasps the polarities of external and internal beauty, and of the devil and Christ, his understanding of the story is assured. Riehl's idealism and the moral purity of his stories have been pointed out above. A by now familiar pattern repeats itself again in the case of *Der Fluch der Schönheit*.

Quite different from the reception of the works of Riehl was that of the works of Friedrich Spielhagen, one of Professor Hosmer's "figures not great, though often respectable" (549). Popular in German-speaking Europe—

particularly during the third quarter of the 1800s—and not unknown in translation in the United States, Spielhagen boasted only one German text, *Das Skelett im Hause*, which appeared in 1913. Bernhardt, though he speaks of Spielhagen in tones of praise, nonetheless reveals a cause of academic inattention:

> Spielhagen ... ist ein geschätzter Erzähler. Seine Hauptstärke liegt im Zeitroman, in dem er mit klarem Blicke brennende Tagesfragen, wie Frauenrechte, Emanzipation der Arbeiter, die sozialistische und Associationsfrage, Freihandel und Schutzzoll und ähnliche soziale Interessen poetisch behandelt. (64–65)

Such social issues and burning questions of the day did not necessarily lend themselves to the consideration of students during the era under consideration.

Indeed, Spielhagen did not seem particularly well suited for the classroom if one shared Professor Wells's point of view:

> Another novelist who made a profound impression on the mind of this generation, though he ministered rather to its moral restlessness than to its social development, is Friedrich Spielhagen. ... The suppressed intensity of the moral life of the German nation during the years that immediately precede the refounding of the empire is to be felt ... the aristocracy is no longer treated with kindly sympathy ... the subject is ... the irrepressible conflict between the stolid landed nobility and the intelligence of the nation. (377)

The overall impression of Spielhagen's writings given here is that they are somewhat explosive. The pronounced leftist tinge of novels such as *Durch Nacht zum Licht* must have rendered Spielhagen's propagandistic works at least somewhat out of place in predominantly right-wing, imperialist America as well as in imperial Germany after 1870—although Spielhagen continued to write until 1889.

The conception of Spielhagen as propagandist and journalist more than artist was further developed by Kummer:

> Spielhagen vertrat die Gedanken der bürgerlichen Revolution von 1848 und der preußischen Fortschrittspartei, deren Hauptschlagworte lauteten: Parlamentsherrschaft und Kampf gegen Junker und Geistliche. Spielhagen führte diese und verwandte Tendenzen ohne Tiefe mit Annäherung an den Leitartikelton in seinen Romanen durch, die wohl als characteristische Zeitwerke, aber niemals als bleibende große Schöpfungen angesehen werden können. (464)

For this commentator, ephemeral novels which dealt with questions of the times were Spielhagen's contribution to German literature. Thus his lack of appeal for later generations may be accounted for.

Calvin Thomas concurs, stating that Spielhagen

was an ideologist, an opinionator, interested as novelist in the clash of doctrines. His characters are schematic embodiments of ideas and tendencies. . . . Withal there is much didacticism. . . . From the nature of the case such fiction loses a large part of its interest when the questions of the hour, with which it deals, have been forgotten. (392–93)

The "German mind" as revealed in Spielhagen's works was, it seems, regarded in much the same way on both sides of the Atlantic.

However, somewhat more favorable was Priest's review of the author's manner of writing. Students were told that "the political or social purpose of Spielhagen's novels is often too conspicuous, but their variety of incident and their smooth narrative still attract many readers" (308). Stroebe and Whitney called Spielhagen an outstanding realistic author who had a thorough psychological understanding of his characters based upon their heredity and environment (234).They apparently regarded him as a forerunner of Naturalism. Certainly, Spielhagen fared better near the beginning and end of the era; the single U.S. Spielhagen text appeared in 1913—a year after Stroebe and Whitney's history (containing a propitious view of Spielhagen) was copyrighted for the first time.

The text, *Das Skelett im Hause*, was edited by M. M. Skinner for Heath. In his introduction, Skinner offered students a dashing characterization of Spielhagen:

> With a fearlessness and impetuosity that compel our admiration, he ever championed the cause of the people, and their claims to greater participation in the affairs of government; he lashed with every weapon in his power class favoritism and caste privilege as well as all kinds of hypocrisy—religious, political and social. (iv)

And *Das Skelett im Hause* is no exception to the rule, although the mood of the tale is far more lighthearted than serious.

The skeleton in the closet, around which the story revolves, is a sign advertising *Nudel Eßwaren*; it has hung on Lebrecht Nudel's mansion for generations. The family fortune began with *Eßwaren*, and a store continues to operate on a lower level of the mansion. However, as Lebrecht has married Ännchen, whose mother is a Rhenish Klüngel-Pütz (word play on "cliquish finery")—one of the most noble families—he has locked the sign in a closet. Through a series of suspenseful and humorous happenings, the skeleton emerges from the closet bringing Lebrecht and Ännchen only happiness.

Perhaps Spielhagen's most pointed slam at the upper class occurs when Ännchen regrets to herself her mother's treatment of Lebrecht during their courtship:

> Die Mama meinte es ja auch nicht bös—gewiß nicht, aber es war für ihren, aller Prahlerei abholden Lebrecht doch sicherlich eine harte Aufgabe, sich fortwährend in Gespräche verwickelt zu sehen, die unverweigerlich dasselbe Ziel hatten: die Verherrlichung des Geschlechtes derer von Klüngel-Pütz: wie

glänzend es einst dagestanden mit seinen fünfzig Burgen am Rhein; und wie es mit höchsten Adelsfamilien verwandt . . . gewesen: und wie der Glanz nun nach und nach verblichen . . . bis—o, des grausamen Geschickes!—eine Klüngel-Pütz—sie selbst—einem Bürgerlichen sich vermählt; und die Tochter aus dieser Ehe sich abermals einem Bürgerlichen vermählen werde! (5)

Spielhagen the socialist pillories the aristocracy here by lightly making fun. The story is harmless, and, had Spielhagen's leftist reputation and World War I not limited his ability to attract a following in academe, *Das Skelett im Hause* might have been a more popular text.

In *Reih und Glied, Hammer und Amboß* and other serious works by Spielhagen did not reach the classroom due to their liberal, socialist, anti-clerical points of view. For example, Charles H. Handschin, himself a German textbook editor during the era surveyed, defined the expectations of language teachers toward their students in *Methods of Modern Language Teaching* as follows:

"When we teach literature, the chief aim is to appreciate it, both as to form and content. Besides getting the meaning . . . the points of value for adolescents are cultural and moral" (238).

Literary works which were socialistic and attacked the church would only with difficulty be regarded as moral.

German philosopher Rudolf Eucken supplied support for Yankee conservatism:

The human race is today confronted by a serious danger; for labor, constantly increasing in volume, threatens to absorb completely the individual, to crush out all spiritual life, and to make us the mere instruments of a mechanical process of culture, which, at the same time, tends to weaken and to cripple the moral faculties. It devolves upon us all unitedly to guard against so serious a danger. (602)

Not only in Germany, but also in America feelings against Spielhagen's socialism and anti-clericalism must have manifested themselves. However, let it be said in Spielhagen's defense that the length of his *Zeitromane* rendered them unlikely choices for classroom editions regardless of the ideas they contained.

Far less propagandistic, though only slightly more successful in the U.S. German textbook trade, were the works of Wilhelm Raabe. Professor Wells explains a basic difficulty encountered by readers of a Raabe text:

The humor of a foreign nation is the most inaccessible part of its literature. To understand the art by which Wilhelm Raabe . . . wins a smile even from the seamy side of life, in spite of a never failing undertone of pessimistic resignation, demands knowledge not only of him but of his countrymen. He lays his stories in out-of-the-way villages, takes for his characters as out-of-the-way people as Dickens. (408–09)

By humor, then, Wells does not signify the farces so popular as textbooks (some of them in Wells's own editions). Elz and Wilhelmi are easily understood; Raabe, who offers humor mixed with disillusionment and resignation, shifts time and place backward and forward and daydreams for pages at a time, is not so easily comprehended. Simply understanding Raabe's basic schematization sometimes requires an effort which dulls a second-year student's appreciation of his subtle humor. If the successful slapstick was an insult to students' intelligence, Raabe's stories may have had a limited appeal as texts due to their taxing a learner's patience.

Along with praise for Raabe, therefore, Priest also apprises the student of certain idiosyncrasies:

> Raabe is very fond of side remarks and of intruding his own personality upon the reader, but in spite of his artificialities of style, he is a convincing, interesting realist, especially in the depiction of life in small towns. . . . For several decades only a small circle of Raabe's countrymen appreciated his power of characterization and his great warm heart. (304–05)

Priest's more negative remarks help to establish why Raabe's works were not popular as textbooks. Once again, his complicated style is the apparent difficulty.

Kummer supplies corroboration of this impression in an entire paragraph within the pages he devotes to Raabe. Some of the thoughts therein expressed are:

> Leser, die in erster Linie Unterhaltung suchen und sonst nichts, werden bei Raabe kein Genüge finden. . . . Gegen Raabes Fehler darf niemand blind sein. Dem Stoff tut er durch seine Neigung zum Seltsamen oft Zwang an; die Darstellung ist oft weitschweifig und verschnörkelt. Der Dichter liebt es . . . die objektive Erzählung bisweilen abzubrechen und den Leser in eigner Person und Sache anzureden. . . . Diese Betrachtungen . . . gefährden . . . oft die Wirkung und schädigen die künstlerische Form. (421)

If a text should entertain the class as it teaches, Raabe would seem to be a poor choice on all but the most advanced levels.

But not all Germanists broached the subject of Raabe's difficult style; nor did they speak of Raabe to any great extent. Calvin Thomas remarked only that "the village tale was cultivated by *Wilhelm Raabe* . . . who belongs to the literary line of Richter and Immermann. His sympathetic pictures of humble life, with their fantastic humor and mild pessimism, have won him many friends" (403). This brief, innocuous statement was echoed three years later by Stroebe and Whitney: "Mit echtem Humor, beeinflußt von Jean Paul und auch von Dickens, stellte Raabe das Leben einfacher, unscheinbarer Menschen dar" (234–35). Had these commentators but written more about Raabe, it seems probable in the light of the other professors' comments that

Raabe's style would have come in for its share of criticism in their assessments as well.

In his introduction to *Eulenpfingsten* (Heath 1912), Marcus Lambert expressed the hope that "the recent recommendation of his [Raabe's] novels and stories as typical texts by the Sub-committee of the Modern Language Association of America will contribute to such a recognition of his writings in the high schools and colleges of this country as they deserve" (iii). The earliest and latest listings of Raabe's works, both for *Else von der Tanne*, were 1911 and 1915. On the one hand, then, Raabe's works came too late to U.S. academe to attain great renown. On the other hand, "his style is so original and unique that a page written by him could not possibly be mistaken for that of another. The wealth of his allusions is at times little short of bewildering" (Raabe iii). Even an editor seeking Raabe's furtherance, then, makes a statement corresponding to "Dem Stoff tut er durch seine Neigung zum Seltsamen oft Zwang an; die Darstellung ist oft weitschweifig und verschnörkelt" (Kummer 421). It was therefore not for moral, religious, or political reasons that there were relatively few Raabe texts; Raabe was simply too difficult.

Slightly higher was the number of texts by Conrad Ferdinand Meyer—five texts, seven listings from 1893 to 1917. An author in whom "the glories of his race roused . . . a patriotic glow," Meyer was viewed by Wells primarily as chronicler of the "Germanic spirit" (397–98). A similar viewpoint was expressed by Priest, who calls Meyer a writer of "vigorous, truthful historical narratives," and places him in associations surprising by today's standards: "With Freytag and Riehl, Meyer is a leader in historical fiction; he reconstructs the past with an intimate understanding of his subject and with the style of a prose artist" (313). The comparison of Meyer to Freytag and Riehl is interesting in retrospect; especially important for students and teachers of the era was the fact that style, so apologized for with regard to the works of Raabe, was praised in those of Meyer.

This difference in style is further commented upon by Kummer:

> Meyers Dichten war ein Schaffen mit stärkster Betätigung des Verstandes. Meyer stand mit kühler Ruhe über den Stoffen. . . . Wie sorgfältig meißelte, schliff und gestaltete er in jedem Zug, und wie führte er über die Einzelheiten so stark, und in seinen besten Sachen sogar gewaltig, die große Linie seiner Erzählung dahin! (483)

Raabe constantly intrudes his own personality into his story; Meyer stands above his plot and carries on the work of the file. Consequently, Meyer's novellas are clearer as far as plot sequence is concerned, helping students comprehend what they are reading.

Thomas, Stroebe and Whitney offer little information on Meyer. Thomas mentions Meyer as "the author of a number of historical novelettes that have hardly been surpassed" (403), while Stroebe and Whitney term Meyer "den Meister des historischen Romans in der neuern [sic] Zeit," who "sucht große, gewaltige Menschen und große Epochen der Weltgeschichte aus, und es gelingt ihm wirklich, die Gestalten der Vergangenheit so zum Leben zu bringen, daß wir sie als unsere Zeitgenossen fühlen" (232–33). If little was written by these commentators about Meyer, their remarks are nonetheless quite complimentary; indeed, Meyer was adversely criticized by none of the professors, which renders his modest reception in U.S. academe surprising.

Martin Haertel, in his preface to *Der Schuß von der Kanzel*, regretted the dearth of Meyer texts, while praising some of the positive qualities of Meyer's writing:

> It has long been the belief of the editor that the work of Conrad F. Meyer is well worthy of increased attention in the American schools. So far as is known to the editor, only one of his works [*Gustav Adolfs Page*] has been made accessible in text-book form. *Der Schuß von der Kanzel* has been selected because of its interest to the student, due to its delightful humor and historic background, and because of the healthy sentiment that inspires it. (iii)

Der Schuß von der Kanzel was interesting, humrous, imparted some historical information on Switzerland, and was a "healthy" (i.e., wholesome) work of art. Against expectation, the text was listed only in 1905.

Most important was the question of style, here hit upon by Alfred Kenngott in his edition of Meyer's *Jürg Jenatsch*:

> In his art Meyer is purely objective; his style is clear and very poetical, and his workmanship perfect, artistic, and refined. He is successful in the art of realistic and plastic presentation, in the careful delineation of character, in his pure objectivity of thought and sentiment, and in his true psychological representation. (ix)

Stylistically, too, therefore, a teacher could hardly choose a finer text than one by Meyer. Yet *Jürg Jenatsch* was also listed only once, in 1911. Only *Gustav Adolfs Page* was listed more than once: three times from 1893 to 1917 (two editions).

Perhaps this is not as surprising as it seems. As it happens, if the average of fifteen years required from the first appearance of a work to its use as a U.S. German textbook is added to the original dates of Meyer's works, *Gustav Adolfs Page* became a textbook in less than the average time. The other Meyer texts are not remarkably late in appearing, but they were introduced a relatively short time before the outbreak of hostilities in World War I; as time passed, the market for German texts began to fall and fewer new editions (or reprints of existing editions) were required. Thus the editors' pleas that

American students should be exposed more to Conrad Ferdinand Meyer" went unheeded.

A similar case is that of Theodor Fontane. Once considered a writer of ballads, he began writing novels and novellas somewhat later in life. In 1901 Professor Wells compared Fontane to Roquette, calling both idle singers of empty days, but added that Fontane should be particularly interesting to Americans "for his popularization of English ballad poetry, though he is noteworthy also as a realistic novelist of kindly and gentle humor" (387).

Some years later, Kummer's assessment is similar to that of the later twentieth century:

> l'Adultera, Irrungen Wirrungen, Stine. . . . Mit ihnen wurde Fontane einer der wichtigsten Schöpfer des modernen Berliner Romans. . . . Seine Schilderung der Berliner Gesellschaft ist echter als die Spielhagens. . . . Klar und scharf sieht Fontane Straßen, Stuben, Menschen. Sein staunenswertes Gedächtnis war ein Magazin von Bildern, in denen auch die kleinste Skizze nicht verloren ging. . . . Mit größter Deutlichkeit versteht Fontane namentlich Gespräche wiederzugeben. Darin war er vor Hauptmann unübertroffen. (620-21)

These points are stressed once more, and another interesting comparison is made by Priest, who, in speaking of Fontane's first novel, *Vor dem Sturm*, states that the author

> showed himself at once the equal of Willibald Alexis in large historical conception and in vivid characterization. The short stories which followed . . . were stepping-stones to realism. Fontane's most striking characteristics, his knowledge and understanding of modern people and his art of characterizing through conversation, are first revealed in his realistic novels of contemporary life. (314)

The comparison of Fontane to the now obscure Alexis makes an interesting comment upon the reception of both in 1909.

Professor Thomas speaks merely of Fontane's conversion from a romantic singer of ballads to a strict realist, noting that at the time of his death he was the acknowledged master of the novel of Berlin life (403). Stroebe and Whitney, however, offer what amounts to a summary of all the opinions on Fontane reviewed. Fontane was

> der einzige Dichter des älteren Richtung, der sich dem neuaufkommenden Naturalismus nicht entgegenstellte. . . . Seine Eigenart ist das realistische Genrebild; er gibt uns ein anschauliches Bild des weltstädtischen Lebens in Berlin und in seiner geliebten Heimat, der Mark Brandenburg. Mit schlichter Wahrhaftigkeit ohne irgend welche [sic] Sentimentalität zeichnet er die Wirklichkeit und auch im Alltagsleben findet er überall Interessantes. (235)

Although compliments fell to Fontane from professors and editors, the space of time between the appearance of a work in Germany and its reception in the U.S. as a German text nonetheless had its role to play. *Vor dem Sturm*, which appeared in 1878, was a text by 1899 and was listed again in 1911. *Grete Minde*, a novella first published in 1880, appeared as a text only in 1911. As these texts were slightly slow in making their initial appearance, time itself was not on the side of a rapid expansion in Fontane texts. Further, Fontane leaned toward Naturalism, with its frank depiction of all sides of life, and its choice of situations not always flattering to order and propriety. Revolution, the questioning of the usefulness of the nobility to the people at large, and thoughts upon the essence of patriotism and its imitations render his works somewhat comparable to those of Spielhagen with respect to their social and political viewpoints. Thus Fontane was not as frequently a *vade mecum* of U.S. German teachers as were moralizers such as Zschokke and Fulda and conservatives such as Wildenbruch.

The didactic historical novels of Felix Dahn and Georg Ebers, often characterized as *Professorenromane*, offered academics an escape from *Zeitdeutung* and *Tendenzdichtung*. Bernhardt termed Dahn "der Verfasser eines der bedeutendsten geschichtlichen Romane der Gegenwart, betitelt 'Ein Kampf um Rom,' in welchem er den Untergang der Ostgoten in Italien unter ihren letzten Königen Totillas und Tejas . . . schildert" (66). Going even further, Wells calls Dahn one of the greatest novelists of any literature, elaborating that

> His "Battle for Rome" (1876) has an epic breadth and swing that that seem to make it kin to the Niebelungen [sic] itself and give it high artistic unity. . . . Here we may watch Germanic virtues as they are gradually softened by the culture of the South, till they fall at last a prey to devious and unscrupulous diplomacy. . . . the tragic end of the Kingdom of the Ostrogoths. No German but feels they are of his race, and his pulse beats quicker in sympathy with the people whose democratic virtues were the causes of their fall. The mass of learning that the work involves is immense. (399)

The professor's effusions continue at length. Not only is a great respect for Dahn and his work perceivable; there may also be at least a hint of Wilhelminian jingoism afoot—the contrast of the Goths with the Romans seems to lend itself to a comparison of the Germans with the French. Indeed, one of the virtues of another of Dahn's novels edited as a German text, *Felicitas*, according to Wells, is that it can "vivify and clarify our ideas of the relation of German and Roman culture" (400)—within the historical frame of the fall of Rome, to be sure, but making a more modern association is facile enough. It seems that from the point of view of at least some teachers, U.S. German students, too, should be aware of the virtues of the Germanic peoples, and this was a didactic plus to Dahn's writings.

In writing of *Ein Kampf um Rom*, Kummer also commented on this equating of Goths with Germans and ancient Romans with Latin peoples: "Der Roman, obwohl erst 1876 erschienen, war nicht, wie man oft gemeint hat, eine Folgeerscheinung des Krieges von 1870, sondern er wurzelte durchweg in den poetischen Stimmungen und politischen Anschaungen der fünfziger Jahre" (428). Therefore, the political interpretation may not apply to the Second Empire versus France—though these feelings made themselves felt, as Kummer indicates—but rather to the German people of the 1850s.

Dahn is not discussed by Professor Thomas and is mentioned only summarily by Priest, Stroebe and Whitney, which is rather surprising after the praise offered by Wells. The three Dahn texts listed date from 1891 to 1904. It seems safe to say that by 1909, when Thomas and Priest published their histories—and certainly by 1913 (Stroebe and Whitney)—Dahn was no longer "one of the great novelists of any literature."

Dahn's contemporary, Georg Ebers, was, if one may judge from the *New York Times* book reviews, one of the most popular German authors of his own time here in the United States (Heinsohn 190–216). However, he was represented by only one text among U.S. German students: *Eine Frage: Idyll zu einem Gemälde seines Freundes Alma Tadema*, copyrighted by Holt in 1887 and listed once more in 1888. The scarcity of Ebers's popular writings in the schools is a condition which deserves investigation.

In writing of German literature of his time, F. H. Geffcken stated that "Ebers continues to write a volume per year of his dull historic novels and so does Felix Dahn in his falsification of history" (671). Professor Wells's comments on Ebers—unlike his deferential assessment of Dahn—are consonant with those of Geffcken:

> This distinguished Egyptologist naturally preferred old Egypt for his scenes, and the attraction of such novels . . . is in the curiosity that this new-old world excites even in the half-cultured. . . . but the thoughts and motives of his characters are thoroughly modern, and the psychology of their development is weak, so that if we could transfer them from their antique setting they would appear dry, unreal, weak, and poor, artificial in sentiment and lacking in all poetic freshness. (396–97)

On the one hand, then, unrealistic modern characters wearing Egyptian costumes amid exotic scenery gave Ebers's books their allure. On the other hand, however, these novels were *Professorenromane* by a distinguished Egyptologist, and as such must have had at least a small share of their appeal from an intellectual point of view.

The latter point of view is supported to some extent by Kummer, who terms Ebers "der lehrreiche, ernsthafte und oft langweilige Professor." Further, however,

> Ebers war moralischer und ehrlicher, aber auch schwerfälliger als andere Modeschriftsteller. . . . Ebers steckte in die bunten Trachten seiner Ägypter moderne Menschen, und ließ sie reden und handeln wie Alltagsmenschen von 1875. Gleichzeitig aber umgab er sie mit dem echten Aberglauben ihrer Zeit. Das war natürlich unsinnig und falsch; aber darauf gründete sich sein großer Erfolg. (524)

The mixture of Egyptology and *Alltagsmenschen* is at once Ebers's greatest fault from a scholarly viewpoint and perhaps his greatest attraction to the reading public at large. Hence the large number of *New York Times* book reviews, at least some of which reflect both opinions (Heinsohn 281–302).

As was the case with Dahn, little or no information on Ebers is offered by Thomas, Priest, Stroebe and Whitney in 1909 and 1913. He had not been reviewed by the *New York Times* since 1899; thus his renown as an author was probably declining on either side of the schoolhouse wall. Most telling is the indictment aimed by Kummer at those who made Ebers a celebrated author:

> Man mag ein vernichtendes Urteil über Ebers fällen, aber über die, die seine Romane immer von neuem begehrten, muß das Urteil nicht weniger vernichtend lauten, und um dieser Leser willen wird Ebers immer in die Literaturgeschichte gehören; denn Ebers war kein Zufall; Ebers war ein Schicksal. (524)

The academics of America who produced German texts during the period under consideration, though their choices are occasionally doubtful, scarcely yielded to the popular appeal of Ebers. Though one of his novels takes place in Nuremberg (and could, therefore, acquaint students with the life of Germany), it is inferior to his Egyptian works (Kummer 524). Finally, somewhat as in the case of Spielhagen, Ebers's novels' length did not recommend them as U.S. German texts.

A similar verdict might have befallen the work of Friedrich Gerstäcker, the follower of Sealsfield, had he not written two works laid in Europe which enjoyed considerable popularity as texts: *Germelshausen* and *Irrfahrten*. Among the sources consulted only Kurz mentions *Heimliche und Unheimliche Geschichten* (4:983), from which *Germelshausen* is taken, while *Irrfahrten* went unmentioned. The third U.S. text by Gerstäcker, *Der Wilddieb*, which is also set in Germany, was listed only in 1915 and likewise received no comment.

The major reason why Gerstäcker's western and South American works were not chosen as texts is that they convey no sense of German life to the student, but another objection was the *Amerikabild* conveyed. As Bernhardt taught, "leider ist Gerstäcker in seinen Schilderungen amerikanischer Verhältnisse nicht unparteiisch genug, da er geneigter ist, die Schattenseiten als die Vorzüge des amerikanischen Volkscharakters zu sehen" (67). One of Kurz's criticisms of Gerstäcker strikes a similar tone; at the same time, Kurz's defense of the United States demonstrates the warm feeling many Germans had for the country to which their friends and relatives had emigrated. Thus he writes of Gerstäcker's popularity and its price that

> Wie andere Schriftsteller verweilt Gerstäcker mit Vorliebe bei den Nachtseiten des Amerikanischen Lebens. Allerdings sicherte er sich dadurch den Beifall des großen Publikums, welches nach Spannendem und Nervenaufregendem verlangt, gern von Mord und andern Gräuelthaten [sic] liest; aber diesen Beifall

> erwarb er sich doch auf Kosten der Wahrheit; denn wenn es auch in Amerika wie überall Schurken und Verbrecher aller Art giebt [sic], so sind sie doch auch dort wie überall nur Ausnahmen, während man aus den Erzählungen Gerstäckers glauben könnte, sie seien daselbst in der Mehrzahl. (4:782)

For Kurz, then, fame at the price of a lack of reality and an excess of gore was Gerstäcker's portion.

Kummer offered students a similarly grim assessment of Gerstäcker: "Sein Stil war drastisch, die Gestalten waren äußerlich gut gesehen, aber die Form war nachläßig und der Gehalt gering. . . . Neben Sealsfield gehalten, erscheint er flach, roh und ideenlos" (435). It is interesting, considering what was then perceived as the negative view of America in Gerstäcker's works, that the most positive estimation came from the American Benjamin Wells, the only U.S. professor other than Bernhardt to recognize Gerstäcker. He stated that Gerstäcker's works, "show a very great gift of description, vigorous character drawing, and a straightforward, rough and ready style that put them quite apart from the scholastic literary tradition" (381). Wells does not indicate that Gerstäcker's writings' "apartness" indicates that his works have no place in the schools. Perhaps one of his western stories would have provided a justifiable change of pace—to see America as outsiders saw it—had any been edited for use in secondary schools and colleges in defiance of the dicta of the Committee of Twelve.

What was edited were three stories already named, which—in keeping with the Committee of Twelve's guidelines for life and literature—are set in Germany: *Der Wilddieb*, listed once in 1915; *Irrfahrten*, listed seven times from 1896 to 1915 (three editions); and *Germelshausen*, listed sixteen times from 1893 to 1916 (eight editions). A look into the review of Walter Myers's edition of *Der Wilddieb* in *The Modern Language Journal* by Bert John Vos (himself an editor of Heine's *Harzreise*) reveals a definitely negative feeling toward Gerstäcker:

> Gerstäcker is certainly 'keiner von den Großen' in the history of German letters and his *Wilddieb* can hardly lay claim to genuine literary worth. None the less [sic], as the editor points out, it offers "a narrative which is rapid and realistic, and which holds the interest from beginning to end." . . . The *Realien* are to be sure not quite those of modern Germany, and the language if "simple and direct," is also not infrequently archaistic, colloquial, and even slovenly. . . . That the 'Schenkmädchen' were gotten rid of is doubtless a sign of the times, as is shown by the almost consistent dropping of references to 'Bier' and 'Wein'— a procedure that in a story dealing so largely with 'Förster' and 'Jäger' does after all to some extent destroy the milieu. (226)

The assessment of Gerstäcker's work as trifling and slovenly seems harsh— especially in view of a recent renewal of interest in the author; the genteel excision of barmaids, beer and wine from the text reflects the era's quest for innocent texts of the sort frequently discussed in this study.

One editor of *Irrfahrten*, Marian Whitney, who in her literary history co-authored by Lillian Stroebe failed to mention Gerstäcker to students, made the following statement about *Irrfahrten* in her preface to the story:

> This is by no means a classic, but it is an amusing modern story, and the interest of the action will be found to carry the pupil over hard constructions; while the fact that it takes place on German ground among German people will teach him much of the customs of the country and the life of its inhabitants. In difficulty it is suited to the second year of high school, or the first year of college, work. (iii)

The text meets the requirements of the Committee of Twelve for a text rather well; a teacher's only objection might be that, by admission of Professor Whitney, *Irrfahrten* is not a work of enduring excellence. It has been forgotten by the contemporary textbook market.

Not so *Germelshausen*, which continues to appear in a simplified form (in *Unheimliche Begegnungen* edited by Edith Bathke) in the catalogs of at least one academic book company in the United States. Carl Osthaus, one of the editors of the tale, explained that among Gerstäcker's stories set in Germany,

> the romance "Germelshausen" ranks as one of the best, not only in consequence of its beautiful style, but also on account of its highly dramatic impersonation of the leading characters and the vivid description of country life. (vi)

Germelshausen is indeed an interesting story based upon German folklore. Due to their refusal to serve the Pope, the people of Germelshausen, together with their town, sank into the earth, to appear on the surface once more only once every hundred years. A young artist named Arnold, who wanders through the region, chances to meet Gertrud, a pretty girl from Germelshausen, and spends the day there as her guest. Because she loves Arnold, Gertrud brings it about that he leaves the cursed village before it sinks again at midnight. Casting an interesting light on the continued reception of the story in the United States, John T. Krumpelmann has suggested that the once very popular textbook was the source for Alan Jay Lerner's Broadway musical *Brigadoon*.

An example of style in *Germelshausen* is offered by Gerstäcker's description of the village:

> Über dem Dorf aber hing der düstere Höhenrauch, den Arnold schon von weitem gesehen, und brach das helle Sonnenlicht, das nur mit einem gelblich unheimlichen Scheine auf die alten grauen verwitterten Dächer fallen konnte. . . . Und wie wunderlich die alten Häuser mit ihren spitzen, mit Schnitzwerk verzierten Giebeln . . . aussahen—und trotz dem Sonntag war kein Fenster blank geputzt, und die runden, in Blei gefaßten Scheiben sahen trüb und angelaufen aus und zeigten auf ihren matten Flächen den schillernden Regenbogenglanz. (13)

Though one may hear the slightest tinkling of *Butzenscheibenlyrik*, *Germelshausen* goes beyond mere externalities of setting. Arnold and Gertrud and their relationship—at once fascinating and tragic—give the story a deeper meaning.

More closely aligned with the literary purveyors of leaded panes is Rudolf Baumbach, who, judging from the statistics in Appendix F, follows Schiller, Goethe and Lessing as an overall academic favorite of the times. As Bernhardt stated,

> Der genialste von Scheffels Schülern und Nachfolgern ist Rudolf *Baumbach* . . . einer der liebenswürdigsten Dichter und Erzähler der Jetztzeit. Alle seine Dichtungen, in Prosa und Vers, zeichnen sich durch denselben frischen Humor, dieselbe gutmütige Satire, natürliche Anmut und gesunde Freude am Leben aus, welche der Scheffelschen Muse eigen sind. (64)

It is worth noting in passing that Bernhardt edited no less than eight Baumbach texts, one prior to and seven after the appearance of his literary history, while other academics tend to ignore Baumbach or mention him to students of literature negatively or cursorily.

Other than Bernhardt, Wells was kindest, writing that Baumbach

> has a natural freshness, a light, pleasing humor, and a charm that belongs rather to the romantic than to the modern period. His epic subjects are taken either from the Slavonic Alps . . . or from old German legend. . . . His lyrics have an even greater joy of life and natural beauty . . . and the same spirit pervades his prose fiction. (393–94)

That Baumbach's work, though recent, seemed rather dated in its singular celebration of life and beauty is evident from Wells's remarks.

Not given to understatement was Kummer, who mentioned Baumbach only as a poet:

> Bedeutungslos, im letzten Grunde prosaisch war Baumbachs Epos. . . . In den Spielmannsliedern träumt sich Baumbach in eine längst vergangene, niemals gewesene Zeit hinein. . . . Der Ton ist altertümelnd, dabei zierlich und leicht; die Baumbachsche Lyrik kam in der Dichtung auf, als in Wohnungsstil die Butzenscheiben und die deutschen Renaissancemöbel Mode wurden. (514)

Meaningless, prosaic and superficial was *Butzenscheibenlyrik*, a thought echoed by Priest, who places Baumbach among "a host of minor poets who fostered so-called . . 'lyrics of leaded panes,' or poetry which aimed at the revival of the spirit and life of olden times, and advanced no farther than casement windows, or mere externalities." At the same time, Priest also notes that Baumbach's works found a large audience (312). Thomas, Stroebe and Whitney offer no information on Baumbach.

It remains to examine why Baumbach's poems and stories were so popular and to speculate upon the scarcity of critical approval in the era under study and in later times. First, it is striking that an author so popular as a pedagogical aid was notably unpopular in translation—an exact reversal of the case of Ebers. Baumbach's lack of popularity is indicated not only by the professors' remarks—or lack of them—above, but by the fact that only one work, the *Sommermärchen* collection, was reviewed by the *New York Times* as follows:

> Their popularity in Germany can be understood. It must be that the adult Germans read a great deal of literature written more especially for young people, and for that reason authors often put into their juvenilities slight little bits of satire, which are appreciated by the older readers. (qtd. in Heinsohn 285)

Yet in the light of the sources consulted Baumbach was not popularly known as a writer of "juvenilities" (unless the lack of reception may be interpreted as stemming from this circumstance), nor must one necessarily suppose that German adults of the era were particularly attracted to children's literature. As the *Sommermärchen* strike the *Times* reviewer as puerile, a brief investigation of the essence of some of Baumbach's stories seems expedient.

However, to begin with, it is well to consider a characterization of Baumbach offered by Edward Meyer in his edition of *Sommermärchen* (Holt 1900), which corresponds in some degree to the image rendered in the *New York Times*:

> The man has a nature so naïve, a sympathy so sincere, a humanity so divine, a realism so ideal, that he sees the soul in everything: he cannot conceive even the elements without their essence, the earth without kobold or gnome, the water without undine or nixie. . . . This is, indeed, to see the soul of Nature and to hear the heart-throbs of humanity, sending the soulfire through all the wonderful world. (iv–v)

The literature produced by such an author must be more than juvenile, one would assume, although the alleged naïveté could account for the child-like impression he gives through his writings.

Meyer proceeds to praise Baumbach's "humanising humor" stating that "there is certainly not a finer bit in German literature than in 'Der Eselsbrunnen'" (Baumbauch, *Sommermärchen* vi). This story explains the origin of the name *Eselsbrunnen*, a resort with a canopy over the healing spring which is topped by a weather vane on which appears an *Esel*. The inner story is a love story between the original donkey, after which the vane was modeled, and a goose. They meet at the spring and engage in flirtation:

> "Jungfräulein, darf ich Euch begleiten?" Sie nickte und wäre gerne errötet, aber das konnte sie nicht, und dann gingen sie selbander durch den Wiesengrund und sprachen vom Wetter. (Baumbach, *Sommermärchen* 44)

There is much word play on *Esel* and *Gans* as used pejoratively regarding people. At last, through the power of the *Wunschfrau*, the spring water and the summer solstice, the two become human. Implied is the knowledge that she is no more a *Gans* than other women, nor is he more an *Esel* than other men. Whether or not the story is merely silly is an open question.

A highly acclaimed plot has been examined; style is the next concern. Bernhardt apprises the student of the riches awaiting him in the *Waldnovellen* in the following manner:

> In wealth, beauty, and lucidity of diction, Rudolf Baumbach is excelled by none of the foremost contemporary writers of Germany. The rhythmical flow of his language . . . the soothing, luring, coaxing, and caressing concord of sweet sounds . . . lull the reason into slumber [with] . . . "a style good enough for a child to dwell upon . . . and good enough for an adult to relish." (Baumbach, *Waldnovellen* v)

Bernhardt seems to describe putting a class to sleep. Nonetheless, juding from the prominence of Baumbach texts, his style was considered by numerous teachers to be most acceptable in the German classroom.

For this reason a sample of Baumbach's prose is offered, from the beginning of the story "Ranunkulus":

> Selbiger Magister war an einem Frühlingsmorgen ins Freie gegangen, um das Gras wachsen zu hören, denn auch das verstand er, und wie er so wandelte im lichten Maiengrün und sah, wie die Grillen im Gras, die Vögel in den Zweigen und die Frösche im Wiesenbach ihr Hochzeitslied sangen, da gedachte er seines Heimatdorfes, das er vor Jahren verlassen, um die hohe Schule zu besuchen, und gedachte auch der kleinen schwarzäugigen Dirne, die ihm zum Abschied ein Herz von Lebzelten geschenkt und dabei bittere Träne vergossen hatte, und es wurde ihm gar wunderlich zu Mute. (Allen and Batt 3)

There is indeed a certain rhythm to the lines; straining for the meter, one becomes aware of something somewhat reminiscent of *Xenien* (Selbiger Magister war an einem Frühlingsmorgen/ins Freie gegangen, um das Gras wachsen zu hören). There are alliteration and assonance to a certain degree after the style of Wagner (an einem Frühlingsmorgen ins Freie; die Grillen im Gras; [and elsewhere] wie die bunten Wunder der Luft um die Sternblumen flogen); thus there may be a concord of sweet sounds to lull the intellect. But nearly every feature of the paragraph is a cliché, whether form or content is examined.

Many captivating stories written in a pleasing style were never edited as texts, so the extras which Baumbach's work offered academe should be pointed out. Bernhardt informed teachers and students that

> Our profoundest interest is from the very start elicited for the exemplary industry, honesty and contented happiness of his sturdy heroes and flaxen-

haired maids. . . . Every age and sex is sure to enjoy these exquisitely light, fascinating and pure stories, fairly bubbling over with wholesome fun, and this, all the more so, as there is nothing tragic in the author's roguish mirth nor a drop of bitterness in his slyly smiling satire . . . who could doubt for a minute that Baumbach ought to be placed in the hands of the youngster as well as the more mature students of language and life? (*Die Nonna* v–vi)

The key word, as so often during the course of this study, is wholesome.

Baumbach's plots and style are Wilhelminian *Kitsch*—tired clichés bring silliness and sentimentality to bear on students, as morals are carefully instilled via the plot. One is at first inclined to find fault with Bernhardt for his promotion of Baumbach's stories. However, as Wells with the trivial plays of Moser, Elz and Wilhelmi, Bernhardt in offering quantitites of Baumbach was tendering U.S. academe what the esteem of the public demanded: innocent mountain folk, sylphs and salamanders, moral and mental innocuousness.

Perhaps nowhere is Bernardt's literary taste so questionable as in the selections of the *Deutsche Novelletten-Bibliothek*, listed from 1867 to 1903. Most of the authors included in this popular volume go unmentioned by all commentators surveyed, including Bernhardt himself, and are unknown to the later twentieth century. However, Henrich Seidel, Ernst Werner and Helene Stökl, some of whose works are included in the small anthology, are discussed in this chapter.

Equally as forgotten as Baumbach in literary studies of today is Wilhelm Jensen, whose novella *Die braune Erika* was apparently a popular text from 1869 to 1910. As Wells writes, "Jensen . . in such early stories as 'The Brown Erica' . . . or 'Eddystone' . . . had written beautiful prose idylls of North German country scenes." However, he then began to write about upper-class society in Berlin, "and drew characters . . . perversely distorted." Later in life Jensen returned to his earlier style of writing. Predictably, the prose idyll in the beautiful country scene was chosen for textbooks over the "perverse" and "psychologic" fiction (Wells 404).

Kummer, who calls *Die braune Erika* one of Jensen's masterworks, makes no mention of the psychological works set in Berlin. Instead, amazing parallels to the art of Baumbach are revealed:

> Die Gestalten Jensens sind selten greifbar; sie führen eine Art von Traumleben, sie . . . können aus ihrer dämmerhaften Welt in die Wirklichkeit . . . kaum hineinversetzt werden. . . . Die Natur steht bei ihm stets in einer bestimmten, manchmal nur zu absichtsvollen Beziehung zur Handlung und Gefühlswelt . . . . Die schwüle Glut des Mittags, der Duft des Sommers, die einsame rotblühende Heide . . . . Die Geschichten sind wie im Rausch oder aus der Vision geschrieben, dabei liegt in ihnen hart neben der Mystik das Triviale. (433)

Unreal characters who inhabit a dream world in which nature plays a vital role in determination of their actions, a world caught between mysticism and triviality, bring thoughts of Baumbach's *Esel, Gans*, spring water and summer solstice.

However, Jensen did not become as imbued with Romanticism as Baumbach; instead, according to Priest, "the romantic elements of the first stories by Wilhelm Jensen . . . *Die braune Erica* and others, suggest a comparison with his model Theodor Storm." But Priest preferred a middle group of stories, whereof *Eddystone* is probably the best, "which mingle romanticism and real life." Poetry of various lengths, as well as dramas, are mentioned in passing. No psychological fiction set in Berlin (e.g., *In der Fremde*, 1886) is brought to the student's attention (Priest 313–14). Stroebe and Whitney write only that Jensen has produced superior novellas (236).

When the choice was made by Edward Payson Evans and Edward Southey Joynes to edit a Jensen text, given all the very successful texts on the market—Andersen's *Märchen*, Lessing's *Minna von Barnhelm*, Benedix's *Der Prozeß*, for example—the "perverse" psychological novels were a dubious choice. The mixtures of romanticism and realism did not bid as fair as the prose idylls of country scenes, the best of which was *Die braune Erika*. As with other authors, so with Jensen: the innocuous work prevailed.

Ferdinand von Saar's *Novellen aus Österreich* began to appear in 1865. Yet a number of years after the first volume of the collection was published, Kurz wrote only of two plays about Emperor Henry IV and Hildebrand: "In beiden Dramen entfaltet der Dichter eine große Meisterschaft in der Zeichnung der Charaktere" (4:648). Kurz's remarks consist mostly of praise; however, the plays were to be forgotten as the novellas became celebrated—a proceeding marked by only gradual change. By 1909, the student was taught that these stories were of considerable merit (Priest 316). Although Saar is also praised in today's literary histories, only two among the consulted sources of the era surveyed mention him. *Die Steinklopfer*, one of the *Novellen aus Österreich*, was listed only in 1906. The story deals with two unfortunate people who rise after the murder of their oppressor to a modest position in life, "womit zugleich die soziale Frage aufgerollt wird" (Krell and Fiedler 308). Perhaps for this reason Saar's novella was resorted to by academe with care.

For the most part, far less caution was necessary when assigning works by Peter Kettenfeier Rosegger, a popular choice for textbooks from 1895 to 1917. Professor Wells termed Rosegger one of those authors "who follow Auerbach with unequal steps and give us village stories of Switzerland, the Tyrol, and the Bavarian Highlands, peopled, as it would seem, by sentimental milkmaids and sighing shepherds, pessimistic yodelers and Alpine disciples of Schopenhauer" (408). Eight years later, Priest chose to accentuate not only sentiment but also didacticism: "Rosegger found his inspiration . . . in the popular life of his native country. His works are not lacking in humor, but they incline rather to the sentimental and didactic" (314). Professor Thomas merely remarked that Rosegger's stories were "winsome" (403), while Stroebe and Whitney described them only as friendly (233).

All these remarks are summarized by Kummer's words:

> Rosegger gehört zu den liebenswürdigsten Poeten der Zeit, doch vor höchsten künstlerischen Ansprüchen wird der Dichter nur in kleineren erzählenden Dichtungen bestehen. . . . Mit Hebel und Auerbach verband ihn im allgemeinen die gleiche volkstümliche und erzieherische Richtung, mit Stifter das Naturgefühl. . . . nur genoß er vor Auerbach den großen Vorzug, daß er zeitlebens in Berührung mit Volk und Natur der Heimat blieb. . . . Die Bedeutung von Rosegger liegt darin, daß er mit seiner reinen, lauteren, sittlichen Natur viel dazu beigetragen hat, die Stadt- und Kulturmenschen wieder . . . zur Natur zurückzuführen. (499–502)

From reading Rosegger, therefore, students are exposed to life in Steiermark, are inculcated with rectitude, and receive a new or expanded feeling for nature.

Since to learn of the life and literature of German-speaking lands while learning German, meanwhile gathering other benefits where he may, is the student's prescribed goal, Rosegger's novellas and short stories seem well suited to the needs of teachers and students. To determine what students derived from Rosegger, his *Der Lex von Gutenhag* will be briefly examined. Edited by B. Q. Morgan and listed in 1911 and 1917, the story is that of a homesick boy (Lex) from Styria who is persecuted by schoolmates—at least partially because of his incessant bragging about his home town, Gutenhag. Only after the arrival of a new schoolmate, Raimund, who becomes Lex's best—and only—friend, does life improve. Yet one day, as the two are climbing a mountain to behold a far-distant view of Gutenhag, there is a quarrel over patriotism. Raimund blames patriotism for wars. Lex defends it. The quarrel over, Lex resolves to speak no more about Gutenhag. At Christmas, all the boys decide to accept Lex and his defender, Raimund. When the school holidays come, Lex and Raimund travel to Gutenhag. The latter and Lex's sister show an interest in each other—there are hints of a serious relationship.

The tendency to didacticism is well illustrated by Raimund's speech contra patriotism:

> Was mich noch am meisten ärgert ist, daß auch die gebildeten Völker gegeneinander Krieg führen. . . . Aber vielleicht, daß, wenn die Menschen um eine Tugend weniger hätten, es besser wäre. Ich meine die allzugroße Vaterlandsliebe, der Patiotismus, führt zum Krieg. (54)

In this manner, Raimund purges Lex of the nemesis which has rendered life at the *landwirtschaftliches Institut* so miserable for him.

The story is—by and large—wholesome, full of local color, and relatively interesting. Yet it was listed only two times. To supply a reason for this relative lack of academic enthusiasm it seems only necessary to consider the following passages from *Lex* and their impression upon a group of American teenagers. First, Raimund to Lex:

"An dir ist ein Mädchen verloren, schön wärest du genug dazu. Alex, ich hab' dich so viel vom Herzen lieb!"
 Er küßte den Jungen; dieser errötete fast und küßte auch. (67)

Then, Lex to Raimund:

"Bei meiner Seele, Raimund, das liebste wäre mir, wenn du ein Sklave wärest!"
"So!"
"Und weißt du warum? damit ich dich kaufen und mit dir machen könnte, was ich wollte." (69)

In an age for which *Werther* and *Käthchen von Heilbronn* were too uncouth, despite the fact that students might be informed that European males exchange kisses, could dialogue such as this fail to excite attention? As the text otherwise meets the requirements laid down by the Committee of Twelve and demostrated by many successful texts of the period, it seems possible that, given the era's desire for wholesome reading, such a conversation could have lessened the prominence of *Lex von Gutenhag*.

A thoroughly delightful story, while absolutely wholesome, is *Leberecht Hühnchen* by Henrich Seidel. Quite prominent in U.S. German texts, Seidel was neglected by professors of literature of the era, having been given cursory mention by only two literary historians consulted. A former civil engineer, Seidel retired from his profession in 1878 in order to devote himself to writing. In the eyes of Kummer, he would seem to have made a mistake: "Seine bekannteste Erzählung war die von Leberecht Hühnchen. Klein und dürftig wie der Inhalt eines Fingerhütchens war Seidels Dichtung" (509). In the same year, Professor Priest termed *Leberecht Hühnchen* a story "of considerable merit" (316).

Arnold Werner-Spanhoofd, who edited the text for Heath, likewise asserted that

> Seidel excels in the production of short stories, many of which, like *Leberecht Hühnchen*, deal with life in and around Berlin. These stories are simple and graceful in style, pervaded by genuine love of nature and many touches of wit and humor. His best creation . . . is Leberecht Hühnchen. (iii–iv)

Werner-Spanhoofd then justifies his choice of *Leberecht Hühnchen* for pedagogical purposes:

> It is confidently believed that a school edition of this famous work will be welcomed by both teacher and student. The graceful, animated style, the wholesome philosophy and the delightful humor cannot fail to stimulate the interest and hold the attention of the reader . . . even the beginner will feel the charm of this masterpiece of modern German literature. (iv)

Judged by the listings, both in anthologies and published separately *Leberecht Hühnchen* was a prominent text, thereby justifying Werner-Spanhoofd's sanguinity.

In demonstrating the work's attraction, a plot summary is of little use, as the plot consists of four visits by a narrator to Leberecht Hühnchen—in his college apartment, some years later at his and his wife's Berlin apartment, at their "new" house in Berlin-Steglitz, and at Christmas in Berlin-Steglitz. It is not what happens, but how Leberecht expresses himself which makes the episodes amusing. The contrast of Leberecht's shabby-genteel efflulgence with the narrator's dry factual statements heightens the reader's amusement.

At the beginning of the third episode, "Weinlese bei Leberecht Hühnchen," the narrator receives an invitation to visit the Hühnchens at their new home in Berlin-Steglitz:

Steglitz, den 28. September 1881.

Villa Hühnchen

Herr und Frau Hühnchen geben sich die Ehre,
Sie zum Sonntag, den 2. Oktober, nachmittags 5 Uhr,
zur Weinlese einzuladen.

Programm

1. Begrüßung der Gäste.
2. Besichtigung der Gartenanlagen und der Menagerie.
3. Eröffnung der Weinlese durch einen Böllerschuß.
4. Weinlese und Nußpflücken.
5. Festzug der Winzer.
6. Feuerwerk.
7. Festessen.
8. Musikalische Abendunterhaltung und Tanz.

The narrator is pleased to accept the invitation, and describes the festivities in part as follows:

Den Garten zeigte mir Hühnchen mit großem Stolz. Die Wasserkunst war fertig und erwies sich als ein kleiner fadendünner Springbrunnen von fast einem Meter Höhe, der sein Gewässer in eine mit bunten Steinchen ausgelegte Schale ergoß.

"Leider ist er ein wenig asthmatisch," sagte Hühnchen, "denn sein Bassin ist nur klein und muß alle halbe Stunde gefüllt werden. Aber es sieht doch opulent und festlich aus."

Am Weinstock waren in diesem Jahr fünfzehn Trauben gewachsen, und der Nußbaum trug einundzwanzig Früchte. . . . Nach Besichtigung der Menagerie, in welcher die Säugetiere durch ein schwarzes Kaninchen, die Vogelwelt durch einen jungen Star ohne Schwanz und die Amphibien durch einen melancholischen Laubfrosch vertreten waren, führte mich Hühnchen in einen schattigen Winkel des kleinen Gärtchens[:]

"Diese Einrichtung bitte ich mit Ehrfurcht zu betrachten," sagte er, "denn hier schlummert die Zukunft. Dies ist nämlich der Komposthaufen. Kraft und Milde, Süßigkeit und Würze liegen hier begraben um in späteren Jahren glanzvoll zur Auferstehung zu gelangen und als köstliches Gemüse oder süße Frucht uns zu nähren und zu laben." (23–26)

All the events listed in the program take place on the scale of the *Weinlese* with fifteen grapes, and are celebrated by Hühnchen in grandiloquent fashion.

What actually happens is indeed "klein und dürftig." However, Hühnchen's mode of operation—reflected here in the *beau monde* invitation, the "opulent und festlich" features of the garden tour, the eloquent apostrophe to the compost heap—is at once humorous and beatific. For Leberecht is truly blessed: as the narrator states at the outset of the Hühnchen stories, Leberecht is one of those rare mortals upon whom "eine gütige Fee das beste Geschenk, die Kunst glücklich zu sein, auf die Wiege gelegt hatte" (1).

The text was well received because it taught German language, life and (at least to a certain extent) literature, and was also amusing. As Professor Bert John Vos stated in a review of William F. Luebke's edition of the text: "*Leberecht Hühnchen* is a text that both for its intrinsic merit and on account of its Berlin milieu deserves to be read more widely" (72).

Less widely read was the prose of poet-dramatist-author Melchior Meyr, whose *Zwei Freier* and *Ludwig und Annemarie*, the latter listed in 1913, the former in 1886 and 1917, were apparently only moderately successful. Only one of the commentators consulted, Heinrich Kurz, included Meyr in his history of German literature. As Kurz seems to suggest, Meyr's inclusion may not be primarily due to artistic excellence:

Es giebt [sic] Dichter, deren Werke uns erfreuen, während ihre eigene Persönlichkeit uns gleichgültig bleibt; Melchoir Meyr gehört zu Denen [sic], welche wir bei Betrachtung ihrer Dichtungen auch persönlich liebgewinnen, weil uns aus denselben nicht bloß ein großes Talent, sondern auch ein edler Charakter entgegentritt. Wir freuen uns über die tief sittliche und auf lebendiger Ueberzeugung beruhende religiöse Haltung seiner Dichtungen. Was er von dem eben so liebenswürdigen als ehrenwerthen Pfarrer in der Erzählung "Ludwig und Annemarie" sagt, läßt sich auch auf ihn selbst anwenden, "Der Glaube an die Grundlehren der evangelischen Kirche war bei ihm ein Trieb und eine Forderung des Herzens, aber sein Christenthum war liebevoller, freundlicher Art." (4:840)

U.S. German students encountered a noble character with a strong religious orientation, whose personality shaped and shone through his works. Though

Meyr has been compared to Auerbach (Krell and Fiedler 267), Zschokke and his moralistic appeal to academe do not stand beyond the confines of comparison. Why Zschokke and Auerbach flourished while Meyr remained lesser known is an inquiry to which the sources consulted remain silent.

One possible detraction, at least in *Ludwig und Annemarie*, is imitation. In defense of Meyr, F. G. G. Schmidt, editor of *Ludwig und Annemarie* for Oxford University Press, American Branch, informed students that

> In the histories of German literature Meyr is generally labeled an imitator or successor of Berthold Auerbach. Against this injustice Meyr protested emphatically in his diary. He did not need, he tells us, the *Schwarzwälder Dorfgeschichten* . . . in order to appreciate the poetry of real rural life or to describe it in his own stories. (v)

Nor is this the end of Schmidt's defense of Meyr against critics who label his works mere copies.

Yet in the same introduction, Schmidt takes pride in pointing out Meyr's penchant for paraphrase:

> The characters of this story are not unlike those in Goethe's *Hermann und Dorothea*. . . . As in Goethe's poem so here is the hero a young villager. In his simple manhood there is nothing of heroic pose. He is brave, strong, faithful . . . exhibiting, in fact, all those genuine qualities typically German. Like Dorothea, Annemarie is a pretty peasant girl, thoroughly Germanic and with many winning touches of feminine grace and charm. . . . The parson of our story, too, owes much to the well-drawn picture of the clergyman in Goethe's poem. (xii)

In this case, imitation is a virtue—the crux of the matter is *whom* one imitates. As Goethe "imitated" Vergil, so Meyr imitated Goethe.

The conclusion one reaches is that if a class is up to Goethe, accepting imitators is unneccessary. Apparently, a number of U.S. *Germanisten* agreed. At best, the "typically German" and "thoroughly Germanic" features of *Ludwig und Annemarie* might have made it an attractive text, especially in the light of the recommendations of the Committee of Twelve. However, for these features as well, recourse might be taken to more original works.

Only slightly better was the reception of novelist Ernst Eckstein in U.S. academe. Among American professors, only Wells deigned to acquaint students with the versatile *Kulturforscher*, dividing his works into three parts: the "classical novels, of which 'Die Claudier' (1881), 'Aphrodite' (1885), 'Nero' (1889), 'Prusias' (1889) may serve as examples" (397); the novels critical of the social order, such as *Jorinda* or *A Cruel Enigma*, "must not be taken seriously, . . . for Eckstein is prominent among the humorists" (405); and lastly, then, the "studies of the comic side of school life, 'The Visit to the Carzer' (1875), 'In Secunda und Prima' (1875), or 'The Boarding-School Girls,' for instance, are already half classic" (409). In the historical division, Wells compares Eckstein to Ebers (397); in the area of the social novel, Eckstein is placed with Heyse and Jensen (405); in the sphere of comic stories, Wells discusses Eckstein between Raabe and Keller (409). For an author neglected by all other U.S. professors and editors consulted, this is celebrity indeed.

Wells favors Eckstein the humorist, but by 1909, Kummer scorned the *alberne Schülerhumoresken* to offer the historical works faint praise. On the one hand, Eckstein was a knowledgeable, cultured author "der sich anschaulicher und lebendiger als Ebers . . . in die alte Kultur hineinzuversetzen wußte." But, for all this, "trotzdem waren seine Charaktere empfindungsstarr, entwicklungslos" (525). As in the cases of Dahn and Ebers, culture, scholarship and a desire to write do not elicit true works of art.

Academic favor decidedly leaned toward Eckstein's *Schülerhumoresken*, and the favorite was *Der Besuch im Carcer* (two editions, three listings). In order to judge between Wells and Kummer regarding the value of Eckstein's story, one must consider at least the basic features of the plot, which follow. The Director of the *Stadtgymnasium* catches one of the most unruly and gifted *Primaner* imitating him before the class and sentences him to three days in the *Carcer*. The Director visits the *Primaner* in the *Carcer* and, because the key is accidently left in the lock, it is only a short time until the Director finds himself a prisoner of the *Primaner*. The Director rages at the Porter, but the latter believes that he hears the rebellious *Primaner* imitating the Director. At length the *Primaner* appears and strikes a bargain. He will release the Director if the *Carcer* sentence is rescinded, and if he will not be expelled. In return, the *Primaner* will say nothing about the Director's stay in the *Carcer* as long as he remains Director. The two agree and all returns to normal—except that the *Primaner* never again imitates the Director (an unexpected benefit). When the Director retires, the story of *Der Besuch im Carcer* comes to light, also to the delight of the former Director, who tells it jovially. And the *Primaner* will never forget the encounter, either.

Here is an amusing little story which could raise a question as to whether Eckstein was an artist of considerable gifts. *Der Besuch im Carcer* seems too simple to be art, but a brief investigation of the dialogue may meliorate the apparently rugged cast of the plot. The following conversation takes place as the Director and *Primaner* Rumpf exchange roles:

> "Sie meinen, Herr Direktor, ich solle mich an Ihre Stelle versetzen . . .?"
> "Ja, Rumpf, das meine ich."
> "Gut, wenn Sie's denn nicht anders haben wollen, so wünsche ich viel Vernügen!"
> Und damit sprang er zur Thüre hinaus, drehte den Schlüssel um und überließ den armen Direktor seinem unverhofften Schicksale.
> "Rumpf! Was fällt Ihnen ein! Ich relegiere Sie noch heute! Wollen Sie augenblicklich öffnen! Augenblicklich, sage ich!"
> "Ach gäbe Ähen härmät zwei Stonden Carcer," antwortete Rumpf mit Würde. "Sä haven sälbst gesagt, äch solle mäch an Ähre Stelle versätzen." (19)

The story was doubless amusing (at least in high school), the language is New High German, the milieu of the *Gymnasium* and its scholars is realistically depicted. Judged by the criteria supplied by the Committee of Twelve, *Der Besuch im Carcer* certainly offered students more of a *Deutschlandbild* than Baumbach's celebrated *Eselsbrunnen*. Though *Der Besuch im Carcer* is at best good entertainment, not great literature, one is nonetheless inclined to agree with Professor Wells's positive estimation of Eckstein's comic stories— though there are presumably few among today's Germanists who would place Eckstein between Raabe and Keller in the pantheon of German authors. Scarcely remembered in modern literary histories, Eckstein is relegated by the Frenzels to fine print, with fellow historical novelists Dahn and Ebers (443). To this extent, Kummer's criticism has outlasted that of Wells.

Another author found for the most part in fine print is Hermann Grimm (son of Wilhelm Grimm), once known for drama and prose fiction, as well as art and literary history (his claims to the meagre fame he still enjoys). His work appeared in four texts listed a total of seven times. As in the case of Eckstein, Grimm's fame is inverse to the number of years which have passed. In Grimm's case, the discussion of the point in time when he was visited by James K. Hosmer sometime before 1875 probably represents the pinnacle of his renown in U.S. *Germanistik*:

> There is not now living a better representative of the writers, so many of whom have been considered as we have traced the course of German literature,— enthusiasts in poetry, history, and criticism, and remarkable in all, the class the illustrious types of which are the greatest men, Lessing, Göthe [sic], Schiller, and Heine,—than Hermann Grimm.

Hosmer goes on to mention by name *Demetrius*, a drama, the *Life of Michelangelo*, the *Venus of Milo* and the lectures on Goethe delivered at the University of Berlin (553–54). Part of the *Life of Michelangelo* and all of the *Venus of Milo* appeared as U.S. textbooks. Two novels, *Das Kind* and *Der Landschaftsmaler*, were also texts.

By 1909 emphasis had shifted entirely to the historical works: "als Kunsthistoriker schrieb er mit feinem Geschmack Das Leben Michelangelos 1860. Als erster Gelehrter von Ruf hielt er . . . 1874 in Berlin an der Universität Vorlesungen über Goethe" (Kummer 534). Priest terms the *Life of Michelangelo* a masterpiece "in biographical art and thorough scholarship" (317). However, the last Hermann Grimm text appeared in the 1890s and recent sources evince no regeneration.

Apparently unknown in the canon of U.S. *Germanistik*, though present in German textbooks, was Emil Frommel, "a noted theologian and writer for the masses" and Chaplain to the Imperial Court. Once again the prototype of such an author, Zschokke, comes to mind; for Frommel "published a large series of popular stories which, on account of their unaffected piety, vigorous language and healthy humor, have become great favorites with the German people" (Bernhardt, *Sonnenseite* vi). These qualitites, as Bernhardt, who included Frommel in his *Auf der Sonnenseite* anthology, was perhaps unconsciously aware, sold textbooks.

However, judging from Frommel's "Das eiserne Kreuz," his stories were not all Sunday school literature, though benign. "Das eiserne Kreuz," which takes place about a year after the Franco-German War, is the story told by a day laborer to a *Gutsherr*, who offers the poor man food and beer in exchange for information as to how such an individual came to win the Iron Cross. This is short to tell: the cross was won through thrift and bravery; in order not to waste bullets, the winner of the decoration continued to shoot at French solidiers until the ammunition was gone—despite the fact that the other German soldiers were following the order to retreat. The episode is recounted with humor which derives to no small extent from the laborer's naïveté.

Yet the story has only begun. The *Gutsherr* now hears how the rustic reasoned and acted as the king's dinner guest after the battle; the tone is reminiscent of *Simplizissimus*:

> Der große Teller kommt an mich zuerst, und ich nehme ihn vor mich und dann auch so ein Assiettchen mit Kartoffeln dazu. Ich denke zwar: "Es ist ein bißchen viel, aber du darfst dich hier nicht lumpen lassen," und esse zu. Die hellen Tropfen sind mir auf der Stirne gestanden, bis die Häppchen alle gegessen waren. Wie ich denn nun fertig war, und der Herr neben mir schenkte immer tapfer ein, daß ich's gut heruntierkriegte, fragt mich seine Majestät der König: "Wie ist's, mein Sohn, möchtest du noch mehr haben?" Ich sage: "Zu Befehl, Majestät, wenn noch ein bißchen da ist." Da lachten alle Herren aus vollem Halse, und auch Seine Majestät hielt sich die Seiten. Ich wußte nicht warum. (Bernhardt, *Sonnenseite* 38–39)

To the relief of the uncomfortable eater of the entire platter of roast veal, the king decides upon another course—the Iron Cross is presented (39).

The tale is interesting and entertainingly written, though plotless in large part in the conventional sense. As in the case of *Leberecht Hühnchen*, how the main character thinks and talks is more important than what happens. In this case, however, there is considerable employment of *Umgangssprache* and even dialect, which contrasts greatly with Leberecht's baroque effusions. In "Das eiserne Kreuz," then, such relative textbook rarities as *Kerl*, *kriegen*, and *ist . . . gestanden*—scarcely encountered in texts in the course of this study through the era of Realism—are very much in evidence.

For Frommel's neglect by German professors, if this story is admissible as evidence, three reasons come to mind. Firstly, the story could be construed as having class prejudice at its core—the court laughs at a man too simple to throw away bullets, then gives him the Iron Cross. On the other hand, the story is told with great good humor by the supposed victim, who feels no more slighted as he speaks than does Huckleberry Finn when he speaks of his efforts to live at the Widow Douglass's. Secondly, it is not beyond question that many educators found *kriegen* or *Kerl* undesirable in classroom reading; yet, once again, American novels read by some students were scarcely free of colloquialism and dialect.

Thirdly, and most importantly, the question of *Deutschlandbild* was doubless a factor, particularly after the turn of the century. Should U.S. German students be handed a chrestomathy glorifying the German war effort, the Kaiser and his retinue, and the Iron Cross? This would, of course, hinge upon individual teachers' predilections; Bernhardt must have found the militaristic story acceptable, as did numerous others, since the anthology is listed five times from 1898 to 1908. Frommel, as a pastor, doubtless meant only to present an interesting story; but in blandness, as in popularity in the U.S. texbook trade, he was no match for his *Vorläufer*, Zschokke.

A more unfortunate case is that presented by Wilhelm Meyer-Förster, whose *Karl Heinrich* was listed in 1904 and 1905 (a possible overlap of copyright date and printing date). Only Kummer includes Meyer-Förster in his literary history:

> Wilhelm Meyer versuchte es zuerst mit einer studentischen Satire (Die Saxo-Saxonen 1885), dann mit mancherlei ernsten und heiteren Dramen (Unsichtbare Ketten 1890, Kriemhild 1891, Der Vielgeprüfte 1898) sowie mit Romanen (Derby 1898, Karl Heinrich 1900), doch alles vergeblich. Da brachte ihm die Dramatisierung des letztgenannten Studentenromans, der teils an Benedix, teils an Nataly von Eschstruth erinnert, einen der größten theatralischen Erfolge. Alles Spätere ist unbedeutend. (706)

That the peak of Meyer-Förster's artistic creativity should result in a comparison to Benedix (*Der Prozeß*) and Eschstruth ("Ihr Ideal") says little from the point of view today. In his own time, Meyer-Förster—who also had an unhappy personal life—had sufficient inducement to dejection.

Unrecognized but in the academic foreground was Richard von Volkmann, who as Richard Leander presented U.S. *Germanistik* with one of its most popular texts (recommended by the Committee of Twelve), *Träumereien an französischen Kaminen: Märchen*. In the preface of one of the editors, Professor William Henry van der Smissen,

> It is hardly necessary to justify the publication of a book written in good easy German prose; there is a great need of many such books, and the one now offered to the schools will speak for itself. (n. pag.)

This is a familiar justification for textbook editions of German literature—if the term may be used loosely. It remains to be seen whether or not Leander's stories should have substituted for *Germelshausen*, *L'Arrabbiata* or *Geschichten aus der Tonne*—all suggested by the Committee for the elementary level. According to catalog listings, the *Träumereien* surpassed *Geschichten aus der*

Tonne, equalled *Germelshausen,* and were slightly bested by *L'Arrabbiata.* Volkmann was recognized in his own time by teachers and students, if not by literary historians.

The fact that Volkmann was slighted by literary historians in his own time and was forgotten thereafter appears to stem from two causes: his shorter *Märchen* are puerile, his longer ones imitations. For example, a nearsighted man finds a baby sparrow in his garden, mistakes it for a nightingale and takes it home. The man and his wife argue violently about the origin of the new pet for two weeks—then the wife opens the cage and the bird escapes. Her husband rages, she feels guilty, recaptures the sparrow and calls it a nightingale. Whereupon her husband declares that he has never seen her so beautiful; he also calls the bird a sparrow. Leander thereupon delivers the moral:

> Die Moral von der Geschichte aber ist: wenn Jemand einen Spatz gefangen hat und denkt, es sei eine Nachtigall—sag's ihm bei Leibe nicht; denn er nimmt's sonst übel, und später wird er's gewiß von selbst merken. (10)

A reading of "Der kleine Vogel" offers an insight into Leander's obscurity.

Far more impressive in its way is "Vom unsichtbaren Königreich," the story of a dreamer—always *in sich gekehrt*—who listens to Nature, marries the Princess of Dreams, and inherits a dream kingdom. The problem is that nearly everything which happens has already happened in someone else's work. The dream kingdom, perceived only by the couple who inhabit it, is all too reminiscent of portions of Tieck's *Der blonde Ekbert*. The singing river, mermaids and magical forest seem to be brought forth directly from Fouqué's *Undine*—the forest is also most certainly a reflection of *Waldeinsamkeit*. Then there is the Garden of Dreams, which contains richly scented flowers which glow in the dark, calling the garden of Novalis's blue flower to mind. A Tannhäuser-style grotto is found not far from several lakes upon which float Spenserian wandering islands. The Princess of Dreams makes her first appearance on Jacob's *scala coeli*—now a gold and silver swing—and appears seven times before the dreamer sets out in search of her.

Although more might be placed in evidence, it should be clear that "Vom unsichtbaren Königreich" is at once delightful and trite. While Leander's works scarcely belong in a category with works by Storm or Heyse or even Gerstäcker—though they were so categorized—the mere richness of representation, even if it is borrowed, renders this tale and others in the *Träumereien* at least mildly intriguing.

If Leander's *Märchen* occasionally display a pronounced juvenile cast, Viktor Blüthgen openly declared his *Das Peterle von Nürnberg* a *Jugenderzählung*. At that same time, the text may have been aimed at college as well as high school classes—for example, Macmillan included it in the

158 Realism—Naturalism—The Early Twentieth Century

same series as Hillern's *Höher als die Kirche* and Wildenbruch's *Das edle Blut*. All three works deal with young people, yet none of them is nursery fare.

Josephine Doniat's reasons for editing *Das Peterle von Nürnberg* echo familiar motifs:

> A new edition of this charming tale of old Nürnberg for the use of students of elementary German hardly requires apology. Both the editor and the illustrator have sought to conjure up a vision of the quaint charm of the old town and of the life so remote from the experience of . . . American youth. (vii)

Thus the justification for placing a third edition of *Peterle*, which takes place in the late Middle Ages, before the eyes of academe is the *Deutschlandbild*; and in 1918, it can well be imagined, there was no time to avoid like the present.

About Blüthgen's art, and *Peterle von Nürnberg* in particular, the student was told that

> His *Jugenderzählungen* . . . strive in a variety of settings to lead the youthful imagination outside of the bounds of personal experience by unrolling in simple words and through the fictitious adventures of sympathetic heroes, a background of historic importance and artistic suggestion. Thus in the *Peterle*, by many intimate touches and without ever becoming pedantic through transparent efforts to instruct, he leads his readers into an appreciation of the life and viewpoint of the artisan, the artist, the churchman of the Middle Ages. (xiv)

Most importantly, however, as in so many other cases, Blüthgen's

> natural love for youth gives him an understanding of what is calculated to attract and hold his readers. His humor is never satiric, his realism never harsh, and the world which he recreates on his pages becomes part and parcel of the reader's inner experience. (xvii)

Stresses fall on humor which is never satiric, realism which is never harsh, and teaching without seeming to teach.

Editor Doniat notwithstanding, *Peterle* is a tale of considerable harshness. The boy, as he grows to a young manhood, is orphaned, adopted by a shoemaker who allows his brutal son to persecute Peterle, is forced to drop out of school to work for his adoptive father's boarders and to take up residence in the rat-infested attic, is wounded as one of the boarders uses him for target practice, and is persecuted for a heinous act he did not commit. This is almost an outline of the plot; the editor attempts to soften the images of Blüthgen and *Peterle* to their discredit, for without these dissonances the text as she describes it would be pedagogical pablum. It was more than that.

In texts by women authors, on the contrary, pablum was occasionally peddled as if piquant. One certain exception to such a procedure was Marie von Ebner-Eschenbach, three of whose works were listed in commercial and scholarly catalogs four times from 1896 to 1908. Described by Bernhardt only as an interesting storyteller (71), she received much more attention in the early twentieth century:

> Ebner-Eschenbach (b. 1830), a high-minded noblewoman . . . knows above all things how to tell a good story, and enjoys the telling of it; but she has also psychologic insight and a polished precision of style . . . Typical alike of her ethics and her art are "The Village and Castle Stories" (1886) and "The Child of the Parish" (1887). What this lady has done for the aristocratic life of Austria has been done for the mercantile aristocracy of Berlin by Theodor Fontane. (Wells 407)

Perhaps most striking as regards textbooks are the careful juxtaposition of ethics and art, and the comparison of Ebner-Eschenbach to Fontane. Fontane's near-naturalism and the relatively late arrival of his work in U.S. German textbooks vaguely parallel the case of Ebner-Eschenbach. Both had a relatively low number of listings from today's viewpoint: neither offered moral lectures for classroom consideration.

Professor Priest notes the unique combination of disparate elements in Ebner-Eschenbach's art, terming the author "a singular combination of feminine kindliness and masculine vigor" who "has keen powers of observation, genuine humor, and a fine sense of artistic proportion" (315). And Kummer notes that, particularly in the shorter works, "glücklicher, sonniger Humor wechselt mit Zügen tiefsten Ernstes" (491). Stroebe and Whitney point out not only the uniting of realism and morality, earnestness and humor, they further state that Ebner-Eschenbach "beschreibt mit dichterisch warmem Empfinden den österreichischen Adel und die Armen und Unbedeutenden in ihrem Lande" (237–38).

In consideration of the polarities found in Ebner-Eschenbach's art, one might think first of the stories *Die Freiherren von Gemperlein* and *Krambambuli*. Both stories unite humorous and serious features; the nobility is dealt with in one story, common people and worse supply the focus of the other; the feminine and masculine principles, kindliness and vigor, are not absent. The two stories appeared together in 1898 and 1904 in a text edited by Alexander R. Hohlfeld.

Hohlfeld's appraisal of the art of Ebner-Eschenbach offers few surprises— the familiar dualities are apparent or implied. The author

> is a realist—a determined and fearless realist. . . . Her eye is just as keen in detecting the sunshine and roses of human existence as in seeking its shadows and thorns, and even her strongest works combine with unflinching devotion to the truth the delicate instinct of a true and noble woman. Womanliness thus adds an irresistable charm to the realism of her works, without detracting from their force and originality. (vii–viii)

In the world of textbooks, however, an imbalance in favor of womanliness, sunshine and roses over realism, shadows and thorns would—judging from the most popular texts—have brought Ebner-Eschenbach greater success in academe. Improbable stories of uncouth characters, as well as stories pervaded by low life and occurring occasionally in bars, could not hope to compete with such gentility as that of Wilhelmine von Hillern.

Hillern, whose *Höher als die Kirche* was one of the era's most popular texts (twenty-six listings, nine editions from the 1870s to 1917), was described by Bernhardt as belonging "zu der Gruppe der den Familienroman kultivierenden Schriftstellerinnen." He took care to inform students that "sehr beliebt ist ihre Novelette 'Höher als die Kirche' " (70). Benjamin Wells, on the contrary, presented a rather radical image of Hillern's "satirizing blue-stockings and all their ways in 'The Physician of the Soul.' . . . The best known of her stories is 'The Geyer-Wally' " (372). No mention of *Höher als die Kirche* is made. If *The Geyer-Wally* is Hillern's best production, why did no editor place it in the schools? It would seem that works by Hillern other than *Höher als die Kirche* were very probably considered unsuitable as texts.

Proof thereof is offered by Kummer, who presents a negative assessment indeed:

> Nach ihrer Vermählung Schriftstellerin, wurde [Hillern] immer mehr zu einer romantischen Schwärmerin, ging in Oberammergau zu einer Art von verliebtläppischem Katholizismus über, Verfasserin der Romane: Geier-Wally 1875 (zum Schrecken aller gesund Empfindenden auch dramatisiert), Am Kreuz 1890 (ein brecherisch süßlicher Oberammergauer Passionsroman). (530)

Once again, the reader is not acquainted with *Höher als die Kirche*.

As all other sources consulted ignore Hillern, and because critical opinions obtained range from at least slight regard to absolute disregard, an examination of the text is desirable. Frederick W. J. Heuser, in his introduction to *Höher als die Kirche*, offered his own evaluation of Hillern and her work:

> Frau von Hillern has written in all some twelve novels, several novelettes and three comedies. Her work has been popular, but it does not rank as great literature. Still it is characterized by great power of visualization and fine dramatic instinct which, however, occasionally degenerates into the purely theatrical, while sentiment sometimes becomes mere sentimentality, and her love for dramatic suspense leads her to what is psychologically untrue. What has endeared her to many is her intensely German feeling and a deep religiosity.
>
> The little story 'Höher als die Kirche' has some of the defects mentioned above, but it is charmingly told and with rare skill combines fact and fiction. It appeared first in the weekly *Bazar* in 1871 and in book-form in 1877. In 1896 it reached its fourth edition. (7)

The editor of the text himself makes little of Hillern's artistry, citing an extremely vague—albeit oft bespoken—"German feeling" and the religiosity reviled by Kummer as the works' main attractions.

Regarding the defects indicated by the editor, theatricality, sentimentality and inanity, the plot of *Höher als die Kirche* does indeed contain such features. Under theatrical might be subsumed the meeting of the children Hans Liefrink and Maili Ruppacher—later star-crossed lovers—and Kaiser Maximilian I and his *Geheimschreiber* Marx Treytz-Sauerwein. The children are planting a rose bush fraught with great significance; the plant is later called the *Kaiserbaum* in honor of the imperial presence. The emperor learns of Hans' desire to be an artist, whereupon he awards the boy an elaborate carving knife, a sum of money, and an entrée to the studio of Dürer: "Geh nach Nürnberg zum Dürer; bring ihm einen Gruß von mir und sag ihm, wie sein Kaiser ihm einst die Leiter gehalten, so solle er nun dir die Leiter halten, damit du recht hoch hinaufsteigen könntest" (21). Such moments may be better described as theatrics than as fiction which reflects real life.

Sentimentality reigns over the *Kaiserbaum* as it functions as Hans and Maili's trysting place. Distressing is the fact that Maili's father, Ratsherr Ruppacher, considers artists the equals of performing gypsies. Although he has forbidden Maili to see Hans—indeed, threatened her with *Fluch und Verstoßung*—the young couple continue to meet furtively until Hans departs for Nürnberg to study with Dürer. As Maili pines, she fits the *Kaiserbaum* into the niche in the wall it occupies. Might this be a sample of the "more or less mawkish love tales" which, according to the Committee of Twelve, caused teachers to "sigh for vigorous stories of adventure with the grand passion left out or made little of" (Report 63)? If so, opposing the Committee is the fact that sentimentality seems to have sold textbooks.

In any case, Hans returns home a master carver to find the lovelorn Maili *todesmüde* and writing her will. Ratsherr Ruppacher remains adamantly opposed to Hans as a son-in-law. After much bitterness aroused by Ruppacher, Hans, upon the recommendation of Dürer, is employed by the *Gemeinderat* to carve an altar for the city, and asks forthwith for Maili's hand. Ruppacher, beside himself with rage, strikes what he considers an impossible wager: "*Schnitz' mir einen Altar, der höher ist als die Kirche, in der er steht—dann sollst du meine Tochter haben—eher nicht, so wahr Gott mir helfe*" (48). All this is plausible, given real individuals who would correspond to Hillern's characters.

At least somewhat improbable is the solution to Hans and Maili's difficulties. Hans goes to the *Kaiserbaum* to think. As he sits, he is struck from behind:

> Das Rosenbäumchen hatte sich endlich durch die eigene Kraft von der Rückwand der Nische fortgerissen, in die Maili es hingebunden, und war im Emporschellen an Hans angeprallt. Da stand es nun kerzengerade, weit über die Wölbung hinausragend. (51)

And so Hans has his answer: he carves an altar which, like the rosebush, is taller than the space it occupies. The flower which began the action provides the denouement. Although the *Kaiserbaum* motif which pervades the book is not unpleasing, Hillern's critics are justified in judging her work rather contrived.

However, let there be no forgetting that *Höher als die Kirche* was one of the era's most popular texts. German culture is much in evidence, and—*Ratsherr* Ruppacher excepted—kindliness and clean living abound. The book presents nothing if not a pleasant, if *kitschig, Deutschlandbild.* For students who were not ready for Storm or Heyse, Hillern was a better choice than Baumbach or Wichert.

A more jejune text was *Fritz auf Ferien* by Hans Arnold (Babette von Bülow). Though none of the literary histories consulted included Arnold, the student was assured by editor Arnold Werner-Spanhoofd that

> The name of the author, Babette von Bülow (Hans Arnold), figures prominently in German magazines; and many a volume of his short stories has been received with unstinted praise and admiration by both the critic and the general reader. (iii)

Nevertheless, judging from the absolute lack of mention in literary histories, Arnold's work was at best *Unterhaltungsliteratur*. Further, if one may infer from listed titles the sort of writing the author frequently indulged in, the predominant genre was the juvenile.

Fritz auf Ferien is a story of the *Pollyanna* variety. Like Pollyanna, Fritz changes the lives of those about him. *Amstrat* Wilhelm Tormann comes to love Fritz in spite of himself; his barren bachelor's life is enriched. Gottlieb, the man-servant, and Hanne, the cook, are capitvated by Fritz. Only Mine, the housekeeper, treats Fritz coldly. In so doing, she loses Gottlieb to Hanne, and possibly jeopardizes her further employment in the home of *Amtsrat* Tormann.

A sample of the text reveals the level of the humor and the style of *Fritz auf Ferien*:

> "Ich habe sie gemolken, Herr Amtsrat, ich habe die große Kuh gemolken," sagte er [Fritz] glückselig, "sie hat mir zweimal mit dem Schwanz ins Auge geschlagen, hier, das ist ein reizendes Tier."
> Gottlieb platzte hinter der vorgehaltenen Hand heraus und entfernte sich erschrocken, als er den strengen Blick seines Herrn auf sich gerichtet fand.
> "Nun setz' dich, mein Sohn, und frühstücke!" sagte der Amtsmann freundlich, aber ernst. (16–17)

If the term inane seems harsh when applied to Hillern, it seems less so when used to describe the work of Arnold; yet *Höher als die Kirche* and *Fritz auf Ferien* were intended for the same groups of students, as Werner-Spanhoofd recommended *Fritz* for "schools and colleges" (Arnold iii).

Werner-Spanhoofd justified his choice of *Fritz* first by not justifying it:

"Fritz auf Ferien" needs no introduction. We will simply leave it to the teacher to judge for himself, whether this charming sketch of boyhood, characteristically German, is worthy of a place in the classroom. (iii)

The usual conundrum of Germanness is Werner-Spanhoofd's first defense of his textbook; another advantage touted is that the story will stimulate curiosity while teaching colloquial German in an "exquisite style." Most importantly, perhaps, "the story is simple and graceful in form with wholesome and delightful humor" (iii). The story is undoubtedly simple and wholesome. The text was rather popular (four editions, seven listings from 1896 to 1915), as were several of the six other Arnold texts listed.

In contrast to Arnold, Luise von François earned professorial praise, but listed only one text, the novella *Phosphorus Hollunder*, in 1887. Kummer mentions *Phosphorus Hollunder* in passing, but devotes the greater part of his appreciation, as did Bernhardt (71), to the novel *Die letzte Reckenburgerin*. In a brief characterization of François, Kummer informed the student that she

> wies . . die starke selbstbewußte Würde einer edlen Frauennatur auf. Sie war eine durch Einfachheit und Gesundheit des Charakters auserlesene Erscheinung; ihr Wesen war weiblich edel und ohne alle Sentimentalität. (506)

Could the lack of sentimentality—a quality quite evident in *Höher als die Kirche* and *Fritz auf Ferien*, to name two successful, sentimental texts—have stunted the popularity of works such as *Phosphorus Holunder*? In the words of the Committee of Twelve, "we must remember that the Germans are more sentimental people than the Americans, and that one of the objects for which we study German in school is to learn what the Germans are like" (Report 63). If, then, the Germans are more sentimental than Americans, sentimental stories should bring across "German life" better than unsentimental ones. The former two works were recommended by the Committee; *Phosphorus Hollunder* was not recommended.

Frieda Schanz (Soyaux), author of *"Der Assistent" and Other Stories* and *Die Alte*, like François, was not entirely ignored by Germanists consulted. For Bernhardt declared that

> zu den interessantesten Erzählerinnen der neusten Zeit [gehört] neben Luise von *François*, der Verfasserin des kulturhistorischen Romans "Die letzte Reckenburgerin" unter manchen andern noch Frida *Schanz*. (71)

However, Schanz's writings apparently interested relatively few teachers. Each of the two texts above mentioned was listed only one time.

Sentimental, successful, and purveyed by editor Bernhardt alone both in his literary history and as editor for Heath, American Book, and Schoenhof, was Helene Stökl, whose *Unter dem Christbaum* was recommended by the

Committee of Twelve. Bernhardt promoted Stökl's writings as follows in 1892:

> An Louisa Alcotts "Little Women" erinnern uns die gefühlvollen Erzählungen der Wienerin Helene *Stökl*, deren Namen schon jetzt weit über die Grenzen ihres Heimatlandes hinaus bekannt ist; ein liebevoller, verständnisiniger und überraschend feiner Blick für das Seelenleben der Kinderwelt ist das charakteristische Merkmal ihrer Novelletten. (71)

The comparison to Alcott causes the reader to recall what made many textbooks popular. In the words of *Encyclopaedia Britannica*, "Alcott's most enduring place is the result of the cheeriness and wholesomeness of her pictures of boy and girl life" (1:546). Thus the familiar pattern in the selection of readings manifests itself again. It seems scarcely necessary to call attention to *liebevoll* and "wholesome," or to reflect upon the fact that qualities such as these frequently caused inferior texts to thrive. Twenty-eight listings for texts or anthologies authored all or in part by Stökl, as well as the fact that her work was disregarded by all but one of the sources consulted, the literary history written by her sole U.S. editor, serve to suggest the presence of a familiar precedent.

Another author popular in German textbooks of the era under investigation who is unknown today was Ernst Werner (Elisabeth Bürstenbinder). Once again, only Bernhardt, who edited Werner's "Der Wilddieb" for the *Deutsche Novelletten-Bibliothek*, noted the author's existence:

> Eine nahe Geistesverwandte von E. Marlitt [who wrote for the *Gartenlaube*] ist die unter dem Pseudonym "E. Werner" schreibende Novellistin Elisabeth Bürstenbinder . . . deren Romane . . . in den siebziger Jahren erschienen und sehr populär waren. (70)

Werner's tenuous relationship to the *Gartenlaube* may offer at least at second hand an idea of what her writing is like. In the words of Benjamin Wells,

> The general effect of . . . prevailing political discouragement was to foster a kindly fiction that, finding it vain to preach, was content to strive to entertain, unless perhaps it aspired to cultivate. These were the palmy days of the "Gartenlaube." (372)

Thus Werner, too, may be said to have been a producer of inferior literature which had the good grace neither to offend nor to suggest unseemly conduct.

Interesting is the opposition of the two editors of Werner's work as German texts. In 1892, Bernhardt at least modestly champions the author; but Marian Whitney, who edited Werner's *Heimatklang* in 1903, made no mention of her in her literary history of 1912 (co-authored with Lilian Stroebe). Werner's short-lived reception among U.S. German students must already have declined.

Like the works of Stökl and Werner, the stories of Ottilie von Wildermuth were promoted in the U.S. solely by the indefatigable Bernhardt—this time, so far as can be ascertained, without self-interest. As he stated: "Ottilie Wildermuths (1817–1877) kunstlos erzählte Lebenserinnerungen ('Bilder und Geschichten aus Schwaben') sind von dauerndem Werte" (71). And in Europe, Kummer concurred that Wildermuth

> war eine sympathische und liebliche Erscheinug. Sie schilderte eine fast schon versunkene Welt: das Kleinleben der Honoratioren in den schwäbischen Landstädtchen, das vormärzliche Beamtentum voll Würde und Behaglichkeit, die friedlich stille Gemütlichkeit des Pfarrhauses. Sie entwickelte dabei höchst gesunde Lebensanschauugen, war heiter, keusch und humorvoll. (435)

The combination of qualities above should have made Wildermuth a major figure in U.S. German classes—it has proved itself repeatedly to be a highly desirable mixture. Yet only one text, *Der Einsiedler im Walde*, was listed three consecutive years beginning in 1891.

Only one edition of *Aus meinem Königreich* by Carmen Sylva (Queen Elizabeth of Rumania) was listed: the editor thereof was also the only U.S. literary historian consulted to mention Carmen Sylva and her work. The editor was Bernhardt. He described the Queen as an interesting storyteller and lyric poet (71), but offered the student no more information.

However, Kummer treats Carmen Sylva in more detail:

> Eine edle, reich begabte Frau, die stets das Höchste anstrebte, deren Vollbringen aber dem Wollen nicht entsprach, schrieb Lieder, Novellen, Märchen, Romane, Dramen . . . teils allein, teils gleichsam mit ihrer Hofdame . . . jedes Buch sollte schnell fertig sein; trotz schöner Einzelheiten waren die Bücher fast immer verfehlt, fantastisch und kritiklos. (530)

The image is that of dilettantism coupled with outbursts of violent mental excitement, and it seems that U.S. German teachers made a proper choice. That there were better things for students to read was proved by the reception of *Aus meinem Königreich*.

Perhaps least satisfying, however, were three stories by Nataly von Eschstruth, "Eine Plauderstunde auf der 'Seehalde,' " "Ihr Ideal," and "Hundert Schimmel." The editor of the stories is again Professor Bernhardt. Yet no mention is made of Eschstruth in any U.S. literary history consulted—perhaps because Bernhardt had not become sufficiently familiar with Eschstruth in 1892, when his *Geschichte der deutschen Literatur* appeared.

Surely the editor did his best to atone for his sin of omission in the preface to *Auf der Sonnenseite*, in which two of the Eschstruth stories appeared:

> At the Summer Festival of the German Authors' Association, held in . . . 1895, a ballot for the most popular writer of the day resulted in a first choice for NATALY VON ESCHSTRUTH; Ernst von Wildenbruch and Paul Heyse taking

the second and third places, respectively, in the hearts of their countrymen. . . . Although now the mother of two children . . . and though personally superintending every detail of her household, she still finds time to present, year after year, the untold number of her admirers with a new product of her prolific pen. (vi–vii)

Amazing is the fact that the great or near-great authors were bested by Eschstruth—until the word popular makes itself evident.

This circumstance is attested to by Kummer, who termed such writing—referring specifically to Eschstruth—

> tiefster Stand der weiblichen Erzählungsliteratur; unwürdige Auffassung, als sei das Leben eines jungen Mädchens von heute nur ein Tanz um den Traualtar, nichtige Darstellung von Toiletten und Äußerlichkeiten, schreiende Unwahrheit des Weltbildes. (530)

The literati of Germany, then, could scarcely have raised Eschstruth to the glory described by Bernhardt. Nor were American professors carried away, though eight listings of the anthologies containing the three stories show that this country was less discriminating in the matter of German textbooks than might be desired. On the other hand, it is to the credit of those professors whose literary histories excluded Eschstruth, Arnold, Stökl, Werner, and Carmen Sylva (among others) that the number of students apparently taught to esteem their writing was not greater than it was.

Naturalism—The Early Twentieth Century

In turning to Naturalism and beyond, one must not overlook at the outset a figure whose works date from both the realistic and naturalistic periods: Ernst von Wildenbruch. In 1892 Wildenbruch was characterized for U.S. students as

> ein höchst talentvoller und vielseitiger Litterat, welcher mit gleichem Geschick die Gebiete der Epik, Lyrik, Novellistik und Dramatik behandelt. Seine Lieder und Balladen zeichnen sich durch einen edlen, wahrhaft vaterländischen Sinn aus, während seine Novellen . . . und Dramen . . . mit Bezug auf Diktion, Komposition, Dialog und Charakterzeichnung zu den Kunstwerken ersten Ranges zählen. (Bernhardt 67)

However, in the era of Naturalism, Wildenbruch, who based his dramatic technique upon that of Schiller, found himself an epigone, although he was much in fashion among the leaders of the Second Reich as well as in U.S. German programs.

As it became apparent that Wildenbruch's plays could not rival those of Naturalism, Wells instructed scholars of 1901 that between 1888 and 1893

Wildenbruch was the most prominent figure in German drama, and his plays remain still, in historical realism, the best since Schiller. With the rise of Sudermann, Wildenbruch returned to fiction. (416)

However, not only were Wildenbruch's plays the prey of changing literary tastes, his novellas likewise received faint praise from some quarters:

> Wildenbruch is often theatrical rather than dramatic, and his plays are weak in characterization [contra Bernhardt]. Wildenbruch's stories, *Das edle Blut* (1893) and others are told with warm feeling, but they are unimportant as compared with his dramas. (Priest 311)

Two dramas, *Die Rabensteinerin* and *Harold* were U.S. German textbooks; but they were greatly outnumbered by texts of Wildenbruch's novellas—above all by *Das edle Blut*.

Kummer criticizes the dramas for four pages before granting the novellas a few lines of praise:

> Wohl aber verdienen seine Gedichte und die kleineren Novellen mit ihrer Psychologie, besonders ihrer Kenntnis der Knabenseele, Hervorhebung. Wildenbruch steht als Novellist, was die Psychologie und die schlichte Darstellung des Lebens betrifft, weit über Wildenbruch dem Dramatiker . . . Der Dichter gibt in den kleinen Novelen mehr Eigenes als in manchen seiner rauschendsten Dramen. (496)

With the *Kenntnis der Knabenseele*, *Das edle Blut* is surely emphasized.

Only the drama is indifferently dealt with by Thomas (493), Stroebe and Whitney (216), but the Wildenbruch known to the greatest number of U.S. German students was almost certainly the author of *Das edle Blut*. Based upon comments by literary historians and the number of editions (8) and listings (18), it may be concluded that *Das edle Blut* was considered Wildenbruch's masterpiece among the novellas.

The story itself is quite simple: in a *Weinstube*, the narrator chances to meet an elderly colonel who reminisces, in a tale revolving around heredity, upon his acquaintance with two brothers, one of whom had *das edle Blut*. One brother is stocky, with heavy arms and legs, the other slim and flexible as a willow branch—and this is not by chance. The narrator and the colonel watch a similar youth defending his fat brother against a tall, slender, shifty boy in the courtyard which the *Weinstube* faces; speaking of the supple, handsome brother the colonel discusses the naturalistic theory at the heart of the story:

> Aus solchen Jungen, da kommt die Natur heraus—alles wie's wirklich ist—nachher, wenn das älter wird, sieht sich das alles gleich—da kann man Studien machen—an solchen Jungen . . . da kommt die Natur 'raus, spritzt ordentlich 'raus—armsdick. Da sieht man ins Blut hinein. Ist aber schade—das edle Blut geht leicht verloren—leichter als das andere. . . . Solche Jungen—da kommt eben die Natur noch 'raus; das ist halb wie bei den Tieren. (Wildenbruch 10, 12, 16)

Blood—"noble" blood—is the axis of the action; those with "noble" blood look alike and, judging from the examples cited above, act alike—the colonel invites studies on the subject. "Noble" blood is not so hardy as common blood; it manifests itself in humans somewhat as it does in "blooded" horses. Other words which tie in here are *Rassegeschöpf*, referring to a lad with noble blood, and the colonel's wish to free himself of the memory of one whom he hates "wie ein Unkraut, das man in den Ofen schmeißt" (8, 41). In the story noble blood is truly pitted against "*Unkraut.*" Defending his heavy, slow brother against a tall, slender troublemaker, the boy with noble blood falls in convulsions and dies of *Nervenfieber*.

The bias of *Das edle Blut* is unlikely to escape a contemporary reader anywhere—indeed it is only with difficulty that the reader avoids making anachronistic parallels to the Third Reich. But one editor of the text, Friedrich G. G. Schmidt, demonstrated the feelings of persons who had not (yet) lived through the Nazi hegemony toward a short story centered on a genetic (and physiognomic) *idée fixe*:

> *Das edle Blut* has already reached its one hundred and ninth thousand in 1910. It is considered one of the best of Wildenbruch's short stories. The descriptions bear witness to the author's power of observation and of realistic reproduction. Each character in the story is clearly and carefully drawn, true to life in every detail. We cannot help admiring his simple, easy style, his keen psychological analyses of boyhood and his wonderful delineation of human nature. (Wildenbruch iv)

It is rather alarming to think of the colonel as true to life, of the concept of "noble" blood as a delineation of human nature, and of keen psychological analyses constituted in large part of descriptions of fist fights and other adolescent violence and cruelty. Yet for whatever reason, *Das edle Blut* was one of the time's most successful texts.

Far more popular without the ivied walls—and significantly less popular within—were the works of Hermann Sudermann:

> Wildenbruch, whose talent in higher dramatic art at first looked promising, has sunk to a court poet. As a novelist he has given some first-rate pictures of small size, but he is certainly surpassed by Sudermann's powerful novels, "*Frau Sorge*," "*Der Katzensteg*," "*Die Geschwister.*" (Geffcken 670–71)

Although less is said by this commentator about Sudermann's dramas, *Honor* receives faint praise (Geffcken 670).

However, like Wildenbruch, Sudermann was known primarily as a dramatist. Thus Benjamin Wells taught students that Sudermann

> was the first to command a place for uncompromising naturalism on the German stage by his "Honor" (1890) and "Sodom's End" (1891). These achieved sensational success. . . . Sudermann, however, was the first to win more than

sensational recognition for this new dramatic art. This he did by "Home" (1893).
... This, like the two preceding dramas, deals earnestly yet serenely with the soul-destroying or soul-numbing effect of social conventions, whether of honor or duty. (417–18)

Because Sudermann's later dramas revolved around moral rather than social problems, and because concessions were made to the public therein, Wells prefers the three plays mentioned above (417–18). An edition of *Heimat* was listed only in 1909. *Johannes* and *Teja*, dramas of moral problems, were both listed three times—1901–1907 and 1905–1909, respectively.

Priest echoed Wells's teachings eight years later:

> *Die Ehre* (1890), a masterly comparison of the ideas of "honor" held by the family of a factory owner and that of one of his employees . . . was followed by *Sodoms Ende* (1891), a play of better construction. . . .The fame of *Die Ehre* and *Sodoms Ende* has, however, been limited to Germany, whereas *Heimat* (1893) has been translated into many languages, and . . . has furnished one of the leading roles of the world's most famous actresses. (326)

The latter plays are considered less effective. Taken as a whole, Sudermann's dramas are said to lack the psychological depth and "truth" of great art (Priest 326). Nonetheless, professorial approval was granted *Heimat* and the earlier works over *Teja* and *Johannes*.

Problematically, Calvin Thomas termed Sudermann "a better playwright than Hauptmann, according to all the old standards, but not so good a poet." Citing only *Honor* in a description of the dramatist's technique—"back and forth between mansion and hovel"—Thomas concludes that

> he has now and then sacrificed the truth to his well-calculated stage effects. Nevertheless . . . his best work . . . seems likely to endure as presenting a fairly just picture of German social conditions at the close of the nineteenth century. (409–10)

Again, the social dramas take precedence over the later plays.

More impartiality is shown by Kummer, inasmuch as he finds fault with all the Sudermann plays he discusses. Least discussed is his favorite, *Heimat*, while *Ehre* receives an unusual amount of disapprobation, as it deals in "Gegensatzfiguren aus der Schablonenkomödie" and a "Raisonneur aus der französischen Komödie." Most informatively, the later moral plays are discussed; for example, *Johannes*

> enthielt einen Anlauf zu einem aus der Bibel entnommenen psychologischen Trauerspiel, das vielverheißend war; es schloß sich aber, gleichsam wie durch ein Verhängnis, das dem Modedichter anhaftet, ein Salondrama von der getäuschten Liebe der Salome daran, das gar keinen innern Zusammenhang mit dem seelischen Erlebnis des Täufers hatte, der plötzlich in den Worten des Galiläers die Sonne der Wahrheit für sich aufgehen sieht. (521–22)

Whatever the faults of *Johannes* may be, there is little need to argue the advantages seen in the "biblical" play (whatever its excesses) by conservative U.S. Germanists over the contemporary unconventionalities of the earlier dramas.

Like Kummer, Stroebe and Whitney presented the student with an overview of both "social" and "moral" dramas by Sudermann. With a lack of impartiality, they take care to point out that the "spätere Dramen sind dichterisch weniger wertvoll." While stressing Sudermann's popularity—not only in Germany—as a playwright, they are careful to record critical disapproval on a large scale. Cautiously it is stated that "nur die Zukunft kann entscheiden, ob seine Dramen dauernden Wert besitzen" (225, 227).

Teja is the story of the conjugal intimacies of a Gothic king who marries and subsequently meets death in frolic welcome, all in one day. At first glance it is curious that *Teja* was probably equal in popularity to the legend of the chaste *Johannes* as classroom fare (though Salome must of course be dealt with in the latter work). The plot of the former play soon dispels misgivings. Teja, the leader of the Goths—now starving fugitives—is forced through the belief of his people to marry on the day upon which he and all the Gothic warriors must knowingly go to their deaths. This folk belief teaches that no man knows what it is to die unless he leaves a wife behind; Teja, as might be expected, is a cynical and bitter bridegroom. However, within the course of only a few hours, he is crying out his bitterness upon the throne which is now only a mockery of true kingship; the sympathetic listener is his wife, Balthilda. Eventually the two resemble carefree children. At last the summons for the last battle is sounded. Teja, once again a warrior, yet not the same acrimonious man who received Balthilda initially, kneels before his queen to receive the death-blessing upon his brow. As the Goths cheer greetings to their king, the curtain falls.

Certainly, there is nothing offensive in this blooming of a thoroughly platonic relationship, in which man and wife meet their dooms as little children:

>Teja. Du—mein Weib! Du . . . (Sie fliegen einander in die Arme. Leise.) Und küssen magst du mich nicht?
>Balthilda. (schüttelt verschämt den Kopf).
>Teja. Warum nicht?
>Balthilda. (schüttelt wieder den Kopf).
>Teja. Sag doch, warum nicht?
>Balthilda. Ich werd's dir ins Ohr sagen.
>Teja. Nun?
>Balthilda. Du hast einen Milchbart.
>Teja. (wischt sich erschrocken über den Mund, dann in geheucheltem Zorne). *Was* hab' ich? Weißt du nicht, wer ich bin? . . . wie darfst

> du zu deinem König sagen, er—sag es noch einmal! Ich will doch mal sehn!
> Balthilda. (lachend). Ei—nen—Milch—bart!
> Teja.   (lachend). Na warte! (Sudermann 30–31)

Innocuous dialog was frequently a seller of texts. Perhaps most striking is the fact that the king and queen of the Goths converse in *Umgangssprache*.

In a discussion of the two leading Sudermann drama texts, Richard Clyde Ford opted for *Teja*:

> Opinions differ as to the artistic merit of *Johannes*, some critics arguing that it is lacking what the French call *vraisemblance* (lifelikeness); but . . . the same objection cannot be urged against *Teja*, its humanness is too real to doubt, the racial pride and feeling which exult through it too unmistakable. (Sudermann v)

As in the case of *Das edle Blut*, a *Rassegeschöpf*—here, in fact, an entire *Rasse*—is the center of the action. But if genetics or physiognomy govern events in *Das edle Blut*, genocide, toward which the victims march unswervingly, is the leitmotif of *Teja*. Ford called the concept one of "loftiness of soul" (Sudermann vi), but perhaps times have changed.

In contrast to Sudermann and Wildenbruch, Hauptmann, the unanimous first choice among the sources consulted with regard to the naturalistic school, was represented by only one text. In 1901 Benjamin Wells calls Hauptmann "probaby the writer of greatest originality and promise now living in Germany" (419). Thereupon the student is informed that

> Hauptmann has given . . . to the German working class the highest artistic expression of their own weakness and of others' selfish strength. He has made himself the poet of the poor, the downtrodden, the lonely, the helpless, the perplexed, even the vicious. He recognizes that individualism must be produced by the material struggle for existence and wealth; but he would convert it to new ends by the inspiration of Christian socialism. (421)

Thus Hauptmann, viewed by Wells as a socialist expositor in his early plays, is nevertheless snugly confined within the capitalistic, imperialistic "struggle for existence and wealth," where the "inspiration of Christian socialism" befits the comforter of the poor and downtrodden. It may be that an attempt was made to render Naturalism acceptable to the American student through association with Christianity and capitalism.

A more realistic, though negative, view was presented eight years later by Calvin Thomas. Although he begins by stating that "it is certainly to him, if to any imaginative writer, that we must turn for a vindication of the new creed," Thomas concludes that Hauptmann "vindicates it very imperfectly." This justification for Naturalism is weak because

What he gives us, whenever he holds fast to the naturalistic faith, is some distressing picture of social wretchedness, family discord or personal infirmity. And that sort of thing soon palls on people whose taste has been trained by the masterpieces of the past. They may acclaim it as a novelty for a season or two, but they presently discover that there is little in it in the way of pleasure, edification or emotional uplift; then they avoid it and look elsewhere for those external desiderata. (407–09)

Though Hauptmann remains one of the greatest German playwrights, Thomas is correct in his description of the rather rapid turning-away from Naturalism.

Yet in the same year in which Thomas's critical remarks went to press, Kummer rushed to Hauptmann's defense:

Mehr als jeder andere Dichter der Gegenwart hat Hauptmann unter jener Beurteilung gelitten, die eine strikte, schulmäßige Entwicklung vom Dichter verlangt und ungeduldig und verständnislos, ja roh ist, wenn ein Werk einmal den gehegten Erwartungen nicht entspricht. Und doch ist diese Entwicklung nach oben da. (641)

Professor Thomas and his cohorts, Kummer seems to say, lack the understanding and the flexibility to esteem a new art form. By 1912, Professors Stroebe and Whitney sided unconditionally with Kummer, describing Hauptmann as "der beste Vertreter des deutschen Naturalismus und der größte Dramatiker der Gegenwart" (220).

Despite such praise, if the findings of this study up to this point are considered, it is not surprising that Hauptmann was a relatively insignificant author in the area of U.S. German texts. Suffice it to say that *Die versunkene Glocke* was the only Hauptmann text, and that it was listed four times from 1900 to 1906. *Die versunkene Glocke* is not a naturalistic play, but deals with an artistically gifted bell-founder torn between everyday reality and the influence exerted by supernatural powers represented particularly by an *Elfin*, with whom he chooses to live. Because he has gone over to the magical world, but is bound to the world of reality, the consequence is death.

Wells saw in *Die versunkene Glocke* "the first strong touch of Symbolism, a reversion to romanticism" (420), but Priest was more effusive:

Die versunkene Glocke is thus far [1909] Hauptmann's masterpiece. A poet of exquisite sensibilities, he gave free rein in this drama to that sympathetic warmth which is always more or less characteristic of him even in his naturalistic plays. No other drama of his contains so many beautiful lines, and no other has figures which are more clearly drawn. (325)

But are sympathetic warmth and beautiful lines really "more or less characteristic" of *Vor Sonnenaufgang* or *Der Biberpelz*? And may *Märchenpersonal* such as sylphs and frogs be more clearly drawn than Johannes Vockerath? It seems that Priest gave students of the era an emphatic "yes."

Thomas reiterated the general approbation in descrying "poetry, romantic charm, and imagination not fettered to the clod, even if the symbolism is at times a little baffling" (409). Further, although Stroebe and Whitney call *Die Weber* Hauptmann's most significant play, they agree with Thomas in stating that

> Trotz des vielfach unklaren Symbolismus hat dieses Drama [*Die versunkene Glocke*] durch die Schönheit der Form und der Sprache, sowie auch durch die Fülle der glänzenden Bilder und der poetischen Gestalten einen starken und dauernden Erfolg errungen. Keine der späteren idealisierenden Dramen Hauptmanns [e.g., *Und Pippa tanzt*] haben eine gleiche Wirkung erzielt. (223)

From 1901 to 1912, Hauptmann's symbolism was one of the U.S. Germanists' major difficulties in evaluation of his work, though only relatively mild criticism was aired.

In Europe, however, the case against Hauptmann's symbolism was made in less measured terms: "Hauptmann verlor in dieser Dichtung [*Die versunkene Glocke*] an Ursprünglichkeit und Selbstverständlichkeit. Die drei ersten Akte der Versunkenen Glocke sind wohl anschaulich, frisch, lebendig, die letzten zwei mühen sich in Deutungen ab" (Kummer 634). Difficulties in interpretation notwithstanding, if U.S. students were to read Hauptmann—whose writings were not recommended by the Committee of Twelve despite praise from members Thomas and Wells—difficult symbolism and an affair between a bell-founder and a sylph took precedence over naturalistic drama.

A better choice for those teachers who preferred "vigorous stories of adventure with the grand passion left out or made little of" (*Report* 63) was Detlev von Liliencron's *Anno 1870: Kriegsnovellen*. These novellas were characterized for students by Priest as "echoes of his part in the war against France" (328), a war described for the class by Bernhardt delightedly as

> the result of French jealousy of Prussia's growth in Germany. . . . Four weeks of fighting and France lay humbled. . . . Like a company of well-drilled actors the generals of Germany played their relentless parts; like a troop of faltering amateurs the marshals of France stumbled, awkward and confused, before the eyes of Europe. (Liliencron iii)

After this gush of cultural chauvinism, the advantages offered by the text were described:

> These war-scenes read with the dramatic interest of a strong novel and yet give us history with the stamp of absolute verity. It is astonishing with what photographic sincerity and scientific minuteness the poet portrays his soldiers. . . . And all this is told in a language, powerful and realistic . . . approaching the minute method of the modern naturalists. (Liliencron v)

Fiction which bears the stamp of truth somewhat after the manner of the naturalists could lead one to expect unsparing war stories.

However, such was not entirely the case. As editor Bernhardt takes care to point out,

> In depicting that struggle in all the minutiae of its reality, the poet—no matter how realistic his report—was forced to exercise a certain reticence, for the whole truth could not be told, as every one [sic] knows who has had a glimpse of a battlefield in modern warfare. (Liliencron iv)

If war could not be wholesome—that most desirable of qualities in German texts of the era—it could be muted. A rather realistic *"Deutschlandbild"* was rendered by the German troops and their experiences, even if the latter happened partially in France. The text was listed three times from 1903 to 1907. Increasing anti-German sentiment was probably responsible for its disappearance.

Liliencron's manner of description and his patriotism are shown by this excerpt describing the aftermath of a battle:

> Alles Leben hatte hier geendet. Mit den Füßen unter einem gefallenen Dragonerpferd, das die Beine in den Himmel streckte, lag das kleine, fünfjährige Kind erdrückt und zerstampft. Die blonden Härchen umzirkelte wie ein Heilingenschein, im milden Sternenlichte glänzend, eine Blutlache. Unter dem blühenden Goldregenbusch, dessen Trauben der volle Mond durchschimmerte, streckte sich Graf Kjerkewanden. Ein Stich ins Herz hatte ihn den glücklichen, beneidenswerten Tod finden lassen, den Tod für seinen König und für sein Vaterland. . . . Von fern herüber tönte Siegesgesang. (Liliencron 37–38)

Liliencron prized military life, valor, and a noble death on the battlefield—he was both a monarchist and a militarist. The *Kriegsnovellen*, once recognized as suitable textbooks, seem likely to reappear in modern classrooms only as an antipodean contrast to *Mann ist Mann* or *Draußen vor der Tür*. Belief in the sincerity of Liliencron's characters' motivations may be difficult to inspire among generations raised to dread death in war rather than to seek glory therein.

As Liliencron, so also Wilhelm von Polenz offered readers "Naturalism in a modified form . . . freed from the doctrines of the microscopic and the brutal" (Priest 329). With emphasis on environment, yet incorporating fantasy and *Vaterlandsliebe*, the works of Polenz are frequently discussed under the term *Heimatkunst*. According to Priest, "Polenz is preeminent among the many recent novelists and story-writers who have dealt with the popular life of their native provinces" (330).

However, portraying provincials was only one of Polenz's motivations to take up the art of fiction. In the words of George M. Baker, editor of "Der arme Grule" for his anthology *German Stories* (1909), Polenz's "works have a pronounced didactic tendency" (132). But exactly what U.S. students were to garner from "Der arme Grule" is uncertain. The story concerns three strikers in a large industrial city—two young bachelors and a middle-aged family man named Grule. The strike fails, and, after having been turned away by their old employers, who have meanwhile hired new workers, the three and many others take to the trains to look for work in other cities. One of the young men uses Socialism to impress others and to con his two associates out of what funds they still possess. Finally jobs are found, Grule earning the largest sum of the three. As the Socialist has arranged that money is placed in a *Genossenschaftskasse* under his (the Socialist's) control, Grule requests from him some money to send to his wife; since the third party of the triumvirate sides with Grule, the Socialist, who opposes such measures, exits with a murderous look. That night he steals everything his two companions possess. Grule, upon awakening, becomes insane upon beholding himself financially ruined. The madman is eventually returned to his family.

Grule is perhaps like no other character so much as Jakob, *der arme Spielmann*: fumbling, credulous, preyed upon by others. These qualities are demonstrated as Grule addresses himself to the exigencies of finding employment:

> "Aber man hat doch sein Handwerk erlernt! Man hat sich doch zwanzig Jahre redlich durchgeschlagen. Und nun mit Frau und Kindern!—Nein, wenn es so zugeht in der Welt. . . ." Er sah sich mit verzweifeltem Blick um und hob die hagere Hand; man wußte nicht gegen wen. (Baker 96–97)

Another representative of *Heimatkunst* is clergyman-author Heinrich Hansjakob. Like Polenz, he was brought to students' attention in a literary history only by Priest (330)—though, in Hansjakob's case, cursorily. But unlike Polenz, whose "Der arme Grule" appeared only once, Hansjakob was more enticing to U.S. editors: four of his stories appeared in three different texts between 1904 and 1918. As Edwin Carl Roedder, who edited three Hansjakob stories for *Schwarzwaldleut'*, expressed it in 1913, the author "is generally regarded to-day [sic], not as the greatest artist in the domain of the village story, but as its most original representative" (ix).

Original indeed, for Roedder proceeds to catalog several eccentricities demonstrated by the author. For example, he is "stubbornly opinionated" and "presents his personal ideas" quite frequently within the larger context of the story being written. He is devoted to the "good old days" and is a bitter opponent of all so-called progress. He hates women. For all that, states Roedder, "the reader is apt and willing to forget such idiosyncrasies of the writer's personality in the many good points of his books." And foremost among these qualities, in fact the only quality cited in support of the preceding statement, is religion:

> Hansjakob's religiousness is genuine and healthy, neither mystic nor ascetic, devoid of sentimentality and narrowness, and without a trace of that unctuous

moralizing sanctimoniousness that so easily creeps into the story books of clerical writers and makes poor Sunday school reading out of what might have become good literature. (xii–xiii)

One expects, therefore, stories in the vein of Zschokke and Frommel. And one is not disappointed. Hansjakob's "Der Ristehansele und der Hansjörgle" provides a means of comparison. The story deals with two friends who are often the butt of jokes played by acquaintances; in this case, Ristehansele and Hansjörgle are told by associates that the newest medicine for treatment of consumption is a preparation made from lizards' flesh. However, the lizards are bought only under the strictest secrecy. They set about catching numerous lizards and skinning them—this last a further improvisation by the jokers. Then they make their delivery, at night and in secret:

> "Herr Apotheker, do hemm'r jetz die g'schellte Heckgaise, Ihr wäre scho wisse, zua was Ihr sie broche könne!"—"Ich glaube, ihr Leute seid verrückt! Wer sagt euch, daß ich Eidechsen kaufe?" fuhr der Apotheker sie scharf an. "In der Zittung isch es g'stande. Nemme sie doch, wir sage nix!"—"Dummheiten! Macht, daß ihr mir zu meinem Haus hinauskommt!" (Roedder 19)

The story and the laughter grow to legendary proportions. Ristehansele tires of the scorn and emigrates to America; Hansjörgle must live with the name *Heckgaisenschäler* until his last hour. Hansjakob's story does what *Heimatkunst* set out to do: to escape the rootless environment of the big city and to portray human beings in a provincial environment. That such regionalism was rooted in Naturalism is shown not only by dialect but also by touches such as the emigration to America.

Friedrich Lienhard, lesser known than Hansjakob in U.S. German studies, 1864–1918, became better known after World War I. Frederick Betz, editor of the anthology *Aus der Jugendzeit*, in which Lienhard's "Der Pandurenstein" appeared, characterized the author as "one of the most interesting writers of the present day in Germany. . . . a master of German prose, full of power and idealism" (iv). These qualities are well blended with thoughts of fatherland and folk—and the enemies thereof—in "Der Pandurenstein."

As frequently in the case of *Heimatkunst*, a rural setting is essential to the action; Lienhard outdoes most others of his school as far as dramatic and vivid impressions are concerned:

> Zwischen Burgtrümmern, an denen armdicker Efeu entlanglief, stand die Meierei. Drei hohe Sandsteinfelsen überragten die Trümmer; zwei davon lagerten nahe beisammen hinter den Gebäuden, gewaltige Klötze, umwachsen und unbesteigbar; der dritte Klotz aber trotzte mit erschreckender Majestät am vorderen Berghang über die Ebene turmhoch und umfangreich, besteigbar nur durch eine schlanke, mehrfach zusammengebundene Leiter. (Betz 35)

It remains to demonstrate how Lienhard's setting shapes the events which unfold.

Namely, the *Meierei* is attacked by the Pandurs, or Hungarian marauders, interrupting a one-sided love affair between a sixteen-year-old shepherd, hero of the tale, and a young beauty intended for the *Großknecht* of the *Meierei*. The lovelorn shepherd returns home one evening to find that the entire staff of the farm has fled for fear of the Pandurs; the lad now climbs the *Pandurenstein*, taking his dog and one of his goats for company, and pulls the ladder up after him. The Pandurs arrive on the following morning and commence pillaging. When one of the marauders puts on a bonnet belonging to the shepherd's love, the lad attacks the Pandurs verbally and with arrows and stones; despite their numbers, the brigands are forced to flee. The shepherd is now a hero. Having received a commission from a neighboring count, the hero says a sad farewell to the girl whose bonnet made him a hero, and walks away without ever looking back.

What would the story have been without the *Pandurenstein*? In consideration of the importance of setting, it is well to remember that *"Friedrich Lienhard erhob den Kampfruf 'Los von Berlin!', d.h. 'los von der wurzellosen Dichtung der Großstadt' "* (Krell and Fiedler 329). The *Deutschlandbild* rendered by rural settings is, then, according to Lienhard, superior to that presented by works which are set in metropolitan areas. However, not all *Heimatdichter* agree.

Foremost in the opposing party is Otto Ernst (Otto Ernst Schmidt), whose works deal for the most part with some aspect of city life. If, as Priest asserts in mentioning *Asmus Sempers Jugendland*, Ernst's work is "literature of the province" (330), that province is almost certainly Hamburg. Significantly, Ernst is grouped by Kummer with Seidel, whose "province" lay in and around Berlin (509–10).

About Ernst's writings, students were informed that

> Vieles in diesen humoristischen Schriften ist allerdings sehr billig; anderes schmeichelt sichtlich dem Philister; mit seinen Komödien . . . gehört Otto Ernst trotz der einseitig schwarz oder weiß gefärbten Charaktere zu den besseren Unterhaltungsschriftstellern. (Kummer 510)

This estimation finds a slightly more favorable echo in the considerations of Stroebe and Whitney:

> In *Flachsmann als Erzieher* gab Otto Ernst . . . ein zwar oberflächliches, aber frisches und anziehendes Bild aus dem Leben der deutschen Volksschule. In dem Drama *Jugend von heute* hat er den übertriebenen Individualismus und die "Herrenmoral" der Nietzscheschwärmer geistreich verspottet. (224)

Stroebe and Whitney favor the dramatic works; Kummer dealt briefly with poetry, essay and drama; only Priest introduced the student to the novel

Asmus Sempers Jugendland, which, as *Heimatkunst* and, probably, one of the more provocative texts of the era, will be briefly investigated.

In a review of Carl Osthaus's edition of *Asmus Sempers Jugendland* (1916), the following remarks recommended the text to uneasy Germanists of the war years.

> *Asmus Sempers Jugendland*, written in 1904 by Otto Ernst (Schmidt), and now edited for American schools by Professor Osthaus, represents a labor of love on the part of both author and editor. The novel, a most artistic portrait of the author's own boyhood, gives us a very realistic view of many institutions of modern Germany. We find in it a wonderful description of the milieu but always by an optimist, and without any plainly visible attempt at dogmatization or moralization. The story grips the heart-strings of the reader, and the book offers splendid opportunities on every page for a study of German 'Realien.' (Klopsch 190)

A better *Deutschlandbild*, judging from Klopsch's evaluation, could scarcely be desired: an autobiographical view of modern Germany which is realistic, but not naturalistic; although the story seeks to touch the heart, there is no preaching per se; and institutions and customs abound.

Editor Osthaus's introduction and the review are strikingly similar. However, the review—aimed at faculty members everywhere—apparently took care not to touch upon the following aspect of *Asmus Sempers Jugendland* placed before the student by Osthaus:

> Through this novel we also learn to understand Otto Ernst's compassionate sympathy with the oppressed, the disinherited among men. Since he himself, like his Asmus, grew up in the midst of these, his knowledge comes first hand. The colors he applied are substantially true to reality. The beginnings of the Socialist movement, the formation of the Socialist party, and the first persecutions of its agitators took place in his own youthful days. Thus also the boy Asmus has frequent opportunity to hear about these things, even to meet some of the prominent Socialists; and his natural indignation against the oppressors wrests from him his first poetical effusions. (x)

If Osthaus was kindly disposed toward the Socialists, his views were not shared by all Americans.

In the article "German Socialism and Literary Sterility," for example, a discussion of leftist politics in Germany pointed out that

> Social democracy in Germany is not so much a party doctrine as a creed. These ignorant masses do not discern that the very name of the party is in itself a contradiction, that in the socialistic state there would be no democracy, but a despotism compared to which Russian autocracy would be liberty, because the state becoming the sole employer, distributing the work and paying for it, everything would be in the hands of the leaders. (Geffcken 664)

Not only were most Americans negative toward European Socialism, they were also leery of Eugene V. Debs and the American Socialist Party here at home. A textbook which spoke well of Socialism would have been at least as unwelcome in the classroom as *Götz von Berlichingen* or *Kabale und Liebe*, since—according to the mores of the era—all three dealt in unhealthy social situations.

But Asmus's *Jugendland* is far more than socialist propaganda, as may be seen from a visit to his attic hideaway, furnished with

> alte Jahrgänge von "Über Land und Meer" und "Gartenlaube," und unvollständige Lieferungen der Werke von Wolfgang von Goethe und anderen. Hier auf dem Boden unter glühenden Dachpfannen begann Asmus Semper die Lektüre der "Wahlverwandtschaften," ohne sie wesentlich zu fördern; dagegen. . . . auf einem angeschmutzten, einsamen Lieferungsbogen fand er einen Kapitelanfang, der also lautete:
>
> "Kennst du das Land, wo die Zitronen blüh'n?
>
> Im dunklen Laub die Goldorangen glühn?—"
>
> O, das war ja das wunderbare Lied, das sein Vater vor Jahren einmal gesungen hatte . . . das Lied, bei dem er sofort sein Spiel hatte ruhen lassen, weil er nur horchen konnte. Er fragte nicht, welches Land es sei. . . . Er wußte nicht, daß es das Land der Sehnsucht war. (82–83)

Asmus is not intellectually impoverished; he is surrounded by poverty, culture and love, and the story of his youth is worth reading. Though research for this study extended only two years past the date of this novel's publication as a U.S. German text, it may be speculated that *Heimatkunst* from Hamburg was limited on the textbook market not only by World War I, but also by Ernst's predilection for Socialism.

A similarly late arrival was that of Rudolf Herzog's *Die Burgkinder* in 1917. Like Otto Ernst, Herzog was subsumed in Priest's literary history under the rubric of provincial literature (330). Similarly, Stroebe and Whitney taught that "Rudolf Herzog zeigt das Leben der größeren Provinzstädte, so gibt er in den *Wiskottens* eine humorvolle Schilderung des Fabrikantenlebens in Wuppertal" (238). Priest, Stroebe and Whitney cite only *Die Wiskottens*, Herzog's first novel, as an example of his work in an urban setting. However, he was known to a relatively small number of U.S. German students for the text *Die Burgkinder*, which, contrary to expectation, takes place not in a provincial city but in a village on the Rhine.

Ottilie Boetzkes, editor of the *Burgkinder* text, justified her edition of the atypical Herzog novel upon the basis of its greater harmony with academic concepts of *Heimatkunst*:

> If less technical and less realistic, Herzog is more poetic and charmingly optimistic in . . . *Die Burgkinder* (1911). All the love for the Rhine and his native soil and a deep fatherly love for humanity prevail throughout. The *Heimatkunst*

is practiced here with all the understanding and devotion that a big-hearted man can have for his homeland. (iv)

As in so many cases, the author's most benign work was preferred over more bracing choices.

The text offered nothing if not a positive—even if rather saccharine and chauvinistic—*Deutschlandbild*. France, malign author of Revolution and warfare, provides the foil, for the plot is laid between the Reign of Terror and the *Völkerschlacht* at Leipzig. Concerning Germany, the student was presented numerous times with passages such as the following:

> Der helle Mond schien über die roten Dächer hinweg, lag auf der Landstraße and ließ die Wellenlinie des Siebengebirges phantastisch im Licht schwimmen. Silbern wälzte sich die Flut des Rheins um den trotzigen Sockel des Drachenfelsen. . . .
> "Wie schön das ist, Oheim . . ."
> "Ja, wie schön—"
> "Du hast viel gesehen von der Welt. Gibt es ein schöneres Land?"
> "Nein, es gibt kein schöneres." (Herzog 2)

And further:

> "Sieh den Rolandsbogen. . . . Die Abendsonne wirft einen Strom von Gold hindurch. Es gibt kein schöner [sic] Land auf der Welt." . . . Und er spürte, wie ihm die tägliche Berührung mit der Heimaterde immer wieder neue Kräfte brachte und der Rheinwind ihn erfrischte. (Herzog 92)

And so on and on, too many times, scenic and sentimental—yet not altogether unpleasing.

On the other hand, little that is good issues from France; one of the characters speaks of the regicide and terror as follows:

> Er [Louis XVI] war nur schwach und ungeschickt und büßte die Schuld seiner Vorgänger. Sie haben ihn aufs Schafott geschickt, und er starb würdig. Vor ihm und nach ihm aber schleppten sie Tausende und aber Tausende unter das Richtbeil. Die Guillotinen konnten ihre Arbeit nicht mehr bewältigen. (Herzog 6)

A monarchist attitude and a negative view of the Revolution were to be expected from militant *Rheinländer* of the era of which Herzog wrote. However, one senses that the same feelings against things French prevailed in 1911 when the novel was written. As Boetzkes points out in her introduction, Herzog "lives in the *Burghaus*, where he places the scene of *Die Burgkinder*. As these lines are being written (1916), he is active in the European War" (iv). Inauspicious for the success of the text was the fact that the designation "European War" lived out its precarious existence on the sixth of April 1917—the year the text was published.

More *Heimatkunst* issued from Schleswig-Holstein, home of Gustav Frenssen, "the author of the enormously successful *Jörn Uhl* (1901)" (Priest 330). Stroebe and Whitney elaborated slightly that

> Sein Roman *Jörn Uhl* war einer der größten Erfolge. Besonders gut gelungen sind darin die Schlachtszenen von Gravelotte. Auch *Hilligenlei* und *Peter Moors Fahrt nach Südwest* zeigen seine glänzende impressionistische Schilderungskunst. (239)

And U.S. students were reading *Jörn Uhl*, *Gravelotte* (chapter 14 of *Jörn Uhl*), and *Peter Moors Fahrt nach Südwest*; in contrast to Herzog's *Die Burgkinder*, the books by Frenssen praised by Germanists were the texts read in German classes.

A primary reason might have been the books' great popularity in Germany: "Frenssens Roman Jörn Uhl ist einer der größten Bucherfolge der Neuzeit. Von 1901 bis 1907 wurden 205 000 Exemplare abgesetzt, von Peter Moors Fahrt binnen einem Jahr 125 000" (Kummer 704). However, popularity is not always—or by any means—a reliable indicator of what will be chosen for pedagogical purposes.

Best of all indicators is that which links Frenssen to the tradition of Zschokke, Frommel and Hansjakob—he was a clergyman:

> Er hat einen geschraubten, manirierten [sic] Ton und liebt gespreizte moralische Betrachtungen. Dichter und Prediger kommen sich einander immer in die Quere, und der Prediger ist meistenteils der stärkere. Seine Breite und Zerfahrenheit ist oft unerträglich, und dabei ist die Schilderung keineswegs besonders anschaulich. Etwas Unklares und Verschwommenes haben alle Frenssenschen Bücher. . . . Das beste, was Frenssen geschrieben, ist seine Schilderung der Kriegsabenteuer von Peter Moor. (Kummer 704–05)

Although he echoes the U.S. professors' choices of *Jörn Uhl* and *Peter Moors Fahrt nach Südwest* as Frenssen's most notable achievements, Kummer's view of his capabilities is considerably diminished: only *Peter Moor* receives faint praise.

In his introduction to *Peter Moors Fahrt nach Südwest*, Herman Babson contradicted the assertion that Frenssen's writing is *zerfahren*, *unklar* and *verschwommen*, and placed him among literary greats:

> Frenssen's style is clear, simple, and charming. His language is not brilliant; he gives us no prose that dazzles with its splendor, but his vocabulary is extensive. No work better typifies the strong points of his simple, unadorned style than *Peter Moors Fahrt nach Südwest*. . . . Frenssen can be—indeed, should be—associated with such writers as Wilhelm Raabe and Gottfried Keller. (x)

182   Realism—Naturalism—The Early Twentieth Century

The comparison to Raabe and Keller surprises modern readers of Babson's estimation; Frenssen's style will speak for itself.

Although both Raabe and Keller were sensitive to social issues of their times, their works are unlikely to have been considered by their contemporaries to be propaganda in actual fact. Quite different the case of Frenssen, who,

> aggrieved that his countrymen . . . should be heartlessly indifferent toward the fighting and suffering soldiers in Southwest Africa . . . set himself the task and duty of writing for the German people an account which when read as an artistic whole would arouse patriotism and awaken a feeling of heartfelt thanks for those who had served their country so well. (Frenssen xi)

To continue the propagandistic thesis, as well as to provide an example of Frenssen's prose, the following lines are offered:

> Er sagte: "In Südwestafrika haben die Schwarzen feige und hinterrücks alle Farmer ermordet, samt Frauen und Kindern." Ich weiß ganz gut in der Erdkunde Bescheid; aber ich war erst doch ganz verwirrt und sagte: "Sind diese Ermordeten deutsche Menschen?" "Natürlich," sagte er: "Schlesier und Bayern und aus allen andern deutschen Stämmen, und auch drei oder vier Holsteiner. Und nun, was meinst du, wir vom Seebataillon. . . ." "Wir müssen hin!" sagte ich. . . . Und ich freute mich. . . . daß wir nach Südwest gingen, um an einem wilden Heidenvolk vergossenes deutsches Blut zu rächen. (6)

A sense of guilt for the "white man's burden" had not yet been awakened. Frenssen was neither Keller nor Raabe. He is known today as "definitely *Blubo*" (Friedrich 274), though he spoke to his times as clergyman and litterateur.

More innocuous was the work of Hans Hoffmann, numbered by Priest among Germany's "less talented authors" (315). Kummer, too, reckoned Hoffmann among the "vorhandene Unterhaltungsschriftsteller," and grouped him with "abhängige Talente" such as Seidel and Otto Ernst—actually a reasonably flattering association. The author's works were, like those of Seidel and Ernst, supposedly shaped by his sunny personality:

> Sein Grundwesen ist optimistisch, ein leichter lyrischer Anflug gab seinen Werken eine gewisse Anmut und Liebenswürdigkeit. Von ihm stammen: Das Gymnasium zu Stolpenburg 1891, in [einem] breiten, behaglichen und humoristischen Charakter gehalten. . . . die Romane: Der eiserne Rittmeister . . . [und] Landsturm. . . . Tiefere Gestaltungskraft fehlt ihm. In seinen Gedichten ist er Baumbach . . . verwandt. (Kummer 510)

Thus Hoffmann's books were said to be pleasant to read, even if shallow. The comparison to Baumbach was not without a sting even then, though in the world of U.S. German texts this is one good reason why students were reading Hoffmann's prose.

Das Gymnasium zu Stolpenburg, one of Hoffmann's best-known works, contains two stories of academic life: "Die Handschrift A" and "Erfüllter Beruf." Valentin Buehner, in his introduction to an edition copyrighted in 1904, acquainted students with Hoffmann and his work in the following way:

> During the past century, German universities have produced a number of writers who, by their broad-mindedness, their elegance of diction, and their cheerful philosophy of life, have raised German literary productions to a high standard. We need only mention such names as Gustav Freytag, Paul Heyse, and Victor von Scheffel, among many others. . . . the works of these authors are instructive, as well as entertaining and elevating. . . . Hans Hoffmann may be classed among such writers. (iii)

The editor esteemed his author too highly; Freytag and Heyse belong to a different sphere. Another apparent inaccuracy is that Buehner—like Kummer—stresses a cheerful quality of Hoffmann's prose which is anything but evident in *Das Gymnasium zu Stolpenburg*.

"Die Handschrift A" is the melancholy narrative of a *Schulamtskandidat* who fails his oral exams because he follows his conscience and defends Lachmann's theory that Manuscript A is the original version of the *Nibelungenlied*. This in spite of the fact that he knows his examiner favors Manuscript C as the original. Exam failed, wedding called off, ex-candidate Dinse accepts a job in the *Gymnasium* at Stolpenburg and proceeds to deteriorate. An attempt by Anna, his former betrothed, to rekindle his former zeal for scholarship ends in Dinse's destruction of his one work of consequence—his manuscript defending Lachmann and Manuscript A.

The end of the tale shows Dinse and Anna—now very old—through the eyes of the citizens of Stolpenburg:

> [Sie] erinnern sich auch genau des altertümlichen Pärchens, das in späterer Zeit täglich die Stadtpromenade von Stolpenburg abwackelte, meist ernst und schweigsam, häufig Hand in Hand. . . . Einige ganz fremde Leute hatten den Mut, über das jugendlose Pärchen am Traualtar zu lächeln, wer aber ein wenig von der Lebensgeschichte der beiden wußte, fand diesen Mut nicht. (Hoffmann 49–50)

The story is interesting, if sentimental, and the *Deutschlandbild* is reasonably realistic if some features of the plot are overlooked. As far as cheerfulness is concerned, let him laugh who will. "Erfüllter Beruf" is at least as dismal.

Offering another reversal of what might have been expected was Helene Böhlau (Madame al Raschid Bey), known as a writer of rather grim novels promoting women's rights; in U.S. German studies her fame was based upon something definitely more cheerful: the *Ratsmädelgeschichten*. Priest stated tersely that these are "very amusing stories" (331); however, the student could take recourse to other sources which elaborated somewhat upon

> die weimarischen Ratsmädelgeschichten, die das engbürgerliche und philiströse Weimar zur Goethe-Schillerzeit mit behaglichem Humor schildern, jenes Klein-Weimar, an das man gewöhnlich nicht denkt, wenn man das klassische Weimar im Auge hat. (Kummer 678–79)

The greatest complement to these modest stories came when Stroebe and Whitney taught about Böhlau that "Ihr Bestes hat sie . . . geleistet . . . in ihren originellen humorvollen Erzählungen aus Altweimar, den *Ratsmädelgeschichten*" (240). The *Ratsmädel*, therefore, would seem to have outlived Böhlau's more outspokenly feminist works in American academe.

Emma Haevernick, editor of the *Ratsmädel* text, discusses the author, the stories and the milieu as follows:

> The author, daughter of the court bookseller and publisher Böhlau, was born November 29, 1859, in Weimar. . . . Marie, one of the *Ratsmädel*, was her grandmother, and perhaps the authoress is able on that account to bring back to us with such vividness the old times of Weimar—the golden days when Goethe and Schiller lived there. . . . She views matters logically, observingly, and a resolute striving for reform, reorganization, elevation, and enrichment of our life is always emphasized. (iii–iv)

As an individual born and raised in Weimar, Böhlau utilized her background to add something enriching to the lives of others in creating the *Ratsmädel*. It is doubtful that today's reader—unless of quite tender years—will agree with the praise once given the stories.

The first of the three stories mixes the engagement of *Ratsmädel* Röse to Ottokar Thon with the search for the ghost of Luise von Göchhausen. However,

> Zu allererst tauchen . . . in unsrer Geschichte ein paar lachende, blütenjunge Gesichter auf, ein paar feste, kindlich behende Körper, blonde, dicke Zöpfe, junge, weiche, noch etwas tollpatschige Hände, helle Kleider, die sich lebendig um diese jungen Körper schmiegen, die sich so jugendsicher auf leichten Füßen bewegen, so kernig, so wohlgebaut und unschuldig. (3)

One is torn between dull, childish and trite in attempting to describe the reader's introduction to the *Ratsmädel*. Nor does the story itself improve matters. The action begins after a mild feminist inference seen in the introduction of the girls' mother:

> Eine rührende Zartheit liegt über der schlanken Gestalt. Der Haushalt mit den wilden Mädchen und Buben, die Kriegsjahre, der überernste Gatte, die Geldsorgen,—das alles ist der fein organisierten Frau zu viel geworden. (7)

Thus the Böhlau of naturalistic, feminist novels discreetly expressed her feelings even in the prim *Ratsmädelgeschichten*.

Concerning the plot, after an engagement dinner held for Röse and Ottokar, the *Ratsmädel* and three young men—one of whom is Schiller's son—chase Göchhausen's ghost by night. However, they discover Ottokar and his hunting dog instead. Ottokar kisses Röse tolerantly and smiles at her three companions. Whereupon Böhlau lauds the purity, tenderness, and bliss of spring by the bright light of the moon.

Reasons for the apparently modest success of the *Ratsmädelgeschichten* fall into the now familiar pattern: unlike Böhlau's feminist, naturalistic novels, the *Ratsmädel* stories are unimpeachably wholesome. There is information on Weimar, Goethe, and Schiller. Weimar is, as indicated by Kummer, viewed in a less accustomed light. By today's standards the work is puerile and sentimental, but in the day of *Fritz auf Ferien* and *Das Peterle von Nürnberg*, works of this type were considered worthwhile by educators and, it is to be hoped, by students.

A cut above Böhlau, according to Priest, was Isolde Kurz, writer of "some beautiful lyrics and several artistic short stories" (331). One of the sources of Kurz's artistic achievement was said to be that

> Isolde gibt ihren Werken vornehm ruhige Umrißlinien; ihre Art ist von einem gediegenen Realismus und ohne viel Nüancen [sic], klar, von stolzer Offenheit in allen Selbstbekenntnissen, sie ist ein ernstes Talent, das keinem Modeerfolg nachstrebt, sondern sich ruhig Pausen gönnt, um immer formvollendeter hervorzutreten. (Kummer 508)

One imagines Kurz's striving for a clarity related to that of Conrad Ferdinand Meyer in the carefully drawn outlines of her work. She was said to stand "auf dem Boden der Romantik, doch hat sich ihre Dichtung mehr an dem Schönheitsempfinden der Griechen und der italienischen Renaissancekünstler gebildet" (Stroebe and Whitney 244–45).

An examination of an excerpt from Kurz's "Die goldenen Träume" makes it seem somewhat similar in its motifs to Leander's "Vom unsichtbaren Königreiche," inasmuch as characters in both stories happily inhabit a dream world. Here, a child receives the gift of dreams from a wise old woman:

> Sowie er das Auge schließt, werden goldene Träume um sein Bett stehen, und werden ihn für alles entschädigen, was er am Tage zu leiden hat, und sie werden nicht von ihm weichen bis zu seinem Lebensende, es wäre denn, daß er selbst sich ihrer entäußerte. Dies soll er ja unterlassen, denn es würde schwerer Kummer für ihn daraus entstehen. Auch soll er nie suchen, andere daran teilnehmen zu lassen oder sie ihnen zeigen zu wollen, er hätte nur Verdruß davon. (3)

Whether Kurz was praised too highly by those who concerned themselves with German literature during the era under investigation is elucidated by more recent sources: the author is recognized as a belated follower of Conrad Ferdinand Meyer, an epigonic adherent of Paul Heyse's "Munich School," and is assessed as an artist "of far less importance" than others of her time (Friedrich 233).

Represented by only one story in period texts, but more important in German studies of today is Clara Viebig. As American students learned in 1909,

> Clara Viebig (born 1860) has written many ultra-modern, erotic stories of little value, but she has also written vivid short stories in the collection *Kinder der Eifel* (1897) and novels such as *Das tägliche Brot* . . . which show fine powers of observation. (Priest 331)

In Germany in the same year there were, similarly, complements underscored by criticism:

> Die Darstellung von Klara Viebig ist ernst und stark. Sie hat eine gewisse derbe Gediegenheit, einen kraftvollen, energischen Stil in der Schilderung von Zuständen. Ihr Naturalismus ist freilich nur im Zuständlichen. . . . Ein Hang zu Effekten, zu grellen Theaterszenen, zu Übertreibungen raubt ihren Lebensschilderungen die tiefere Wahrheit. (Kummer 704)

The truth of this assessment will be demonstrated below.

Near the end of the era, Stroebe and Whitney were relatively commendatory, though bland; Viebig

> steht mitten in der brutalen Wirklichkeit des Lebens; ihre Sprache und ihr Stil sind hart und realistisch. Sie wählt besonders die Eifelgegend westlich vom Rhein zum Hintergrund ihrer herben, ernsten Romane, auch behandelt sie soziale Probleme aus dem Berliner Großstadtleben und aus den deutschpolnischen Grenzgebieten. (234)

The brutal "reality" presented to students as an example of Viebig's work is laid in the area of the German-Polish border. How real the story is is a difficult question, for "Jaschu" (included in George Merrick Baker's *German Stories*) is a story about a girl who loved a pig.

Namely, Marinka, *Schweinemagd* in Przysienowo, pines for her intended, Jasch, who is away in military service. Then she transfers her feelings for Jasch to a tender, white, blossom-like newborn piglet, which she names Jaschu after her human admirer. Marinka sometimes sleeps in Jaschu's pen. A terrible drought attacks the region, and animals die in great numbers of thirst and disease; Jaschu, too, falls ill. Despite all that Marinka can do—including prayers to the Mother of God—Jaschu dies. The starving villagers eat the diseased corpse, and a number of them consequently die. Marinka is the only healthy peasant in Pryzysienowo, as she could not eat Jaschu. She collects all his bones in her best scarf and gives them a solemn burial.

Here is a peculiar mixture of baroque and naturalistic tendencies. As Kummer stated, the depiction of conditions—on a country estate during a severe dought—is naturalistic to the point of coarseness. On the other hand, the strange effects and theatrical happenings—Marinka's fulsome infatuation with a pig, the furtive exhumation and devouring of Jaschu's diseased corpse, the devout gathering of Jaschu's bones like holy relics—render the story chimerical, fairy-tale like.

This one story, Viebig's only listed entry into the U.S. German textbook market, probably suffices to demonstrate why her work was not widely accepted in the classroom. *L'Arrabbiata* and *Höher als die Kirche* were doubtlessly thought to be better suited to romantically awakened young adults than "Jaschu," though the nearness of the appearance of the text (1909) to World War I doubtless limited its appeal. (Another edition appeared in 1926.)

A contrast of super-refined subtlety is offered by *Hansen*, one of four stories by Ilse Leskien in *"Schuld" and Other Stories*. Professor L. E. Cannon, who reviewed the text for *The Modern Language Journal*, made a significant statement which places Leskien's work at the oposite pole from Viebig's: "We have in this volume four delightful stories. I question, however, whether the average student will appreciate the subtle psychological suggestion of Hansen" (113). Whereas the student is made entirely aware of Marinka's transfer of affection from Jasch to Jaschu, and what follows is clearly delineated, the non-action and disordered dialogue of "Hansen" do indeed leave the reader somewhat perplexed.

Regarding what actually happens, a fifty-year-old schoolmaster is sitting in the garden of the village castle, to which his former pupil—now the Frau Gräfin—and her husband of a short time have recently returned. The schoolmaster has a key to the gardens, presumably because he formerly taught at the castle. He plans to return the key tomorrow. As he enjoys the silent stars and forest, he becomes aware of a woman in a white dress, weeping. With a shock he realizes it is his former pupil. The rest of the story proceeds as follows:

> Sie versuchte Haltung zu gewinnen: "Was . . . tun Sie hier, jetzt, . . . was?" sank aber plötzlich in sich zusammen.
>
> Ihm stand der kalte Schweiß auf der Stirn, seine Knie zitterten, die Zunge wollte ihm nicht gehorchen; und doch mußte er sprechen, daß sie nur nicht zum Denken kamen, daß sie nur Zeit gewannen, sprachen, als wäre nichts geschehen! . . .
>
> "Ich muß Frau Gräfin um Verzeihung bitten . . . nichts habe ich hier zu tun, gar nichts . . . morgen bringe ich den Schlüssel." (Leskien 44)

And so on, for a number of pages; after an undetermined amount of time, to the surprise of the villagers, the Frau Gräfin has the Schoolmaster buried in the castle cemetery.

Several solutions to Leskien's riddles presented themselves as the student read the story. As in the case of Annette von Droste-Hülshoff's *Judenbuche*, such ambiguity need not be regarded as a weakness. "Hansen," however, is not the usual, innocuous text. *"Schuld" and Other Stories* was listed only in 1915. It is possible that more than World War I precluded further listings during the era.

An obscure author in her own time, according to literary histories consulted, yet known to German students in this country through her short stories was Charlotte Niese. Textbook editor George Merrick Baker informed the scholar that

> Although she has attempted works of more considerable size, as for example the historical novel *Cajus Rungholt*, her greatest success has been in the field of the short story. She has especially succeeded in faithfully reproducing the atmosphere and life in Schleswig-Holstein. (120)

Perhaps more realistic was editor Frederick Betz's assessment:

> Niese . . . is known to American students only by a few of her short stories. . . . Simple and unpretentious in her style, she knows how to tell of the happy days of her childhood in a most delightful manner. (iv)

Betz writes indirectly of "Die Seeräuberburg," an adventurous tale of sunshine, piracy and ghosts, a blend of *Nancy Drew* and Poetic Realism—a story included in his anthology. But not all of Niese's stories "tell of happy days."

For example, Baker included the tale of "Tante Feddersen," an ungenial kindergarten teacher, in *German Stories*. One morning, *Tante* discovers Ehlers the grocer, whom she has amorously pursued for several years, hanging from a meat hook in an attempted suicide due to debts. *Tante* relieves Ehlers of his pecuniary difficulties, whereupon the two are wed. The once jovial Ehlers finds his new circumstances painful; within a year he is dead. His widow is quick to reveal that her opinion of men was not improved by her experiences with Ehlers: "Sie taugen alle nix! . . . Kaum hat man sie, dann kneifen sie wieder aus! Was ich mich bloß denke, was Ehlers mich für bar Geld gekostet hat . . ." (16). *Tante*'s pride was that her tombstone would read *Ehefrau* and *Wittwe*; but the grave of Ehlers is the one which receives an occasional wreath.

As *Tante* Feddersen's speech implies, Niese, like Viebig, inclined to a naturalistic idiom, making her stories a rather unusual choice for students of the era. The visualization of Ehlers on the meat hook and *Tante*'s subsequent reckoning of what he cost her inform the story with a tincture of the raw and uncouth. All this notwithstanding, Niese's work (included in three anthologies listed a total of five times from 1901 to 1913) was at least somewhat successful in the textbook field; as has been pointed out, not all her tales are so lugubrious. From all indications, Niese's idiom represented another small crack in the wall of academe—which by and large remained the bulwark of gentility, of Viktor von Scheffel and Wilhelmine von Hillern, and of "those works of emotional literature which contain the proper ideals" (Handschin 249).

V

Conclusion

As shown in Appendix B, a considerable amount of German literature was shared in the United States between German classes and readers of the translations reviewed by the *New York Times*. Volkmar Sander notes the importance of the *Times* in bringing German literature to a privileged audience, and Wolfgang Heinsohn demonstrates that this was the case from 1870 to 1918. This audience doubtless included some of the university, college, and high school teachers involved in editing and selecting texts and in teaching German classes. Thus the editors of German texts were probably guided in some cases by the *Times* reviews. Yet certainly, as shown in Appendix B, a number of German works were in the schools as texts before they were reviewed in translation by the *Times*. Thus a reciprocal action between journalism and academe appears probable in the era under consideration.

Not all of the sharing from 1864 to 1918 involved great authors; there were also writers such as Werner (Bürstenbinder), Ebers, Roquette, and Zschokke; but many of the correspondences involve authors considered great or near-great today. Especially significant is the fact that this correspondence of authors received in academe and reviewed in translation does indeed seem—in the light of statements by Sander and others—to have been rather more widespread in the era investigated than it is today. However, only an investigation centered on German literature as presented in U.S. high school, college, and university textbooks after World War I will decide this issue.

A related point is that—as some present-day academics feel—students should read *Groschenromane* and *Trivialliteratur*—not Goethe, Schiller, and Lessing, as many continue to do. From 1864 to 1918, students received not only the classics, but the likes of Benedix, Baumbach, Wichert and Wilhelmi—contemporary and trivial. Prefaces and introductions to texts of the latter type very often state that such books need no introduction, hardly require apology, necessitate no justification, have been favorites in American schools for thirty years, and so on. (It seems that only inferior works required such introductions.) Thus students of the era surveyed, as has been clarified by the Committee of Twelve, got a balance between *Unterhaltungsliteratur* and the classics.

Regarding classical literature, those works which might be expected to cultivate the personality type desired by the era—incorporating morality, decency, industriousness, wholesomeness—were listed particularly frequently: *Hermann und Dorothea, Wilhelm Tell,* and *Minna von Barnhelm* met all the requirements and were probably the largest-selling texts. This is in contrast to the present, when students may be familiar with *Götz von Berlichingen, Kabale und Liebe,* and *Emilia Galotti.* These more wordly plays, particularly *Götz* and *Kabale und Liebe* (*Emilia* was relatively popular), were labeled by nineteenth- and early twentieth-century professors as unwholesome.

The assertion of some contemporary literati that classical literature drove (and is driving) students away from *Germanistik* is inept for 1864–1918. Had this been the case, German, with its liberal dose of the classics, could not have vied for the number one position in high schools, colleges, and universities. Further, since the classics were said to cultivate character while inculcating the German language, they were definitely felt—in opposition to the viewpoints of some today—to have a value in the real world.

Yet there is another side to be considered. It is true that Germanists of the day sought, by and large, to convey what they considered a discerning *Deutschlandbild.* This interpretation of "the German mind" presented by editors and publishers to teachers and students must above all be wholesome, it must be entertaining, lively, adventurous and not too difficult. Culture and literary worth, as has been shown, might or might not be present, though even inferior works can convey culture—if thereby "German life" is signified.

The fact is, however, that students were severely limited in their view of German life (and literature) by the prescription for textbook materials cited above. There was, above all, practically no social activism, a contrast to the German studies of today, though the heyday of the sociological slant of literary criticism and political activism is over. Not only were works such as *Die Räuber* barred from academe, the works of Hauptmann likewise found but scant acceptance. Julius Sachs addressed the Association of Modern Language Teachers on this subject in 1917 as follows:

> Before we recommend it, we ought to reach definite conclusions about the applicability of a piece of literature to our class requirements. How lightly we have hitherto regarded these serious questions! No one but a teacher of long experience realizes the pitfalls that result from a lack of forethought; it is criminal to ignore what the possible reaction of his class to a certain piece of literature may be. Forewarned is forearmed! (145)

This conservative mood manifested itself in the 1860s as students looked back to the classics—as they would repeatedly do throughout the era. In U.S. *Germanistik,* Lessing, Goethe, and Schiller continued their hegemony which had begun in the later 1700s; they are constants throughout the years surveyed. The most socially positive works—*Hermann und Dorothea, Wilhelm*

Tell and *Minna von Barnhelm*—prevailed, for reasons outlined above. On the other hand, Lessing was harshly criticized for his *Erziehung des Menschengeschlechts*, while Goethe and Schiller were sharply taken to task for the excesses of their earlier creations.

Romanticism manifested itself most strikingly during the sixties in the works of Andersen, some of which were actually written in German, not translated from Danish. The one Tieck edition, containing "Die Elfen" and "Leben und Tod des kleinen Rotkäppchens," was probably surpassed in reception by two editions of Andersen's stories. Eichendorff and Fouqué, as well as Körner, who is sometimes reckoned a romantic, were also represented. Andersen probably bested the other romantic authors in academe of the 1860s because his works best projected the distanced innocence of fairy land.

Biedermeier and Young Germany were represented by the works of Benedix and Mügge, respectively, each with three listings from 1864 to 1869. Benedix, because his farces were said to be entertaining for classroom reading, were clean and offered a reasonably good—if silly—*Deutschlandbild*, was one of the most popular authors in U.S. *Germanistik* during the era surveyed. As far as can be ascertained, Mügge went largely unrecognized here throughout the period 1864–1918, although his texts enjoyed a small amount of scholastic popularity. He was a freedom fighter with Bolivar in South America, and ever remained on the side of the oppressed. In the U.S. of the age, it may be that Mügge's writings induced fear of the left—thus the lack of professorial praise.

Regarding Realism, textbooks of the 1860s could boast of Storm, Heyse, Wilhelmi (Zechmeister), Putlitz, Jensen, and Hermann Grimm. Putlitz and Storm were labeled romantics, their works were termed wistful and idealized. Actually, with the prominent exception of his banal farces, some of Putlitz's sentimental works—the *Blumen- und Elfenmarchen*—may indeed seem best fitted for inclusion in books of fairy tales. The so-called mawkish quality of *Immensee* likewise suited it well to instruction which, as has been shown, was to be directed to the feelings at least as much as to the intellect. Nor is Heyse, who was influenced by Tieck and Hoffmann, totally free of the romantic tradition; *L'Arrabbiata* features a curious love affair in a faraway place. Its ending smacks at least slightly of sentimentality—which is apparently what helped to sell texts by Storm and Putlitz as well. Jensen was known for both romantic pastorals and novels of social engagement. Only *Die braune Erika*, a work of romantic stamp, became a U.S. German text—and a popular one. Like Benedix, Wilhelmi (Zechmeister) was the author of shallow farces; his inane *Einer muß heiraten* presented the brothers Grimm as imbeciles. However, the text was wholesome and—perhaps—entertaining; it, too, was a leading text of the era. Hermann Grimm, son of Wilhelm Grimm, was popular in texts of the earlier years of the time period surveyed for his essays on Renaissance artists.

Although not all the authors of texts published in the 1860s have been considered in this brief summary, the majority—and the most popular—have been touched upon. It may therefore be concluded that, with few exceptions, students were allowed to read only the most moral, idealistic works of the Enlightenment and Classicism, only the more innocent manifestations of Romanticism—and these only in moderation, only an innocently romanticized Realism free from social issues, or, for comic relief, farces. The prevailing national conservatism in politics and morals held sway in the classroom.

The decade of the seventies, during which the authors read in the sixties continued their prevalence, saw an even more conservative drift in texts. Hugo Müller and Alexander Elz—all but unknown on either side of the Atlantic—contributed farces. Some amusement and a *Deutschlandbild* better than that provided by stories or plays set outside the German-speaking area of Europe are the only advantages offered by these texts, which were apparently popular. More serious and sentimental were the texts by Marie Nathusius, Heinrich Zschokke, and Wilhelmine von Hillern. Nathusius was the author of a "Christian family novel," *Tagebuch aus dem Leben eines armen Fräuleins.* Zschokke was a pastor known to U.S. German students not for his most famous work, *Aballino, der große Bandit*—a work regretted by the author in old age—but rather for his innocent novellas, such as *Das Wirtshaus zu Cransac*. Hillern was given to Catholic mysticism, as is proved reasonably well by *Höher als die Kirche*, in which a rosebush planted near a cathedral by two children becomes the key to their eventual success and happiness. Without a doubt, works with a religious cast and farces were the primary trends among texts by authors who were first listed in the seventies.

The eighties saw a broad expansion in textual offerings, with the first appearance of relatively liberal readings. With Gellert the *Empfindsamkeit* arrived at school, while Romanticism was strengthened by the addition of Jakob and Wilhelm Grimm, Chamisso, Hauff and Uhland. Roquette, with his belated–*Biedermeier* songs of the Rhine and wine, prepared the way for the author who was probably most popular in German textbooks after Lessing, Goethe and Schiller: Rudolf Baumbach. Both Roquette and Baumbach, *Butzenscheiben* conservatives, have ebbed far short of present-day artistic recognition.

Moritz Hartmann, Heine and Gutzkow represented liberal Young Germany in new editions of the eighties. Hartmann, who dealt in political satire, was a veteran of the movement of 1848. U.S. students apparently read only *Die Ausgestoßenen*, an unpopular novel listed only once. The fate of Gutzkow would have been similar had he not written the relatively innocent historical comedy *Zopf und Schwert*, which was listed frequently from 1881 to 1910. Heine, as has been demonstrated, was received only in carefully censored editions, though these are quite numerous.

A warm reception was granted the representatives of the school of Realism. Foremost among this group were Gustav Freytag and Wilhelm Riehl, originators of *deutsche Kulturgeschichte* and celebrators of German virtues, especially as reflected in *Bürgertum*. In distinct opposition to Young Germany, commendation rather than criticism marked the *Deutschlandbild* offered by the works of these men. The prolific and popular Professor Ebers was, to American academics' credit, not strongly represented in German classes, but the inevitable *Schwänke*, predominently the products of Gustav von Moser, Oskar Blumenthal and Julius Rosen, brought their share of humor to language students. In the field of the *Dorfgeschichte*, Berthold Auerbach and Melchior Meyr vied for the attention of teachers and students, much to the advantage of Auerbach. That moral tales peopled by sturdy, steadfast characters were adopted as chrestomathies is not out of character for the age. On the lighter side came Heinrich Seidel, whose *Leberecht Hühnchen* is still rather entertaining, and Richard Leander (Richard von Volkmann), whose *Träumereien* are definitely romantic in nature.

On the one hand, the eighties demonstrated a slight tendency toward liberalism and social engagement, even if carefully muffled. On the other hand, late *Biedermeier* and middle-class Realism far exceeded the modest gains of Young Germany in U.S. pedagogy—particularly when one reflects that conservative textbooks previously published had by and large stayed on the market, and that authors first published in textbook editions in the sixties and seventies were frequently the object of further editions. Classical ideals, romantic fairy-tale innocence, *Biedermeier* views beheld through leaded panes, and honest middle-class Realism produced an image of Germany, Austria, and Switzerland not conceived to engender liberal thinking, social or political, among American students.

The nineties brought more Realism with an extremely moderate dash of Naturalism. From periods prior to that of Realism, Bürger's *Leonore*, selections from Jean Paul, and three works by Kleist were the earliest literary works to appear for the first time in textbook editions during the decade. Kleist enjoyed a moderate success. Next chronologically are two of academe's more prominent authors, Grillparzer and Scheffel—a strange juxtaposition of dramatic genius and sentimentalization which demonstrates the taste of the times quite well. In point of fact, Scheffel's work outlisted that of Grillparzer; as has been indicated, Scheffel's *Der Trompeter von Säkkingen* is unmarred by anything morally untoward. Then, too, two of the Grillparzer plays take place far from the German-speaking area of Europe. Thus Grillparzer's dramas were subordinated to Scheffel's careless verse and anachronistic *Deutschlandbild*. Perhaps due to what literary historians of the time termed their lack of vigor and dearth of plot, the works of Stifter fared less well than those of Grillparzer in the struggle against mediocre talents.

Rather belated was the appearance in U.S. German texts of Gottfried Keller, about whom widely varying opinions prevailed among German professors. Keller's works, with their instructive Swiss milieu, were reasonably prominent in academe, but they were apparently no match for the clean and wholesome Scheffel. Roughcast yet clear were the writings of Gerstäcker adopted for school use. *Germelshausen*, the leading Gerstäcker text, is a love/ghost story set in Germany during the 1840s; it is still utilized in American schools today. Not so prominent then as now, judging from the listings, was Conrad Ferdinand Meyer; though justly famed for their realistic quality, something which often proved an attraction in academe, Meyer's novellas and *Jürg Jenatsch* were only moderately successful texts.

Quite popular in the world at large, Felix L. S. Dahn's historical novels and stories did not flourish in proportion to their acceptance outside academe; as has been pointed out, they were perceived by some scholars as distortions of history. Also limited in its appeal was Ernst Eckstein's *Der Besuch im Carcer*, a humorous though intellectually uninspiring little book—and entirely clean, if a daring adolescent's insubordination is regarded by the reader as amusing. On the other hand, the books of Peter Rosegger (e.g., *Der Lex von Gutenhag*) struck the academic fancy: they were didactic and sentimental. A similar appeal was exerted by the work of Emil Frommel, author of "Das eiserne Kreuz," who was known for his unaffected piety and healthy humor. The inevitable farce of the nineties was presented in Ernst Wichert's *Als Verlobte empfehlen sich—*. With the exception of two short passages in *Der Lex von Gutenhag* which could strike an American reader as questionable, the last four stories are unimpeachably pure; they show at least a few aspects of life in Germany or Austria, and could be expected not to put a class to sleep, if not always to entertain.

Wildenbruch and Fontane stood at the onset of Naturalism. Fontane questioned the politics and mores of his time (the aristocracy, sexual arrangements); Wildenbruch lauded the house of Hohenzollern. Wildenbruch was the favorite, not only of the Second Empire, but also of U.S. teachers of German (e.g., *Das edle Blut*, a naturalistic story based on heredity and physiognomy). The apparent popularity of Hermann Sudermann in U.S. schools of the day indicates that, at least in certain quarters, farces, juvenile fiction and other ultra-light readings were, as in the eighties, at least slightly challenged by social and moral criticism. But Sudermann and, to a lesser degree, Fontane, could make at best a limited impact upon German programs thriving largely upon the more controlled classics of the past and conservative or apolitical authors of the relative present.

Among female authors of the nineties, Hans Arnold (Babette von Bülow) instilled respect for one's elders, while Nataly von Eschstruth portrayed for students a silly woman in an improbable situation ("Ihr Ideal"), and paraphrased an anecdote by *Butzenscheibendichter* Scheffel. Johanna Spyri offered scholars *Moni der Geißbub*. The one true exception to this mediocrity is Marie von Ebner-Eschenbach, who should perhaps be better known for *Die Freiherren von Gemperlein*, the story of two eccentric brothers, than for the dog story *Krambambuli*.

Textbooks published between 1900 and 1910 demonstrated less concern with social issues and conventions than those of the preceding decade. In a literary climate uncongenial to Gutzkow and Spielhagen, the student might be entertained by Raspe's *Münchhausen*, Campe's *Robinson der Jüngere*, or Kotzebue's *Die deutschen Kleinstädter*. A degree of dated political engagement was offered by Arndt's description of German patriots in Russia during the Napoleonic era, while E. T. A. Hoffmann's fantasies were offered only in the form of what professors called his two most realistic tales. Mörike's *Mozart auf der Reise nach Prag* and Droste-Hülshoff's *Die Judenbuche* were representative of the *Biedermeierzeit*. Hebbel, Otto Ludwig, and Wagner appeared in German textbooks for the first time. Charles Sealsfield (Karl Postl) praised American democracy and opposed European imperialism and clericalism. Sealsfield's *Die Prärie am Jacinto* was published as a text in 1905.

Concerning literature published in texts 1900–1910 contemporary to the period surveyed, probably most popular was the work of Ludwig Fulda, who was best known for his dramatized fairy tale, *Der Talisman*. This is a blend of Andersen's "The Emperor's New Clothes" and Lessing's "Ring Parable" written in iambic pentameter with frequent rhymes. Less popular as a text but more impressive was Wilbrandt's *Der Meister von Palmyra*, a play set in antiquity which deals with the transmigration of souls. Perhaps for this reason the text was not widely chosen by educators.

The muffling of social criticism is nowhere more striking than in academe's reception of Gerhart Hauptmann. Only the symbolist drama *Die versunkene Glocke*, with mythological background and magical beings, was considered wholesome enough for student use. On the other hand, the war reminiscences of Liliencron and the bogus war reminiscences of Frenssen were desirable texts in the estimation of professors of the day.

One socialist sympathizer somehow penetrated U.S. *Germanistik* during these ten years. Otto Ernst (Otto Ernst Schmidt) created the novel *Asmus Sempers Jugendland*, a good text if faculty and students could tolerate occasional lapsings into socialism, or simply skipped these soapbox addresses. Apparently, teachers felt apprehensive; *Asmus Sempers Jugendland* was listed only once. If the predominantly serious tone of *Asmus* was not desired, Heinrich Hansjakob's stories of the Black Forest were apolitical and amusing, and Viktor Blüthgen's puerile but enjoyable *Das Peterle von Nürnberg* clearly appealed to a number of teachers. Hans Hoffmann offered students a view of the negative side of academic life in Germany in two stories from *Das Gymnasium zu Stolpenburg*.

Prominent among women authors was Isolde Kurz, a formalist whose works recall those of Heyse and Meyer. Better known today is Clara Viebig, whose works are a blend of Naturalism and *Heimatkunst*; though her writings contain considerable agitation on social problems, she was safely presented to U.S. German students as the author of "Jaschu," the story of a peasant girl's love for her pet pig. A similar case was that of Helene Böhlau, who was celebrated in Germany for her innocent *Ratsmädelgeschichten* as well as other works dealing with social issues; she was known to American students only for the former stories. Carmen Sylva, actually Queen Elizabeth of Rumania, and Charlotte Niese also made appearances in academe.

The final eight years of the era reinforce the familiar pattern. First, there was a looking-back to something innocent—in this case Hebel's homespun *Schatzkästlein*. Probably because of his pessimism and the difficulty of his prose, Raabe only now appeared in textbooks; despite the comments on society made by his view of Germany, Raabe cannot be called a reformer. However, in 1913 students were offered Carl Schurz's *Lebenserinnerungen* (actually German-American literature) and Spielhagen's *Das Skelett im Hause*; neither text was listed more than once. That Spielhagen was not read in academe until 1913, although his works, which had appeared years earlier, were frequently translated and were reviewed by the *New York Times*, is doubtless due to his leftist tendencies. As for Schurz, who was perhaps most controversial in America as a leader of the Liberal Republican movement, the revolutionary activities of his earlier years in Germany could have weakened his standing among conservative Germanists.

An escape from liberal literature which had already proved its usefulness was resorted to once more during these last years surveyed: texts containing conservative *Heimatkunst* were adopted. Herzog's *Die Burgkinder* and Lienhard's "Der Pandurenstein" both deal soberly with valor in battle and striving—those most "German" qualities in middle-class American credence of years past. Because both works appeared late in the era surveyed, their popularity at that time—especially that of Herzog's book, which appeared in 1917—is difficult to assess (though Lienhard is recognized in German studies of today).

The impact of women authors of the last eight years of the era is weak. If Frieda Schanz (Soyaux), Ilse Leskien and two exponents of *Heimatkunst*, Auguste Supper and Hermine Villinger, ever became popular authors of U.S. German texts, it was after 1918. It would appear that all four are forgotten by the *Germanistik* of the later twentieth century.

A significant question which arises from a consideration of the data presented, a question which each person must ultimately answer for himself, is this: Has the study of German literature in the classrooms of the United States improved since the era surveyed, or have German textbooks produced in America declined in quality as well as in quantity? Concerning German studies of the past, many would agree with Edwin Zeydel, who wrote in 1964 that beginning with the 1870s

> Reading texts offering works of contemporary authors became more plentiful, giving teachers wider opportunity to select more modern materials. Many of these works were also edited better than those of earlier days. The editions of Wilhelm Bernhardt from about 1885 on furnish good examples. But prudishness still reigned in the classroom, and such contemporaneous works as the dramas

and novels of the early Naturalists were unthinkable in the schoolroom, which no writer, old or recent, could enter unless he was as pure as the driven snow. What is perhaps even worse, the usual reading fare gave no inkling of the Germany of that day, and offered mostly innocuous, romantic tales with little or no local color. (354)

Or, as Levin Schücking wrote of nineteenth-century editors, "bezeichnend ist hier die strenge Verantwortung, die der Herausgeber sich für seine Leser auferlegt. Sie erscheint uns recht eigentlich biedermeierlich" (64). The problem is where to draw the line between editorial responsibility and prudery.

But there is another aspect of German texts, 1864–1918, which should be considered apart from the question of prudery: How many German students—even German majors—of today are familiar with Kaiser Maximilian I and Marx Treitsauerwein, with "real" people of Goethe's Weimar or an orphan in medieval Nuremberg, or with the last of the Gothic emperors, Teja? Today's student may experience Lenz's "Die Nacht im Hotel" or Bichsel's "Der Milchmann" and learn relatively little about Germany. Certainly, 1864–1918 was the era of Scheffel and Baumbach, but was the student of those years necessarily worse off amidst *Butzenscheiben*, the *Wunschfrau* and the summer solstice than the student of today, with his regimen of sometimes depressing postwar literature?

Indeed, the greatest differences between then and now—as far as literature textbooks are concerned—are an increase in political and social activism and a decrease in virtuousness accompanied by a general darkening of outlook. What the texts of the years surveyed contained, what the professors of those years have written about them, and what Germanists of today have decided about them shows not only what students then were reading and why, but holds up a mirror to the *Germanistik* of the present. And when the comparison of the two pedagogical approaches is made, the German texts of the earlier era do not, taken as a whole, compare altogether disadvantageously with those of today.

Selected Bibliography

SOURCES CITED

1. Primary

Allen, Phillip Schuyler, and Max Batt, eds. *Easy German Stories*. Chicago: Scott, Foresman and Co., 1903.

Arnold, Hans (Babette von Bülow). *Fritz auf Ferien*. Edited by Arnold Werner-Spanhoofd. Boston: D.C. Heath and Co., 1896.

Baker, George Merrick, ed. *German Stories*. New York: Henry Holt and Co., 1909.

Baumbach, Rudolf. *Die Nonna*. Edited by Wilhelm Bernhardt. Boston: D. C. Heath and Co., 1897.

———. *Sommermärchen*. Edited by Edward Meyer. New York: Henry Holt and Co., 1900.

———. *Waldnovellen*. Edited by Wilhelm Bernhardt. Boston: D. C. Heath and Co., 1899.

Benedix, Roderich. *Der Prozeß*. Edited by Benjamin Willis Wells. Boston: D. C. Heath and Co., 1900.

Benedix, Roderich, and Alexander Wilhelmi (Alexander Viktor Zechmeister). *Drei kleine Lustspiele*. Edited by Benjamin Willis Wells. Boston: D. C. Heath and Co., 1897.

Bernhardt, Wilhelm, ed. *Auf der Sonnenseite*. Boston: D. C. Heath and Co., 1904.

Betz, Frederick, ed. *Aus der Jugendzeit*. Boston: D. C. Heath and Co., 1913.

Bierwirth, Heinrich C., and Asbury H. Herrick, eds. *Ährenlese*. Boston: D. C. Heath and Co., 1918.

Blüthgen, Victor. *Das Peterle von Nürnberg*. Edited by Josephine C. Doniat. New York: Macmillan, 1918.

Böhlau, Helene. *Ratsmädelgeschichten*. Edited by Emma Haevernick. Boston: D. C. Heath and Co., 1908.

Campe, Joachim Heinrich. *Robinson der Jüngere*. Edited by Carl Henry Ibershoff. Boston: D. C. Heath and Co., 1904.

Ebner-Eschenbach, Marie von. *Die Freiherren von Gemperlein* and *Krambambuli*. Edited by Alexander R. Hohlfeld. Boston: D. C. Heath and Co., 1898.

Eckstein, Ernst. *Der Besuch im Carcer*. Edited by T. A. Stephens. New York: Maynard, Merrill and Co., 189-.

Eichendorff, Joseph Freiherr von. *Aus dem Leben eines Taugenichts*. Edited by George M. Howe. New York: Henry Holt and Co., 1906.

Elz, Alexander. *Er ist nicht eifersüchtig*. Edited by Benjamin Willis Wells. New York: Henry Holt and Co., 1870.

Ernst, Otto (Otto Ernst Schmidt). *Asmus Sempers Jugendland*. Edited by Carl Osthaus. Boston: D. C. Heath and Co., 1916.

Fouqué, Friedrich Baron de LaMotte. *Undine*. Edited by Joachim Henry Senger. New York: American Book Co., 1903.

Frenssen, Gustav. *Peter Moors Fahrt nach Südwest*. Edited by Herman Babson. New York: Henry Holt and Co., 1914.

Freytag, Gustav. *Die Journalisten*. Edited by Hermann Hager; re-edited by Walter Dallam Toy. Boston: D. C. Heath and Co., 1901.

Fulda, Ludwig. *Der Talisman*. Edited by C. William Prettyman. Boston: D. C. Heath and Co., 1902.

Gerstäcker, Friedrich. *Germelshausen*. Edited by Carl Osthaus; re-edited by Orlando F. Lewis. Boston: D. C. Heath and Co., 1902.

———. *Irrfahrten*. Edited by Marian P. Whitney. New York: Henry Holt and Co., 1896.

Goethe, Johann Wolfgang von. *Faust I*. Edited by Calvin Thomas. Boston: D. C. Heath and Co., 1892.

———. *Hermann und Dorothea*. Edited by Warren Austin Adams. Boston: D. C. Heath and Co., 1904.

Hauff, Wilhelm. *Das kalte Herz*. Edited by Neil C. Brooks. New York: Henry Holt and Co., 1912.

———. *Der Zwerg Nase*. Edited by Otto R. Patzwald and Charles W. Robson. Boston: D. C. Heath and Co., 1913.

Heine, Heinrich. *Die Harzreise*. Edited by Robert Porter Keep. Boston: Allyn and Bacon, 1916.

Herzog, Rudolf. *Die Burgkinder*. Edited by Ottilie G. Boetzkes. Boston: D. C. Heath and Co., 1917.

Heyse, Paul. *L'Arrabbiata*. Edited by Max Lenz. New York: American Book Co., 1897.

———. *Niels mit der offenen Hand*. Edited by Edward Southey Joynes. Boston: D. C. Heath and Co., 1902.

Hillern, Wilhelmine von. *Höher als die Kirche*. Edited by Frederick W. J. Heuser. New York: Charles E. Merrill Co., 1910.

Hoffmann, Ernst Theodor Amadeus. *Meister Martin der Küfner und seine Gesellen*. Edited by Robert Herndon Fife, Jr. New York: Henry Holt and Co., 1907.

Hoffmann, Hans. *Das Gymnasium zu Stolpenburg*. Edited by Valentin Buehner. Boston: D. C. Heath and Co., 1904.

Keller, Gottfried. *Romeo und Julia auf dem Dorfe*. Edited by Warren Austin Adams. Boston: D. C. Heath and Co., 1900.

Kurz, Isolde. *Zwei Märchen*. Edited by Charles Marshall Poor. New York: Oxford University Press, American Branch, 1914.

Leander, Richard (Richard von Volkmann). *Träumereien an französischen Kaminen*. Edited by William Henry van der Smissen. Boston: D. C. Heath and Co., 1984.

Leskien, Ilse. *"Schuld" and Other Stories*. Edited by Bayard Quincy Morgan. New York: Oxford University Press, American Branch, 1915.

Lessing, Gotthold Ephraim. *Emilia Galotti*. Edited by Max Winkler. Boston: D. C. Heath and Co., 1885.

———. *Emilia Galotti*. Edited by Max Poll. Boston: Ginn and Co., 1894.

———. *Minna von Barnhelm*. Edited by Sylvester Primer. rev. ed. Boston: D. C. Heath and Co., 1889.

Liliencron, Detlev von. *Anno 1870: Kriegsnovellen*. Edited by Wilhelm Bernhardt. Boston: D. C. Heath and Co., 1903.

Ludwig, Otto. *Der Erbförster*. Edited by Morton C. Stewart. New York: Henry Holt and Co., 1910.

Meyer, Conrad Ferdinand. *Der Schuß von der Kanzel*. Edited by Martin H. Haertel. Boston: Ginn and Co., 1905.

―――. *Jürg Jenatsch*. Edited by Alfred Kenngott. Boston: D. C. Heath and Co., 1911.

Meyr, Melchior. *Ludwig und Annemarie*. Edited by Friedrich Georg Gottlob Schmidt. New York: Oxford University Press, American Branch, 1913.

Mörike, Eduard. *Mozart auf der Reise nach Prag*. Edited by William Guild Howard. Boston: D. C. Heath and Co., 1904.

Moser, Gustav von. *Der Bibliothekar*. Edited by Benjamin Willis Wells. Boston: D. C. Heath and Co., 1897.

Raabe, Wilhelm. *Eulenpfingsten*. Edited by Marcus B. Lambert. Boston: D. C. Heath and Co., 1912.

Riehl, Wilhelm Heinrich. *Burg Neideck*. Edited by Garrett W. Thompson. New York: American Book Co., 1916

―――. *Der Fluch der Schönheit*. Edited by Arthur N. Leonard. Boston: Ginn and Co., 1908.

Roedder, Edwin Carl, ed. *Schwarzwaldleut'*. New York: Henry Holt and Co., 1913.

Rosegger, Peter Kettenfeier. *Der Lex von Gutenhag*. Edited by Bayard Quincy Morgan. Boston: D. C. Heath and Co., 1911.

Scheffel, Joseph Viktor von. *Der Trompeter von Säkkingen*. Edited by Carla Wenckebach. Boston: D. C. Heath and Co., 1895.

Schiller, Friedrich. *Wilhelm Tell*. Edited by Carl Schlenker. Boston: Allyn and Bacon, 1913.

Schönberg, Hans Friedrich von. *Die Schildbürger*. Edited by Frederick Betz. Boston: D. C. Heath and Co., 1910.

Seidel, Heinrich. *Leberecht Hühnchen*. Edited by Arnold Werner-Spanhoofd. Boston: D. C. Heath and Co., 1901.

Spielhagen, Friedrich. *Das Skelett im Hause*. Edited by M. M. Skinner. Boston, D. C. Heath and Co., 1913.

Stifter, Adalbert. *Brigitta*. Edited by Robert Warner Crowell. New York: Oxford University Press, American Branch, 1914.

Storm, Theodor. *Immensee*. Edited by Wilhelm Bernhardt. Boston: D. C. Heath and Co., 1902.

Sudermann, Hermann. *Teja*. Edited by Richard Clyde Ford. Boston: D. C. Heath and Co., 1906.

Wichert, Ernst. *Als Verlobte empfehlen sich—*. Edited by George T. Flom. Boston: D. C. Heath and Co., 1902.

Wilbrandt, Adolf. *Der Meister von Palmyra*. Edited by Théodore Henckels. New York: American Book Co., 1900.

Wildenbruch, Ernst von. *Das edle Blut*. Edited by Friedrich Georg Gottlob Schmidt. Boston: D. C. Heath and Co., 1898.

Zschokke, Johann Heinrich Daniel. *Das Wirtshaus zu Cransac*. Edited by Edward Southey Joynes. Boston: D. C. Heath and Co., 1900.

2. Bibliographical

Frenzel, Herbert A., and Elizabeth Frenzel. *Daten deutscher Dichtung.* Cologne: Verlag Kiepenheuer und Witsch, 1953.
Kelly, James, ed. *The American Catalogue of Books (Original and Reprints) Published in the United States.* New York: J. Wiley and Son, 1866–71.
Kurian, George T. *The Directory of American Book Publishing.* New York: Simon and Schuster, 1975.
Leypoldt, Frederick, et al. *The American Catalogue.* New York: A. C. Armstrong, 1880–1911.
Library of Congress Catalogue. Totowa, N. Y.: Roman and Littlefield, Inc., 1898–1942.
Morgan, Bayard Q. *German Literature in English Translation: 1481–1927.* 2nd ed. rev. and augm. New York and London: Scarecrow Press, 1965.
———. *German Literature in English Translation, Supplement Embracing the Years 1928–1955.* New York and London: Scarecrow Press, 1965.
National Union Catalog: Pre-1956 Imprints. Chicago: Mansell Information/Publishing, Ltd. and The American Library Association, 1968–1980.
Pochmann, Henry A., and Arthur R. Schultz, *Bibliography of German Culture in America to 1940.* Madison: University of Wisconsin Press, 1953.
Publishers Trade List Annual. New York: *Publishers Weekly* (later R. R. Bowker), 1873-.
Publishers Weekly. New York: F. Leypoldt (later Office of *Publishers Weekly*; then R. R. Bowker), 1872-.
Schultz, Arthur R. *German-American Relations and German Culture in America: A Subject Bibliography, 1941–1980.* 2 vols. Milwood, N. Y.: Kraus International Publications, 1984.
Tanselle, Thomas. *Guide to the Study of U. S. Imprints.* Cambridge, Mass.: Belknap Press, 1971.
Tebbel, John W. *A History of Book Publishing in the United States.* 2 vols. New York: Xerox, 1975.
The United States Catalog: Books in Print. Minneapolis (later New York): H. W. Wilson, 1900–1928.

3. Critical

Auerbach, Doris. "The Reception of German Literature in America as Exemplified by the *New York Times*: 1945–1970." Ph.D. dissertation, New York University, 1974.
Beitter, Ursula. "The Cultural Image of Germans and Germany in First-year American College Texts." Ph.D. dissertation, New York University, 1975.
Bernhardt, Wilhelm. *Geschichte der deutschen Literatur.* Boston: Carl Schoenhof, 1892; New York: F. W. Christern, 1892; Chicago: Koelling and Klappenbach, 1892.
Brett-Evans, David. "Theodor Storm: An Enduring 'College Classic.'" Edited by Brigitte Schludermann et al. *Deutung und Bedeutung.* The Hague: Mouton, 1973, pp. 181–191.
Cannon, Lee E. Review of Ilse Leskien's *"Schuld" and Other Stories,* ed. by Bayard Quincy Morgan." *The Modern Language Journal* 1 (October 1916-May 1917):113.
Carse, Alice F. "The Reception of German Literature in America as Exemplified by the *New York Times*: 1919–1944." Ph.D. dissertation, New York University, 1973.
Durzak, Manfred. "Die Rezeption der deutschen Literatur nach 1945 in den USA." *Die deutsche Literatur der Gegenwart.* Stuttgart: Reclam, 1971.

Ehlert K., H. Hoffacker, and H. Ide. "Thesen über Erziehung zu kritischem Lesen." *Diskussion Deutsch* 4 (1971):101.
Eucken, Rudolf. "Are the Germans Still a Nation of Thinkers?" *The Forum* 26 (September 1898-February 1899):592–602.
Friedrich, Werner P. *History of German Literature*. 2nd ed. New York: Barnes and Noble. 1961.
Geffcken, F. H. "German Socialism and Literary Sterility." *The Forum* 14 (September 1892-February 1893):660–672.
Gordon, John. "The Reception of German Literature in America as Exemplified by the *New York Herald Tribune*: 1935–1966." Ph.D. dissertation, New York University, 1974.
Handschin, Charles H. *Methods of Teaching Modern Languages*. Yonkers-on-Hudson, N. Y.: World Book Co., 1923.
Hatfield, Henry C., and Joan Merrick. "Studies of German Literature in the United States, 1939–1946." *Modern Language Review* 42 (1948): 353–392.
Heinsohn, Wolfgang. "The Reception of German Literature in America as Exemplified by the *New York Times*: Part I: 1870–1918." Ph.D. dissertation, New York University, 1974.
Heuser, Frederick W. J. "Nineteenth Century German Literature for Undergraduates." *The Modern Language Journal* 2 (October 1917–May 1918): 248–259.
Hosmer, James K. *A Short History of German Literature*. 2nd ed. St. Louis: G. I. Jones and Co., 1879.
Klopsch, O. P. "Otto Ernst, *Asmus Sempers Jugendland*, edited by Carl Osthaus." *The Modern Language Journal* 1 (October 1916–May 1917):190.
Kolbe, P. R. "Heinrich Heine, *Die Harzreise*, edited by Robert Porter Keep." *The Modern Language Journal* 2 (October 1917–May 1918): 180.
Kopp, W. LaMarr. *German Literature in the United States 1945–1960*. Chapel Hill: University of North Carolina Press, 1967.
Krell, Leo, and Leonhard Fiedler. *Deutsche Literaturgeschichte*. 11th ed. Bamberg: C. C. Buchners Verlag, 1965.
Krumpelmann, John T. "Gerstaecker's 'Germelshausen' and Lerner's 'Brigadoon.'" *Monatshefte* 40 (November 1948):396–400.
Kummer, Friedrich. *Deutsche Literaturgeschichte*. Dresden: Verlag von Carl Reißner, 1909.
Kurz, Heinrich. *Geschichte der deutschen Literatur*. Vols. II–IV. 8th ed. Leipzig: B. G. Teubner, 1888.
"Louisa May Alcott." *Encyclopaedia Britannica*, 1957. Vol. I.
"Ludvig Holberg." *Encyclopaedia Britannica*, 1957. Vol. XI.
Mews, Siegfried E. "'The Evil Spirit Journalism': The Press in the Context of Literature." *South Atlantic Bulletin* 43 (November 1978): 5–21.
Nollen, John S. "*Goethe's Poems*, edited by Martin Schütze." *The Modern Language Journal* 1 (October 1916-May 1917):320–322.
Pochmann, Henry A., Arthur R. Schultz et al. *German Culture in America: Philosophical and Cultural Influences: 1600–1900*. Madison: University of Wisconsin Press, 1957.
Priest, George M. *A Brief History of German Literature*. New York: Charles Scribner's Sons, 1909.
Report of the Committee of Twelve. Calvin Thomas, chairman. Boston: D. C. Heath and Co., 1900.

Sachs, Julius. "Desirability of a Syllabus of French and German Texts." *The Modern Language Journal* 2 (October 1917–May 1918):139–145.
Sander, Volkmar. "Zur Rezeption der deutschen Literatur in der *New York Times*." *Festschrift Gerhard Loose*. Munich-Bern: Francke Verlag, 1973, pp. 161–173.
Schücking, Levin L. *Soziologie der literarischen Geschmacksbildung*. 3rd ed. Munich-Bern: Francke Verlag, 1961.
Schulz-Behrend, George. "Forever *Immensee*." *The German Quarterly* 22 (May 1949):159–163.
Stroebe, Lilian E., and Marian P. Whitney. *Geschichte der Deutschen Literatur*. New York: Henry Holt and Co., 1913.
Thomas, Calvin. *A History of German Literature*. New York: Appleton and Co., 1909.
Twain, Mark (Samuel L. Clemens). "About 'Play-Acting.'" *The Forum* 26 (September 1898–February 1899):143–151.
Vilmar, A. F. C. *Geschichte der deutschen National-Literatur*. 16th ed. Marburg and Leipzig: N. G. Elwert'sche Universitäts-Buchhandlung, 1874.
Vos, Bert John. "Goethe's *Hermann and Dorothea*, edited by Ernst Feise." *The Modern Language Journal* 2 (October 1917–May 1918):181-183.
―――. "Friedrich Gerstäcker, *Der Wilddieb*, ed. by Walter R. Myers." *The Modern Language Journal* 1 (October 1916-May 1917):226-227.
―――. "Heinrich Seidel, *Leberecht Hühnchen*, ed. by William F. Luebke." *The Modern Language Journal* 1 (October 1916–May 1917):72–73.
Webster's Seventh New Collegiate Dictionary. 13th edition, 1963.
Weisstein, Ulrich W. *Einführung in die Vergleichende Literaturwissenschaft*. Stuttgart: Kohlhammer Verlag, 1968.
Wells, Benjamin W. *Modern German Literature*. 2nd ed. Boston: Little, Brown and Co., 1901.
Wittke, Carl. *The German-language Press in America*. Lexington: University of Kentucky Press, 1957.
Zeydel, Edwin H. "The Teaching of German in the United States from Colonial Times to the Present." *The German Quarterly* 37 (September 1964):315–392.

Sources Consulted—Other Relevant Works

Allaire, Joseph L. "Foreign Languages and the Founding Fathers." *South Atlantic Bulletin* 42 (January 1977):3–9.
Allen, Phillip Schuyler. *Hints on Teaching of German Conversation, Together with a List of the Text-Books in German Published by Ginn and Company, 1912*. [German Texts for High School and College Reading: pp. 37–56.] New York: Ginn and Co., 1912.
Alt, Arthur Tilo. "Die kritische Rezeption Friedrich Hebbels in den USA." *Hebbel-Jahrbuch 1978*, 163–180.
Bagley, William C. *The Educative Process*. New York: Macmillan, 1908.
Bagster-Collins, E. W. "History of Modern Language Teaching in the United States." *Publications of the American and Canadian Committees on Modern Languages*, vol. 42. New York: Macmillan, 1930.
Bathke, Edith, ed. *Unheimliche Begegnungen*. Stuttgart: Ernst Klett Verlag, 1983.
Belgardt, Raimund. "Dichtertum als Existenzproblem: Zur Deutung von Storms *Immensee*." *Schriften der Theodor Storm-Gesellschaft* 18 (1969):77–78.
"Biography and Bibliography of Ernst Steiger, German-American Publisher and

Collector of Americana." Philadephia: *American Philosophical Society Year Book 1967* (1968), 453–456.

Boerner, Peter. "Erika Diehl: *Deutsche Literatur im französischen Deutschlesebuch 1870–1970.*" *Germanistik* 18 (Jahrgang 1977), Heft I, 110.

Bosse, Georg von. *Das heutige Deutschtum in den Vereinigten Staaten von Amerika.* Stuttgart: C. Belser-sche Verlagshandlung, 1904.

British Museum. *The Catalogues of the British Museum.* London: Trustees of the British Museum, 1951–1952.

Cazden, Robert. "Johann Georg Wesselhöft and the German Book Trade in America." *The German Contribution to the Building of the Americas, Studies in Honor of Karl J. R. Arndt.* Edited by Gerhard K. Friesen and Walter Schatzberg. Hanover: Clark University Press, 1977.

"Der Begriff der humanistischen Bildung in den Erziehungssystemen der Vereinigten Staaten." *Paedagogische Provinz* 4 (1949):237–242.

Dick, Charles, and James E. Homans, eds. *The Cyclopedia of American Biography.* 2nd ed. 11 vols. New York: The Press Association Compilers, 1915.

Durzak, Manfred. *Das Amerika-Bild in der deutschen Gegenwartsliteratur.* Stuttgart: Kohlhammer Verlag, 1979.

Faust, Albert Bernhardt. *The German Element in the United States.* Boston and New York: Houghton, Mifflin and Co., 1909.

Fick, Henry H. "Was soll die Jugend lesen?" *Vortrag.* Chicago: Franz Cindele Printing Co., 1880.

Florer, Warren Washburn. *German Liberty Authors.* Boston: The Gorham Press, 1918.

Francke, Kuno. *German Ideals of To-day and Other Essays on German Culture.* Boston and New York: Houghton, Mifflin and Co., 1907.

———. *A History of German Literature as Determined by Social Forces.* 4th ed. New York: Henry Holt and Co., 1901.

Goedeke, Karl. *Grundrisz zur Geschichte der deutschen Dichtung aus den Quellen.* 15 vols. [later 25 vols., 1940]. Dresden: L. Ehlermann, 1884.

Hewett, Waterman Thomas. "The Aims and Methods of Collegiate Instruction in Modern Languages." *Modern Language Association Publications* 1 (1886):25–36.

———, ed. *Methods of Teaching Modern Languages and on Methods of Modern Language Instruction.* Boston: D. C. Heath and Co., 1893.

Jantz, Harold S. "German Thought and Literature in New England, 1620–1820, A Preliminary Survey." *Journal of English and Germanic Philology* 41 (January 1942);i, 1–45.

Kayser, Christian Gottlob. *Vollständiges Literaturlexikon.* 42 vols. Leipzig: Schumann (1834–41); Weigel (1848–87); Weigel Nachfolger (1891); Tauschnitz (1895–1912).

Kelly, L. G. *Twenty-five Centuries of Language Teaching: 500 BC-1969.* Rowley, Mass.: Newbury House, 1969.

Klenze, Camillo von. "Die Zukunft der deutschen Kultur in Amerika." An address before the German University League, New York, N. Y., March 17, 1915. New York: F. C. Stechert, 1915.

Kluge, Hermann. *Geschichte der deutschen Nationalliteratur.* 3rd ed. Altenburg: O. Bonde, 1871.

Koenig, Robert. *Deutsche Litteraturgeschichte* [sic]. 19th ed. Bielefeld and Leipzig: Verlag von Velhagen und Klasing, 1887.

Kosch, Wilhelm. *Deutsches Literatur-Lexikon.* 2nd ed. Bern: A. Francke, 1949.

Lehmann-Haupt, Helmut. *The Book in America*. In collaboration with Lawrence C. Wroth and Rollo G. Silver. 2nd ed. New York: Bowker, 1952.

Link, Hannelore. *Rezeptionsforschung: Eine Einführung in Methoden und Probleme*. Urban-Taschenbücher, vol. 215. Stuttgart: Kohlhammer Verlag, 1976.

Mencken, H. L. "Shocking Stuff." *Smart Set* 52 (May 1917):398–99.

Mosher, William Eugene. *The Promise of the Christ-age in Recent Literature*. New York: G. P. Putnam's Sons, 1912.

Müller, Margarethe. *Carla Wenckebach, Pioneer*. Boston: Ginn and Co., 1908.

Newmark, Maxim, ed. *Twentieth Century Modern Language Teaching: Sources and Readings*. New York: The Philosophical Library, 1948.

The New York Times Theater Reviews: 1870–1919. 5 vols. New York: Arno Press, 1976.

Paulsen, Wolfgang, ed. *Die USA und Deutschland: Wechselseitige Spiegelungen in der Literatur der Gegenwart*. Bern: Francke Verlag, 1976.

Peddie, Robert Alexander, and Waddington, Quintin, eds. *The English Catalog of Books*. London: S. Low, 1914.

Pillet, Roger A. *Foreign Language Study: Perspective and Prospect*. Chicago: University of Chicago Press, 1973.

Reichmann, Eberhardt, comp. *The Teaching of German. Problems and Methods*. Philadelphia: Teaching Aid Project, National Carl Schurz Association, 1970.

Rippley, La Vern J. *The German-Americans*. Boston: Twayne Publishers, 1976.

Silz, Walter. *Realism and Reality; Studies in the German Novelle [sic] of Poetic Realism*. Studies in the Germanic Languages and Literatures, Number 11. Chapel Hill: University of North Carolina Press, 1954.

Springfield (Mass.) *Daily Republican*. "Recent School Textbooks," 20 August 1895, p. 8.

Thierfelder, Franz, et al. *Das deutsche Buch im Ausland*. Leipzig: Paul List, 1935.

Trommler, Frank, and Joseph McVeigh. *America and the Germans, An Assessment of a Three-Hundred-Year History*. 2 vols. Philadelphia: University of Pennsylvania Press, 1985.

Wenckebach, Carla, and Helene Wenckebach. *Deutscher Anschauungs-Unterricht für Amerikaner*. New York: Henry Holt and Co., 1888.

Who Was Who in America: 1607–1896. 4 vols. Chicago: Marquis, 1963.

Wilpert, Gero von. *Sachwörterbuch der Literatur*. Kröners Taschenausgabe, vol. 231. Stuttgart: A. Kröner, 1955.

Witkowski, Georg. *The German Drama of the Nineteenth Century*. Translated from the 2nd German edition by L. E. Horning. New York: Henry Holt and Co., 1909.

APPENDIX A

AUTHOR OR AUTHOR/TITLE CORRESPONDENCE: *NEW YORK TIMES* REVIEWS AND U.S. GERMAN TEXTS
ONLY YEARS IN WHICH CORRESPONDENCE OCCURS ARE LISTED.

Publication Date of Book Reviews	Number of Reviews of German Literature Also in Texts	Total Number of Reviews of German Books	Percentage of Overall Agreement between German Texts and *NYT* Reviews
1870	6	19	32
1871	3	11	27
1872	3	13	23
1874	1	4	25
1875	2	6	33
1876	1	4	25
1877	5	15	33
1878	1	11	10
1879	1	8	13
1880	9	22	41
1881	14	20	70
1882	7	20	35
1883	5	18	28
1884	7	28	25
1885	8	19	42
1886	6	25	24
1887	7	24	29
1888	10	17	59
1889	1	14	7
1890	2	10	20
1891	4	15	27
1892	9	16	56
1893	7	20	45
1894	4	17	24
1895	4	17	24
1896	1	10	10
1897	1	4	25
1898	1	6	17
1900	1	9	11
1901	5	11	45
1902	2	9	22

APPENDIX A (Continued)

Publication Date of Book Reviews	Number of Reviews of German Literature Also in Texts	Total Number of Reviews of German Books	Percentage of Overall Agreement between German Texts and NYT Reviews
1903	2	21	10
1904	2	20	10
1905	8	29	28
1906	3	13	23
1907	3	27	11
1908	1	15	7
1909	3	35	9
1910	2	24	8
1911	7	22	32
1912	5	18	28
1913	7	21	33
1914	6	21	29
1915	3	25	12
1916	1	12	8
1917	2	13	15

APPENDIX B

GERMAN AUTHORS APPEARING IN U. S. GERMAN TEXTS, REVIEWED IN TRANSLATION, AND LISTED BY POCHMANN

Authors Titles When Shared First and Last Dates of Texts Indicated	Reviews	Pochmann
Arndt, E. M.		0
Auerbach, B.		47
Brigitta. Boston: Ginn, 1893–1913.	*Brigitta.* New York: Holt, 1880.	
Brigitta. Boston: Allyn and Bacon, 1917–1918.		
Baumbach, R.		0
Sommermärchen. New York: Holt, 1900.	*Summer Legends.* New York: T. Y. Crowell, 1888.	
Carové, F. W.		0
Das Märchen ohne Ende. New York: Holt, 1864–1887.	*Story without an End.* New York: James Miller, 1875.	
Dahn, F. L. S.		0
Felicitas. New York: Longmans, Green, 1891.	*Felizitas.* New York: Wm. S. Gottesberger, 1883.	
Ebers, G. M.		85
Eine Frage, Idyll zu einem Gemälde. New York: Holt, 1887–1888.	*A Question, The Idyll.* New York: Wm. S. Gottesberger, 1881.	
Ebner-Eschenbach, M. v.		0
Eckstein, E.		16
Eichendorff, J. v.		0
Aus dem Leben eines Taugenichts. New York: Holt, 1864–1906.	*Leaves from the Life of a Good-for-Nothing.* Philadelphia: J. B. Lippincott, 1889.	
Aus dem Leben eines Taugenichts. Boston: De Vries, Ibarra, 1864–1870.		
Aus dem Leben eines Taugenichts. New York: Leypoldt and Holt, 1870.		
Aus dem Leben eines Taugenichts. Boston: Heath, 1892–1911.		

APPENDIX B *(Continued)*

Authors Titles When Shared First and Last Dates of Texts Indicated	Reviews	Pochmann
Ernst, O. (Schmidt, O.E.)		0
Flachsmann als Erzieher. Boston: Ginn, 1904.	*Master Flachsmann.* New York: Duffield, 1912.	
Eschstruth, N. v.		0
François, M. L. v.		0
Frenssen, G.		0
Jörn Uhl. Boston: Heath, 1914.	*Joern Uhl.* Boston: Dana, Estes, 1905.	
Freytag, G.		26
Soll und Haben. Boston: Ginn, 1892–1898.	*Debit and Credit.* New York: Harper, 1893.	
Soll und Haben. New York: Macmillan, 1893.		
Soll und Haben. Boston: Heath, 1901–1911.		
Goethe, J. W. v.		311
Egmont. Boston: DeVries, Ibarra, 1866.	*Egmont.* New York: Holt, 1903.	
Egmont. New York: Holt, 1866–1903.		
Egmont. New York: Leypoldt and Holt, 1870.		
Egmont. New York: Christern, 1870.		
Egmont. Boston: Ginn, 1898–1902.		
Egmont. New York: Macmillan, 1898–1901.		
Egmont. Syracuse: Bardeen, 1902.		
Egmont. Boston: Heath, 1904.		
Faust I. Boston: Urbino, 1864–1865.	*Faust I.* New York: Harper, 1886.	
Faust I. New York: Holt, 1866–1907.	*Faust I.* Washington, D. C.: Morrison, 1886.	
Faust I. Boston: Schoenhof and Moeller, 1866.	*Faust.* Boston: Roberts Brothers, 1870.	
Faust I. New York: Christern, 1866.		
Faust I. New York: Leypoldt and Holt, 1870.		
Faust I. New York: Putnam, 1888.		
Faust I. New York: Macmillan, 1886–1893.		
Faust I. Boston: Heath, 1892.		

APPENDIX B *(Continued)*

Authors Titles When Shared First and Last Dates of Texts Indicated	Reviews	Pochmann
Goethe, J. W. v. (cont.)		
Faust I and II. Boston: Heath, 1892–1912.	*Faust I and II*. Boston: Fields, Osgood and Co., 1870.	
Faust II. Boston: Heath, 1897.	*Faust II*. Boston: J. R. Osgood and Co., 1870.	
Hermann und Dorothea. New York: Christern, 1866.	*Hermann and Dorothea*. Boston: Roberts, 1870.	
Hermann und Dorothea. New York: Steiger, 1866.		
Hermann und Dorothea. New York: Holt, 1866–1915.		
Hermann und Dorothea. Boston: Urbino, 1866–1870.		
Hermann und Dorothea. New York: Putnam, 1875–1912.		
Hermann und Dorothea. Boston: Heath, 1891–1911.		
Hermann und Dorothea. Boston: Schoenhof, 1891.		
Hermann und Dorothea. New York: G. Bell and Sons, 1892.		
Hermann und Dorothea. New York: Hinds and Noble, 1899.		
Hermann und Dorothea. New York: Macmillan, 1899–1907.		
Hermann und Dorothea. New York: Appleton, 1903.		
Hermann und Dorothea. Boston: Ginn, 1904.		
Hermann und Dorothea. New York: Merrill, 1908.		
Hermann und Dorothea. New York: Scribner, 1917.		
Hermann und Dorothea. New York: Oxford University Press, 1917.		
Hermann und Dorothea. Boston: Allyn and Bacon, 1917.		
Poems. Boston: Ginn, 1874–1916.	*Poems and Ballads*. New York: Holt and Williams, 1871.	
Poems. Boston: Heath, 1899–1904.	*Poems*. New York: F. W. Christern, 1878.	
Poems. New York: Holt, 1901–1909.	*Poems*. New York: Holt, 1886.	
Reineke Fuchs. New York: Holt, 1901.	*Reynard the Fox*. New York: T. Stoeffer, 1870.	

APPENDIX B *(Continued)*

Authors Titles When Shared First and Last Dates of Texts Indicated	Reviews	Pochmann
Grillparzer, F.		0
Sappho. New York: Macmillan, 1898.	*Sappho*. Boston: Roberts Brothers, 1898.	
Sappho. Boston: Ginn, 1899–1904.		
Sappho. New York: Oxford University Press, 1916.		
Grimm, J. and W.		106
Kinder- und Hausmärchen. New York: Holt, 1881–1887.	*Household Stories*. New York: Macmillan, 1882.	
Kinder- und Hausmärchen. Boston: Heath, 1885–1907.	*Household Stories*. New York: Scribner and Welford, 1884.	
Kinder- und Hausmärchen. New York: Macmillan, 1885–1889.	*Grimm's Fairy Tales*. New York: Frederick Warne, 1884.	
Kinder- u. Hausmärchen. Boston: Schoenhof, 1887.	*Fairy Tales*. Philadelphia: J. B. Lippincott, 1902.	
Kinder- und Hausmärchen. New York: American Book, 1903.		
Märchen. Boston: Allyn and Bacon, 1903.		
Stories. New York: Holt, 1895.		
Märchen and Schiller's "Der Taucher." Boston: Heath, 1894–1909.		
Hauff, W.		24
Tales. Boston: Ginn, 1896–1901.	*Fairy Tales*. New York: Scribner and Welford, 1886.	
Lichtenstein. Boston: Heath, 1901–1911.	*Lichtenstein*. New York: E. P. Dutton, 1901.	
Lichtenstein. New York: Holt, 1910.		
Lichtenstein. Boston: Ginn, 1914.		
Hauptmann, G.		8
Heine, H.		72
Lieder u. Gedichte. New York: Macmillan, 1897–1907.	*Poems & Ballads*. New York: Worthington, 1881.	
Selections from the Reisebilder (and other prose). New York: Macmillan, 1891.	*Travel Pictures*. New York: Scribner and Welford, 1887.	
Herzog, R.		0
Hillern, W. v.		25
Höher als die Kirche. New York: Holt, 187- to 1894.	*Higher than the Church*. New York: W. S. Gottesberger, 1881.	
Höher als die Kirche. Boston: Heath, 1891–1916.		
Höher als die Kirche. New York: American Book, 1895–1896.		

APPENDIX B (Continued)

Authors Titles When Shared First and Last Dates of Texts Indicated	Reviews	Pochmann
Hillern, W. v. (con't)		
Höher als die Kirche. Boston: Allyn and Bacon, 1901.		
Höher als die Kirche. Boston: Ginn, 1906.		
Höher als die Kirche. New York: Merrill, 1910.		
Höher als die Kirche. New York: Scribner, 1917.		
Höher als die Kirche. New York: Macmillan, 1917.		
Hoffmann, E. T. A.		22
Jensen, W.		0
Keller, G.		0
Romeo und Julia auf dem Dorfe. Boston: Heath, 1900–1914.	*A Village Romeo and Juliet.* New York: Scribner, 1914.	
Romeo und Julia auf dem Dorfe. New York: Holt, 1912.		
Lessing, G. E.		41
Laokoon. New York: Macmillan, 1892.	*Laokoon.* Boston: Roberts Brothers, 1874.	
Laokoon. New York: Holt, 1910.	*Laokoon.* New York: Scribner and Welford, 1888.	
Minna von Barnhelm. New York: Christern, 1864.	*Minna von Barnhelm.* New York: Holt, 1917.	
Minna von Barnhelm. New York: Holt, 1864–1908.		
Minna von Barnhelm. Boston: Urbino, 1864.		
Minna von Barnhelm. New York: Holt and Williams, 1864.		
Minna von Barnhelm. Boston: DeVries, Ibarra, 1866.		
Minna von Barnhelm. New York: Leypoldt and Holt, 1870.		
Minna von Barnhelm. Boston: Schoenhof and Moeller, 1876.		
Minna von Barnhelm. Boston: Schoenhof, 1880–1898.		
Minna von Barnhelm. Boston: Heath, 1889–1911.		
Minna von Barnhelm. New York: Macmillan, 1896–1914.		
Minna von Barnhelm. New York: American Book, 1897–1898.		
Minna von Barnhelm. New York: Hinds and Noble, 1898–1899.		

214 *Appendix B*

APPENDIX B *(Continued)*

Authors Titles When Shared First and Last Dates of Texts Indicated	Reviews	Pochmann
Lessing, G. E. (cont.)		
Minna von Barnhelm. New York: Appleton, 1902–1907.		
Minna von Barnhelm. Boston: Ginn, 1904.		
Minna von Barnhelm. New York: Merrill, 1907.		
Minna von Barnhelm. Chicago: Scott, Foresman, 1909.		
Minna von Barnhelm. New York: Oxford University Press, 1910–1914.		
Luther, M.		18
Moltke, H. v.		0
Nathusius, M.		0
Pauli, R.		0
Zwei Aufsätze: Cromwell; Robert Blake. New York: Maynard and Merrill, 1893.	*Oliver Cromwell.* New York: Scribner and Welford, 1888.	
Zwei Aufsätze: Cromwell; Robert Blake. New York: Merrill, 1912.		
Ranke, L. v.		0
Raspe, R.		23
Münchhausen: Reisen und Abenteuer. Boston: Heath, 1906.	*The Adventures of Baron Münchhausen.* New York: Putnam, 1888.	
Richter, J. P. F.		0
Roquette, O.		0
Rosegger, P.		0
Die Schriften des Waldschulmeisters. New York: Holt, 1898–1904.	*The Forest Schoolmaster.* New York: Putnam, 1901.	
Scheffel, J. V. v.		0
Ekkehard. Boston: Heath, 1893–1906.	*Ekkehardt* [sic]. New York: Gottesberger, 1890.	
Ekkehard. Boston: Schoenhof, 1895.		
Ekkehard. New York: Holt, 1895–1899.		
Ekkehard; Audifax und Hadumoth. New York: American Book, 1911.		
Schurz, C.		0
Lebenserinnerungen bis 1850. Boston: Allyn and Bacon, 1913.	*Reminiscences.* New York: McClure, 1907.	

APPENDIX B *(Continued)*

Authors Titles When Shared First and Last Dates of Texts Indicated	Reviews	Pochmann
Spielhagen, F.		21
Das Skelett im Hause. Boston: Heath, 1913.	*A Skeleton in the House.* New York: G. W. Harlan, 1881.	
Spyri, J.		0
Stifter, A.		0
Das Heidedorf. Boston: Heath, 1891–1905.	*The Village on the Heath.* Newburgh: C. B. Martin, 1872.	
Das Heidedorf. New York: American Book, 1895.		
Storm, T.		0
Immensee. Boston: Urbino, 1864–1870.	*Immensee.* New York: T. Y. Cromwell [sic], 1904.	
Immensee. New York: Holt, 1875–1914.		
Immensee. Boston: Heath, 1890–1916.		
Immensee. New York: Maynard and Merrill, 1895.		
Immensee. New York: American Book, 1896–1916.		
Immensee. Boston: Ginn, 1901.		
Immensee. Boston: Allyn and Bacon, 1901.		
Immensee. Ann Arbor, Mich.: G. Wahr, 1901–1904.		
Immensee. New York: Merrill, 1912.		
Immensee. New York: Scribner, 1915.		
Immensee. New York: Macmillan, 1917.		
Storm, *Immensee*; Gerstäcker, *Germelshausen*; and Seidel, *Der Lindenbaum.* Chicago: Scott, Foresman, 1909.		
Sudermann, H.		8
Sybel, H. v.		0
Sylva, C. (Elizabeth of Rumania)		0
Aus meinem Königreich. Boston: Heath, 1900.	*A Real Queen's Fairy Tales.* Chicago: Davis, 1901.	
Treitschke, H. v.		0
Trojan, J.		0
Wagner, R.		128
Werner, E. (Bürstenbinder, E.)		98
Wilbrandt, A.		0
Zschokke, J. H. D.		25

APPENDIX C

AUTHORS OF HIGH SCHOOL AND COLLEGE TEXTS UNRECOGNIZED BY THE *NEW YORK TIMES* OR POCHMANN

Group I: (a) "German" works by foreign authors
         (b) German versions of foreign works
  (a) Hans Christian Andersen   (b) Gustav Weil
     Ludvig Holberg   Albert Ludwig Grimm

Group II: Period of greatest creativity beyond 1899 or 1918

    Clara Viebig   Friedrich Lienhard

Group III: Great or near-great authors then and today

Gottfried Bürger	Detlev von Liliencron
Annette von Droste-Hülshoff	Otto Ludwig
Theodor Fontane	C. F. Meyer
C. F. Gellert	Eduard Mörike
Karl Gutzkow	Wilhelm Raabe
Friedrich Hebbel	Karl Simrock
J. P. Hebel	Ludwig Tieck
J. G. Herder	Ludwig Uhland
Heinrich von Kleist	C. M. Wieland
Theodor Körner	

Group IV: Other authors once read by U.S. German students

P. Albersdorf	Helene von Götzendorff-Grabowski
Ludwig Bechstein	Leo Goldhammer
Roderich Benedix	Baldwin Groller
Oscar Blumenthal	Friedrich Halm
Helene Böhlau	Heinrich Hansjakob
M. Boyen	Friedrich Helbig
Emma Buchheim	Otto Hoffmann
Ernest Budde	Hans Hoffmann
Emil Claar	W. O. von Horn
Otto Elster	Karl Jacobsen
Alexander Elz	Jungmann
Natalie von Eschstruth	Heinrich Jung-Stilling
Wilhelm Fischer	T. Kerkhoff
Emil Frommel	Anton Klausmann
Ludwig Fulda	W. Müller von Königswinter
Ferdinand Goebel	Anna von Krane
Karl August Görner	Johannes Kraner

APPENDIX C *(Continued)*

Group IV (continued)
- Isolde Kurz
- Max von La Roche
- Richard Leander
- Ilse Leskien
- Julius Lohmeyer
- Wilhelm Meyer-Förster
- Melchoir Meyr
- Theodor Mügge
- Hugo Müller
- Charlotte Niese
- C. A. Paul (B. Scheiden)
- Anton Perfall
- Emil Peschkau
- Marie Petersen
- Emil Pohl
- Wilhelm Polenz
- Gustav zu Putlitz
- Albert Richter
- Wilhelm Riehl
- Clara E. Ries
- Wilhelm F. Riese
- Julius Rosen
- Ferdinand von Saar
- Ludwig Salomon
- Frieda Schanz (Soyaux)
- J. Schlicht
- Else Schmieden
- A. Schmitthenner
- Hans Schönberg
- Levin Schücking
- Heinrich Seidel
- Johann Seume
- K. Stoeber
- J. Sturm
- Auguste Supper
- J. Trojan
- Villamaria (Marie Timme)
- Hermine Villinger
- Ernst A. Wichert
- A. C. Wiesner
- Ernst von Wildenbruch
- Alexander Wilhelmi

Group V: Juvenile
- Viktor Blüthgen
- Niklaus Bolt
- Babette von Bülow
- J. H. Campe
- Helene Stökl

Group VI: Histories, literary essays, studies in mythology, etc.
- Karl F. Becker
- F. K. Biedermann
- Theodor Ebner
- Oscar Faulhaber
- G. G. Gervinus
- August W. Grube
- Isidor Keller
- Friedrich Khull
- H. F. T. Kohlrausch
- Heinrich Kurz
- Bernhard Rogge
- Richard Roth
- Friedrich Schrader
- Johannes Schrammen
- Adolf E. Stern
- A. F. C. Vilmar
- Hans Wachenhusen
- Karl Zastrow

APPENDIX D

Recommendations of the Committee of Twelve

Literature Recommended for the Elementary Level:

Andersen's *Märchen* and *Bilderbuch ohne Bilder*; Arnold's *Fritz auf Ferien*; Baumbach's *Die Nonna* and *Der Schwiegersohn*; Gerstäcker's *Germelshausen*; Heyse's *L'Arrabbiata, Das Mädchen von Treppi,* and *Anfang und Ende*; Hillern's *Höher als die Kirche*; Jensen's *Die braune Erika*; Leander's *Träumereien,* and *Kleine Geschichten*; Seidel's *Märchen*; Stökl's *Unter dem Christbaum*; Storm's *Immensee* and *Geschichten aus der Tonne*; Zschokke's *Der zerbrochene Krug*. . . .Benedix's *Der Prozesz, Der Weiberfeind* and *Guñstige Vorzeichen*; Elz's *Er ist nicht eifersüchtig*; Wichert's *An der Majorsecke*; Wilhelmi's *Einer muß heiraten*. (63–64)

Selections especially recommended:

Andersen's *Märchen*, or *Bilderbuch*, or Leander's *Träumereien*; to the extent of . . . forty pages. . . . *Das kalte Herz*, or *Der zerbrochene Krug*; then *Höher als die Kirche*, or *Immensee*; next a . . . story by Heyse, Baumbach or Seidel; lastly *Der Prozesz*. [For sight reading] Grimm's [sic] *Märchen* . . . Meissner's *Aus meiner Welt* or Volkmann's *Kleine Geschichten*. (64; 69)

Literature Recommended for the Intermediate Level:

Ebner-Eschenbach's *Die Freiherren von Gemperlein*; Freytag's *Die Journalisten* and *Bilder aus der deutschen Vergangenheit*, for example *Karl der Grosse, Aus den Kreuzzügen, Doktor Luther, Aus dem Staat Friedrichs des Grossen*; Fouque's *Undine*; Gerstäcker's *Irrfahrten*; Goethe's *Hermann und Dorothea* and *Iphigenie*; Heine's poems and *Reisebilder*; Hoffmann's *Historische Erzählungen*; Lessing's *Minna von Barnhelm*; Meyer's *Gustav Adolphs* [sic] *Page*; Moser's *Der Bibliothekar*; Riehl's *Novellen*, for example, *Burg Neideck, Der Fluch der Schönheit, Der stumme Ratsherr, Das Spielmannskind*; Rosegger's *Waldheimat*; Schiller's *Der Neffe als Onkel, Der Geisterseher, Wilhelm Tell, Die Jungfrau von Orleans, Das Lied von der Glocke, Balladen*; Scheffel's *Der Trompeter von Säkkingen*; Uhland's poems; Wildenbruch's *Das edle Blut*. (71)

Selections especially recommended:

A good selection would be: (1) one of Riehl's novelettes; (2) one of Freytag's "pictures;" (3) part of *Undine* or *Der Geisterseher*; (4) a short course of reading in lyrics and ballads; (5) a classical play by Schiller, Lessing, or Goethe. (71)

Literature Recommended for the Advanced Level:

> Freytag's *Soll und Haben*; Fulda's *Der Talisman*; Goethe's dramas (except *Faust*) and prose writings (say extracts from *Werther* and *Dichtung und Wahrheit*); Grillparzer's *Ahnfrau* or *Der Traum ein Leben*; Hauff's *Lichtenstein*; Heine's more difficult prose (for example, *Über Deutschland*); Kleist's *Prinz von Homburg*; Körner's *Zriny*; Lessing's *Emilia Galotti* and prose writings (say extracts from the *Hamburgische Dramaturgie* or *Laokoon*); Scheffel's *Ekkehard*; Schiller's *Wallenstein, Maria Stuart, Braut von Messina*, and historical prose (say the third book of the *Geschichte des dreiszigjahrigen* [sic] *Krieges*); Sudermann's *Johannes*; Tieck's *Genoveva*; Wildenbruch's *Heinrich*. (73)

The list of suggested works for the advanced level includes the *Aufklärung, Sturm and Drang*, and *Klassik* in a suitable proportion to the other works included. The nineteenth century having been previously read through, the student might now proceed to enlightenment and classicism.

Selections especially recommended:

> (1) A recent novel, such as *Ekkehard* or *Soll und Haben*, read not in its entirety, but in extracts sufficient to give a good idea of the plot, the style, and the characters; (2) *Egmont* or *Götz*; (3) a short course of reading in Goethe's prose (say the *Sesenheim* episode from *Dichtung und Wahrheit*); (4) *Wallenstein's* [sic] *Lager* and *Wallenstein's* [sic] *Tod*, with the third book of the Thirty Years' War [not italicized]; (5) *Emilia Galotti*; (6) a romantic drama, such as *Genoveva* or *Der Prinz von Homburg*. (73–74)

No *Genoveva* text was located in advertisements, commercial or scholarly catalogs. Indeed, not all the recommended works had appeared in textbook form when the Committee recommended them as texts.

APPENDIX E

Recommendations on German Texts Presented by Frederick W. J. Heuser Before the MLA in 1917

1. Open to Freshmen (=4th to 5th year): Short-Story, Drama, Contemporary Literature, Lyrics and Ballads, Modern Novelists, History of German Literature from the Romantic School to the Present. More in detail are announced: a) Kleist, Grillparzer, and Hebbel. b) Goethe, Schiller, Kleist, Grillparzer, Hebbel, Poems, Modern Novel. c) Hauptmann, Sudermann, Wildenbruch, Fulda. d) Nathan, Götz, Iphigenie, Wallenstein, Prinz von Homburg, Johannes, Versunkene Glocke.
2. Sophomores (5th to 6th year) may elect: Short-Story, Drama, Poets of Patriotism, Contemporary Literature, Early Nineteenth Century Literature with study of tendencies. More specifically again are offered: a) Kleist, Grillparzer, Hebbel, Hauptmann, Sudermann. b) Lenau, Anzengruber and Rosegger. c) Heine, Hebbel, Wagner, Keller, Grillparzer, Nietzsche, Sudermann and Hauptmann. d) Grillparzer, Hebbel, and Hauptmann. e) Sudermann, Hauptmann and Heyse. f) Kleist, Grillparzer, Raimund, Gutzkow, Halbe, Ludwig, Anzengruber, Wildenbruch, Sudermann, Hauptmann, Fulda, Lienhard and Otto Ernst. g) Kleist, Hauff, Hoffmann, Immermann, Stifter, Grillparzer, Ludwig, Meyer, Spielhagen, Storm, Heyse, Raabe, Wildenbruch, Sudermann, Frenssen. h) Auerbach, Scheffel, Freytag, Spielhagen. Then there are several more intensive courses on one author for a semester: Heine, Kleist, Grillparzer, Hebbel, Hauptmann, Wagner.
3. Restricted to Juniors and Seniors we find: Drama from Lessing to the Present, Recent German Drama, Present Literature (Novel and Drama), the Younger Romantic School and *das Junge Deutschland*, Romantic School to 1850 with special reference to the *Weltanschauung* of the period, Literature from 1850 to the present with reference to the influence of French, Russian and Scandinavian Literatures; Literature of the nineteenth century with some reference to Strauss, Mommsen, Nietzsche and Wagner; Modern Novel and Drama—Hauptmann,

Sudermann, Fontane, Kretzer, Halbe, Wildenbruch and Fulda. There are also one-semester courses on special authors: Heine, Grillparzer, Wagner, Kleist and Hebbel.

Apparently, works by Anzengruber, Halbe, Kretzer, Lenau, Mommsen, Nietzsche, and Emil Strauß had not been adopted by U.S. publishers for texts of the type surveyed by this study before the end of World War I.

APPENDIX F

Texts in Chronological Order by Year

Appendix F is a chronological listing by year, then alphabetically by author (then alphabetically by title), of the texts copyrighted, printed, reprinted, re-edited, or listed by commercial and scholarly catalogs during the years investigated. Information other than author and title—offered when established—is publisher, editor, number of pages, price, name of series, and individual works contained in the volume; in the case of small anthologies containing stories by a number of authors, these works are listed individually by author.

APPENDIX F

1864

Author	Title	Publisher/Editor	Pages	Price	Series and Contents
Andersen, H. C.	Bilderbuch ohne Bilder	DeVries, Ibarra/Simonson, Leopold		.50	De Vries German Series
	Bilderbuch ohne Bilder	Holt/Simonson, Leopold	61		Unterhaltungs-Bibliothek
Carové	Das Märchen ohne Ende	Holt	45		
Eichendorff, Joseph von	Aus dem Leben eines Taugenichts	DeVries, Ibarra		.75	
	Aus dem Leben eines Taugenichts	Holt		.75	
Fouqué, Friedrich de la Motte	Undine	Holt	88	.50	Unterhaltungs-Bibliothek
Goethe, J. W. von	Faust. Erster Teil	Urbino	195	1.25	
Grimm, Herman F.	Die Venus von Milo and Rafael und Michel-Angelo	DeVries, Ibarra	139	.75	
Heyse, Paul	Anfang und Ende	DeVries, Ibarra	54	.40	DeVries German Series
	Die Einsamen	DeVries, Ibarra	44	.40	DeVries German Series
	L'Arrabbiata and Das Mädchen von Treppi	Urbino		.25	
Lessing, G. E.	Minna von Barnhelm.	Holt and Williams/Wrankmore, W. C.	123		
	Minna von Barnhelm.	Christern/Wrankmore, W. C.	123		
	Minna von Barnhelm.	Urbino/Wrankmore, W. C.	123		
Petersen, Marie	Prinzessin Ilse	DeVries, Ibarra	38		DeVries German Series
	Prinzessin Ilse	Holt/Merrick, John Mudge	45		Unterhaltungs-Bibliothek

Putlitz, Gustav zu	Badekuren	DeVries, Ibarra	61	.50
	Das Herz vergessen	DeVries, Ibarra/ Merrick, John Mudge	73	.50
	Vergißmeinnicht	Christern	46	
	Vergißmeinnicht	Urbino	46	.40
	Was sich der Wald erzählt	DeVries, Ibarra	62	.50	DeVries German Series
	Was sich der Wald erzählt	Holt		
Schiller, J. C. F. von	Die Piccolomini	Holt/Krauss, Ernst Carl F.	139	
	Wilhelm Tell	Urbino	161	
	Wilhelm Tell	Holt/Krauss, Ernst Carl F.			Classic German Plays
Storm, Theodor	Immensee	Urbino	36	.40
Tieck, Ludwig	Zwei Märchennovellen: Die Elfen, Das Rothkäppchen	DeVries, Ibarra	74	.50

1865

Benedix, Roderich	Der Prozeß and Wilhelmi's Einer muß heiraten	Urbino/Lambert, Marcus B.	112	.40
	Eigensinn and Wilhelmi's Einer muß heiraten	Urbino	55	.40
Fouqué, Friedrich de la Motte	Undine	Urbino	88	.50
	Undine	Christern	88	
Görner, Karl August	Englisch	Urbino	59	.50
Goethe, J. W. von	Faust. Erster Teil	Urbino	195	1.25
	Iphigenie auf Tauris	Urbino/Krauss, Ernst Carl F.	94	1.00

225

APPENDIX F (Continued)

Author	Title	Publisher/Editor	Pages	Price	Series and Contents
Schiller, J. C. F. von	Iphigenie auf Tauris	Christern/Krauss, Ernst Carl F.	94	1.00	
	Die Jungfrau von Orleans	DeVries, Ibarra/Bernays, Adolphus	135		Classic German Plays
	Die Jungfrau von Orleans	Holt	135		
	Die Piccolomini	Urbino/Krauss, Ernst Carl F.	139		
	Die Piccolomini	Christern/Krauss, Ernst Carl F.	139		
	Maria Stuart	DeVries, Ibarra/Bernays, Adolphus	173	.60	DeVries German Series
	Maria Stuart	Holt/Bernays, Adolphus	173	.60	
	Wallenstein Trilogie	Urbino/Krauss, Ernst Carl F.	210	.50	
	Wallenstein Trilogie	Christern/Krauss, Ernst Carl F.	210		
	Wilhelm Tell	Eggers and Wilde/Oehlschlager, James	168		
	Wilhelm Tell	Urbino/Krauss, Ernst Carl F.	171	.50	
Tieck, Ludwig	Zwei Märchennovellen: Die Elfen, Das Rothkäppchen	DeVries, Ibarra	74	.50	
Wilhelmi, Alexander (Zechmeister, Alexander Viktor)	Einer muß heiraten and Benedix's Der Prozeß	Urbino/Lambert, Marcus B.	112	.40	
	Einer muß heiraten and Benedix's Eigensinn	Urbino	55	.40	

1866

Andersen, H. C.	Die Eisjungfrau und andere Geschichten	DeVries, Ibarra/Krauss, Ernst Carl F.		Includes: Die Eisjungfrau, Die Psyche, Die Schnecke und der Rosenstock, Der Schmetterling, Der silberne Schilling, Die Glocke
	Die Eisjungfrau und andere Geschichten	Holt/Krauss, Ernst Carl F.		
	Die Eisjungfrau und andere Geschichten	Christern/Krauss, Ernst Carl F.		
	Die Eisjungfrau und andere Geschichten	Urbino/Krauss, Ernst Carl F.		
Benedix, Roderich	Eigensinn and Wilhelmi's Einer muß heiraten	Holt	63	.40
Eichendorff, Joseph von	Aus dem Leben eines Taugenichts	DeVries, Ibarra	132		DeVries German Series
Goethe, J. W. von	Egmont.	DeVries, Ibarra/Steffen, William	113	.50	Classic German Plays
	Egmont.	Holt/Steffen, William	113	.50	
	Faust. Erster Teil	Holt	195		
	Faust. Erster Teil	Christern	195		
	Faust. Erster Teil	Schoenhof and Moeller	195		
	Hermann und Dorothea	Urbino/Krauss, Ernst Carl F.	99		
	Hermann und Dorothea	Steiger/Krauss, Ernst Carl F.	99		
	Hermann und Dorothea	Christern/Krauss, Ernst Carl F.	99		
	Hermann und Dorothea	Holt/Krauss, Ernst Carl F.	99		

APPENDIX F (Continued)

Author	Title	Publisher/Editor	Pages	Price	Series and Contents
Grimm, Hermann F.	Iphigenie auf Tauris	Holt/Krauss, Ernst Carl F.			
	Die Venus von Milo and Rafael und Michel-Angelo	Holt			
Heyse, Paul	Anfang und Ende	Holt			
Körner, Theodor	Zriny	DeVries, Ibarra/Ruggles, Edward Rush	116	.60	
	Zriny	Holt/Ruggles, Edward Rush	116	.60	
Lessing, G. E.	Minna von Barnhelm	DeVries, Ibarra/Wrankmore, W. C.	123	.50	
Nathusius, Marie	Tagebuch eines armen Fräuleins	DeVries, Ibarra	163	1.00	DeVries German Series
	Tagebuch eines armen Fräuleins	Holt	163		
Putlitz, Gustav zu	Badekuren	Holt	69		College Series of German Plays
Schiller, J. C. F. von	Die Piccolomini	Holt/Krauss, Ernst Carl F.	139		
	Die Piccolomini	Christern/Krauss, Ernst Carl F.	139		
	Maria Stuart	Holt/Krauss, Ernst Carl F.	197		Students' Collection of Classic German Plays
	Maria Stuart	Urbino/Krauss, Ernst Carl F.	197		
	Maria Stuart	Christern/Krauss, Ernst Carl F.	197		

	Maria Stuart	Eggers and Wilde/ Oehlschlager, James	190	
	Wallenstein Trilogie	Urbino/Krauss, Ernst Carl F.	210	.50
	Wallenstein Trilogie	Christern/Krauss, Ernst Carl F.	210	
	Wallenstein Trilogie	Steiger/Krauss, Ernst Carl F.	210	
	Wallenstein Trilogie	Holt/Krauss, Ernst Carl F.	210	
	Wallensteins Lager	Holt/Krauss, Ernst Carl F.	60	
Tieck, Ludwig	Zwei Märchennovellen: Die Elfen, Das Rothkäppchen	Holt/Simonson, Leopold		
Wilhelmi, Alexander (Zechmeister, Alexander Viktor)	Einer muß heiraten and Benedix's Eigensinn	Holt	63	.40

1867

Boyen, M.	Mein erster Patient In: Deutsche Novelletten-Bibliothek	n.p./Bernhardt, Wilhelm		1.20	Modern Language Series
Götzendorff-Grabowski, Helene von	Der Simpel and Vor Sonnenaufgang In: Deutsche Novelletten-Bibliothek	n.p./Bernhardt, Wilhelm		1.20	Modern Language Series
Juncke, E. (Schmieden, Else)	Ein Frühlingstraum In: Deutsche Novelletten-Bibliothek	n.p./Bernhardt, Wilhelm		1.20	Modern Language Series
Peschkau Emil	Sphinx In: Deutsche Novelletten-Bibliothek	n.p./Bernhardt, Wilhelm		1.20	Modern Language Series
Schiller, J. C. F. von	Maria Stuart	Urbino/Krauss, Ernst Carl F.	197		

APPENDIX F (Continued)

Author	Title	Publisher/Editor	Pages	Price	Series and Contents
Seidel, Heinrich	Leberecht Hühnchen and Der gute alte Onkel In: Deutsche Novelletten-Bibliothek	n.p./Bernhardt, Wilhelm		1.20	Modern Language Series
Stökl, Helene	Am Heiligen Abend and Eine Weihnachtsgeschichte In: Deutsche Novelletten-Bibliothek	n.p./Bernhardt, Wilhelm		1.20	Modern Language Series
Werner, Ernst (Bürstenbinder, Elizabeth)	Der Wilddieb In: Deutsche Novelletten-Bibliothek	n.p./Bernhardt, Wilhelm		1.20	Modern Language Series
Wiesner, A. C.	Die schwarze Dame In: Deutsche Novelletten-Bibliothek	n.p./Bernhardt, Wilhelm		1.20	Modern Language Series
		1868			
Heyse, Paul	Die Einsamen	Holt			
Schiller, J. C. F. von	Maria Stuart	Leypoldt and Holt/ Bernays, Adolphus	173	.60	
	Wallenstein Trilogie	Urbino/Krauss, Ernst Carl F.			
	Wilhelm Tell	Eggers and Wilde/ Oehlschlager, James	168		
		1869			
Fouqué, Friedrich de la Motte	Undine	Urbino	88	.50	
	Undine	Leypoldt and Holt	88	.50	
Jensen, Wilhelm	Die braune Erika	Urbino/Evans, Edward Payson	63	.50	
	Die braune Erika	Holt		.40	

230

Lessing, G. E.	Emilia Galotti	Urbino	77	.40
	Emilia Galotti	Holt		.40
Mügge, Theodor	Riukan-Voss	Urbino	55	.40
	Riukan-Voss	Holt	55	.40
	Signa die Seterin	Urbino	71	.40
	Signa die Seterin	Holt	71	.40
Schiller, J. C. F. von	Die Jungfrau von Orleans	Leypoldt and Holt		
	Wallensteins Lager	Urbino		
Storm, Theodor	Immensee	Urbino	36	

187-

Hillern, Wilhelmine von	Höher als die Kirche	Holt	46	Unterhaltungs-Bibliothek
Jensen, Wilhelm	Die braune Erika	Schoenhof/Joynes, Edward S.	80	
	Die braune Erika	Christern/Joynes, Edward S.	80	
Nathusius, Marie	Tagebuch eines armen Fräuleins	DeVries, Ibarra	163	DeVries German Series

1870

Andersen, H. C.	Die Eisjungfrau und andere Geschichten	Leypoldt/Krauss, Ernst Carl F.	150	Includes: Die Eisjungfrau, Die Psyche, Die Schnecke und der Rosenstock, Der Schmetterling, Der silberne Schilling, Die Glocke
Benedix, Roderich	Der Weiberfeind	Urbino	26	
	Der Weiberfeind, with Elz's Er ist nicht eifersüchtig and Müller's Im Wartesalon erster Klasse	Leypoldt and Holt	82	

APPENDIX F (Continued)

Author	Title	Publisher/Editor	Pages	Price	Series and Contents
Eichendorff, Joseph von	Aus dem Leben eines Taugenichts	Leypoldt and Holt	132		
	Aus dem Leben eines Taugenichts	DeVries, Ibarra	132		
Elz, Alexander	Er ist nicht eifersüchtig, with Benedix's Der Weiberfeind and Müllers Im Wartesalon erster Klasse	Leypoldt and Holt	82		
	Er ist nicht eifersüchtig	Urbino	32		
	Er ist nicht eifersüchtig	Holt	32		College Series of German Plays
Goethe, J. W. von	Egmont	Leypoldt and Holt/ Steffen, William	113	.50	Classic German Plays
	Egmont	Christern/Steffen, William	113	.50	Classic German Plays
	Faust. Erster Teil	Leypoldt and Holt	195		Classic German Plays
	Hermann und Dorothea	Urbino/Krauss, Ernst Carl F.	99		
Heyse, Paul	Anfang und Ende	Leypoldt and Holt	123		Unterhaltungs-Bibliothek
Lessing, G. E.	Minna von Barnhelm	Leypoldt and Holt/ Wrankmore, W. C.	82		
Müller, Hugo	Im Wartesalon erster Klasse, with Benedix's Der Weiberfeind and Elz's Er ist nicht eifersüchtig	Leypoldt and Holt			
	Im Wartesalon erster Klasse	Urbino	24		

Putlitz, Gustav zu	Das Herz vergessen	Leypoldt and Holt		
	Was sich der Wald erzählt	Leypoldt and Holt	.50	College Series of German Plays
Schiller, J. C. F. von	Wallenstein Trilogie	Urbino/Krauss, Ernst Carl F.		
	Wallenstein Trilogie	Leypoldt and Holt/ Krauss, Ernst Carl F.	210	
	Wallensteins Lager	Leypoldt and Holt	60	
	Wilhelm Tell	Eggers and Wilde/ Oehlschlager, James	168	Classic German Plays
	Wilhelm Tell	Urbino/Krauss, Ernst Carl F.	171	Standard Educational Works
Storm Theodor	Immensee	Urbino	36	

1871

Putlitz, Gustav zu	Vergißmeinnicht	Holt	44	.50	
Zschokke, Heinrich	Das Wirtshaus zu Cransac	Schoenhof and Moeller			
	Der zerbrochene Krug	Schoenhof and Moeller	24	.30	

1872

Benedix, Roderich	Eigensinn and Wilhelmi's Einer muß heiraten	Holt and Williams/ Krauss, Ernst Carl F.	63	.40	College Series of German Plays
Carové	Das Märchen ohne Ende	Holt	45	.25	
Schiller, J. C. F. von	Maria Stuart	Eggers and Wilde	190		
Wilhelmi, Alexander (Zechmeister, Alexander Viktor)	Einer muß heiraten and Benedix's Eigensinn	Holt and Williams/ Krauss, Ernst Carl F.	63	.40	College Series of German Plays

APPENDIX F *(Continued)*

Author	Title	Publisher/Editor	Pages	Price	Series and Contents
\multicolumn{6}{c}{1873}					
Benedix, Roderich	Der Weiberfeind with Elz's Er ist nicht eifersüchtig and Müller's Im Wartesalon erster Klasse	Holt and Williams	82	.50	College Series of German Plays
	Eigensinn and Wilhelmi's Einer muß heiraten	Holt	63	.40	College Series of German Plays
Elz, Alexander	Er ist nicht eifersüchtig, with Benedix's Der Weiberfeind and Müller's Im Wartesalon erster Klasse	Holt and Williams	82	.50	College Series of German Plays
Lessing, G. E.	Emilia Galotti	Holt	82	.40	
Müller, Hugo	Im Wartesalon erster Klasse, with Benedix's Der Weiberfeind and Elz's Er ist nicht eifersüchtig	Holt and Williams	82	.50	College Series of German Plays
Putlitz, Gustav zu	Das Herz vergessen	DeVries, Ibarra/Merrick, John Mudge	79		
Wilhelmi, Alexander (Zechmeister, Alexander Viktor)	Einer muß heiraten and Benedix's Eigensinn	Holt	63	.40	College Series of German Plays
\multicolumn{6}{c}{1874}					
Goethe, J. W. von	Poems	Ginn/Schütze, Martin			International Modern Language Series

234

		1875		
Benedix, Roderich	Der Weiberfeind with Elz's Er ist nicht eifersüchtig and Müller's Im Wartesalon erster Klasse	Holt	82	.50
	Eigensinn and Wilhelmi's Einer muß heiraten	Holt	63	.40
Elz, Alexander	Er ist nicht eifersüchtig, with Benedix's Der Weiberfeind and Müller's Im Wartesalon erster Klasse	Holt	82	.50
Goethe, J. W. von	Hermann und Dorothea	Putnam/Hart, James Morgan	155	1.00	German Classics for American Students
Grimm, Hermann F.	Die Venus von Milo and Rafael und Michel-Angelo	Holt	139	.75	Unterhaltungs-Bibliothek
Heyse, Paul	Anfang und Ende	Holt	54	.40	
Müller Hugo	Im Wartesalon erster Klasse, with Benedix's Der Weiberfeind and Elz's Er ist nicht eifersüchtig	Holt	82	.50	Unterhaltungs-Bibliothek
Schiller, J. C. F. von	Der Neffe als Onkel	Holt/Clement, Alfred	99	.40	
	Der Neffe als Onkel	Schoenhof and Moeller/Clement, Alfred	99	.40	
	Die Piccolomini	Putnam	178	1.25	German Classics for American Students
Storm, Theodor	Immensee	Holt		.40	
Wilhelmi, Alexander (Zechmeister, Alexander Viktor)	Einer muß heiraten and Benedix's Eigensinn	Holt	63	.40	

235

APPENDIX F (Continued)

1876

Author	Title	Publisher/Editor	Pages	Price	Series and Contents
Andersen, H. C.	Bilderbuch ohne Bilder	Holt/Simonson, Leopold	104	.50	
	Die Eisjungfrau und andere Geschichten	Holt/Krauss, Ernst Carl F.	150	.50	Includes: Die Eisjungfrau, Die Psyche, Die Schnecke und der Rosenstock, Der Schmetterling, Der silberne Schilling, Die Glocke
Eichendorff, Joseph von	Aus dem Leben eines Taugenichts	Holt		.75	
Fouqué, Friedrich de la Motte	Undine	Holt		.50	
Goethe, J. W. von	Ausgewählte Prosa	Putnam/Hart, James Morgan	199	1.00	German Classics for American Students. Readings from: Dichtung und Wahrheit, Die Leiden des jungen Werthers, Ein Brief aus der Schweiz, Italienische Reise, Wilhelm Meisters Lehrjahre
	Faust. Erster Teil	Holt	195	.75	
	Hermann und Dorothea	Holt/Krauss, Ernst Carl F.	99		
	Iphigenie auf Tauris	Holt/Krauss, Ernst Carl F.		.40	
	Poems	Ginn/Schütze, Martin			International Modern Language Series
Heyse, Paul	Die Einsamen	Holt	44	.40	

236

Author	Title	Publisher	Page	Price	Series
Körner, Theodor	Zriny	Holt/Ruggles, Edward Rush	116	.60	Classic German Plays
Lessing, G. E.	Minna von Barnhelm	Holt/Whitney, William D.	138	.50	Whitney's German Texts
	Minna von Barnhelm	Schoenhof and Moeller/Whitney, William D.	138		Whitney's German Texts
Nathusius, Marie	Tagebuch eines armen Fräuleins	Holt		.75	
Petersen, Marie	Prinzessin Ilse	Holt/Merrick, John Mudge		.50	
Putlitz, Gustav zu	Badekuren	Holt		.50	
	Das Herz vergessen	Holt	79	.40	
Schiller, J. C. F. von	Die Jungfrau von Orleans	Holt		.50	
	Die Piccolomini	Holt/Krauss, Ernst Carl F.	139		
	Die Piccolomini	Schoenhof and Moeller/Krauss, Ernst Carl F.	139		
	Maria Stuart	Holt/Krauss, Ernst Carl F.		.50	
	Maria Stuart.	Holt/Bernays, Adolphus		.60	
	Wallenstein Trilogie	Holt/Krauss, Ernst Carl F.		.50	
	Wallensteins Lager	Holt		.50	
	Wilhelm Tell	Holt/Krauss, Ernst Carl F.		.50	
Tieck, Ludwig	Zwei Märchennovellen: Die Elfen, Das Rothkäppchen	Holt/Simonson, Leopold		.60	
Zschokke, Heinrich	Das Wirtshaus zu Cransac	Schoenhof and Moeller	43	.40	

237

APPENDIX F (*Continued*)

Author	Title	Publisher/Editor	Pages	Price	Series and Contents
	Das Wirtshaus zu Cransac	Christern	43	.40	
	Der zerbrochene Krug	Schoenhof and Moeller/Roelker, Bernard	24	.30	
1877					
Schiller, J. C. F. von	Wilhelm Tell	Schoenhof and Moeller/Sachtleben, Augustus	199		Whitney's German Texts
	Wilhelm Tell	Holt/Sachtleben, Augustus	199		Whitney's German Texts
1878					
Görner, Karl August	Englisch	Holt/Edgren, August H.	61		College Series of German Plays
	Englisch	Schoenhof/Edgren, August H.	61		College Series of German Plays
Goethe, J. W. von	Faust. Erster Teil	Putnam/Hart, James Morgan	257	1.25	German Classics for American Students
	Faust. Erster Teil	Holt/Whitney, William D.	229	1.20	Whitney's German Texts
	Faust. Erster Teil	Schoenhof and Moeller/Whitney, William D.	229	1.20	Whitney's German Texts
	Hermann und Dorothea	Putnam/Hart, James Morgan	155	1.00	German Classics for American Students
Heyse, Paul	Anfang und Ende	Holt	54		Unterhaltungs-Bibliothek

Lessing, G. E.	Minna von Barnhelm	Holt/Whitney, William D.	138		Whitney's German Texts
Schiller, J. C. F. von	Die Piccolomini	Putnam/Hart, James Morgan	178		German Classics for American Students
	Historische Skizzen	Macmillan/Buchheim, Carl Adolf	162	1.00	German Classics. Includes: Egmonts Leben und Tod and Die Belagerung von Antwerpen
	Wilhelm Tell	Eggers and Wilde/Oehlschlager, James	168		
	Wilhelm Tell	Holt/Sachtleben, Augustus	199		Whitney's German Texts

1879

Goethe, J. W. von	Ausgewählte Prosa	Putnam/Hart, James Morgan	199	1.00	German Classics for American Students. Readings from: Dichtung und Wahrheit, Die Leiden des jungen Werthers, Ein Brief aus der Schweiz, Italienische Reise, Wilhelm Meisters Lehrjahre
	Iphigenie auf Tauris	Holt/Whitney, William D.	113	.95	Whitney's German Texts
	Iphigenie auf Tauris	Schoenhof/Whitney, William D.	113	.95	Whitney's German Texts
	Poems	Ginn/Schütze, Martin			International Modern Language Series
Schiller, J. C. F. von	Die Piccolomini	Putnam/Hart, James Morgan	178		German Classics for American Students

239

APPENDIX F (Continued)

Author	Title	Publisher/Editor	Pages	Price	Series and Contents
		188-			
Heyse, Paul	Er soll dein Herr sein	Steiger/Ahn	40	.20	Ahn's Series of German Novels
Lessing, G. E.	Emilia Galotti	Holt	82		Classic German Plays
Putlitz, Gustav zu	Badekuren	Holt			
Seidel, Heinrich	Leberecht Hühnchen	Steiger/Ahn		.20	Ahn's Series of German Novels
		1880			
Goethe, J. W. von	Ausgewählte Prosa	Putnam/Hart, James Morgan	199	1.00	German Classics for American Students. Readings from: Dichtung und Wahrheit, Die Leiden des jungen Werthers, Ein Brief aus der Schweiz, Italienische Reise, Wilhelm Meisters Lehrjahre
	Hermann und Dorothea	Putnam/Hart, James Morgan	155	1.00	German Classics for American Students
Lessing, G. E.	Minna von Barnhelm	Holt/Whitney, William D.	158		Whitney's German Texts
	Minna von Barnhelm	Schoenhof/Whitney, William D.	158		Whitney's German Texts
Schiller, J. C. F. von	Die Piccolomini	Putnam/Hart, James Morgan	178		German Classics for American Students
	Maria Stuart	Schoenhof/Whitney, William D.	222		Whitney's German Texts
	Maria Stuart	Holt/Whitney, William D.	222		Whitney's German Texts
Zschokke, Heinrich	Der zerbrochene Krug	Schoenhof/Roelker, Bernard	28	.30	

1881				
Grimm, Jakob and Wilhelm	Kinder- und Hausmärchen	Holt	228	Unterhaltungs-Bibliothek
Gutzkow, Karl F.	Zopf und Schwert	Macmillan/Wolstenholme, Henry J.	197	.90	Pitt Press Series
1882				
Uhland, Ludwig	Herzog Ernst von Schwaben	Macmillan/Wolstenholme, Henry J.		.90	Pitt Press Series
1883				
Claar, Emil	Simson und Delila	Holt/Stern, Sigmon Martin	55	.30	Stern's German Comedies
	Simson und Delila	Schoenhof/Stern, Sigmon Martin	55	.30	Stern's German Comedies
Goethe, J. W. von	Götz von Berlichingen	Macmillan/Bull, H. A.	179	.55	Foreign School Classics
Heine, Heinrich	Die Harzreise and Das Buch Le Grand	Holt/Harrison, James A.	164	.50	Unterhaltungs-Bibliothek
	Die Harzreise and Das Buch Le Grand	Schoenhof/Harrison, James A.	164	.50	
Jungmann	Er sucht einen Vetter	Holt/Stern, Sigmon Martin	49	.25	Stern's German Comedies
	Er sucht einen Vetter	Schoenhof/Stern, Sigmon Martin	49	.25	
Königswinter, W. M. von	Sie hat ihr Herz entdeckt	Holt/Stern, Sigmon Martin	79	.40	Stern's German Comedies
Moser, Gustav von	Der Schimmel	Holt/Stern, Sigmon Martin	55	.25	Stern's German Comedies
	Der Schimmel	Schoenhof/Stern, Sigmon Martin	55	.25	Stern's German Comedies
Paul, C. A. (Scheiden, B.)	Er muss tanzen	Holt/Stern, Sigmon Martin	51	.25	Stern's German Comedies

APPENDIX F *(Continued)*

Author	Title	Publisher/Editor	Pages	Price	Series and Contents
	Er muß tanzen	Schoenhof/Stern, Sigmon Martin	51	.25	Stern's German Comedies
Rosen, Julius	Ein Knopf	Holt/Stern, Sigmon Martin	41	.30	Stern's German Comedies
	Ein Knopf	Schoenhof/Stern, Sigmon Martin	41	.30	Stern's German Comedies
Schiller, J. C. F. von	Die Jungfrau von Orleans	Macmillan/Gostwick, Joseph		.60	Foreign School Classics
	Maria Stuart	Macmillan/Sheldon, Charles	264	.65	Foreign School Classics

1884

Author	Title	Publisher/Editor	Pages	Price	Series and Contents
Benedix, Roderich	Die Phrenologen	Steiger/Ahn	52	.25	Ahn's Series of German Comedies
Claar, Emil	Simson und Delila	Holt/Stern, Sigmon Martin	55	.25	Stern's German Comedies
Fouqué, Friedrich de la Motte	Sintram und seine Gefährten	Holt	114	.40	Unterhaltungs-Bibliothek
Friedrich, W. (Riese, Wilhelm Friedrich)	Gänschen von Buchenau	Holt/Stern, Sigmon Martin	88	.35	Stern's German Comedies
Jungmann	Er sucht einen Vetter	Holt/Stern, Sigmon Martin	49	.25	Stern's German Comedies
Königswinter, W. M. von	Sie hat ihr Herz entdeckt	Holt/Stern, Sigmon Martin	79	.40	Stern's German Comedies
Moser, Gustav von	Der Schimmel	Holt/Stern, Sigmon Martin	55	.25	Stern's German Comedies

Paul, C. A. (Scheiden, B.)	Er muß tanzen	Holt/Stern, Sigmon Martin	51	.25	Stern's German Comedies
Riehl, Wilhelm H.	Culturgeschichtliche Novellen	Macmillan/Wolstenholme, Henry J.	301	1.00	Includes: Der stumme Ratsherr, Der Dachs auf Lichtmeß, Der Leibmedikus, Der Zopf des Herrn Guillemain
Rosen, Julius	Ein Knopf	Holt/Stern, Sigmon Martin	41	.25	Stern's German Comedies
Zschokke, Heinrich	Das Wirtshaus zu Cransac	Schoenhof			

1885

Blumenthal, Oscar	Paulas Geheimnis	Steiger/Ahn	45	.25	Ahn's Series of German Comedies
Claar, Emil	Simson und Delila	Holt/Stern, Sigmon Martin	55	.25	Stern's German Comedies
Friedrich, W. (Riese, Wilhelm Friedrich)	Gänschen von Buchenau	Holt/Stern, Sigmon Martin	88	.35	Stern's German Comedies
Grimm, Jakob and Wilhelm	Kinder- und Hausmärchen	Heath/Smissen, W. H. van der	190	.75	Modern Language Series
	Kinder- und Hausmärchen	Macmillan/Fasnacht, G. Eugene	160	.50	Primary Series
Hillern, Wilhelmine von	Höher als die Kirche	Holt	46	.25	Unterhaltungs-Bibliothek
Königswinter, W. M. von	Sie hat ihr Herz entdeckt	Holt/Stern, Sigmon Martin	79	.40	Stern's German Comedies

APPENDIX F (*Continued*)

Author	Title	Publisher/Editor	Pages	Price	Series and Contents
Leander, Richard (Volkmann, Richard von)	Träumereien an französischen Kaminen	American Book/ Hanstein, Amalie			Includes: Der kleine Vogel, Das kleine bucklige Mädchen, Die himmlische Musik, Die künstliche Orgel, Der Wunschring, Die drei Schwestern mit den gläsernen Herzen, Von der Königin, die keine Pfeffernüsse backen, und dem König, der nicht das Brummeisen spielen konnte, Vom unsichtbaren Königreiche, Pechvogel und Glückskind, Die Traumbuche, Der kleine Mohr und die Goldprinzessin
Lessing, G. E.	Emilia Galotti	Heath/Winkler, Max	128		Modern Language Series
Moser, Gustav von	Er soll dein Herr sein	Steiger/Ahn	51	.25	Ahn's Series of German Comedies
Paul, C. A. (Scheiden, B.)	Er muß tanzen	Holt/Stern, Sigmon Martin	70	.25	Stern's German Comedies
Schiller, J. C. F. von	Das Lied von der Glocke	Holt/Otis, Charles Pomeroy	70	.40	
	Das Lied von der Glocke	Schoenhof/Otis, Charles Pomeroy	70	.40	

244

		Holt/Simonson, Leopold	74	Unterhaltungs-Bibliothek
Tieck, Ludwig	Zwei Märchennovellen: Die Elfen, Das Rothkäppchen			
		1886		
Auerbach, Berthold	Joseph und Benjamin	Steiger/Ahn	52	.20	Ahn's Series of German Novels
Benedix, Roderich	Die Phrenologen	Steiger/Ahn	63	.25	Ahn's Series of German Comedies
	Eigensinn and Wilhelmi's Einer muß heiraten	Holt			
	Eigensinn and Wilhelmi's Einer muß heiraten	Schoenhof	63		
	Günstige Vorzeichen	Steiger/Ahn		.25	Ahn's Series of German Comedies
Goethe, J. W. von	Faust. Erster Teil	Macmillan/Lee, Jane	363	1.10	Foreign School Classics
	Hermann und Dorothea	Putnam/Hart, James Morgan	155	1.00	German Classics for American Students
Grimm Hermann F.	Das Kind	Steiger/Ahn	47	.20	Ahn's Series of German Novels
	Der Landschaftsmaler	Steiger/Ahn		.20	Ahn's Series of German Novels
Grimm Jakob and Wilhelm	Kinder- und Hausmärchen	Heath/Smissen, W. H. van der	190	.75	Modern Language Series
	Kinder- und Hausmärchen	Holt/Otis, Charles Pomeroy	351	1.00	
Hartmann, Moritz	Die Ausgestoßenen	Steiger/Ahn	184	.20	Ahn's Series of German Novels
Hauff, Wilhelm	Das kalte Herz	Heath/Smissen, W. H. van der			
	Die Karawane	Macmillan/Schlottmann, A.		.90	
Heine, Heinrich	Die Harzreise	Macmillan/Buchheim, Carl Adolf		.60	German Classics
Heyse, Paul	Am Toten See	Steiger/Ahn		.20	Ahn's Series of German Novels
	Das Mädchen von Treppi	Steiger/Ahn	58	.20	Ahn's Series of German Novels
	Die Blinden	Steiger/Ahn		.20	Ahn's Series of German Novels
	L'Arrabbiata	Steiger/Ahn	21	.20	Ahn's Series of German Novels
	Vetter Gabriel	Steiger/Ahn	53	.20	Ahn's Series of German Novels
Jensen, Wilhelm	Die braune Erika	Schoenhof			

APPENDIX F *(Continued)*

Author	Title	Publisher/Editor	Pages	Price	Series and Contents
Meyr, Melchior	Zwei Freier	Steiger/Ahn	38	.20	Ahn's Series of German Novels
Müller, Max	Deutsche Liebe	Holt	121	.35	Unterhaltungs-Bibliothek
	Deutsche Liebe	Schoenhof	121	.35	Unterhaltungs-Bibliothek
Niebuhr, B. G.	Griechische Heroengeschichten	Macmillan/Buchheim, Emma S.	131	.50	Clarendon Press. Includes: Die Fahrt der Argonauten, Geschichten von Herakles, Die Herakliden, Orestes, Meroppe und Apytos
Pohl, Emil	Die Schulreiterin	Steiger/Ahn	47	.25	Ahn's Series of German Comedies
Riehl, Wilhelm H.	Burg Neideck	Steiger/Ahn	45	.20	Ahn's Series of German Novels
Schiller, J. C. F. von	Ausgewählte Briefe	Putnam/Buchheim, Pauline H.	206	1.00	German Classics for American Students
	Selections from Lyrical Poems	Macmillan/Turner, Edward J., and Edmund D. Morshead,	203	.65	Foreign School Classics
Storm, Theodor	Auf der Universität	Steiger/Ahn	95	.20	Ahn's Series of German Novels
Wilhelmi, Alexander (Zechmeister, Alexander Viktor)	Einer muß heiraten and Benedix's Eigensinn	Holt	63		
	Einer muß heiraten and Benedix's Eigensinn	Schoenhof	63		

1887

Author	Title	Publisher/Editor	Pages	Price	Series and Contents
Andersen, H. C.	Bilderbuch ohne Bilder	Holt/Simonson, Leopold		.25	Unterhaltungs-Bibliothek
	Bilderbuch ohne Bilder	Schoenhof/Simonson, Leopold			

246

Author	Title	Publisher	Price	Series
	Die Eisjungfrau und andere Geschichten	Holt	.40	Unterhaltungs-Bibliothek. Includes: Die Eisjungfrau, Die Psyche, Die Schnecke und der Rosenstock, Der Schmetterling, Der silberne Schilling, Die Glocke
Auerbach, Berthold	Auf Wache and Roquette's Der gefrorene Kuß	Holt/MacDonnell, Arthur A.	126	.35	Unterhaltungs-Bibliothek
Boyen, M.	Mein erster Patient In: Deutsche Novelletten-Bibliothek	Heath/Bernhardt, Wilhelm		1.20	Modern Language Series
Carové	Das Märchen ohne Ende	Holt	45	.20	Unterhaltungs-Bibliothek
Ebers, Georg M.	Eine Frage. Idyll zu einem Gemälde	Holt/Storr, Francis	117	.35	Unterhaltungs-Bibliothek
Eichendorff, Joseph von	Aus dem Leben eines Taugenichts	Holt	132	.40	Unterhaltungs-Bibliothek
Fouqué, Friedrich de la Motte	Undine	Holt	88	.35	Unterhaltungs-Bibliothek
	Undine	Schoenhof Christern	88	.35	Unterhaltungs-Bibliothek
	Undine		88	.35	Unterhaltungs-Bibliothek
Francois, Marie L. von	Phosphorus Hollunder	Heath/Faulhaber, Oscar	77	.30	Unterhaltungs-Bibliothek
Gellert, C. F.	Fabeln und Erzählungen, with fables by Lessing	Macmillan/Breul, Karl Hermann		.75	
Goethe, J. W. von	Hermann und Dorothea	Putnam/Hart, James Morgan	155	1.00	German Classics for American Students
Götzendorff-Grabowski, Helene von	Der Simpel and Vor Sonnenaufgang In: Deutsche Novelletten-Bibliothek	Heath/Bernhardt, Wilhelm		1.20	Modern Language Series

APPENDIX F (Continued)

Author	Title	Publisher/Editor	Pages	Price	Series and Contents
Grimm, Hermann F.	Die Venus von Milo and Rafael und Michel-Angelo	Holt	139	.40	Unterhaltungs-Bibliothek
Grimm, Jakob and Wilhelm	Kinder- und Hausmärchen	Heath/Smissen, W. H. van der	190	.75	Modern Language Series
	Kinder- und Hausmärchen	Holt	228	.40	Unterhaltungs-Bibliothek
	Kinder- und Hausmärchen	Holt/Otis, Charles Pomeroy	351	1.00	
	Kinder- und Hausmärchen	Schoenhof/Otis, Charles Pomeroy	351	1.00	
Heine, Heinrich	Die Harzreise and Das Buch Le Grand	Holt/Harrison, James A.	164	.50	Unterhaltungs-Bibliothek
Heyse, Paul	Anfang und Ende	Holt	54	.25	Unterhaltungs-Bibliothek
	Die Einsamen	Holt	44	.20	Unterhaltungs-Bibliothek
	Die Einsamen	Schoenhof	44	.20	Unterhaltungs-Bibliothek
Hillern, Wilhelmine von	Höher als die Kirche	Holt	46	.20	Unterhaltungs-Bibliothek
Juncke, E. (Schmieden, Else)	Ein Frühlingstraum In: Deutsche Novelletten-Bibliothek	Heath/Bernhardt, Wilhelm		1.20	Modern Language Series
Lessing, G. E.	Fabeln, with fables and stories by Gellert	Macmillan/Breul, Karl Hermann		.75	
Moser, Gustav von	Der Bibliothekar	Holt/Lange, Franz	161	.40	Unterhaltungs-Bibliothek
Mügge, Theodor	Riukan-Voss	Holt	55	.25	Unterhaltungs-Bibliothek
	Signa die Seterin	Holt	71	.25	Unterhaltungs-Bibliothek
Nathusius, Marie	Tagebuch eines armen Fräuleins	Holt		.50	Unterhaltungs-Bibliothek
Peschkau, Emil	Sphinx In: Deutsche Novelletten-Bibliothek	Heath/Bernhardt, Wilhelm		1.20	Modern Language Series
Petersen, Marie	Prinzessin Ilse	Holt/Merrick, John Mudge		.20	Unterhaltungs-Bibliothek

Putlitz, Gustav zu	Vergißmeinnicht	Holt	44	.20	Unterhaltungs-Bibliothek
	Was sich der Wald erzählt	Holt		.25	Unterhaltungs-Bibliothek
Roquette, Otto	Der gefrorene Kuß and Auerbach's Auf Wache	Holt/MacDonnell, Arthur A.	126	.35	Unterhaltungs-Bibliothek
Schiller, J. C. F. von	Das Lied von der Glocke	Holt/Otis, Charles Pomeroy	70	.35	Unterhaltungs-Bibliothek
	Der Taucher	Heath/Smissen, W. H. van der	24	.12	Modern Language Series
	Die Jungfrau von Orleans	Holt/Nichols, Alfred Bull	203		
	Die Jungfrau von Orleans	Schoenhof/Nichols, Alfred Bull	203		
	Wallensteins Lager	Macmillan/Cotterill, Henry B.	113	.50	Foreign School Classics
	Wilhelm Tell	Schoenhof/Sachtleben, Augustus	199		Whitney's German Texts
	Wilhelm Tell	Holt/Sachtleben, Augustus	199		Whitney's German Texts
	Wilhelm Tell	Macmillan/Fasnacht, G. Eugene	238	.60	Foreign School Classics
Seidel, Heinrich	Leberecht Hühnchen and Der gute alte Onkel In: Deutsche Novelletten-Bibliothek	Heath/Bernhardt, Wilhelm		1.20	Modern Language Series
Stökl, Helene	Am Heiligen Abend and Eine Weihnachtsgeschichte In: Deutsche Novelletten-Bibliothek	Heath/Bernhardt, Wilhelm		1.20	Modern Language Series
Storm, Theodor	Immensee	Holt		.20	Unterhaltungs-Bibliothek
Tieck, Ludwig	Zwei Märchennovellen: Die Elfen, Das Rothkäppchen	Holt/Simonson, Leopold	74	.30	Unterhaltungs-Bibliothek
Werner, Ernst (Bürstenbinder, Elizabeth)	Der Wilddieb In: Deutsche Novelletten-Bibliothek	Heath/Bernhardt, Wilhelm		1.20	Modern Language Series

APPENDIX F (*Continued*)

Author	Title	Publisher/Editor	Pages	Price	Series and Contents
Wiesner, A. C.	Die schwarze Dame In: Deutsche Novelletten-Bibliothek	Heath/Bernhardt, Wilhelm		1.20	Modern Language Series
1888					
Baumbach, Rudolf	Im Zwielicht	Schoenhof/Bernhardt, Wilhelm			
	Im Zwielicht	Christern/Bernhardt, Wilhelm			
	Im Zwielicht	American Book/Bernhardt, Wilhelm			
Becker, Karl F.	Friedrich der Große	Macmillan/Buchheim, Carl Adolf	175	.90	
Benedix, Roderich	Doktor Wespe	Macmillan/Breul, Karl Hermann	208	.75	Pitt Press Series
	Eigensinn and Wilhelmi's Einer muß heiraten	Holt	75		
	Eigensinn and Wilhelmi's Einer muß heiraten	Schoenhof	75		
Boyen, M.	Mein erster Patient In: Deutsche Novelletten-Bibliothek	Heath/Bernhardt, Wilhelm	85	1.20	Modern Language Series
Chamisso, Adelbert von	Peter Schlemihls wundersame Geschichte	Kilborn/Primer, Sylvester		.25	Select German Texts
Ebers, Georg M.	Eine Frage. Idyll zu einem Gemälde	Holt/Storr, Francis	117	.35	Unterhaltungs-Bibliothek
	Eine Frage. Idyll zu einem Gemälde	Schoenhof/Storr, Francis	117	.35	Unterhaltungs-Bibliothek
Faulhaber, Oscar	Onkel und Nichte	Heath		.15	

250

Freytag, Gustav	Die Journalisten	Holt/Lange, Franz	178	.40	College Series of German Plays
	Die Journalisten	Schoenhof/Hochdörfer, Richard	128		
Goethe, J. W. von	Ausgewählte Prosa	Putnam/Hart, James Morgan	199	1.00	German Classics for American Students. Readings from: Dichtung und Wahrheit, Die Leiden des jungen Werthers, Ein Brief aus der Schweiz, Italienische Reise, Wilhelm Meisters Lehrjahre
	Faust. Erster Teil	Putnam/Hart, James Morgan	257	1.25	German Classics for American Students
	Hermann und Dorothea	Putnam/Hart, James Morgan	155	1.00	German Classics for American Students
	Torquato Tasso	Heath/Thomas, Calvin	181	.75	Heath's German Series
Götzendorff-Grabowski, Helene von	Der Simpel and Vor Sonnenaufgang In: Deutsche Novelletten-Bibliothek	Heath/Bernhardt, Wilhelm	103	1.20	Modern Language Series
Grimm, Jakob and Wilhelm	Kinder- und Hausmärchen	Heath/Smissen, W. H. van der	163	.40	Modern Language Series
Gutzkow, Karl F.	Zopf und Schwert	Holt/Lange, Franz	184		
Hauff, Wilhelm	Das kalte Herz	Heath/Smissen, W. H. van der			
	Der Zwerg Nase	Kilborn	38	.15	Selected German Texts
	Die Karawane	Macmillan		.75	
Heine, Heinrich	Die Harzreise	Kilborn/Daell, Alphonse N. van	79	.25	Selected German Texts
	Prose	Macmillan/Buchheim, Carl Adolf	322	1.10	German Classics
Juncke, E. (Schmieden, Else)	Ein Frühlingstraum In: Deutsche Novelletten-Bibliothek	Heath/Bernhardt, Wilhelm		1.20	Modern Language Series

251

APPENDIX F (*Continued*)

Author	Title	Publisher/Editor	Pages	Price	Series and Contents
Leander, Richard (Volkmann, Richard von)	Träumereien an französischen Kaminen	Heath/Daell, Alphonse N. van	103	.25	Heath's German Series. Includes: Der kleine Vogel, Das kleine bucklige Mädchen, Die himmlische Musik, Die künstliche Orgel, Der Wunschring, Die drei Schwestern mit den gläsernen Herzen, Von der Königin, die keine Pfeffernüsse backen, und dem König, der nicht das Brummeisen spielen konnte, Vom unsichtbaren Königreiche, Pechvogel und Glückskind, Die Traumbuche, Der kleine Mohr und die Goldprinzessin
Lessing, G. E.	Ausgewählte Prosa und Briefe	Putnam/White, Horatio S.	236	1.00	German Classics for American Students. Includes: Fabeln, Siebzehnter Literaturbrief, Gedanken über die Herrnhuter, Eine Parabel, Hamburgische Dramaturgie, Ernst und Falk, Ausgewählte Briefe
	Nathan der Weise	Macmillan/Buchheim, Carl Adolf	301	1.10	Clarendon Press
Peschkau, Emil	Sphinx In: Deutsche Novelletten-Bibliothek	Heath/Bernhardt, Wilhelm		1.20	Modern Language Series
Richter, Albert	Walther und Hildegund and Vilmar's Die Nibelungen	Holt	100	.35	Unterhaltungs-Bibliothek
Schiller, J. C. F. von	Ballads	Heath/Johnson, Henry	165	.60	Modern Language Series
	Der Taucher	Heath/Smissen, W. H. van der	24	.12	Modern Lanugage Series
	Die Jungfrau von Orleans	Holt/Nichols, Alfred Bull	203	.40	

	Die Jungfrau von Orleans	Heath/Wells, Benjamin W.		.60	Heath German Series
	Die Jungfrau von Orleans Die Piccolomini	Macmillan Putnam/Hart, James Morgan	178	.60	Foreign School Classics German Classics for American Students
	Maria Stuart	Macmillan/Sheldon, Charles	264		Foreign School Classics
Seidel, Heinrich	Leberecht Hühnchen and Der gute alte Onkel In: Deutsche Novelletten-Bibliothek	Heath/Bernhardt, Wilhelm		1.20	Modern Language Series
Stökl, Helene	Am Heiligen Abend and Eine Weihnachtsgeschichte In: Deutsche Novelletten-Bibliothek	Heath/Bernhardt, Wilhelm		1.20	Modern Language Series
Vilmar, A. F. C.	Die Nibelungen and Richter's Walther und Hildegund	Holt	100	.35	Unterhaltungs-Bibliothek
Werner, Ernst (Bürstenbinder, Elizabeth)	Der Wilddieb In: Deutsche Novelletten-Bibliothek	Heath/Bernhardt, Wilhelm		1.20	Modern Language Series
Wiesner, A. C.	Die Schwarze Dame In: Deutsche Novelletten-Bibliothek	Heath/Bernhardt, Wilhelm		1.20	Modern Language Series
Wilhelmi, Alexander (Zechmeister, Alexander Viktor)	Einer muß heiraten and Benedix's Eigensinn	Holt	75		
	Einer muß heiraten and Benedix's Eigensinn	Schoenhof	75		

1889

Baumbach, Rudolf	Im Zwielicht	Schoenhof/Bernhardt, Wilhelm			
	Im Zwielicht	Christern/Bernhardt, Wilhelm			

253

APPENDIX F (*Continued*)

Author	Title	Publisher/Editor	Pages	Price	Series and Contents
	Im Zwielicht	American Book Bernhardt, Wilhelm	155	.50	
Chamisso, Adelbert von	Peter Schlemihls Wundersame Geschichte	Macmillan/Buchheim, Emma S.		.25	
	Peter Schlemihls Wundersame Geschichte	Heath/Primer, Sylvester	96		Modern Language Series
Fouqué, Friedrich de la Motte	Undine	Holt/Jagemann, Hans Carl G.	229	.50	
Freytag, Gustav	Aus dem Staat Friedrichs des Großen	Heath/Hager, Hermann	115	.30	Modern Language Series
	Die Journalisten	Heath/Toy, Walter Dallam	160	.50	Modern Language Series
	Die Journalisten	Holt/Thomas, Calvin	134	.30	College Series of German Plays
	Die Journalisten	Schoenhof/Thomas, Calvin	134	.30	College Series of German Plays
Goethe, J. W. von	Goethe's Sesenheim	Heath/Huss, Hermann Carl O.	83	.25	Modern Language Series
	Hermann und Dorothea	Putnam/Hart, James Morgan	155	1.00	German Classics for American Students
Hauff, Wilhelm	Das Bild des Kaisers	Macmillan/Breul, Karl Hermann	216	.75	Pitt Press Series
	Das Bild des Kaisers	Schoenhof/Davis, John Francis	206		
	Der Zwerg Nase	Heath	38		Heath German Series
Heine, Heinrich	Die Harzreise	Heath/Daell, Alphonse N. van	80	.25	Heath German Series
	Die Harzreise	Holt/Burnett, A. W.	97	.30	Unterhaltungs-Bibliothek
	Die Harzreise	Schoenhof/Burnett, A. W.	97	.30	Unterhaltungs-Bibliothek

Holberg, Ludvig	Niels Klims Wallfahrt in die Unterwelt	Heath/Babbitt, Eugene H.	63	.20	Modern Language Series
Jensen, Wilhelm	Die braune Erika	Heath/Joynes, Edward S.	80	.25	Heath German Series
Lessing, G. E.	Minna von Barnhelm	Heath/Primer, Sylvester	178	.60	Modern Language Series
Schiller, J. C. F. von	Der Neffe als Onkel	Allyn and Bacon/Raddatz, Charles F.	125	.50	Allyn and Bacon's German Texts
	Die Jungfrau von Orleans	Heath/Wells, Benjamin W.	224	.60	Heath German Series
Schmid, Chr. von	Heinrich von Eichenfels	Macmillan/Fasnacht, G. Eugene	150	.60	Foreign School Classics
Wachenhusen, Hans	Vom ersten bis zum letzten Schuß	Macmillan/Bayley, Thomas Henry		.60	

189-

Benedix, Roderich	Der Prozeß	Steiger/Ahn	47	.25	Ahn's Series of German Comedies
	Der Weiberfeind, with Elz's Er ist nicht eifersüchtig and Müller's Im Wartesalon erster Klasse	Holt	82	.50	
	Der Weiberfeind, with Elz's Er ist nicht eifersüchtig and Müller's Im Wartesalon erster Klasse	Schoenhof	82	.50	
	Günstige Vorzeichen	Steiger/Ahn		.25	Ahn's Series of German Comedies
Blumenthal, Oscar	Paulas Geheimnis	Steiger/Ahn	45	.25	Ahn's Series of German Comedies
Eckstein, Ernst	Der Besuch im Carcer	Maynard and Merrill/Stephens, T. A.	86	.25	Maynard's German Texts

255

APPENDIX F *(Continued)*

Author	Title	Publisher/Editor	Pages	Price	Series and Contents
Eichendorff, Joseph von	Aus dem Leben eines Taugenichts and Grimm's Die Venus von Milo	DeVries, Ibarra	132		
Elz, Alexander	Er ist nicht eifersüchtig, with Benedix's Der Weiberfeind and Müllers Im Wartesalon erster Klasse	Holt	82	.50	
	Er ist nicht eifersüchtig, with Benedix's Der Weiberfeind and Müllers Im Wartesalon erster Klasse	Schoenhof	82	.50	
Grimm, Hermann F.	Die Venus von Milo and Eichendorff's Aus dem Leben eines Taugenichts	DeVries, Ibarra	132		
Heyse, Paul	Anfang und Ende	Holt	54	.25	Unterhaltungs-Bibliothek
Hoffmann, Otto	Episodes from Andreas Hofer	Maynard and Merrill/ Powell, O. B.	96		Maynard's German Texts
Moser, Gustav von	Der Bibliothekar	Holt/Lange, Franz	161	.50	College Series of German Plays
Müller, Hugo	Im Wartesalon erster Klasse, with Benedix's Der Weiberfeind und Elz's Er ist nicht eifersüchtig	Holt	82		
	Im Wartesalon erster Klasse, with Benedix's Der Weiberfeind and Elz's Er ist nicht eifersüchtig	Schoenhof	82	.50	

Putlitz, Gustav zu	Das Herz vergessen	Holt	79		Classic German Plays
Schiller, J. C. F. von	Wallenstein Trilogie	Holt/Krauss, Ernst Carl F.			
Seidel, Heinrich	Weihnachten bei Leberecht Hühnchen	Maynard and Merrill/ Morich, R. J.	94	.25	Maynard's German Texts
		1890			
Auerbach, Berthold	Tales of the Black Forest	Longmans, Green/Fox-Strangeways, A. H.	123	.45	Modern German Authors
Boyen, M.	Mein erster Patient In: Deutsche Novelletten-Bibliothek	Heath/Bernhardt, Wilhelm		1.20	Modern Language Series
Freytag, Gustav	Aus dem Staat Friedrichs des Großen	Heath/Hager, Hermann	115	.30	Modern Language Series
	Die Journalisten	Heath/Toy, Walter Dallam	160	.50	Modern Language Series
Goethe, J. W. von	Dichtung und Wahrheit	Holt/Jagemann, Hans Carl G.	373	1.12	
Götzendorff-Grabowski, Helene von	Der Simpel and Vor Sonnenaufgang In: Deutsche Novelletten-Bibliotek	Heath/Bernhardt, Wilhelm		1.20	Modern Language Series
Gutzkow, Karl F.	Zopf und Schwert	Holt/Lange, Franz	163	.20	College Series of German Plays
	Zopf und Schwert	Schoenhof/Lange, Franz	163		College Series of German Plays
Hauff, Wilhelm	Das kalte Herz	Holt	61	.20	Unterhaltungs-Bibliothek
Heine, Heinrich	Die Harzreise	Macmillan		.40	
	Die Harzreise	Heath/Daell, Alphonse N. van			
	Poems	Heath/White, Horatio S.	220	.75	Modern Language Series
Hoffmann, Hans F.	Historische Erzählungen	Heath/Beresdford-Webb, H. S.	107	.25	Modern Language Series

APPENDIX F (Continued)

Author	Title	Publisher/Editor	Pages	Price	Series and Contents
Juncke, E. (Schmieden, Else)	Ein Frühlingstraum In: Deutsche Novelletten-Bibliothek	Heath/Bernhardt, Wilhelm		1.20	Modern Language Series
Lessing, G. E.	Minna von Barnhelm	Heath/Primer, Sylvester	245		Modern Language Series
Peschkau, Emil	Sphinx In: Deutsche Novelletten-Bibliothek	Heath/Bernhardt, Wilhelm		1.20	Modern Language Series
Richter, Albert	Walther und Hildegund and Vilmar's Die Nibelungen	Holt		.35	
Riehl, Wilhelm H.	Der Fluch der Schönheit	Heath/Thomas, Calvin	70	.25	Modern Language Series
Schiller, J. C. F. von	Der Geisterseher. Erstes Buch	Heath/Joynes, Edward S.	118	.25	Modern Language Series
	Der Neffe als Onkel	Allyn and Bacon/Raddatz, Charles F.	125	.50	Allyn and Bacon's German Texts
	Die Jungfrau von Orleans	Heath/Wells, Benjamin W.	224	.60	Heath German Series
	Die Jungfrau von Orleans	Macmillan/Buchheim, Carl Adolf		1.10	German Classics
Schmid, Chr. von	Heinrich von Eichenfels	Macmillan/Fasnacht, G. Eugene	150	.60	Foreign School Classics
Seidel, Heinrich	Leberecht Hühnchen and Der gute alte Onkel In: Deutsche Novelletten-Bibliothek	Heath/Bernhardt, Wilhelm		1.20	Modern Language Series
Stökl, Helene	Am Heiligen Abend and Eine Weihnachtsgeschichte In: Deutsche Novelletten-Bibliothek	Heath/Bernhardt, Wilhelm		1.20	Modern Language Series
Storm, Theodor	Immensee	Heath/Bernhardt, Wilhelm	113	.30	Modern Language Series

Sudermann, Hermann	Der Katzensteg	Heath/Wells, Benjamin W.		Modern Language Series
Vilmar, A. F. C.	Die Nibelungen and Richter's Walther und Hildegund	Holt	.35	
Werner, Ernst (Bürstenbinder, Elizabeth)	Der Wilddieb In: Deutsche Novelletten-Bibliothek	Heath/Bernhardt, Wilhelm	1.20	Modern Language Series
Wiesner, A. C.	Die schwarze Dame In: Deutsche Novelletten-Bibliothek	Heath/Bernhardt, Wilhelm	1.20	Modern Language Series
1891				
Andersen, H. C.	Bilderbuch ohne Bilder	Heath/Bernhardt, Wilhelm	.35	Modern Language Series
Auerbach, Berthold	Tales of the Black Forest	Longmans, Green/Fox-Strangeways, A. H.	123	.45	Modern German Authors
Baumbach, Rudolf	Im Zwielicht	Schoenhof/Bernhardt, Wilhelm		
Boyen, M.	Mein erster Patient In: Deutsche Novelletten-Bibliothek	Heath/Bernhardt, Wilhelm		1.20	Modern Language Series
Chamisso, Adelbert von	Peter Schlemihls wundersame Geschichte	Holt/Hitzig, Julius H.	126	.25	
	Peter Schlemihls wundersame Geschichte	Christern/Hitzig, Julius H.	126	.25	
	Peter Schlemihls wundersame Geschichte	Schoenhof/Hitzig, Julius H.	126	.25	
Dahn, Felix L. S.	Felicitas	Longmans, Green/Bienemann, G. A.	193	.60	Modern German Authors
Freytag, Gustav	Aus dem Staat Friedrichs des Großen	Heath/Hager, Hermann	115	.30	Modern Language Series
Goethe, J. W. von	Einführung in Goethe's [sic] Meisterwerke	Heath/Bernhardt, Wilhelm	275	1.50	Modern Language Series

APPENDIX F *(Continued)*

Author	Title	Publisher/Editor	Pages	Price	Series and Contents
	Hermann und Dorothea	Putnam/Hart, James Morgan	155	1.00	German Classics for American Students
	Hermann und Dorothea	Holt/Thomas, Calvin	104		
	Hermann und Dorothea	Schoenhof/Thomas, Calvin	104		
	Hermann und Dorothea	Heath/Hewett, Waterman T.	243	1.00	Modern Language Series
	Torquato Tasso	Heath/Thomas, Calvin	181	.75	Heath German Series
Götzendorff-Grabowski, Helene von	Der Simpel and Vor Sonnenaufgang In: Deutsche Novelletten-Bibliothek	Heath/Bernhardt, Wilhelm		1.20	Modern Language Series
Hauff, Wilhelm	Das kalte Herz	Heath/Smissen, W. H. van der	184		
	Die Karawane	Macmillan/Hager, Hermann	251	.65	Primary Series
Heine, Heinrich	Poems	Heath/White, Horatio S.	220	.75	Modern Language Series
	Selections from the Reisebilder	Macmillan/Colbeck, Charles	230		Foreign School Classics
Hillern, Wilhelmine von	Höher als die Kirche	Heath/Clary, Stedman W.	102	.15	Modern Language Series
Juncke, E. (Schmieden, Else)	Ein Frühlingstraum In: Deutsche Novelletten-Bibliothek	Heath/Bernhardt, Wilhelm		1.20	Modern Language Series
Lessing, G. E.	Ausgewählte Prosa und Briefe	Putnam/White, Horatio S.	236	1.00	German Classics for American Students. Includes: Fabeln, Siebzehnter Literaturbrief, Gedanken über die Herrnhuter, Eine Parabel, Hamburgische Dramaturgie, Ernst und Falk, Ausgewählte Briefe

Peschkau, Emil	Sphinx In: Deutsche Novelletten-Bibliothek	Heath/Bernhardt, Wilhelm		1.20	Modern Language Series
Riehl, Wilhelm H.	Der Fluch der Schönheit	Heath/Thomas, Calvin	70	.35	Modern Language Series
	Der Fluch der Schönheit	Holt/Kendall, Francis L.	77		Unterhaltungs-Bibliothek
	Der Fluch der Schönheit	Schoenhof/Kendall, Francis L.	77	.35	Unterhaltungs-Bibliothek
Schiller, J. C. F. von	Das Lied von der Glocke	Holt/Otis, Charles Pomeroy	70	.35	
	Der Geisterseher. Erstes Buch	Heath/Joynes, Edward S.	118		Modern Language Series
	Wilhelm Tell	Macmillan/Breul, Karl Hermann		.50	
Seidel, Heinrich	Leberecht Hühnchen and Der gute alte Onkel In: Deutsche Novelletten-Bibliothek	Heath/Bernhardt, Wilhelm		1.20	Modern Language Series
Stifter, Adalbert	Das Heidedorf	Heath/Heller, Otto	50	.20	Modern Language Series
Stökl, Helene	Am Heiligen Abend and Eine Weihnachtsgeschichte In: Deutsche Novelletten-Bibliothek	Heath/Bernhardt, Wilhelm		1.20	Modern Language Series
Storm, Theodor	Immensee	Heath/Bernhardt, Wilhelm	113	.30	Modern Language Series
Werner, Ernst (Bürstenbinder, Elizabeth)	Der Wilddieb In: Deutsche Novelletten-Bibliothek	Heath/Bernhardt, Wilhelm		1.20	Modern Language Series
Wiesner, A. C.	Die schwarze Dame In: Deutsche Novelletten-Bibliothek	Heath/Bernhardt, Wilhelm		1.20	Modern Language Series
Wildermuth, Ottilie	Der Einsiedler im Walde	Holt/Fischer, A. Albin			

APPENDIX F (*Continued*)

1892

Author	Title	Publisher/Editor	Pages	Price	Series and Contents
Baumbach, Rudolf	Im Zwielicht	Schoenhof/Bernhardt, Wilhelm			
Benedix, Roderich	Doktor Wespe	Holt	116	.25	College Series of German Plays
	Doktor Wespe	Schoenhof	116	.25	College Series of German Plays
Boyen, M.	Mein erster Patient In: Deutsche Novelletten-Bibliothek	Heath/Bernhardt, Wilhelm		1.20	Modern Language Series
Eichendorff, Joseph von	Aus dem Leben eines Taugenichts	Heath/Osthaus, Carl Wilhelm	176	.40	Modern Language Series
Fischer, Wilhelm	Die wandelnde Glocke	Maynard and Merrill/Allpress, Robert H.	96	.25	Maynard's German Texts
Freytag, Gustav	Die Journalisten	Heath/Toy, Walter Dallam	160	.50	Modern Language Series
	Soll und Haben	Ginn/Bultmann, Ida W.	220	.70	International Modern Language Series
Goethe, J. W. von	Ausgewählte Prosa	Putnam/Hart, James Morgan	199	1.00	German Classics for American Students. Readings from: Dichtung und Wahrheit, Die Leiden des jungen Werthers, Ein Brief aus der Schweiz, Italienische Reise, Wilhelm Meisters Lehrjahre
	Faust. Erster Teil	Heath/Thomas, Calvin	365	1.20	Modern Language Series
	Faust. Erster und zweiter Teil	Heath/Thomas, Calvin			Modern Language Series
	Hermann und Dorothea	Bell/Bell, Ernest, and E. Wölfel	139	.50	Foreign Classics
	Hermann und Dorothea	Heath/Hewett, Waterman T.	243	1.00	Modern Language Series

Götzendorff-Grabowski, Helena von	Der Simpel and Vor Sonnenaufgang In: Deutsche Novelletten-Bibliothek	Heath/Bernhardt, Wilhelm		1.20	Modern Language Series
Grimm, Jakob and Wilhelm	Kinder- und Hausmärchen	Heath/Smissen, W. H. van der			Modern Language Series
Hauff, Wilhelm	Der Zwerg Nase	Heath	38		Heath German Series
Heyse, Paul	L'Arrabbiata	Heath/Bernhardt, Wilhelm	76	.25	Modern Language Series
Hillern, Wilhelmine von	Höher als die Kirche	Holt/Whitlesey, Mills	96	.25	Unterhaltungs-Bibliothek
Juncke, E. (Schmieden, Else)	Ein Frühlingstraum In: Deutsche Novelletten-Bibliothek	Heath/Bernhardt, Wilhelm		1.20	Modern Language Series
Keller, Gottfried	Dietegen	Ginn/Gruener, Gustav	75	.40	International Modern Language Series
Lessing, G. E.	Laokoon	Macmillan/Hamann, Albert	302	1.25	Clarendon Press
	Minna von Barnhelm	Heath/Primer, Sylvester	250		Modern Language Series
Peschkau, Emil	Sphinx In: Deutsche Novelletten-Bibliothek	Heath/Bernhardt, Wilhelm		1.20	Modern Language Series
Riehl, Wilhelm H.	Der Fluch der Schönheit	Heath/Thomas, Calvin	70		Modern Language Series
	Die Werke der Barmherzigkeit	Maynard and Merrill/ Voegelin, Ada	94	.25	Maynard's German Texts
Schiller, J. C. F. von	Ballads	Heath/Johnson, Henry	165	.60	Modern Language Series
	Die Jungfrau von Orleans	Heath/Wells, Benjamin W.	224		Modern Language Series
	Geschichte des Dreißigjährigen Kriegs	Macmillan/Breul, Karl Hermann		.80	Pitt Press Series
Seidel, Heinrich	Leberecht Hühnchen and Der gute alte Onkel In: Deutsche Novelletten-Bibliothek	Heath/Bernhardt, Wilhelm		1.20	Modern Language Series

APPENDIX F (*Continued*)

Author	Title	Publisher/Editor	Pages	Price	Series and Contents
Stökl, Helene	Am Heiligen Abend and Eine Weihnachtsgeschichte In: Deutsche Novelletten-Bibliothek	Heath/Bernhardt, Wilhelm		1.20	Modern Language Series
Storm, Theodor	Immensee	Holt/Burnett, Arthur W.	109		Unterhaltungs-Bibliothek
	Immensee	Schoenhof/Burnett, Arthur W.	109		Unterhaltungs-Bibliothek
	Psyche	Koelling and Klappenbach		.20	High School Series
Werner, Ernst (Bürstenbinder, Elizabeth)	Der Wilddieb In: Deutsche Novelletten-Bibliothek	Heath/Bernhardt, Wilhelm		1.20	Modern Language Series
Wiesner, A. C.	Die schwarze Dame In: Deutsche Novelletten-Bibliothek	Heath/Bernhardt, Wilhelm		1.20	Modern Language Series
Wildenbruch, Ernst von	Das edle Blut	Heath/Schmidt, Friedrich G.	52		Modern Language Series
	Der Letzte	Heath/Schmidt, Friedrich G.	73		Modern Language Series
Wildermuth, Ottilie	Der Einsiedler im Walde	Holt/Fischer, A. Albin	110		
1893					
Andersen, H. C.	Märchen	Heath/Super, Ovando B.		.90	Modern Language Series
Auerbach, Berthold	Brigitta	Ginn/Gore, J. Howard		.55	International Modern Language Series
Baumbach, Rudolf	Die stumme Königstochter In: Freudvoll und leidvoll	American Book/Bernhardt, Wilhelm	125		
	Es war einmal (stories by Baumbach and Wildenbruch)	American Book/Bernhardt, Wilhelm	174	.65	

Author	Title	Publisher	Pages	Price	Series
Boyen, M.	Mein erster Patient In: Deutsche Novelletten-Bibliothek	Heath/Bernhardt, Wilhelm		1.20	Modern Language Series
Chamisso, Adelbert von	Peter Schlemihls wundersame Geschichte	Heath/Primer, Sylvester	96	.25	Modern Language Series
Faulhaber, Oscar	Onkel und Nichte	Heath		.15	
Freytag, Gustav	Karl der Große/Aus dem Klosterleben/Aus den Kreuzzügen	Holt/Nichols, Alfred Bull	200	.75	
	Soll und Haben	Macmillan/Crump, William Haney		.60	
Gerstäcker, Friedrich	Germelshausen	Schoenhof/Osthaus, Carl Wilhelm	56		
Goethe, J. W. von	Dichtung und Wahrheit	Heath/Buchheim, Carl Adolf	317	1.05	Modern Language Series
	Einführung In Goethe's [sic] Meisterwerke	Heath/Bernhardt, Wilhelm	275	1.50	Modern Language Series
	Faust. Erster Teil	Macmillan/Lee, Jane	363	1.10	Foreign School Classics
	Faust. Erster Teil	Putnam/Hart, James Morgan	257	1.25	German Classics for American Students
	Hermann und Dorothea	Heath/Hewett, Waterman T.	243	1.00	Modern Language Series
Götzendorff-Grabowski, Helene von	Der Simpel and Vor Sonnenaufgang In: Deutsche Novelletten-Bibliothek	Heath/Bernhardt, Wilhelm		1.20	Modern Language Series
	"Long Long Ago" In: Freudvoll und leidvoll	American Book/ Bernhardt, Wilhelm	125		
Hauff, Wilhelm	Das kalte Herz	Heath/Smissen, W. H. van der	184		
	Das Wirtshaus im Spessart	Macmillan/Fasnacht, G. Eugene		.70	Primary Series

APPENDIX F (Continued)

Author	Title	Publisher/Editor	Pages	Price	Series and Contents
Heine, Heinrich	Die Harzreise	Heath/Daell, Alphonse N. van	96		Modern Language Series
Heyse, Paul	L'Arrabbiata	Heath/Bernhardt, Wilhelm	76	.25	Modern Language Series
Hillern, Wilhelmine von	Höher als die Kirche	Heath/Clary, Stedman W.	102	.15	Modern Language Series
Jensen, Wilhelm	Die braune Erika	Heath/Joynes, Edward S.	80	.25	Heath German Series
Juncke, E. (Schmieden, Else)	Ein Frühlingstraum In: Deutsche Novelletten-Bibliothek	Heath/Bernhardt, Wilhelm		1.20	Modern Language Series
Lessing, G. E.	Ausgewählte Prosa und Briefe	Putnam/White, Horatio S.	236	1.00	German Classics for American Students. Includes: Fabeln, Siebzehnter Literaturbrief, Gedanken über die Herrnhuter, Eine Parabel, Hamburgische Dramaturgie, Ernst und Falk, Ausgewählte Briefe
Meyer, Conrad F.	Gustav Adolfs Page	Heath/Heller, Otto	79	.30	Modern Language Series
Pauli, Reinhold	Zwei ausgewählte Aufsätze: Robert Blake, ein Seestück; Cromwell	Maynard and Merrill/Corser, Charles W. S.	143		Maynard's German Texts
Peschkau, Emil	Meine Freunde In: Freudvoll und leidvoll Sphinx In: Deutsche Novelletten-Bibliothek	American Book/Bernhardt, Wilhelm Heath/Bernhardt, Wilhelm	125	1.20	Modern Language Series
Riehl, Wilhelm H.	Burg Neideck	Schoenhof/Palmer, Arthur H.	66		Unterhaltungs-Bibliothek
	Burg Neideck	Holt/Palmer, Arthur H.	66		Unterhaltungs-Bibliothek

	Das Spielmannskind and Der stumme Ratsherr	Heath/Eaton, Abbie Fiske	91	.25	Modern Language Series
Scheffel, Joseph Viktor von	Ekkehard. Geschichte aus dem zehnten Jahrhundert	Heath/Wenckebach, Carla	235	.75	Modern Language Series
Seidel, Heinrich	Leberecht Hühnchen and Der gute alte Onkel In: Deutsche Novelletten-Bibliothek	Heath/Bernhardt, Wilhelm		1.20	Modern Language Series
	Leberecht Hühnchen and Weinlese bei Leberecht Hühnchen In: Freudvoll und leidvoll	American Book/Bernhardt, Wilhelm	125		
Stökl, Helene	Am Heiligen Abend and Eine Weihnachtsgeschichte In: Deutsche Novelletten-Bibliothek	Heath/Bernhardt, Wilhelm		1.20	Modern Language Series
	Reiselust In: Freudvoll und leidvoll	American Book/Bernhardt, Wilhelm	125		
	Unter dem Christbaum	Heath/Bernhardt, Wilhelm	168	.35	Modern Language Series. Includes: Vom Bübchen vor der Himmelsthür, Der vergessene Koffer, Eingeschneit, In der Weihnachtszeit, Am Heiligen Abend
Storm, Theodor	Immensee	Heath/Bernhardt, Wilhelm	113	.30	Modern Language Series
Sybel, Heinrich von	Die Erhebung Europas gegen Napoleon I.	Ginn/Nichols, Alfred Bull	126	.66	International Modern Language Series
Werner, Ernst (Bürstenbinder, Elizabeth)	Der Wilddieb In: Deutsche Novelletten-Bibliothek	Heath/Bernhardt, Wilhelm		1.20	Modern Language Series
Wiesner, A.C.	Die schwarze Dame	Heath/Bernhardt, Wilhelm		1.20	Modern Language Series

APPENDIX F (Continued)

Author	Title	Publisher/Editor	Pages	Price	Series and Contents
Wildenbruch, Ernst von	Es war einmal (stories by Wildenbruch and Baumbach)	American Book/ Bernhardt, Wilhelm	174	.65	
	Mein nervöser Onkel In: Freudvoll und leidvoll	American Book/ Bernhardt, Wilhelm	125		
Wildermuth, Ottilie	Der Einsiedler im Walde	Holt/Fischer, A. Albin	110	.65	
	Der Einsiedler im Walde	Schoenhof/Fischer, A. Albin	110	.65	
1894					
Andersen, H. C.	Bilderbuch ohne Bilder	Heath/Bernhardt, Wilhelm		.35	Modern Language Series
	Märchen	Heath/Super, Ovando B.		.90	Modern Language Series
Arnold, Hans (Bülow, Babette von)	Fritz auf dem Lande	Maynard and Merrill/ Morich, R. J.	92	.25	Maynard's German Texts
Auerbach, Berthold	Brigitta	Ginn/Gore, J. Howard		.55	International Modern Language Series
Baumbach, Rudolf	Die stumme Königstochter In: Freudvoll und leidvoll	Schoenhof/Bernhardt, Wilhelm	125		Bernhardt's German Series
	Frau Holde	Schoenhof/Fossler, Laurence	105	.25	
	Im Zwielicht	Schoenhof/Bernhardt, Wilhelm			
Becker, Karl F.	Ulysses und der Kyklop	Maynard and Merrill/ Lyon, Walter Sidney	71	.25	Maynard's German Texts
Boyen, M.	Mein erster Patient In: Deutsche Novelletten-Bibliothek	Heath/Bernhardt, Wilhelm		1.20	Modern Language Series
Chamisso, Adelbert von	Peter Schlemihls wundersame Geschichte	Heath/Primer, Sylvester	96	.25	Modern Language Series

Freytag, Gustav	Aus dem Jahrhundert des großen Krieges	Maynard and Merrill/Morich, R. J.	126	.40	Maynard's German Texts
	Der Rittmeister von Altrosen	Heath/Hatfield, James Taft	201	.75	Modern Language Series
	Doktor Luther	Ginn/Goodrich, Frank P.	177	.70	International Modern Language Series
	Karl der Große/Aus dem Klosterleben/Aus den Kreuzzügen	Holt/Nichols, Alfred Bull	200	.75	
	Soll und Haben	Ginn/Bultmann, Ida W.	220	.70	International Modern Language Series
Gerstäcker, Friedrich	Germelshausen	Heath/Osthaus, Carl Wilhelm	83	.25	Modern Language Series
Goethe, J. W. von	Ausgewählte Prosa	Putnam/Hart, James Morgan	199	1.00	German Classics for American Students. Readings from: Dichtung und Wahrheit, Die Leiden des jungen Werthers, Ein Brief aus der Schweiz, Italienische Reise, Wilhelm Meisters Lehrjahre
	Dichtung und Wahrheit	Heath/Buchheim, Carl Adolf	317	1.05	Modern Language Series
Götzendorff-Grabowski, Helene von	Der Simpel and Vor Sonnenaufgang In: Deutsche Novelletten-Bibliothek	Heath/Bernhardt, Wilhelm	125	1.20	Modern Language Series
	"Long Long Ago" In: Freudvoll und leidvoll	Schoenhof/Bernhardt, Wilhelm	125		Bernhardt German Series
Grimm, Jakob and Wilhelm	Kinder- und Hausmärchen and Schiller's Der Taucher	Heath/Smissen, W. H. von der	214	.65	Modern Language Series
Halm, Friedrich (Münch-Bellinghausen, E. F. J. von)	Griseldis	Macmillan/Buchheim, Carl Adolf	154	.90	German Classics
Heyse, Paul	Das Mädchen von Treppi	Holt/Brusie, Charles F.	111	.25	
	Das Mädchen von Treppi and Marion	American Book/Bernhardt, Wilhelm	136		

APPENDIX F (*Continued*)

Author	Title	Publisher/Editor	Pages	Price	Series and Contents
	Das Mädchen von Treppi and Marion	Schoenhof/Bernhardt, Wilhelm	94		
	Das Mädchen von Treppi and Marion	Christern/Bernhardt, Wilhelm	94		
	Das Mädchen von Treppi and Marion	Holt/Brusie, Charles F.	88		
	Das Mädchen von Treppi and Marion	Schoenhof/Brusie, Charles F.	88		
	Kolberg	Maynard and Merrill/Allpress, Robert H.	137	.40	Maynard's German Texts
	L'Arrabbiata	Heath/Bernhardt, Wilhelm	76	.25	Modern Language Series
Hillern, Wilhelmine von Jensen, Wilhelm	Höher als die Kirche Die braune Erika	Holt/Fischer, A. A. Heath/Joynes, Edward S.	80	.60 .25	Heath German Series
Juncke, E. (Schmieden, Else)	Ein Frühlingstraum In: Deutsche Novelletten-Bibliothek	Heath/Bernhardt, Wilhelm		1.20	Modern Language Series.
Leander, Richard (Volkmann, Richard von)	Träumereien an französischen Kaminen	Heath/Smissen, W. H. van der			Modern Language Series. Includes: Der kleine Vogel, Das kleine bucklige Mädchen, Die himmlische Musik, Die künstliche Orgel, Der Wunschring, Die drei Schwestern mit den gläsernen Herzen, Von der Königin, die keine Pfeffernüsse backen, und dem König, der nicht das Brummeisen spielen konnte, Vom unsichtbaren Königreiche, Pechvogel und Glückskind, Die Traumbuche, Der kleine Mohr und die Goldprinzessin

Author	Title	Editor	Pages	Price	Series
Lessing, G. E.	Emilia Galotti	Holt/Super, Ovando B.	83	.30	
	Emilia Galotti	Schoenhof/Super, Ovando B.	83	.30	
	Emilia Galotti	Ginn/Poll, Max	131	.70	International Modern Language Series
	Minna von Barnhelm	Heath/Primer, Sylvester			Modern Language Series
	Nathan der Weise	Heath/Primer, Sylvester	300	1.10	Modern Language Series
Meyer, Conrad F.	Gustav Adolfs Page	Heath/Heller, Otto	79	.30	Modern Language Series
Peschkau, Emil	Meine Freunde In: Freudvoll und leidvoll	Schoenhof/Bernhardt, Wilhelm	125		Bernhardt German Series
	Sphinx In: Deutsche Novelletten-Bibliothek	Heath/Bernhardt, Wilhelm		1.20	Modern Language Series
Riehl, Wilhelm H.	Burg Neideck	Ginn/Wilson, Charles B.	86	.35	International Modern Language Series
	Die Lehrjahre eines Humanisten	Maynard and Merrill/Morich, R. J.	102	.40	Maynard's German Texts
	Meister Martin Hildebrand	Maynard and Merrill/Beredsford-Webb, H.S.	88	.40	Maynard's German Texts
Scheffel, Joseph Viktor von	Ekkehard. Geschichte aus dem zehnten Jahrhundert	Heath/Wenckebach, Carla	235	.75	Modern Language Series
Schiller, J. C. F. von	Der Neffe als Onkel	Allyn and Bacon/Raddatz, Charles F.	125	.50	Allyn and Bacon's German Texts
	Der Taucher and the Grimms' Kinder- und Hausmärchen	Heath/Smissen, W. H. van der	214	.65	Modern Language Series
	Die Jungfrau von Orleans	Holt/Nichols, Alfred Bull	237	.60	
	Die Jungfrau von Orleans	Heath/Wells, Benjamin W.	224		Modern Language Series

APPENDIX F (*Continued*)

Author	Title	Publisher/Editor	Pages	Price	Series and Contents
	Gustav Adolf in Deutschland	American Book/Bernhardt, Wilhelm	143	.45	
	Maria Stuart	Holt/Joynes, Edward S.	265	.60	Whitney's German Texts
	Maria Stuart	Heath/Rhoades, Lewis A.	232	.65	Modern Language Series
	Wallenstein Trilogie	Holt/Carruth, William H.	456	1.00	
	Wallensteins Lager and Die Piccolomini	Macmillan/Breul, Karl Hermann		.90	Pitt Press Series
	Wilhelm Tell	Holt/Sachtleben, Augustus	197	.48	Whitney's German Texts
	Wilhelm Tell	Heath/Deering, Robert W.	242	.65	Modern Language Series
Seidel, Heinrich	Die Monate	American Book/Arrowsmith, Robert	72	.25	
	Leberecht Hühnchen and Der gute alte Onkel In: Deutsche Novelletten-Bibliothek	Heath/Bernhardt, Wilhelm		1.20	Modern Language Series
	Leberecht Hühnchen and Weinlese bei Leberecht Hühnchen In: Freudvoll und leidvoll	Schoenhof/Bernhardt, Wilhelm	125		Bernhardt German Series
Stökl, Helene	Am Heiligen Abend and Eine Weihnachtsgeschichte In: Deutsche Novelletten-Bibliothek	Heath/Bernhardt, Wilhelm		1.20	Modern Language Series
	Reiselust In: Freudvoll und leidvoll	Schoenhof/Bernhardt, Wilhelm	125		Bernhardt German Series

Storm, Theodor	Unter dem Christbaum	Heath/Bernhardt, Wilhelm	168	.35	Modern Language Series. Includes: Vom Bübchen vor der Himmelsthür, Der vergessene Koffer, Eingeschneit, In der Weihnachtszeit, Am Heiligen Abend
Treitschke, Heinrich von	Geschichten aus der Tonne	Ginn/Brusie, Charles F.	127	.65	International Modern Language Series
	Das deutsche Ordensland Preußen	Maynard and Merrill/ Lyon, Walter Sidney	139		Maynard's German Texts
Werner, Ernst (Bürstenbinder, Elizabeth)	Der Wilddieb In: Deutsche Novelletten-Bibliothek	Heath/Bernhardt, Wilhelm		1.20	Modern Language Series
Wiesner, A. C.	Die schwarze Dame In: Deutsche Novelletten-Bibliothek	Heath/Bernhardt, Wilhelm		1.20	Modern Language Series
Wildenbruch, Ernst von	Harold	Maynard and Merrill/ Voegelin, Ada	133	.40	Maynard's German Texts
	Mein nervöser Onkel In: Freudvoll und leidvoll	Schoenhof/Bernhardt, Wilhelm	125		Bernhardt German Series

1895

Andersen, H. C.	Ein Besuch bei Charles Dickens	Holt/Bernhardt, Wilhelm	62	.25
	Stories, with the Grimms' Märchen and Hauff's Die Karawane	Holt/Bronson, Thomas B.	424	.90
	Stories, with the Grimms' Märchen and Hauff's Die Karawane	Schoenhof/Bronson, Thomas B.	424	.90
Baumbach, Rudolf	Frau Holde Im Zwielicht	Holt/Fossler, Laurence Schoenhof/Bernhardt, Wilhelm	105	.25
Benedix, Roderich	Der Dritte	Holt/Whitney, Marian P.	36	.20

273

APPENDIX F *(Continued)*

Author	Title	Publisher/Editor	Pages	Price	Series and Contents
	Die Hochzeitsreise	Heath/Schiefferdecker, Natalie	64	.25	Modern Language Series
Boyen, M.	Mein erster Patient In: Deutsche Novelletten-Bibliothek	Heath/Bernhardt, Wilhelm		1.20	Modern Language Series
Bürger, Gottfried	Leonore	American Book/Werner-Spanhoofd, Arnold	32	.10	Germania Texts
Chamisso, Adelbert von	Peter Schlemihls wundersame Geschichte	Holt/Hitzig, Julius H.	126	.25	
	Peter Schlemihls wundersame Geschichte	Christern/Hitzig, Julius H.	126	.25	
	Peter Schlemihls wundersame Geschichte	Schoenhof/Hitzig, Julius H.	126	.25	
Eichendorff, Joseph von	Aus dem Leben eines Taugenichts	Heath/Osthaus, Carl Wilhelm	176	.40	Modern Language Series
Freytag, Gustav	Aus dem Staat Friedrichs des Großen	Heath/Hager, Hermann	115	.30	Modern Language Series
	Soll und Haben	Ginn/Bultmann, Ida W.	220	.70	International Modern Language Series
Gerstäcker Friedrich	Germelshausen	Heath/Osthaus, Carl Wilhelm	83	.25	Modern Language Series
Gervinus, Georg	Lessings Hamburgische Dramaturgie and Kurz's Lessings Minna von Barnhelm	American Book/Werner-Spanhoofd, Arnold	23	.10	Germania Texts
	Vergleichung Goethes und Schillers, Vergleichung Lessings und Herders	American Book/Werner-Spanhoofd, Arnold	22	.10	Germania Texts

Goethe, J. W. von	Die Krönung Josefs II.	American Book/Werner-Spanhoofd, Arnold	19	.10	Germania Texts
	Die neue Melusine, with Kleist's Die Verlobung in Santo Domingo and Zschokke's Der tote Gast In: Three German Tales	Holt/Nichols, Alfred Bull	226	.60	
Götzendorff-Grabowski, Helene von	Der Simpel and Vor Sonnenaufgang In: Deutsche Novelletten-Bibliothek	Heath/Bernhardt, Wilhelm		1.20	Modern Language Series
Grimm, Jakob and Wilhelm	Märchen, with stories by Andersen and Hauff's Die Karawane	Holt/Bronson, Thomas B.	424	.90	
	Märchen, with stories by Andersen and Hauff's Die Karawane	Schoenhof/Bronson, Thomas B.	424	.90	
Hauff, Wilhelm	Die Karawane	Holt/Bronson, Thomas B.		.75	
	Stories, i.e., Die Karawane, with stories by Andersen and the Grimms' Märchen	Holt/Bronson, Thomas B.	424	.90	
	Stories, i.e., Die Karawane, with stories by Andersen and the Grimms' Märchen	Schoenhof/Bronson, Thomas B.	424	.90	
Heine, Heinrich	Die Harzreise	Heath/Daell, Alphonse N. van	96		Modern Language Series
	Poems	Heath/White, Horatio S.	220	.75	Modern Language Series

275

APPENDIX F *(Continued)*

Author	Title	Publisher/Editor	Pages	Price	Series and Contents
Heyse, Paul	L'Arrabbiata	Heath/Bernhardt, Wilhelm	76	.25	Modern Language Series
Hillern, Wilhelmine von	Höher als die Kirche	American Book/Dauer, F. A.	96	.25	German Readings
Juncke, E. (Schmieden, Else)	Ein Frühlingstraum In: Deutsche Novelletten-Bibliothek	Heath/Bernhardt, Wilhelm		1.20	Modern Language Series
Keller, Gottfried	Dietegen	Ginn/Gruener, Gustav	75	.40	International Modern Language Series
Keller, Isidor	Bilder aus der deutschen Literatur	American Book	225		
Kleist, Heinrich	Die Verlobung in Santo Domingo, with Goethe's Die neue Melusine and Zschokke's Der tote Gast In: Three German Tales	Holt/Nichols, Alfred Bull	226	.60	
Kurz, Heinrich	Lessings Minna von Barnhelm and Gervinus's Lessings Hamburgische Dramaturgie	American Book/Werner-Spanhoofd, Arnold	23	.10	Germania Texts
	Reineke Fuchs	American Book/Werner-Spanhoofd, Arnold	23	.10	Germania Texts
Leander, Richard (Volkmann, Richard von)	Kleine Geschichten und andere Erzählungen	Heath/Bernhardt, Wilhelm	90	.35	Modern Language Series

Author	Title	Editor	Pages	Price	Series
	Träumereien an französischen Kaminen	American Book/ Hanstein, Amalie	163	.35	Includes: Der kleine Vogel, Das kleine bucklige Mädchen, Die himmlische Musik, Die künstliche Orgel, Der Wunschring, Die drei Schwestern mit den gläsernen Herzen, Von der Königin, die keine Pfeffernüsse backen, und dem König, der nicht das Brummeisen spielen konnte, Vom unsichtbaren Königreiche, Pechvogel und Glückskind, Die Traumbuche, Der kleine Mohr und die Goldprinzessin Modern Language Series
Lessing, G. E.	Träumereien an französischen Kaminen Emilia Galotti	Heath/Smissen, W. H. van der Ginn/Poll, Max	131	.70	International Modern Language Series
	Emilia Galotti	Heath/Winkler, Max	128	.60	Modern Language Series
	Minna von Barnhelm	Holt/Brandt, Hermann C. G.	227	.60	
	Minna von Barnhelm	Schoenhof/Brandt, Hermann C. G.	227		
	Minna von Barnhelm	Heath/Primer, Sylvester	178		Modern Language Series
Peschkau, Emil	Sphinx In: Deutsche Novelletten-Bibliothek	Heath/Bernhardt, Wilhelm		1.20	Modern Language Series
Riehl, Wilhelm H.	Burg Neideck	Ginn/Wilson, Charles B.	86	.35	International Modern Language Series
	Die Ganerben and Die Gerechtigkeit Gottes	Macmillan/Wolstenholme, Henry J.	201	.90	Pitt Press Series
	Die Werke der Barmherzigkeit	Maynard and Merrill/ Voegelin, Ada	94	.25	Maynard's German Texts
Rosegger, Peter	Waldheimat. Selections	Ginn/Fossler, Laurence	103	.55	International Modern Language Series
Scheffel, Joseph Viktor von	Der Trompeter von Säkkingen	Heath/Wenckebach, Carla	181	.70	Modern Language Series

277

APPENDIX F (*Continued*)

Author	Title	Publisher/Editor	Pages	Price	Series and Contents
	Der Trompeter von Säkkingen	Holt/Frost, Mary Adeline	284	.80	
	Ekkehard. Geschichte aus dem zehnten Jahrhundert	Holt/Carruth, William H.	493	1.25	
	Ekkehard. Geschichte aus dem zehnten Jahrhundert	Schoenhof/Carruth, William H.	493	1.25	
Schiller, J. C. F. von	Ballads	Heath/Johnson, Henry	165		Modern Language Series
	Die Jungfrau von Orleans	Holt/Nichols, Alfred Bull	237	.60	
	Maria Stuart	Macmillan/Breul, Karl Hermann	271	1.00	Pitt Press Series
	Wilhelm Tell	Heath/Deering, Robert W.	242	.65	Modern Language Series
Schrammen, Johannes	Legends of German Heroes	Maynard and Merrill/Lechner, A. R.	158		Maynard's German Texts
Seidel, Heinrich	Der Lindenbaum and Other Stories	American Book/Richard, Ernst	71	.25	
	Die Monate	American Book/Arrowsmith, Robert	72	.25	
	Herr Omnia	American Book/Matthewman, J.	85	.25	
	Leberecht Hühnchen and Der gute alte Onkel In: Deutsche Novelletten-Bibliothek	Heath/Bernhardt, Wilhelm		1.20	Modern Language Series
	Leberecht Hühnchen und andere Sonderlinge	Schoenhof/Bernhardt, Wilhelm	52	.30	
	Leberecht Hühnchen und andere Sonderlinge	Christern/Bernhardt, Wilhelm	52	.30	

Stifter, Adalbert	Das Heidedorf	American Book/Lentz, Max	80	.25	
Stökl, Helene	Am Heiligen Abend and Eine Weihnachtsgeschichte In: Deutsche Novelletten-Bibliothek	Heath/Bernhardt, Wilhelm		1.20	Modern Language Series
Storm, Theodor	Immensee	Heath/Bernhardt, Wilhelm	113	.30	Modern Language Series
Sybel, Heinrich von	Die Erhebung Europas gegen Napoleon I.	Ginn/Nichols, Alfred Bull	126	.66	International Modern Language Series
Werner, Ernst (Bürstenbinder, Elizabeth)	Der Wilddieb In: Deutsche Novelletten-Bibliothek	Heath/Bernhardt, Wilhelm		1.20	Modern Language Series
Wichert, Ernst A.	An der Majorsecke	Holt/Harris, Charles	41	.20	
Wiesner, A. C.	Die schwarze Dame In: Deutsche Novelletten-Bibliothek	Heath/Bernhardt, Wilhelm		1.20	Modern Language Series
Zschokke, Heinrich	Das Abenteuer der Neujahrsnacht and Der zerbrochene Krug	Holt/Faust, Albert B.	110	.25	
	Der tote Gast, with Goethe's Die neue Melusine and Kleist's Die Verlobung in Santo Domingo In: Three German Tales	Holt/Nichols, Alfred Bull	226	.60	

APPENDIX F (*Continued*)

1896

Author	Title	Publisher/Editor	Pages	Price	Series and Contents
Andersen, H. C.	Bilderbuch ohne Bilder	Heath/Bernhardt, Wilhelm		.35	Modern Language Series
	Märchen	Heath/Super, Ovando B.		.90	Modern Language Series
Arnold, Hans (Bülow, Babette von)	Ein Regentag auf dem Lande	American Book/Kern, Albert J. W.		.25	
	Fritz auf Ferien	Heath/Werner-Spanhoofd, Arnold	99	.20	Modern Language Series
Baumbach, Rudolf	Der Schwiegersohn	Heath/Bernhardt, Wilhelm	121	.30	Modern Language Series
	Im Zwielicht	Schoenhof/Bernhardt, Wilhelm			
Benedix, Roderich	Die Hochzeitsreise	Heath/Schiefferdecker, Natalie	46	.25	Modern Language Series
	Plautus und Terence and Der Sonntagsjäger	Heath/Wells, Benjamin W.	109	.25	Modern Language Series
Boyen, M.	Mein erster Patient In: Deutsche Novelletten-Bibliothek	Heath/Bernhardt, Wilhelm		1.20	Modern Language Series
Ebner-Eschenbach, Marie von	Krambambuli and Klausmann's Memoiren eines Offizierburschen	American Book/Werner-Spanhoofd, Arnold	77	.25	Modern German Text Series
Eckstein, Ernst	Preisgekrönt	Holt/Wilson, Charles B.	83	.30	Selected German Tales
Eichendorff, Joseph von	Aus dem Leben eines Taugenichts	Heath/Osthaus, Carl Wilhelm	176	.40	Modern Language Series
Eschstruth, Nataly von	Hundert Schimmel In: Aus Herz und Welt	Heath/Bernhardt, Wilhelm	92	.25	Modern Language Series
Freytag, Gustav	Aus dem Staat Friedrichs des Großen	Heath/Hager, Hermann	115	.30	Modern Language Series

	Die Journalisten	Heath/Toy, Walter Dallam	160	.50	Modern Language Series
Gerstäcker, Friedrich	Germelshausen	Heath/Osthaus, Carl Wilhelm	83	.25	Modern Language Series
	Irrfahrten	Holt/Whitney, Marian P.	221	.30	Whitney-Klemm German Series
Goethe, J. W. von	Dichtung und Wahrheit	Holt/Jagemann, Hans Carl G.	373	1.12	Modern Language Series
	Dichtung und Wahrheit	Heath/Buchheim, Carl Adolf	317	1.05	Modern Language Series
	Die Krönung Josefs II.	American Book/Werner-Spanhoofd, Arnold	19	.10	Germania Texts
	Einführung in Goethe's [sic] Meisterwerke	Heath/Bernhardt, Wilhelm	275	1.50	Modern Language Series
	Götz von Berlichingen	Holt/Goodrich, Frank P.	170	.70	Modern Language Series
	Iphigenie auf Tauris	Heath/Rhoades, Lewis A.	139	.70	Modern Language Series
	Wieland. Aus Goethes Gedächtnisrede	American Book/Werner-Spanhoofd, Arnold	24	.10	Germania Texts
Götzendorff-Grabowski, Helene von	Der Simpel and Vor Sonnenaufgang In: Deutsche Novelletten-Bibliothek	Heath/Bernhardt, Wilhelm		1.20	Modern Language Series
Hauff, Wilhelm	Tales: Die Sage vom Hirschgulden, Die Höhle von Steenfoll, Saids Schicksale	Ginn/Goold, Charles B.	200	.80	International Modern Language Series
Heine, Heinrich	Die Harzreise	Heath/Daell, Alphonse N. van	96		Modern Language Series

APPENDIX F (*Continued*)

Author	Title	Publisher/Editor	Pages	Price	Series and Contents
Heyse, Paul	L'Arrabbiata	Holt/Frost, Mary Adeline	73	.25	
Hillern, Wilhelmine von	Höher als die Kirche	Heath/Clary, Stedman W.	102		Modern Language Series
	Höher als die Kirche	American Book/Dauer, F. A.	96	.25	German Readings
Jensen, Wilhelm	Die braune Erika	Heath/Joynes, Edward S.	80	.35	Modern Language Series
Juncke, E. (Schmieden, Else)	Ein Frühlingstraum In: Deutsche Novelletten-Bibliothek	Heath/Bernhardt, Wilhelm		1.20	Modern Language Series
Jungmann	Er sucht einen Vetter	Holt/Stern, Sigmon Martin	49		Selected German Comedies
Khull, Ferdinand	Meier Helmbrecht	American Book/Werner-Spanhoofd, Arnold	16	.10	Germania Texts
Klausmann, Anton	Memoiren eines Offizierburschen and Ebner-Eschenbach's Krambambuli	American Book/Werner-Spanhoofd, Arnold	77	.25	Modern German Text Series
Kurz, Heinrich	Reineke Fuchs	American Book/Werner-Spanhoofd, Arnold	23	.10	Germania Texts
	Wielands Oberon	American Book/Werner-Spanhoofd, Arnold	22	.10	Germania Texts
Leander, Richard (Volkmann, Richard von)	Kleine Geschichten und andere Erzählungen	Heath/Bernhardt, Wilhelm	90	.35	Modern Language Series

Author	Title	Publisher	Pages	Price	Series
	Träumereien an französischen Kaminen	Heath/Smissen, W. H. van der			Modern Language Series. Includes: Der kleine Vogel, Das kleine bucklige Mädchen, Die himmlische Musik, Die künstliche Orgel, Der Wunschring, Die drei Schwestern mit den gläsernen Herzen, Von der Königin, die keine Pfeffernüsse backen, und dem König, der nicht das Brummeisen spielen konnte, Vom unsichtbaren Königreiche, Pechvogel und Glückskind, Die Traumbuche, Der kleine Mohr und die Goldprinzessin
Lessing, G. E.	Minna von Barnhelm	Macmillan/Merk, Charles	224	.75	Foreign School Classics
	Nathan der Weise	Heath/Primer, Sylvester	300	1.10	Modern Language Series
Peschkau, Emil	Sphinx In: Deutsche Novelletten-Bibliothek	Heath/Bernhardt, Wilhelm	125	1.20	Modern Language Series
Riehl, Wilhelm H.	Die vierzehn Nothelfer and Trost um Trost	American Book/Sihler, Katherine E.	125	.30	
Rosegger, Peter	Waldheimat. Selections	Ginn/Fossler, Laurence	103	.55	International Modern Language Series
Scheffel, Joseph Viktor von	Ekkehard. Geschichte aus dem zehnten Jahrhundert	Heath/Wenckebach, Carla	235		Modern Language Series
Schillier, J. C. F. von	Das Lied von der Glocke	American Book/Werner-Spanhoofd, Arnold		.10	Germania Texts
	Die Jungfrau von Orleans	Heath/Wells, Benjamin W.	226		Modern Language Series
	Die Kraniche des Ibykus and Das eleusische Fest	American Book/Werner-Spanhoofd, Arnold	20	.10	Germania Texts
	Maria Stuart	Heath/Rhoades, Lewis A.	232	.65	Modern Language Series

APPENDIX F (*Continued*)

Author	Title	Publisher/Editor	Pages	Price	Series and Contents
	Wilhelm Tell	Heath/Deering, Robert W.	242		Modern Language Series
Seidel, Heinrich	Leberecht Hühnchen and Der gute alte Onkel In: Deutsche Novelletten-Bibliothek	Heath/Bernhardt, Wilhelm		1.20	Modern Language Series
Stökl, Helene	Alle fünf In: Aus Herz und Welt	Heath/Bernhardt, Wilhelm	92	.25	Modern Language Series
	Am Heiligen Abend and Eine Weihnachtsgeschichte In: Deutsche Novelletten-Bibliothek	Heath/Bernhardt, Wilhelm		1.20	Modern Language Series
Storm, Theodor	Geschichten aus der Tonne	Ginn/Brusie, Charles F.	127	.65	International Modern Language Series
	Immensee	Heath/Bernhardt, Wilhelm	113	.30	Modern Language Series
	Immensee	American Book/Dauer, F. A.	85	.25	
Sybel, Heinrich von	Die Erhebung Europas gegen Napoleon I.	Ginn/Nichols, Alfred Bull	126	.66	International Modern Language Series
Uhland, Ludwig	Poems	Macmillan/Hewett, Waterman T.	352	.60	German Classics
Werner, Ernst (Bürstenbinder, Elizabeth)	Der Wilddieb In: Deutsche Novelletten-Bibliothek	Heath/Bernhardt, Wilhelm		1.20	Modern Language Series
Wiesner, A. C.	Die schwarze Dame In: Deutsche Novelletten-Bibliothek	Heath/Bernhardt, Wilhelm		1.20	Modern Language Series
Zschokke, Heinrich	Das Abenteuer der Neujahrsnacht and Der zerbrochene Krug	Holt/Faust, Albert B.	110	.25	

1897

Andersen, H. C.	Märchen	Heath/Super, Ovando B.	.90	Modern Language Series
Baumbach, Rudolf	Die Nonna. Blaustrumpfgeschichte	Heath/Bernhardt, Wilhelm	97	.30	Modern Language Series
	Es war einmal (stories by Baumbach and Wildenbruch)	American Book/Bernhardt, Wilhelm	174	.65	
Benedix, Roderich	Der Prozeß	Heath/Wells, Benjamin W.	61	.20	Modern Language Series
	Der Prozeß and Günstige Vorzeichen, with Wilhelmi's Einer muß heiraten	Heath/Wells, Benjamin W.	121		Modern Language Series
	Die Hochzeitsreise	Heath/Schiefferdecker, Natalie	64	.25	Modern Language Series
Boyen, M.	Doktor Wespe	Holt	116	.25	College Series of German Plays
	Mein erster Patient In: Deutsche Novelletten-Bibliothek	Heath/Bernhardt, Wilhelm		1.20	Modern Language Series
Freytag, Gustav	Aus dem Staat Friedrichs des Großen	Heath/Hager, Hermann	115	.30	Modern Language Series
	Die Journalisten	Heath/Toy, Walter Dallam	160	.50	Modern Language Series
	Die Journalisten	American Book/Johnson, J. Norton	171	.35	
Goethe, J. W. von	Faust. Zweiter Teil	Heath/Thomas, Calvin	457	1.50	Classic German Plays (sic)
	Hermann und Dorothea	Holt/Thomas, Calvin	150	.40	Heath German Series
	Torquato Tasso	Heath/Thomas, Calvin	181	.75	Modern Language Series
Götzendorff-Grabowski, Helene von	Der Simpel and Vor Sonnenaufgang In: Deutsche Novelletten-Bibliothek	Heath/Bernhardt, Wilhelm		1.20	
Hauff, Wilhelm	Das kalte Herz	Heath/Smissen, W. H. van der	92		Modern Language Series

285

APPENDIX F (*Continued*)

Author	Title	Publisher/Editor	Pages	Price	Series and Contents
	Das kalte Herz	Holt/Beck, George A. D.	87	.35	
	Tales: Die Sage vom Hirschgulden, Die Höhle von Steenfoll, Saids Schicksale	Ginn	200		International Modern Language Series
Heine, Heinrich	Die Harzreise	Heath/Daell, Alphonse N. van	96		Modern Language Series
	Lieder und Gedichte	Macmillan/Buchheim, Carl Adolf	376	1.00	Golden Treasury
Heyse, Paul	Das Mädchen von Treppi and Marion	American Book/Bernhardt, Wilhem		.30	
	L'Arrabbiata	Heath/Bernhardt, Wilhelm	76	.25	Modern Language Series
	L'Arrabbiata	American Book/Lentz, Max Carl G.	87	.30	
Juncke, E. (Schmieden, Else)	Ein Frühlingstraum In: Deutsche Novelletten-Bibliothek	Heath/Bernhardt, Wilhelm		1.20	Modern Language Series
Lessing, G. E.	Minna von Barnhelm	Macmillan Merck, Charles	224	.75	Foreign School Classics
	Minna von Barnhelm	American Book/Lambert, Marcus B.	159	.50	
Moser, Gustav von	Der Bibliothekar	Heath/Wells, Benjamin W.	138	.30	Modern Language Series
	Köpnickerstraße 120	Heath/Wells, Benjamin W.	159	.30	Modern Language Series
Peschkau, Emil	Sphinx In: Deutsche Novelletten-Bibliothek	Heath/Bernhardt, Wilhelm		1.20	Modern Language Series
Riehl, Wilhelm H.	Das Spielmannskind and Der stumme Ratsherr	Heath/Eaton, Abbie Fiske	91	.25	Modern Language Series

	Der Fluch der Schönheit	Heath/Thomas, Calvin	70		Modern Language Series
	Der Fluch der Schönheit	Holt/Kendall, Francis	112	.35	Unterhaltungs-Bibliothek
	Der Fluch der Schönheit	American Book/Frost, Mary Adeline	107	.30	
Scheffel, Joseph Viktor von	Ekkehard. Geschichte aus dem zehnten Jahrhundert	Heath/Wenckebach, Carla	235		Modern Language Series
Schiller, J. C. F. von	Ballads	Heath/Johnson, Henry	165		Modern Language Series
	Der Geisterseher. Erstes Buch	Heath/Joynes, Edward S.	126		Modern Language Series
	Der Neffe als Onkel	Heath/Beredsford-Webb, H. S.	121	.30	Modern Language Series
	Die Jungfrau von Orleans	Heath/Wells, Benjamin W.	226		Modern Language Series
	Gustav Adolf in Deutschland	American Book/Bernhardt, Wilhelm	143	.45	
	Gustav Adolf in Deutschland	Schoenhof/Bernhardt, Wilhelm	143		
Seidel, Heinrich	Leberecht Hühnchen and Der gute alte Onkel In: Deutsche Novelletten-Bibliothek	Heath/Bernhardt, Wilhelm		1.20	Modern Language Series
	Leberecht Hühnchen und andere Sonderlinge	American Book/Bernhardt, Wilhelm	75	.30	
Spyri, Johanna	Moni der Geißbub	Heath/Guerber, Helene A.	74	.25	Modern Language Series
	Rosenresli and Der Toni von Kandergrund	American Book		.25	
Stifter, Adalbert	Das Heidedorf	Heath/Heller, Otto	50		Modern Language Series
Stökl, Helene	Am Heiligen Abend and Eine Weihnachtsgeschichte In: Deutsche Novelletten-Bibliothek	Heath/Bernhardt, Wilhelm		1.20	Modern Language Series
Storm, Theodor	Immensee	Heath/Bernhardt, Wilhelm	113	.30	Modern Language Series

APPENDIX F (Continued)

Author	Title	Publisher/Editor	Pages	Price	Series and Contents
Werner, Ernst (Bürstenbinder, Elizabeth)	Der Wilddieb In: Deutsche Novelletten-Bibliothek	Heath/Bernhardt, Wilhelm		1.20	Modern Language Series
Wiesner, A. C.	Die schwarze Dame In: Deutsche Novelletten-Bibliothek	Heath/Bernhardt, Wilhelm		1.20	Modern Language Series
Wildenbruch, Ernst von	Es war einmal (stories by Wildenbruch and Baumbach)	American Book/ Bernhardt, Wilhelm	174	.65	
Wilhelmi, Alexander (Zechmeister, Alexander Viktor)	Einer muß heiraten, with Benedix's Der Prozeß and Günstige Vorzeichen In: Drei kleine Lustspiele	Heath/Wells, Benjamin W.	121		Modern Language Series
Zschokke, Heinrich	Der zerbrochene Krug	American Book/ Roelker, Bernard	33	.25	

1898

Author	Title	Publisher/Editor	Pages	Price	Series and Contents
Andersen, H. C.	Eight Stories	Macmillan/Rippmann, Walter		.60	Pitt Press Series
Auerbach, Berthold	Brigitta	Ginn/Gore, J. Howard		.55	International Modern Language Series
Baumbach, Rudolf	Der Schwiegersohn	Heath/Bernhardt, Wilhelm	121	.30	Modern Language Series
	Die Nonna. Blaustrumpfgeschichte	Heath/Bernhardt, Wilhelm	97	.30	Modern Language Series
	Nicotiana und andere Erzählungen	Heath/Bernhardt, Wilhelm	106	.30	Modern Language Series

Benedix, Roderich	Der Prozeß and Günstige Vorzeichen, with Wilhelmi's Einer muß heiraten In: Drei kleine Lustspiele	Heath/Wells, Benjamin W.	121	Modern Language Series
Bruneck, Otto von (Elster, Otto)	Zwischen den Schlachten	Macmillan/Hirsch, Ludwig	254 .75	Siepmann's German Series
Ebner-Eschenbach, Marie von	Die Freiherren von Gemperlein and Krambambuli	Heath/Hohlfeld, Alexander R.	128 .30	Modern Language Series
Eschstruth, Nataly von	Ihr Ideal and Eine Plauderstunde auf der "Seehalde" In: Auf der Sonnenseite	Heath/Bernhardt, Wilhelm	146 .35	Modern Language Series
Freytag, Gustav	Aus dem Staat Friedrichs des Großen	Heath/Hager, Hermann	115 .30	Modern Language Series
	Die verlorene Handschrift	Macmillan/Hewett, Katherine M.	223 .60	Modern Language Series
	Soll und Haben	Ginn/Bultmann, Ida W.	220 .70	International Modern Language Series
Frommel, Emil	Das eiserne Kreuz In: Auf der Sonnenseite	Heath/Bernhardt, Wilhelm	146 .35	Modern Language Series
Gerstäcker, Friedrich	Germelshausen	Heath/Osthaus, Carl Wilhelm	83 .25	Modern Language Series
Goethe, J. W. von	Dichtung und Wahrheit	Heath/Buchheim, Carl Adolf	317 1.05	Modern Language Series
	Egmont	Macmillan/Primer, Sylvester	174 .60	
	Egmont	Ginn/Winkler, Max	276 1.00	International Modern Language Series
	Iphigenie auf Tauris	Macmillan/Eggert, Charles A.	180 .60	German Classics
	Selections from Correspondence with Schiller	Ginn/Robertson, John G.	210 .80	International Modern Language Series
Grillparzer, Franz	Sappho	Macmillan/Rippmann, Walter	157 .75	Siepmann's German Series

APPENDIX F (Continued)

Author	Title	Publisher/Editor	Pages	Price	Series and Contents
Hauff, Wilhelm	Der Zwerg Nase	Heath/Grandgent, C. H.	96		Modern Language Series
Heine, Heinrich	Die Harzreise	Heath/Daell, Alphonse N. van			
	Lieder und Gedichte	Macmillan/Buchheim, Carl Adolf	376	1.00	Golden Treasury
Helbig, Friedrich	Die Komödie auf der Hochschule	Heath/Wells, Benjamin W.	134	.30	Modern Language Series
Heyse, Paul	L'Arrabbiata	Heath/Bernhardt, Wilhelm	76	.25	Modern Language Series
Hillern, Wilhelmine von	Höher als die Kirche	Heath/Clary, Stedman W.	102		Modern Language Series
Jensen, Wilhelm	Die braune Erika	Heath/Joynes, Edward S.	101	.35	Modern Language Series
Leander, Richard (Volkmann, Richard von)	Kleine Geschichten und andere Erzählungen	Heath/Bernhardt, Wilhelm	90		Modern Language Series
	Träumereien an französischen Kaminen	Holt/Watson, Idelle B.	151		Includes: Der kleine Vogel, Das kleine bucklige Mädchen, Die himmlische Musik, Die künstliche Orgel, Der Wunschring, Die drei Schwestern mit den gläsernen Herzen, Von der Königin, die keine Pfeffernüsse backen, und dem König, der nicht das Brummeisen spielen konnte, Vom unsichtbaren Königreiche, Pechvogel und Glückskind, Die Traumbuche, Der kleine Mohr und die Goldprinzessin
Lessing, G. E.	Emilia Galotti	Ginn/Poll, Max	131		International Modern Language Series

	Emilia Galotti	Hinds and Noble/ Granger, E. M.	132	.50	Hinds and Noble's German Classics
	Minna von Barnhelm	Holt/Brandt, Hermann C. G.	227	.60	
	Minna von Barnhelm	Schoenhof/Brandt, Hermann C. G.	227	.60	
	Minna von Barnhelm	Holt/Nichols, Alfred Bull	163	.80	Pitt Press Series
	Minna von Barnhelm	Macmillan/Wolstenholme, Henry J.	214	.60	German Classics
	Minna von Barnhelm	Macmillan/Cutting, Starr Willard	224		Modern Language Series
	Minna von Barnhelm	Heath/Primer, Sylvester			
	Minna von Barnhelm	American Book/ Lambert, Marcus B.	159	.50	
	Minna von Barnhelm	Hinds and Noble/ Granger, E. M.	142	.50	Hinds and Noble's German Classics
	Nathan der Weise	Hinds and Noble/ Granger, E. M.	160	.50	Hinds and Noble's German Classics
	Nathan der Weise	Macmillan/Curme, George Oliver	300	.60	German Classics
Richter, Jean Paul	Selections	American Book/ Collins, George S.	163	.60	Includes: Leichenrede auf den blinden Bergmann, Erinnerungen aus den schönsten Stunden, Schreiben des Rektor Seemaus, Leben des vergnügten Schulmeisterleins Maria Wuz, Der Tod eines Engels, Rede des toten Christus, Aus Jean Pauls Leben, Über das Immergrün unserer Gefühle
Riehl, Wilhelm H.	Der Fluch der Schönheit	Heath/Thomas, Calvin	70		Modern Language Series
Rosegger, Peter	Die Schriften des Waldschulmeisters	Holt/Fossler, Laurence	158	.40	

APPENDIX F *(Continued)*

Author	Title	Publisher/Editor	Pages	Price	Series and Contents
Scheffel, Joseph Viktor von	Ekkehard. Geschichte aus dem zehnten Jahrhundert	Heath/Wenckebach, Carla	235	.30	Modern Language Series
Schiller, J. C. F. von	Der Neffe als Onkel	Heath/Beredsford-Webb, H. S.	121	.30	Modern Language Series
	Der Neffe als Onkel	Hinds and Noble/Granger, E. M.	237	.50	Hinds and Noble's German Classics
	Die Jungfrau von Orleans	Holt/Nichols, Alfred Bull		.60	
	Die Jungfrau von Orleans	Macmillan/Humphreys, Willard C.	259	.50	German Classics
	Maria Stuart	Heath/Rhoades, Lewis A.	232		Modern Language Series
	Selections from Correspondence with Goethe	Ginn/Robertson, John G.	210	.80	International Modern Language Series
	Wilhelm Tell	Macmillan/Carruth, William H.	246	.50	German Classics
	Wilhelm Tell	Hinds and Noble/Granger, E. M.	185	.50	Hinds and Noble's German Classics
	Wilhelm Tell	Holt/Palmer, Arthur H.	404	1.00	
	Wilhelm Tell	Holt/Palmer, Arthur H.	300		
	Wilhelm Tell	Heath/Deering, Robert W.	242		Modern Language Series
Seidel, Heinrich	Der ruhige Mieter and Wie man einen Weinreisenden los wird In: Auf der Sonnenseite	Heath/Bernhardt, Wilhelm	146	.35	Modern Language Series
Spyri, Johanna	Rosenresli	Heath/Boll, Helene H.	62	.25	Modern Language Series

Stökl, Helene	Unter dem Christbaum	Heath/Bernhardt, Wilhelm	168	.35	Modern Language Series. Includes: Vom Bübchen vor der Himmelsthür, Der vergessene Koffer, Eingeschneit, In der Weihnachtszeit, Am Heiligen Abend
Storm, Theodor	Immensee	Heath/Bernhardt, Wilhelm	113	.30	Modern Language Series
Sudermann, Hermann	Der Gänsehirt In: Auf der Sonnenseite	Heath/Bernhardt, Wilhelm	146	.35	Modern Language Series
Wachenhusen, Hans	Vom ersten bis zum letzten Schuß	Macmillan/Bayley, Thomas Henry		.60	Siepmann's German Series
Wildenbruch, Ernst von	Das edle Blut	Heath/Schmidt, Friedrich G.	52	.30	Modern Language Series
Wilhelmi, Alexander (Zechmeister, Alexander Viktor)	Einer muß heiraten, with Benedix's der Prozeß and Günstige Vorzeichen In: Drei kleine Lustspiele	Heath/Wells, Benjamin W.	121		Modern Language Series
Zschokke, Heinrich	Der zerbrochene Krug	Heath/Joynes, Edward S.	80	.25	Modern Language Series

1899

Andersen, H. C.	Bilderbuch ohne Bilder	Heath/Bernhardt, Wilhelm	126	.35	Modern Language Series
Auerbach, Berthold	Auf Wache and Roquette's Der gefrorene Kuß	Holt/McDonnell, Arthur A.		.35	Unterhaltungs-Bibliothek
Baumbach, Rudolf	Der Schwiegersohn	Heath/Bernhardt, Wilhelm	187	.40	Modern Language Series
	Die Nonna. Blaustrumpfgeschichte	Heath/Bernhardt, Wilhelm	97	.30	Modern Language Series
	Nicotiana und andere Erzählungen	Heath/Bernhardt, Wilhelm	106	.30	Modern Language Series

293

APPENDIX F *(Continued)*

Author	Title	Publisher/Editor	Pages	Price	Series and Contents
	Waldnovellen	Heath/Bernhardt, Wilhelm	155	.35	Modern Language Series. Includes: Das stählerne Schloß, Warum die Großmutter nicht schreiben kann, Sankt Huberti Wunder, Schleierweiß, Der Kobold im Keller, Die gefangene Drude
Boyen, M.	Mein erster Patient In: Deutsche Novelletten-Bibliothek	Heath/Bernhardt, Wilhelm		1.20	Modern Language Series
Chamisso, Adelbert von	Peter Schlemihls wundersame Geschichte	Heath/Primer, Sylvester	96	.25	Modern Language Series
Eichendorff, Joseph von	Aus dem Leben eines Taugenichts	Heath/Osthaus, Carl Wilhelm	176	.40	Modern Language Series
Fontane, Theodor	Vor dem Sturm	Macmillan/Weiss, Aloys	268	.75	
Freytag, Gustav	Aus dem Jahrhundert des großen Krieges	Heath/Rhoades, Lewis A.	158	.35	Modern Language Series
	Die Journalisten	Heath/Toy, Walter Dallam	160	.50	Modern Language Series
	Doktor Luther	Ginn/Goodrich, Frank P.	177	.70	International Modern Language Series
Frommel, Emil	Eingeschneit. Studentengeschichte	Heath/Bernhardt, Wilhelm	114	.30	Modern Language Series
Goethe, J. W. von	Egmont	Ginn/Winkler, Max	276	1.00	International Modern Language Series
	Einführung in Goethes Meisterwerke	Heath/Bernhardt, Wilhelm	275	1.50	Modern Language Series
	Götz von Berlichingen	Holt/Goodrich, Frank P.	170	.70	
	Hermann und Dorothea	Hinds and Noble/Hervey, William A.	150	.50	Hinds and Noble's German Classics

	Hermann und Dorothea	Heath/Hewett, Waterman T.	243	1.00	Modern Language Series
	Hermann und Dorothea	Macmillan/Hatfield, James Taft	187	.60	German Classics
	Iphigenie auf Tauris	Macmillan/Cotterill, Henry B.	183	.70	Siepmann's German Series
	Poems	Heath/Harris, Charles	286	.90	Modern Language Series
Götzendorff-Grabowski, Helene von	Der Simpel and Vor Sonnenaufgang In: Deutsche Novelletten-Bibliothek	Heath/Bernhardt, Wilhelm		1.20	Modern Language Series
Grillparzer, Franz	Sappho	Ginn/Ferrell, Chiles C.	143	.65	International Modern Language Series
Grimm, Jakob and Wilhelm	Kinder- und Hausmärchen	Macmillan/Fasnacht, G. Eugene	160	.50	Primary Series
Hauff, Wilhelm	Das Wirtshaus im Spessart	Macmillan/Fasnacht, G. Eugene	283		Primary Series
Heine, Heinrich	Die Harzreise	Heath/Daell, Alphonse N. van	96		Modern Language Series
	Prose	Macmillan/Faust, Albert B.	341	.60	German Classics
Heyse, Paul	L'Arrabbiata	American Book/Lentz, Max Carl G.	87	.30	
Hillern, Wilhelmine von	Höher als die Kirche	Heath/Clary, Stedman W.	102		Modern Language Series
Hoffmann, Hans F.	Der faule Beppo In: Stille Wasser	Heath/Bernhardt, Wilhelm	149	.35	Modern Language Series
Jensen, Wilhelm	Die braune Erika	Heath/Joynes, Edward S.	101	.35	Modern Language Series
Juncke, E. (Schmieden, Else)	Ein Frühlingstraum In: Deutsche Novelletten-Bibliothek	Heath/Bernhardt, Wilhelm		1.20	Modern Language Series
Jung-Stilling, Heinrich	Lebensgeschichte	Holt/Stern, Sigmon Martin	285	1.20	New Modern Language Series

APPENDIX F (Continued)

Author	Title	Publisher/Editor	Pages	Price	Series and Contents
Kleist, Heinrich von	Prinz Friedrich von Homburg	Ginn/Nollen, John Scholte	172	.90	International Modern Language Series
Krane, Anna von	Solitaria In: Stille Wasser	Heath/Bernhardt, Wilhelm	149	.35	Modern Language Series
Leander, Richard (Volkmann, Richard von)	Klein Geschichten und andere Erzählungen	Heath/Bernhardt, Wilhelm	90		Modern Language Series
	Träumereien an französischen Kaminen	Holt/Watson, Idelle B.	170		Includes: Der kleine Vogel, Das kleine bucklige Mädchen, Die himmlische Musik, Die künstliche Orgel, Der Wunschring, Die drei Schwestern mit den gläsernen Herzen, Von der Königin, die keine Pfeffernüsse backen, und dem König, der nicht das Brummeisen spielen konnte, Vom unsichtbaren Königreiche, Pechvogel und Glückskind, Die Traumbuche, Der kleine Mohr und die Goldprinzessin Modern Language Series
Lessing, G. E.	Träumereien an französischen Kaminen Emilia Galotti	Heath/Smissen, W. H. van der Hinds and Noble/Granger, E. M.	132	.50	Hinds and Noble's German Classics
	Emilia Galotti	Heath/Winkler, Max	128		Modern Language Series
	Minna von Barnhelm	Holt/Whitney, William D.	191		Whitney's German Texts
	Minna von Barnhelm	Macmillan/Cutting, Starr Willard	224	.60	German Classics
	Minna von Barnhelm	Hinds and Noble/Granger, E. M.	142	.50	Hinds and Noble's German Classics
	Nathan der Weise	Heath/Primer, Sylvester	300		Modern Language Series

Luther, Martin	Nathan der Weise	Hinds and Noble/ Granger, E. M.	160	.50	Hinds and Noble's German Classics
	Auswahl aus Luthers deutschen Schriften	Ginn/Carruth, William H.	362	1.10	International Modern Language Series
Peschkau, Emil	Sphinx In: Deutsche Novelletten-Bibliothek	Heath/Bernhardt, Wilhelm		1.20	Modern Language Series
Ranke, Leopold von	Kaiserwahl Karls V.	American Book/ Schoenfeld, Hermann	94	.35	
Riehl, Wilhelm H.	Das Spielmannskind and Der stumme Ratsherr	Heath/Eaton, Abbie Fiske	70		Modern Language Series
	Der Fluch der Schönheit	Heath/Thomas, Calvin	126	.35	Modern Language Series
Roquette, Otto	Der gefrorene Kuß and Auerbach's Auf Wache	Holt/MacDonnell, Arthur A.			Unterhaltungs-Bibliothek
Rosegger, Peter	Die Schriften des Waldschulmeisters	Holt/Fossler, Laurence	158	.40	
Scheffel, Joseph Viktor von	Der Trompeter von Säkkingen	Heath/Wenckebach, Carla	181		Modern Language Series
	Ekkehard. Geschichte aus dem zehnten Jahrhundert	Holt/Carruth, William H.	493		
Schiller, J. C. F. von	Der Geisterseher. Erstes Buch	Heath/Joynes, Edward S.	126		Modern Language Series
	Der Neffe als Onkel	Heath/Beredsford-Webb, H. S.	121	.30	Modern Language Series
	Der Neffe als Onkel	Hinds and Noble/ Granger, E. M.		.50	Hinds and Noble's German Classics
	Die Jungfrau von Orleans	Heath/Wells, Benjamin W.	226		Modern Language Series
	History of the Thirty Years' War	Holt/Palmer, Arthur H.	202	.80	
	Maria Stuart	Heath/Rhoades, Lewis A.	232		Modern Language Series
	Maria Stuart	Hinds and Noble/ Hervey, William A.	273	.50	Hinds and Noble's German Classics

APPENDIX F (*Continued*)

Author	Title	Publisher/Editor	Pages	Price	Series and Contents
	Maria Stuart	Macmillan/Schoenfeld, Hermann	322	.60	German Classics
	Wilhelm Tell	Macmillan/Carruth, William H.	317	.60	German Classics
	Wilhelm Tell	Hinds and Noble/Granger, E. M.	185	.50	Hinds and Noble's German Classics
	Wilhelm Tell	Heath/Deering, Robert W.	242		Modern Language Series
Seidel, Heinrich	Drei Rosen an einem Zweige	Steiger/Ahn	51	.20	Ahn's Series of German Novels
	Leberecht Hühnchen and Der gute alte Onkel In: Deutsche Novelletten-Bibliothek	Heath/Bernhardt, Wilhelm		1.20	Modern Language Series
Seume, Johann G.	Mein Leben	Ginn/Senger, Joachim Henry	136	.65	International Modern Language Series
Stökl, Helene	Am Heiligen Abend and Eine Weihnachtsgeschichte In: Deutsche Novelletten-Bibliothek	Heath/Bernhardt, Wilhelm		1.20	Modern Language Series
Sudermann, Hermann	Der Katzensteg	Heath/Wells, Benjamin W.	203		Modern Language Series
Wachenhusen, Hans	Vom ersten bis zum letzten Schuß	Macmillan/Bayley, Thomas Henry			Siepmann's German Series
Werner, Ernst (Bürstenbinder, Elizabeth)	Der Wilddieb In: Deutsche Novelletten-Bibliothek	Heath/Bernhardt, Wilhelm		1.20	Modern Language Series
Wiesner, A. C.	Die schwarze Dame In: Deutsche Novelletten-Bibliothek	Heath/Bernhardt, Wilhelm		1.20	Modern Language Series
Wildenbruch, Ernst von	Der Letzte	Heath/Schmidt, Friedrich G.	124		Modern Language Series

Zschokke, Heinrich	Das Orakel In: Stille Wasser	Heath/Bernhardt, Wilhelm	149	.35	Modern Language Series
	Der zerbrochene Krug	Heath/Joynes, Edward S.	76		Modern Language Series

19--

Eichendorff, Joseph von	Aus dem Leben eines Taugenichts	Holt	132		
Gerstäcker, Friedrich	Germelshausen	Schoenhof/Osthaus, Carl Wilhelm	56		
Goethe, J. W. von	Torquato Tasso	Heath/Thomas, Calvin	181	.75	Heath German Series
Körner, Theodor	Zriny	Holt/Ruggles, Edward Rush	116	.60	Classic German Plays
Moser, Gustav von	Der Bibliothekar	Holt/Lange, Franz	161		College Series of German Plays
Müller, Hugo	Im Wartesalon erster Klasse	Holt	24		College Series of German Plays

1900

Andersen, H. C.	Bilderbuch ohne Bilder	Heath/Bernhardt, Wilhelm	99	.35	Modern Language Series
Arnold, Hans (Bülow, Babette von)	Fritz auf Ferien	Heath/Werner-Spanhoofd, Arnold	99	.20	Modern Language Series
Baumbach, Rudolf	Der Schwiegersohn	Heath/Bernhardt, Wilhelm	187	.40	Modern Language Series
	Sommermärchen	Holt/Meyer, Edward S.	142	.35	Includes: Ranunkulus, Der Fiedelbogen des Neck, Das Wasser des Vergessens, Die Teufel auf der Himmelswiese, Warum die Großmutter nicht schreiben kann, Theolinde und der Wassermann, Der Eselsbrunnen, Sankt Huberti Wunder
Benedix, Roderich	Der Prozeß	Heath/Wells, Benjamin W.	61	.20	Modern Language Series

299

APPENDIX F (Continued)

Author	Title	Publisher/Editor	Pages	Price	Series and Contents
	Nein	Heath/Werner-Spanhoofd, Arnold	69	.25	Modern Language Series
Boyen, M.	Mein erster Patient In: Deutsche Novelletten-Bibliothek	Heath/Bernhardt, Wilhelm		1.20	Modern Language Series
Dahn, Felix L. S.	Ein Kampf um Rom	Heath/Wenckebach, Carla	220	.70	Modern Language Series
	Sigwalt und Sigridh	Heath/Schmidt, Friedrich G.		.25	Modern Language Series
Ebner, Theodor	Herr Walther von der Vogelweide	Macmillan/North, E. G.	115	.50	Siepmann's German Series
Eichendorff, Joseph von	Aus dem Leben eines Taugenichts	Heath/Osthaus, Carl Wilhelm	176	.40	Modern Language Series
Elz, Alexander	Er ist nicht eifersüchtig	Heath/Wells, Benjamin W.	57	.20	Modern Language Series
Freytag, Gustav	Aus dem Jahrhundert des großen Krieges	Heath/Rhoades, Lewis A.	158	.35	Modern Language Series
	Aus dem Staat Friedrichs des Großen	Heath/Hager, Hermann	115	.30	Modern Language Series
	Der Rittmeister von Altrosen	Heath/Hatfield, James Taft	201	.75	Modern Language Series
Frommel, Emil	Eingeschneit. Studentengeschichte	Heath/Bernhardt, Wilhelm	114	.30	Modern Language Series
	Mutterliebe In: Krieg und Frieden	Ginn/Bernhardt, Wilhelm	120	.55	International Modern Language Series
Gerstäcker, Friedrich	Germelshausen	Allyn and Bacon/Minckwitz, Richard A.	114	.50	Allyn and Bacon's German Texts

Author	Title	Editor	Pages	Price	Series
Götzendorff-Grabowski, Helene von	Der Simpel and Vor Sonnenaufgang In: Deutsche Novelletten-Bibliothek	Heath/Bernhardt, Wilhelm		1.20	Modern Language Series
Grillparzer, Franz	Sappho	Ginn/Ferrell, Chiles C.	143	.65	International Modern Language Series
Gutzkow, Karl F.	Zopf und Schwert	Holt/Lange, Franz Schoenhof/Lange, Franz	163 163		College Series of German Plays College Series of German Plays
	Zopf und Schwert	Christern/Lange, Franz	163		College Series of German Plays
Hauff, Wilhelm	Das kalte Herz	Heath/Smissen, W. H. van der	184	.40	
	Scheik von Alessandria und seine Sklaven	Macmillan/Rippmann, Walter	183	.60	Pitt Press Series
Hauptmann, Gerhart	Die versunkene Glocke	Holt/Baker, Thomas S.	205	.80	
Heine, Heinrich	Poems	Heath/White, Horatio S.	220	.75	Modern Language Series
Heyse, Paul	Anfang und Ende	American Book/Lentz, Max Carl G.	105	.30	
	Das Mädchen von Treppi	Heath/Joynes, Edward S.	124	.30	Modern Language Series
	L'Arrabbiata	Heath/Bernhardt, Wilhelm	76	.25	Modern Language Series
Hillern, Wilhelmine von	Höher als die Kirche	Heath/Clary, Stedman W.	102		Modern Language Series
Hoffmann, Hans F.	Publius In: Krieg und Frieden	Ginn/Bernhardt, Wilhelm	120	.55	International Modern Language Series
Juncke, E. (Schmieden, Else)	Ein Frühlingstraum In: Deutsche Novelletten-Bibliothek	Heath/Bernhardt, Wilhelm		1.20	Modern Language Series
Keller, Gottfried	Kleider machen Leute	Heath/Lambert, Marcus B.	140	.35	Modern Language Series
	Romeo und Julia auf dem Dorfe	Heath/Adams, Warren Austin	185	.30	Modern Language Series

APPENDIX F *(Continued)*

Author	Title	Publisher/Editor	Pages	Price	Series and Contents
Kurz, Isolde	Die Humanisten	Macmillan/Voegelin, Ada	141	.60	Siepmann's German Series
Lessing, G. E.	Minna von Barnhelm	Heath/Primer, Sylvester			Modern Language Series
Peschkau, Emil	Sphinx In: Deutsche Novelletten-Bibliothek	Heath/Bernhardt, Wilhelm		1.20	Modern Language Series
Schanz, Frida (Soyaux, Frida Schanz)	Der Assistent and Other Stories	American Book/Beinhorn, A.	140	.35	Includes: Der Assistent, Aus der Tanzstunde, Ein Schwalbenstreich
Scheffel, Joseph Viktor von	Ekkehard. Geschichte aus dem zehnten Jahrhundert	Heath/Wenckebach, Carla	235		Modern Language Series
Schiller, J. C. F. von	Das Lied von der Glocke	Heath/Chamberlin, Willis A.	43	.20	Modern Language Series
	Die Jungfrau von Orleans	Heath/Wells, Benjamin W.	224	.60	Heath German Series
	Die Jungfrau von Orleans	Hinds and Noble/Hervey, William A.	268	.50	Hinds and Noble's German Classics
	Die Jungfrau von Orleans	Macmillan/Buchheim, Carl Adolf	259	.50	German Classics
	Maria Stuart	Ginn/Müller, Margarethe, and Carla Wenckebach	262	1.00	
	Wilhelm Tell. Erster Aufzug	Languages Printing/Pierce, Robert M.	239		Ideophonic Texts
	Wilhelm Tell. Erster Aufzug	Hinds, Noble and Eldridge/Pierce, Robert M.	239	1.00	Ideophonic Texts
	Wilhelm Tell	Macmillan/Carruth, William H.	246	.50	German Classics
	Wilhelm Tell	Holt/Palmer, Arthur H.	404	.70	

	Wilhelm Tell (without vocabulary) Wilhelm Tell	Holt/Palmer, Arthur H. Heath/Deering, Robert W.	300 333	.60 .75 Modern Language Series
Seidel, Heinrich	Der Tausendmarkschein und andere Erzählungen	Reuschel/Demeter, Ludwig, and Samuel P. Capen	58	.25 Includes: Der Tausendmarkschein, Eine Sperlingsgeschichte, Der Hagelschlag, Hundegeschichten, Sonnenuntergang
	Leberecht Hühnchen and Der gute alte Onkel In: Deutsche Novelletten-Bibliothek Wintermärchen	Heath/Bernhardt, Wilhelm Holt/Crook, Corinth LeDuc	129	1.20 Modern Language Series .35 Includes: Die grüne Eidechse, Die Wetterhexe, Die schwimmende Insel, Der Wassermann
Spyri, Johanna	Moni der Geißbub	Heath/Guerber, Helene A.	74	.25 Modern Language Series
Stökl, Helene	Am Heiligen Abend and Eine Weihnachtsgeschichte In: Deutsche Novelletten-Bibliothek Unter dem Christbaum	Heath/Bernhardt, Wilhelm Heath/Bernhardt, Wilhelm	168	1.20 Modern Language Series .60 Modern Language Series. Includes: Vom Bübchen vor der Himmelsthür, Der vergessene Koffer, Eingeschneit, In der Weihnachtszeit, Am Heiligen Abend
Storm, Theodor	Immensee	Heath/Bernhardt, Wilhelm	113	.30 Modern Language Series
Sudermann, Hermann	Frau Sorge	Holt/Gruener, Gustav	268	.80 Modern Language Series
Sylva, Carmen (Elizabeth of Roumania)	Aus meinem Königreich	Heath/Bernhardt, Wilhelm	132	.35 Modern Language Series
Villamaria (Timme, Marie)	Der Sohn der Puszta In: Krieg und Frieden	Ginn/Bernhardt, Wilhelm	120	.55 International Modern Language Series

303

APPENDIX F (Continued)

Author	Title	Publisher/Editor	Pages	Price	Series and Contents
Werner, Ernst (Bürstenbinder, Elizabeth)	Der Wilddieb In: Deutsche Novelletten-Bibliothek	Heath/Bernhardt, Wilhelm		1.20	Modern Language Series
Wiesner, A. C.	Die schwarze Dame In: Deutsche Novelletten-Bibliothek	Heath/Bernhardt, Wilhelm		1.20	Modern Language Series
Wilbrandt, Adolf	Der Meister von Palmyra	American Book/Henckels, Théodore	212	.80	
Wildenbruch, Ernst von	Das edle Blut	Heath/Schmidt, Friedrich G.		.20	Modern Language Series
Zschokke, Heinrich	Das Wirtshaus zu Cransac	Heath/Joynes, Edward S.	115	.30	Modern Language Series
	Der zerbrochene Krug	Heath/Joynes, Edward S.	76		Modern Language Series

1901

Author	Title	Publisher/Editor	Pages	Price	Series and Contents
Albersdorf, P.	Cand. Phil. Lauschmann and Groller's Inkognito	American Book/Lentz, Max Carl G.	118	.30	
Andersen, H. C.	Märchen	Heath/Super, Ovando B.		.90	Modern Language Series
Baumbach, Rudolf	Der Schwiegersohn	Heath/Bernhardt, Wilhelm	121	.30	Modern Language Series
	Bruder Klaus und die treuen Tiere, Der Eselsbrunnen, Der Fiedelbogen des Neck, Die Siebenmeilenstiefel In: Edelsteine	Ginn/Minckwitz, Richard A. von, and Frida von Unwerth	132	.65	International Modern Language Series
	Nicotiana und andere Erzählungen	Heath/Bernhardt, Wilhelm	106	.30	Modern Language Series

Author	Title	Editor	Pages	Price	Series
Benedix, Roderich	Der Prozeß and Wilhelmi's Einer muß heiraten	American Book/ Lambert, Marcus B.	112	.30	
	Nein	Heath/Werner-Spanhoofd, Arnold	69	.25	Modern Language Series
Boyen, M.	Mein erster Patient In: Deutsche Novelletten-Bibliothek	Heath/Bernhardt, Wilhelm		1.20	Modern Language Series
Chamisso, Adelbert von	Peter Schlemihls wundersame Geschichte	Heath/Primer, Sylvester	96	.25	Modern Language Series
Ebner, Theodor	Herr Walther von der Vogelweide	Macmillan/North, E. G.	115	.50	Siepmann's German Series
Eichendorff, Joseph von	Aus dem Leben eines Taugenichts	Heath/Osthaus, Carl Wilhelm	176	.40	Modern Language Series
Eschstruth, Nataly von	Ihr Ideal and Eine Plauderstunde auf der "Seehalde" In: Auf der Sonnenseite	Heath/Bernhardt, Wilhelm	146	.35	Modern Language Series
Freytag, Gustav	Aus dem Staat Friedrichs des Großen	Heath/Hager, Hermann	115	.30	Modern Language Series
	Die Journalisten	Heath/Toy, Walter Dallam	140	.30	Modern Language Series
	Die Journalisten	Allyn and Bacon/ Manley, Edward	262	.60	Allyn and Bacon's German Texts
	Die Journalisten	Appleton/Bronson, Thomas B.	194	.45	Twentieth Century Textbooks
	Die Journalisten	Wahr/Hildner, Jonathan K. A., and Tobias J. C. Diekhoff	174		
	Die Journalisten	Macmillan/Eve, Henry Weston	183	.60	Pitt Press Series
	Soll und Haben	Heath/Files, George Taylor	255	.65	Modern Language Series

305

APPENDIX F (Continued)

Author	Title	Publisher/Editor	Pages	Price	Series and Contents
Friedrich, W. (Riese, Wilhelm F.)	Gänschen von Buchenau	Holt/Stern, Sigmon Martin			Selected German Comedies
Frommel, Emil	Das eiserne Kreuz In: Auf der Sonnenseite Eingeschneit. Studentengeschichte	Heath/Bernhardt, Wilhelm	146	.35	Modern Language Series
		Heath/Bernhardt, Wilhelm	114	.30	Modern Language Series
	Mutterliebe In: Krieg und Frieden	Ginn/Bernhardt, Wilhelm	120	.55	International Modern Language Series
Goethe, J. W. von	Dichtung und Wahrheit	Holt/Jagemann, Hans Carl G.	373	1.12	
	Egmont	Macmillan/Primer, Sylvester	174	.60	
	Faust. Erster und zweiter Teil	Heath/Thomas, Calvin			Modern Language Series
	Hermann und Dorothea	Heath/Hewett, Waterman T.	243	1.00	Modern Language Series
	Iphigenie auf Tauris	Heath/Rhoades, Lewis A.	139	.70	Modern Language Series
	Poems	Holt/Goebel, Julius	244	.80	
	Reineke Fuchs	Holt/Holman, Louis Arthur	71	.50	
Götzendorff-Grabowski, Helene von	Der Simpel and Vor Sonnenaufgang In: Deutsche Novelletten-Bibliothek	Heath/Bernhardt, Wilhelm		1.20	Modern Language Series
Groller, Balduin	Inkognito and Albersdorf's Cand. phil. Lauschmann	American Book/Lentz, Max Carl G.	118	.30	
Hauff, Wilhelm	Der Zwerg Nase	Heath	38		Modern Language Series
	Lichtenstein	Heath/Vogel, Frank	274	.75	Modern Language Series

Author	Title	Editor/Publisher	Pages	Price	Series
	Tales	Ginn/Goold, Charles B.	200		International Modern Language Series. Includes: Die Sage vom Hirschgulden, Die Höhle von Steenfoll, Saids Schicksale
Hauptmann, Gerhart	Die versunkene Glocke	Holt/Baker, Thomas S.	206		
Heine, Heinrich	Lieder und Gedichte	Macmillan/Buchheim, Carl Adolf	376	1.00	Golden Treasury
Heyse, Paul	Hochzeit auf Capri	Heath/Bernhardt, Wilhelm	128	.30	Modern Language Series
	Unter Brüdern	Silver, Burdett/Keppler, Emil A. C.	68	.30	Silver Series of Modern Language Textbooks
Hillern, Wilhelmine von	Höher als die Kirche	Allyn and Bacon/Jonas, Johannes B. E.	124	.50	Allyn and Bacon's German Texts
Hoffman, Hans F.	Publius In: Krieg und Frieden	Ginn/Bernhardt, Wilhelm	120	.55	International Modern Language Series
Juncke, E. (Schmieden, Else)	Ein Frühlingstraum In: Deutsche Novelletten-Bibliothek	Heath/Bernhardt, Wilhelm		1.20	Modern Language Series
Leander, Richard (Volkmann, Richard von)	Die Rumpelkammer In: Edelsteine	Ginn/Minckwitz, Richard A. von, and Frida von Unwerth	132	.65	International Modern Language Series
Lessing, G. E.	Hamburgische Dramaturgie	Holt/Harris, Charles	356	1.00	
	Minna von Barnhelm	Holt/Whitney, William D.	191		Whitney's German Texts
	Minna von Barnhelm	Macmillan/Cutting, Starr Willard	224		German Classics
	Nathan der Weise	Heath/Primer, Sylvester	300		Modern Language Series
Niese, Charlotte	Aus dänischer Zeit	Ginn/Fossler, Laurence	103	.50	International Modern Language Series
Peschkau, Emil	Sphinx In: Deutsche Novelletten-Bibliothek	Heath/Bernhardt, Wilhelm		1.20	Modern Language Series

307

APPENDIX F (Continued)

Author	Title	Publisher/Editor	Pages	Price	Series and Contents
Riehl, Wilhelm H.	Culturgeschichtliche Novellen	Heath/Joynes, Edward S.		.50	Modern Language Series. Includes: Der Stumme Ratsherr, Der Dachs auf Lichtmeß, Der Leibmedikus, Der Zopf des Herrn Guillemain
	Das Spielmannskind and Der stumme Ratsherr	American Book/Priest, George M.	134	.35	
	Der Fluch der Schönheit	Heath/Thomas, Calvin			
Scheffel, Joseph Viktor von	Der Trompeter von Säkkingen	Heath/Wenckebach, Carla	181		Modern Language Series
	Ekkehard. Geschichte aus dem zehnten Jahrhundert	Heath/Wenckebach, Carla	235		Modern Language Series
Schiller, J. C. F. von	Die Braut von Messina	Holt/Palmer, Arthur H., and Jay G. Eldridge	193	.60	
	Die Braut von Messina	Silver, Burdette/Carruth, William H.	185	.60	Silver Series of Modern Language Textbooks
	Die Jungfrau von Orleans	Holt/Nichols, Alfred Bull	309	.60	
	Die Jungfrau von Orleans	Heath/Wells, Benjamin W.	292	.75	Modern Language Series
	Die Jungfrau von Orleans	Appleton/Rhoades, Lewis A.	276	.60	
	Maria Stuart	Holt/Joynes, Edward S.	350	.70	Twentieth Century Textbooks
	Maria Stuart	Heath/Rhoades, Lewis A.	232		Modern Language Series
	Wallenstein Trilogie	Holt/Carruth, William H.	456	1.00	
	Wallenstein Trilogie	Macmillan/Winkler, Max	446	1.00	

Seidel, Heinrich	Wilhelm Tell	Heath/Deering, Robert W.	333	.75	Modern Language Series
	Der gute alte Onkel In: Edelsteine	Ginn/Minckwitz, Richard A. von, and Frida von Unwerth	132	.65	International Modern Language Series
	Der ruhige Mieter and Wie man einen Weinreisenden los wird In: Auf der Sonnenseite	Heath/Bernhardt, Wilhelm	146	.35	Modern Language Series
	Leberecht Hühnchen and Der gute alte Onkel In: Deutsche Novelletten-Bibliothek	Heath/Bernhardt, Wilhelm		1.20	Modern Language Series
	Leberecht Hühnchen	Heath/Werner-Spanhoofd, Arnold	120	.30	Modern Language Series
Stökl, Helene	Am Heiligen Abend and Eine Weihnachtsgeschichte In: Deutsche Novelletten-Bibliothek	Heath/Bernhardt, Wilhelm		1.20	Modern Language Series
Storm, Theodor	Immensee	Heath/Bernhardt, Wilhelm	113	.30	Modern Language Series
	Immensee	Ginn/Minckwitz, Richard A. von, and Ann Crombie Wilder	89	.50	International Modern Language Series
	Immensee	Allyn and Bacon/Whitenack, Erastmus A.	111	.50	Allyn and Bacon's German Texts
	Immensee	Wahr/Hildner, Karl A. J., and Tobias J. C. Diekhoff	70	.35	
	In St. Jürgen	Heath/Wright, Arthur Silas	129	.30	Modern Language Series
Sudermann, Hermann	Der Gänsehirt In: Auf der Sonnenseite	Heath/Bernhardt, Wilhelm	146	.35	Modern Language Series

APPENDIX F *(Continued)*

Author	Title	Publisher/Editor	Pages	Price	Series and Contents
Johannes		Heath/Schmidt, Friedrich G.	126	.35	Modern Language Series
Sybel, Heinrich von	Die Erhebung Europas gegen Napoleon I.	Ginn/Nichols, Alfred Bull	126		International Modern Language Series
Villamaria (Timme, Marie)	Der Sohn der Puszta In: Krieg und Frieden	Ginn/Bernhardt, Wilhelm	120	.55	International Modern Language Series
Wagner, Richard	Das Rheingold	Newson/Minckwitz, Richard A. von	102	.75	
Werner, Ernst (Bürstenbinder, Elizabeth)	Der Wilddieb In: Deutsche Novelletten-Bibliothek	Heath/Bernhardt, Wilhelm		1.20	Modern Language Series
Wiesner, A. C.	Die schwarze Dame In: Deutsche Novelletten-Bibliothek	Heath/Bernhardt, Wilhelm		1.20	Modern Language Series
Wildenbruch, Ernst von	Harold	Heath/Eggert, Charles A.	145	.35	Modern Language Series
Wilhelmi, Alexander (Zechmeister, Alexander Viktor)	Einer muß heiraten and Benedix's Der Prozeß	American Book/Lambert, Marcus B.	112	.30	

1902

Author	Title	Publisher/Editor	Pages	Price	Series and Contents
Andersen, H. C.	Märchen	Heath/Super, Ovando B.		.90	Modern Language Series
Arnold, Hans (Bülow, Babette von)	Fritz auf Ferien	Heath/Werner-Spanhoofd, Arnold	99	.20	Modern Language Series
Baumbach, Rudolf	Der Schwiegersohn	Heath/Bernhardt, Wilhelm	187	.40	Modern Language Series
	Es war einmal (stories by Baumbach and Wildenbruch)	American Book/Bernhardt, Wilhelm	174	.65	

Becker, Karl F.		Friedrich der Große	Oxford University Press/Buchheim, Carl Adolf	175	.50	German Classics
Benedix, Roderich		Der Prozeß and Fulda's Unter vier Augen	Holt/Hervey, William A.	135	.35	
		Der Prozeß and Günstige Vorzeichen, with Wilhelmi's Einer muß heiraten In: Drei kleine Lustspiele	Heath/Wells, Benjamin W.	121	.30	Modern Language Series
		Die Hochzeitsreise	Heath/Schiefferdecker, Natalie	94	.25	Modern Language Series
		Doktor Wespe	Macmillan/Breul, Karl Hermann	208	.75	Pitt Press Series
		Plautus und Terence and Der Sonntagsjäger	Heath/Wells, Benjamin W.	109	.25	Modern Language Series
Eschstruth, Nataly von		Ihr Ideal and Eine Plauderstunde auf der "Seehalde" In: Auf der Sonnenseite	Heath/Bernhardt, Wilhelm	146	.35	Modern Language Series
Fischer, Wilhelm		Die wandelnde Glocke	Maynard and Merrill/Allpress, Robert H.	96	.25	Maynard's German Texts
Freytag, Gustav		Der Rittmeister von Altrosen	Heath/Hatfield, James Taft	201	.75	Modern Language Series
		Die Journalisten	Heath/Toy, Walter Dallam	191	.30	Modern Language Series
		Die Journalisten	Appleton/Bronson, Thomas B.	194	.45	Twentieth Century Textbooks
Frommel, Emil		Das eiserne Kreuz In: Auf der Sonnenseite	Heath/Bernhardt, Wilhelm	146	.35	Modern Language Series
Fulda, Ludwig		Unter vier Augen and Benedix's Der Prozeß	Holt/Hervey, William A.	135	.35	
		Der Talisman	Heath/Prettyman, Cornelius	125	.35	Modern Language Series
		Der Talisman	Holt/Meyer, Edward S.	170	.35	

APPENDIX F *(Continued)*

Author	Title	Publisher/Editor	Pages	Price	Series and Contents
Gerstäcker, Friedrich	Germelshausen	Heath/Lewis, Orlando F.	91	.25	Modern Language Series
Goebel, Ferdinand	Hermann der Cherusker	Macmillan/Esser, G. J.	163	.35	Siepmann's German Series
Goethe, J. W. von	Ausgewählte Prosa	Putnam/Hart, James Morgan	199	1.00	German Classics for American Students. Readings from: Dichtung und Wahrheit, Die Leiden des jungen Werthers, Ein Brief aus der Schweiz, Italienische Reise, Wilhelm Meisters Lehrjahre
	Dichtung und Wahrheit	Heath/Buchheim, Carl Adolf	317	1.05	Modern Language Series
	Egmont	Ginn/Winkler, Max	276	1.00	International Modern Language Series
	Egmont	Bardeen	180	.40	
	Iphigenie auf Tauris	Macmillan/Eggert, Charles A.		.60	German Classics
	Italienische Reise	Maynard/Beredsford-Webb, H. S.	146	.50	Maynard's German Texts
	Selections from Correspondence with Schiller	Ginn/Robertson, John G.	210	.80	International Modern Language Series
Grillparzer, Franz	Der Traum ein Leben	Heath/Meyer, Edward S.	128	.60	Modern Language Series
Grube, August W.	Bilder aus der Turkei	Maynard and Merrill/Lyon, W. S.	92	.25	Maynard's German Texts
Hauff, Wilhelm	Das kalte Herz	Holt/Beck, George A. D.	87	.35	
Heine, Heinrich	Die Harzreise	Heath/Daell, Alphonse N. van	96		Modern Language Series
	Die Harzreise	Ginn/Gregor, Leigh R.	183	.40	International Modern Language Series

Author	Title	Editor	Pages	Price	Series
Heyse, Paul	Das Mädchen von Treppi and Marion Kolberg	Holt/Brusie, Charles F.	137	.25	Maynard's German Texts
	L'Arrabbiata	Maynard and Merrill/Allpress, Robert H.	76	.40	Modern Language Series
	L'Arrabbiata	Heath/Bernhardt, Wilhelm	85	.25	Modern Language Series
	Niels mit der offenen Hand	Wahr/Florer, Warren W.	105	.35	Modern Language Series
	Unter Brüdern	Heath/Joynes, Edward S.	68	.30	Modern Language Series
Hillern, Wilhelmine von	Höher als die Kirche	Silver, Burdett/Keppler, Emil A. C.	105	.30	Silver Series of Modern Language Textbooks
Hoffmann, Otto	Episodes from Andreas Hofer	Heath/Clary, Stedman W.	96	.25	Modern Language Series
Holberg, Ludvig	Niels Klims Wallfahrt in die Unterwelt	Maynard and Merrill/Powell, O. B.	63	.25	Maynard's German Texts
Keller, Gottfried	Dietegen	Heath/Babbitt, Eugene H.	75	.20	Modern Language Series
	Legenden	Ginn/Gruener, Gustav	145	.35	International Modern Language Series
		Holt/Müller, Margarethe, and Carla Wenckebach			Includes: Eugenia, Die Jungfrau und der Teufel, Die Jungfrau als Ritter, Die Jungfrau und die Nonne, Dorotheas Blumenkörbchen
Kleist, Heinrich von	Michael Kohlhaas	Holt/Kurrelmeyer, William	149	.50	Modern Language Series
Körner, Theodor	Zriny	Heath/Holzwarth, Franklin J.	126	.35	Modern Language Series
Leander, Richard (Volkmann, Richard von)	Kleine Geschichten und andere Erzählungen	Heath/Bernhardt, Wilhelm	90		Modern Language Series
Lessing, G. E.	Emilia Galotti	Ginn/Poll, Max	131		International Modern Language Series
	Minna von Barnhelm	Heath/Primer, Sylvester	218		Modern Language Series

APPENDIX F (*Continued*)

Author	Title	Publisher/Editor	Pages	Price	Series and Contents
	Minna von Barnhelm	Appleton/Wilson, Charles B.	196	.50	Twentieth Century Textbooks
	Nathan der Weise	Heath/Primer, Sylvester	300		Modern Language Series
	Nathan der Weise	American Book/Diekhoff, Tobias J. C.	368	.80	
Moser, Gustav von	Der Bibliothekar	American Book/Cooper, William A.	187	.45	
	Köpnickerstrasse 120	Heath/Wells, Benjamin W.	159		Modern Language Series
Niebuhr, B. G.	Griechische Heroengeschichten	Longmans, Green/Lechner, A. R.	296	.60	Includes: Die Fahrt der Argonauten, Geschichten von Herakles, Die Herakliden, Orestes, Merope und Apytos
Niese, Charlotte	Aus dänischer Zeit	Ginn/Fossler, Laurence	156	.45	International Modern Language Series
Petersen, Marie	Prinzessin Ilse	Holt/Merrick, John Mudge	134	.20	
Riehl, Wilhelm H.	Culturgeschichtliche Novellen	Macmillan/Wolstenholme, Henry J.	134	.90	Includes: Der stumme Ratsherr, Der Dachs auf Lichtmeß, Der Leibmedikus, Der Zopf des Herrn Guillemain
	Das Spielmannskind and Der stumme Ratsherr	American Book/Priest, George M.	134	.35	Modern Language Series
	Der Fluch der Schönheit	Heath/Thomas, Calvin	116		
Rosegger, Peter	Waldheimat: Selections	Ginn/Fossler, Laurence	103	.30	International Modern Language Series
Scheffel, Joseph Viktor von	Der Trompeter von Säkkingen	Heath/Wenckebach, Carla	181		Modern Language Series
Schiller, J. C. F. von	Ballads	Heath/Johnson, Henry	165		Modern Language Series

314

	Das Lied von der Glocke	Holt/Otis, Charles Pomeroy	70	.35	
	Der Neffe als Onkel	Holt/Clement, Alfred	99	.40	
	Die Jungfrau von Orleans	Appleton/Rhoades, Lewis A.	276	.60	Twentieth Century Textbooks
	Die Jungfrau von Orleans	Longmans, Green/ Bevir, Joseph Louis Bardeen		.60	
	Die Jungfrau von Orleans	Heath/Prettyman, Cornelius	170	.40 .35	Modern Language Series
	Geschichte des Dreißig-jährigen Kriegs	Holt/Joynes, Edward S.	350	.70	
	Maria Stuart	Heath/Rhoades, Lewis A.			Modern Language Series
	Maria Stuart	Longmans, Green/ Bevir, Joseph Louis Ginn/Robertson, John G.	210	.80	International Modern Language Series
	Selections from Correspondence with Goethe	Heath/Eggert, Charles A.	189	.60	Modern Language Series
	Wallensteins Tod	Macmillan/Carruth, William H.	317	.60	German Classics
	Wilhelm Tell	Longmans, Green/ Bevir, Joseph Louis		.60	
	Wilhelm Tell	Oxford University Press/Schoenfeld, Hermann	256	.50	Clarendon Press
	Wilhelm Tell	Heath/Deering, Robert W.	242	.50	Modern Language Series
	Der ruhige Mieter and Wie man einen Weinreisenden los wird In: Auf der Sonnenseite	Heath/Bernhardt, Wilhelm	146	.35	Modern Language Series
Seidel, Heinrich	Drei Rosen an einem Zweige	Steiger/Ahn	51	.20	Ahn's Series of German Novels

315

APPENDIX F (Continued)

Author	Title	Publisher/Editor	Pages	Price	Series and Contents
Spyri, Johanna	Weihnachten bei Leberecht Hühnchen	Maynard and Merrill/Morich, R. J.	94	.25	Maynard's German Texts
Stökl, Helene	Moni der Geißbub	Heath/Guerber, Helene A.	74	.25	Modern Language Series
	Unter dem Christbaum	Heath/Bernhardt, Wilhelm	168	.60	Modern Language Series. Includes: Vom Bübchen vor der Himmelsthür, Der vergessene Koffer, Eingeschneit, In der Weihnachtszeit, Am Heiligen Abend
Storm, Theodor	Immensee	Heath/Bernhardt, Wilhelm	120	.30	Modern Language Series
	Immensee	Holt/Burnett, Arthur W.	109	.25	Unterhaltungs-Bibliothek
Sudermann, Hermann	Der Gänsehirt In: Auf der Sonnenseite	Heath/Bernhardt, Wilhelm	146	.35	Modern Language Series
Sybel, Heinrich von	Prinz Eugen von Savoyen	Macmillan/Quiggin, Edmund C.	180	.60	Pitt Press Series
Treitschke, Heinrich von	Das deutsche Ordensland Preußen	Maynard and Merrill/Lyon, Walter Sidney	139	.40	Maynard's German Texts
Wagner, Richard	Das Rheingold	Newson/Minckwitz, Richard A. von	102	.75	
Wichert, Ernst A.	Als Verlobte empfehlen sich—	Heath/Flom, George Tobias	64	.25	Modern Language Series
Wilbrandt, Adolf	Das Urteil des Paris	Heath/Wirt, Anne Grace	125	.30	Modern Language Series
Wildenbruch, Ernst von	Das edle Blut	American Book/Eggert, Charles A.	86	.30	
	Es war einmal (stories by Wildenbruch and Baumbach)	American Book/Bernhardt, Wilhelm	174	.65	
	Harold	Maynard and Merrill/Voegelin, Ada	133	.40	Maynard's German Texts

316

Wilhelmi, Alexander (Zechmeister, Alexander Viktor)	Einer muß heiraten, with Benedix's Der Prozeß and Günstige Vorzeichen In: Drei kleine Lustspiele	Heath/Wells, Benjamin W.	121	.30	Modern Language Series
Zastrow, Karl	Wilhelm der Siegreiche	Macmillan/Ash, E. P.		.50	Siepmann's German Series
Zschokke, Heinrich	Der zerbrochene Krug	American Book/Berkefeld, Rosalie O.	59	.25	Modern German Readings

1903

Andersen, H. C.	Märchen	Heath/Super, Ovando B.		.90	Modern Language Series
Baumbach, Rudolf	Der Schwiegersohn	Heath/Bernhardt, Wilhelm	121	.30	Modern Language Series
	Nicotiana und andere Erzählungen	Heath/Bernhardt, Wilhelm	106	.30	Modern Language Series
	Ranunkulus and Der Fiedelbogen des Neck In: Easy German Stories	Scott, Foresman/Allen, Phillip S., and Max Batt	241		Lake German Series
Benedix, Roderich	Die Hochzeitsreise	Heath/Schiefferdecker, Natalie	64	.25	Modern Language Series
	Nein	Heath/Werner-Spanhoofd, Arnold	69	.25	Modern Language Series
Boyen, M.	Mein erster Patient In: Deutsche Novelletten-Bibliothek	Heath/Bernhardt, Wilhelm		1.20	Modern Language Series
Eschstruth, Nataly von	Hundert Schimmel In: Aus Herz und Welt	Heath/Bernhardt, Wilhelm	92	.25	Modern Language Series
Fouqué, Friedrich de la Motte	Undine	American Book/Senger, Joachim Henry	174	.50	Modern Language Series
Freytag, Gustav	Die Journalisten	Appleton/Bronson, Thomas B.	194	.45	Twentieth Century Textbooks
Fulda, Ludwig	Der Talisman	Holt/Meyer, Edward S.	170	.35	

317

APPENDIX F (Continued)

Author	Title	Publisher/Editor	Pages	Price	Series and Contents
Gerstäcker, Friedrich	Irrfahrten	Holt/Whitney, Marian P.	221	.30	Whitney-Klemm German Series
Goethe, J. W. von	Ausgewählte Prosa	Putnam/Hart, James Morgan	199	1.00	German Classics for American Students. Readings from: Dichtung und Wahrheit, Die Leiden des jungen Werthers, Ein Brief aus der Schweiz, Italienische Reise, Wilhelm Meisters Lehrjahre
	Egmont	Holt/Deering, Robert W.		.60	
	Goethe's Sesenheim	Heath/Huss, Hermann Carl O.	83	.25	Modern Language Series
	Hermann und Dorothea	Appleton/Palmer, Arthur H.	202	.50	Twentieth Century Textbooks
	Hermann und Dorothea	Heath/Hewett, Waterman T.	243	1.00	Modern Language Series
	Hermann und Dorothea	Macmillan/Hatfield, James Taft	187	.60	German Classics
Götzendorff-Grabowski, Helene von	Der Simpel and Vor Sonnenaufgang In: Deutsche Novelletten-Bibliothek	Heath/Bernhardt, Wilhelm		1.20	Modern Language Series
Grimm, Jakob and Wilhelm	Kinder- und Hausmärchen Märchen	American Book/Vos, Bert John	191	.45	
		Allyn and Bacon/Merkley, George E.	132	.50	
Gutzkow, Karl F.	Zopf und Schwert	Holt/Lange, Franz	163		College Series of German Plays
Heine, Heinrich	Die Harzreise	Ginn/Gregor, Leigh R.	183	.40	International Modern Language Series

318

Heyse, Paul	L'Arrabbiata In: Easy German Stories	Scott, Foresman/Allen, Phillips S., and Max Batt	241	Lake German Series
	L'Arrabbiata	Heath/Bernhardt, Wilhelm	86 .25	Modern Language Series
Juncke, E. (Schmieden, Else)	Ein Frühlingstraum In: Deutsche Novelletten-Bibliothek	Heath/Bernhardt, Wilhelm	1.20	Modern Language Series
Keller, Gottfried	Dietegen	Ginn/Gruener, Gustav	75	International Modern Language Series
Kotzebue, A. F. F. von	Die deutschen Kleinstädter	Maynard and Merrill/Matthews, J. H. O. and W. H. Witherby	115	Maynard's German Texts
Leander, Richard (Volkmann, Richard von)	Träumereien an französischen Kaminen	Heath/Smissen, W. H. van der	185 .40	Modern Language Series. Includes: Der kleine Vogel, Das kleine buck-lige Mädchen, Die himmlische Musik, Die künstliche Orgel, Der Wunschring, Die drei Schwestern mit den gläsernen Herzen, Von der Königin, die keine Pfeffernüsse backen, und dem König, der nicht das Brummeisen spielen konnte, Vom unsichtbaren Königreiche, Pechvogel und Glückskind, Die Traumbuche, Der kleine Mohr und die Goldprinzessin
Lessing, G. E.	Emilia Galotti	Ginn/Poll, Max	131	International Modern Language Series
	Emilia Galotti	Heath/Winkler, Max	128	Modern Language Series
	Minna von Barnhelm	Heath/Primer, Sylvester	178	Modern Language Series
Liliencron, Detlev von	Anno 1870. Kriegsbilder	Heath/Bernhardt, Wilhelm	138 .40	Modern Language Series
Ludwig, Otto	Zwischen Himmel und Erde	Heath/Meyer, Edward S.	240 .65	Modern Language Series

APPENDIX F (*Continued*)

Author	Title	Publisher/Editor	Pages	Price	Series and Contents
Peschkau, Emil	Sphinx In: Deutsche Novelletten-Bibliothek	Heath/Bernhardt, Wilhelm		1.20	Modern Language Series
Rosegger, Peter	Als ich das erste Mal auf dem Dampfwagen saß and Wie der Meisensepp gestorben ist In: Easy German Stories	Scott, Foresman/Allen, Phillip S. and Max Batt	241		Lake German Series
Scheffel, Joseph Viktor von	Der Trompeter von Säkkingen	Macmillan/Milner-Barry, E. L.	280	.80	Siepmann's German Series
	Der Trompeter von Säkkingen	American Book/Buehner, Valentin	328	.75	
	Ekkehard. Geschichte aus dem zehnten Jahrhundert	Heath/Wenckebach, Carla	235		Modern Language Series
Schiller, J. C. F. von	Die Jungfrau von Orleans	Heath/Wells, Benjamin W.	226		Modern Language Series
	Maria Stuart	Ginn/Müller, Margarethe, and Carla Wenckebach	262	1.00	
	Maria Stuart	Scott, Foresman/Eggert, Carl Edgar	276	.70	Lake German Classics
	Wallensteins Tod	Heath/Eggert, Charles A.	189	.60	Modern Language Series
	Wilhelm Tell	Oxford University Press/Schoenfeld, Hermann		.60	German Classics
Schücking, Levin	Die drei Freier	Ginn/Heller, Otto	81	.30	International Modern Language Series

Seidel, Heinrich	Leberecht Hühnchen and Der gute alte Onkel In: Deutsche Novelletten-Bibliothek	Heath/Bernhardt, Wilhelm		1.20	Modern Language Series
Stökl, Helene	Alle fünf! In: Aus Herz und Welt	Heath/Bernhardt, Wilhelm	92	.25	Modern Language Series
	Am Heiligen Abend and Eine Weihnachtsgeschichte In: Deutsche Novelletten-Bibliothek	Heath/Bernhardt, Wilhelm		1.20	Modern Language Series
Werner, Ernst (Bürstenbinder, Elizabeth)	Der Wilddieb In: Deutsche Novelletten-Bibliothek	Heath/Bernhardt, Wilhelm		1.20	Modern Language Series
	Heimatklang	Holt/Whitney, Marian P.	232	.35	
Wiesner, A. C.	Die schwarze Dame In: Deutsche Novelletten-Bibliothek	Heath/Bernhardt, Wilhelm		1.20	Modern Language Series
Wilbrandt, Adolf	Jugendliebe	Holt/Henckels, Théodore	87	.30	
Zschokke, Heinrich	Der zerbrochene Krug	Heath/Joynes, Edward S.	76		Modern Language Series

1904

Baumbach, Rudolf	Das Habichtsfräulein	Heath/Bernhardt, Wilhelm	191	.40	Modern Language Series
	Der Schwiegersohn	Heath/Bernhardt, Wilhelm	187	.40	Modern Language Series
	Nicotiana und andere Erzählungen	Heath/Bernhardt, Wilhelm	106	.30	Modern Language Series
	Ranunkulus and Der Fiedelbogen des Neck In: Easy German Stories	Scott, Foresman/Allen, Phillip S., and Max Batt	241		Lake German Series

APPENDIX F *(Continued)*

Author	Title	Publisher/Editor	Pages	Price	Series and Contents
Benedix, Roderich	Der Prozeß	Heath/Wells, Benjamin W.	61	.20	Modern Language Series
	Der Prozeß and Fulda's Unter vier Augen	Holt/Hervey, William A.	135	.35	
	Die Hochzeitsreise	Christern/Ascher, David	68		Englische Übungsbibliothek
Campe, Joachim H.	Robinson der Jüngere	Heath/Ibershoff, Carl Henry	201	.40	Modern Language Series
Chamisso, Adelbert von	Peter Schlemihls wundersame Geschichte	Heath/Primer, Sylvester	96	.25	Modern Language Series
Dahn, Felix L. S.	Ein Kampf um Rom	Heath/Wenckebach, Carla	220	.70	Modern Language Series
Ebner-Eschenbach, Marie von	Die Freiherren von Gemperlein and Krambambuli	Heath/Hohlfeld, Alexander R.	128	.30	Modern Language Series
Eichendorff, Joseph von	Aus dem Leben eines Taugenichts	Heath/Osthaus, Carl Wilhelm	176	.40	Modern Language Series
Ernst, Otto (Schmidt, Otto Ernst)	Flachsmann als Erzieher	Ginn/Kingsbury, Elizabeth	190	.40	International Modern Language Series
Eschstruth, Nataly von	Ihr Ideal and Eine Plauderstunde auf der "Seehalde" In: Auf der Sonnenseite	Heath/Bernhardt, Wilhelm	146	.35	Modern Language Series
Freytag, Gustav	Aus dem Jahrhundert des großen Krieges	Heath/Rhoades, Lewis A.	158	.35	Modern Language Series
	Die Journalisten	Ginn/Gregor, Leigh R.	231	.45	International Modern Language Series
Frommel, Emil	Das eiserne Kreuz In: Auf der Sonnenseite	Heath/Bernhardt, Wilhelm	146	.35	Modern Language Series
	Mutterliebe In: Krieg und Frieden	Ginn/Bernhardt, Wilhelm	120	.55	International Modern Language Series

Fulda, Ludwig	Unter vier Augen and Benedix's Der Prozeß	Holt/Hervey, William A.	135	.35	
Gerstäcker, Friedrich	Germelshausen	Holt/McLouth, Lawrence A.	124	.30	
	Germelshausen	Heath/Lewis, Orlando F.	90	.25	Modern Language Series
	Germelshausen	Ginn/Lovelace, Griffin M.	107	.30	International Modern Language Series
Goebel, Ferdinand	Hermann der Cherusker	Macmillan/Esser, G. J.	163	.35	Siepmann's German Series
Goethe, J. W. von	Das Märchen	Heath/Eggert, Charles A.	109	.30	Modern Language Series
	Egmont	Heath/Hatfield, James Taft	134	.60	Modern Language Series
	Hermann und Dorothea	Heath/Adams, Warren Austin	189	.65	Modern Language Series
	Hermann und Dorothea	Ginn/Allen, Phillip S.	257	.60	International Modern Language Series
	Iphigenie auf Tauris	Macmillan/Eggert, Charles A.	180	.60	German Classics
	Poems	Holt/Goebel, Julius	244	.80	Modern Language Series
	Poems	Heath/Harris, Charles	286	.90	
Grillparzer, Franz	Sappho	Ginn/Ferrell, Chiles C.	143	.65	International Modern Language Series
Hansjakob, Heinrich	Aus dem Leben eines Unglücklichen	Macmillan/Dixon, E.	149	.50	Siepmann's German Series
Hauff, Wilhelm	Das kalte Herz	Heath/Smissen, W. H. van der	184	.40	
	Lichtenstein	Heath/Vogel, Frank	274		Modern Language Series
Hauptmann, Gerhart	Die versunkene Glocke	Holt/Baker, Thomas S.	206		
Heine, Heinrich	Die Harzreise	Ginn/Gregor, Leigh R.	183	.40	International Modern Language Series
	Prose	Macmillan/Faust, Albert B.	341	.60	German Classics

APPENDIX F (Continued)

Author	Title	Publisher/Editor	Pages	Price	Series and Contents
Heyse, Paul	L'Arrabbiata In: Easy German Stories	Scott, Foresman/Allen, Phillip S., and Max Batt	241	.25	Lake German Series
Hillern, Wilhelmine von	Höher als die Kirche	Heath/Clary, Stedman W.	105	.35	Modern Language Series
Hoffmann, Hans F.	Das Gymnasium zu Stolpenburg	Heath/Buehner, Valentin	145	.55	Modern Language Series
	Publius In: Krieg und Frieden	Ginn/Bernhardt, Wilhelm	120		International Modern Language Series
Jensen, Wilhelm	Die braune Erika	Heath/Joynes, Edward S.	101	.35	Modern Language Series
Kleist, Heinrich von	Michael Kohlhaas	Holt/Kurrelmeyer, William	149	.50	
Kohlrausch, F.	Das Jahr 1813	Macmillan/Cartmell, James W.	156	.50	Pitt Press Series
Leander, Richard (Volkmann, Richard von)	Träumereien an französischen Kaminen	Heath/Smissen, W. H. van der	185	.40	Modern Language Series. Includes: Der kleine Vogel, Das kleine bucklige Mädchen, Die himmlische Musik, Die künstliche Orgel, Der Wunschring, Die drei Schwestern mit den gläsernen Herzen, Von der Königin, die keine Pfeffernüsse backen, und dem König der nicht das Brummeisen spielen konnte, Vom unsichtbaren Königreiche, Pechvogel und Glückskind, Die Traumbuche, Der kleine Mohr und die Goldprinzessin
Lessing, G. E.	Minna von Barnhelm	Holt/Whitney, William D.	191		Whitney's German Texts

324

	Minna von Barnhelm	Ginn/Minckwitz, Richard A. von, and Anne Crombie Wilder	202	.45	International Modern Language Series
Meyer-Förster, Wilhelm	Karl Heinrich	Newson/Sanborn, Herbert C.	391	.80	Modern Language Series
Mörike, Eduard	Mozart auf der Reise nach Prag	Heath/Howard, William G.	125	.35	
Niebuhr, B. G.	Griechische Heroengeschichten	Allyn and Bacon/ Merkley, George E.	122	.50	Allyn and Bacon's German Texts Includes: Die Fahrt der Argonauten, Geschichten von Herakles, Die Herakliden, Orestes, Merope und Apytos
Niese, Charlotte	Aus dänischer Zeit	Ginn/Fossler, Laurence	156	.45	International Modern Language Series
Rosegger, Peter	Als ich das erste mal auf dem Dampfwagen saß and Wie der Meisensepp gestorben ist In: Easy German Stories	Scott, Foresman/Allen, Phillip S., and Max Batt	241		Lake German Series
	Die Schriften des Waldschulmeisters	Holt/Fossler, Laurence	158		
Scheffel, Joseph Viktor von	Der Trompeter von Säkkingen	Holt/Osthaus, Carl Wilhelm	319	.80	
	Der Trompeter von Säkkingen	Macmillan/Milner-Barry, E. L.	280	.80	Siepmann's German Series
	Der Trompeter von Säkkingen	American Book/ Buehner, Valentin	328	.75	
	Ekkehard. Geschichte aus dem zehnten Jahrhundert	Heath/Wenckebach, Carla	235		Modern Language Series
Schiller, J. C. F. von	Ballads	Heath/Johnson, Henry	165		Modern Language Series
	Der Neffe als Onkel	Allyn and Bacon/ Raddatz, Charles F.	147	.50	Allyn and Bacon's German Texts

APPENDIX F (Continued)

Author	Title	Publisher/Editor	Pages	Price	Series and Contents
	Der Neffe als Onkel	Heath/Beredsford-Webb, H. S.	121		Modern Language Series
	Die Jungfrau von Orleans	Heath/Wells, Benjamin W.			Modern Language Series
	Die Jungfrau von Orleans	Oxford University Press/Buchheim, Carl Adolf	272	.50	German Classics
	Die Jungfrau von Orleans	Appleton/Rhoades, Lewis A.	276	.60	Twentieth Century Textbooks
	Maria Stuart	Heath/Rhoades, Lewis A.	314		Modern Language Series
	Wilhelm Tell	Macmillan/Carruth, William H.	317	.60	German Classics
	Wilhelm Tell	Oxford University Press/Schoenfeld, Hermann		.60	Clarendon Press
	Wilhelm Tell	Heath/Deering, Robert W.	333	.75	Modern Language Series
Schücking, Levin	Die drei Freier	Ginn/Heller, Otto	81	.30	International Modern Language Series
Seidel, Heinrich	Der ruhige Mieter and Wie man einen Weinreisenden los wird In: Auf der Sonnenseite	Heath/Bernhardt, Wilhelm	146	.35	Modern Language Series
Spyri, Johanna	Rosenresli	Heath/Boll, Helene H.	62		Modern Language Series
Storm, Theodor	Immensee	Heath/Bernhardt, Wilhelm	120	.30	Modern Language Series
	Immensee	Wahr/Hildner, Karl A. J., and Tobias J. C. Diekhoff	112	.35	
	In St. Jürgen	Ginn/Beckmann, John Henry	120	.35	International Modern Language Series

	Pole Poppenspäler	Heath/Bernhardt, Wilhelm	172	.35	Modern Language Series
Sudermann, Hermann	Der Gänsehirt In: Auf der Sonnenseite	Heath/Bernhardt, Wilhelm	146	.35	Modern Language Series
	Der Katzensteg	Heath/Wells, Benjamin W.	203		Modern Language Series
Uhland, Ludwig	Poems	Macmillan/Hewett, Waterman T.	352		German Classics
Villamaria (Timme, Marie)	Der Sohn der Puszta In: Krieg und Frieden	Ginn/Bernhardt, Wilhelm	120	.55	International Modern Language Series
Wagner, Richard	Die Meistersinger von Nürnberg	American Book/ Bigelow, William P.	178	.70	
Wildenbruch, Ernst von	Der Letzte	Heath/Schmidt, Friedrich G.		.25	Modern Language Series
	Harold	Heath/Eggert, Charles A.	145		Modern Language Series
Zschokke, Heinrich	Der zerbrochene Krug	Ginn/Sanborn, Herbert C.	76	.25	International Modern Language Series

1905

Arnold, Hans (Bülow, Babette von)	Aprilwetter	Heath/Fossler, Laurence		.35	Modern Language Series. Includes: Nicht lügen, Von Taufe zu Taufe, Logierbesuch zum Künstlerfest, Warum die Leute nicht heiraten, Des Rittmeisters erste Liebe, Der Amateurphotograph, Junge Gäste, Tante Clementine
Baumbach, Rudolf	Der Schwiegersohn	Heath/Bernhardt, Wilhelm	187	.40	Modern Language Series
	Die Nonna. Blaustrumpf- geschichte	Heath/Bernhardt, Wilhelm	97	.30	Modern Language Series

APPENDIX F (*Continued*)

Author	Title	Publisher/Editor	Pages	Price	Series and Contents
Benedix, Roderich	Ranunkulus and Der Fiedelbogen des Neck In: Easy German Stories	Scott, Foresman/Allen, Phillip S., and Max Batt	241		Lake German Series
	Der Prozeß	Heath/Wells, Benjamin W.	61	.20	Modern Language Series
	Eigensinn and Wilhelmi's Einer muß heiraten	Holt/Hervey, William A.	124	.25	
	Eigensinn and Jagderfolge, with Buchheim's Der ungebetene Gast and Ernst's Wie man sich bildet In: Short German Plays	Oxford University Press/Buchheim, Emma S.	91	.60	
Biedermann, Friedrich Karl	Deutsche Bildungszustände	Holt/Walz, John A.	205	.70	
Buchheim, Emma S.	Der ungebetene Gast, with Benedix's Eigensinn and Jagderfolge and Ernst's Wie man sich bildet In: Short German Plays	Oxford University Press/Buchheim, Emma S.	91	.60	
Campe, Joachim H.	Robinson der jüngere	Heath/Ibershoff, Carl Henry	201	.40	Modern Language Series
Eichendorff, Joseph von	Aus dem Leben eines Taugenichts	Holt/Howe, George Maxwell	227		
Ernst, Otto (Schmidt, Otto Ernst)	Wie man sich bildet, with Benedix's Eigensinn and Jagderfolge and Buchheim's Der ungebetene Gast In: Short German Plays	Oxford University Press/Buchheim, Emma S.	91	.60	

Author	Title	Editor	Page	Price	Series
Eschstruth, Nataly	Hundert Schimmel In: Aus Herz und Welt	Heath/Bernhardt, Wilhelm	92	.25	Modern Language Series
Freytag, Gustav	Die Journalisten	Heath/Toy, Walter Dallam	191	.30	Modern Language Series
	Die Journalisten	Scott, Foresman/Wilson, Charles B.	218	.50	Lake German Classics
	Soll und Haben	Heath/Files, George Taylor	255	.65	Modern Language Series
Gerstäcker, Friedrich	Irrfahrten	Heath/Sturm, Frederick B.	203	.45	Modern Language Series
Görner, Karl A.	Englisch	Holt/Edgren, August H.	61	.25	
Goethe, J. W. von	Die neue Melusine and Zschokke's Der tote Gast In: Two German Tales	Holt/Nichols, Alfred Bull	256	.40	
	Iphigenie auf Tauris	Holt/Winkler, Max	211	.60	Modern Language Series
	Der arme Spielmann	Heath/Howard, William G.	143	.35	
Grillparzer, Franz					
Hebbel, Friedrich	Herodes und Mariamne	Holt/Meyer, Edward S.	192	.60	
Heine, Heinrich	Die Harzreise Poems	Heath/Vos, Bert John Heath/White, Horatio S.	196	.45	Modern Language Series Modern Language Series
Heyse, Paul	Die Blinden	Holt/Carruth, William H.	131	.35	
	L'Arrabbiata In: Easy German Stories	Scott, Foresman/Allen, Phillip S., and Max Batt	241	.25	Lake German Series
	L'Arrabbiata	Heath/Bernhardt, Wilhelm	86	.25	Modern Language Series
Jacobsen, Karl	Wigo and Kraner's Der Tschokoi In: Two German Tales	Silver, Burdett/Lentz, Max Carl G.	108	.40	Silver Series of Modern Language Textbooks

APPENDIX F (*Continued*)

Author	Title	Publisher/Editor	Pages	Price	Series and Contents
Keller, Isidor	Bilder aus der deutschen Literatur	American Book	359	1.00	
Kraner, Johannes	Der Tschokoi and Jacobsen's Wigo In: Two German Tales	Silver, Burdett/Lentz, Max Carl G.	108	.40	Silver Series of Modern Language Textbooks
Lessing, G. E.	Emilia Galotti	Heath/Winkler, Max	128	.40	Modern Language Series
	Nathan der Weise	Heath/Primer, Sylvester	300		Modern Language Series
Liliencron, Detlev von	Anno 1870. Kriegsbilder	Heath/Bernhardt, Wilhelm	138	.40	Modern Language Series
Lohmeyer, Julius	Geißbub von Engelberg	Heath/Bernhardt, Wilhelm	182	.40	Modern Language Series
Meyer, Conrad F.	Das Amulett	American Book/ Glascock, Clyde C.	165	.35	
	Der Schuß von der Kanzel	Ginn/Haertel, Martin H.	141	.35	International Modern Language Series
Meyer-Förster, Wilhelm	Karl Heinrich	Newson/Sanborn, Herbert C.	391	.80	
Moser, Gustav von	Ein amerikanisches Duell, with Müller's Im Wartesalon erster Klasse, Pohl's Die Schulreiterin and Rosen's Ein Knopf In: Four German Comedies	Ginn/Allen, Phillip S., and Edward Manley	210	.45	International Modern Language Series
Müller, Hugo	Im Wartesalon erster Klasse, with Moser's Ein amerikanisches Duell, Pohl's Die Schulreiterin and Rosen's Ein Knopf In: Four German Comedies	Ginn/Allen, Phillip S., and Edward Manley	210	.45	International Modern Language Series

Müller, Max	Deutsche Liebe	Ginn/Johnston, James C.	185	.45	International Modern Language Series
Pohl, Emil	Die Schulreiterin, with Moser's Ein amerikanisches Duell, Müller's Im Wartesalon erster Klasse, and Rosen's Ein Knopf In: Four German Comedies	Ginn/Allen, Phillip S., and Edward Manley	210	.45	International Modern Language Series
Rosegger, Peter	Als ich das erste Mal auf dem Dampfwagen saß and Wie der Meisensepp gestorben ist In: Easy German Stories	Scott, Foresman/Allen, Phillip S., and Max Batt	241		Lake German Series
	Das Holzknechthaus und zwei andere Geschichten (Wie ich dem lieben Herrgott mein Sonntagsjöppel schenkte and Als dem kleinen Maxel das Haus niederbrannte)	Wahr/Diekhoff, Tobias J. C.	86	.40	
Rosen, Julius	Ein Knopf, with Moser's Ein amerikanisches Duell, Müller's Im Wartesalon erster Klasse and Pohl's Die Schulreiterin In: Four German Comedies	Ginn/Allen, Phillip S., and Edward Manley	210	.45	International Modern Language Series
Scheffel, Joseph Viktor von	Der Trompeter von Säkkingen	Heath/Wenckebach, Carla	181		Modern Language Series
Schiller, J. C. F. von	Der Neffe als Onkel	Allyn and Bacon/Raddatz, Charles F.	147	.50	Allyn and Bacon's German Texts
	Der Neffe als Onkel	Heath/Beredsford-Webb, H. S.	121		Modern Language Series

APPENDIX F (Continued)

Author	Title	Publisher/Editor	Pages	Price	Series and Contents
	Die Jungfrau von Orleans	Heath/Wells, Benjamin W.	292		Modern Language Series
	Die Jungfrau von Orleans	Macmillan/Humphreys, Willard C.	259		German Classics
	Geschichte des Dreißigjährigen Kriegs Historische Skizzen	Holt/Palmer, Arthur H.	183	.35	
		Oxford University Press/Buchheim, Emma S.		.50	German Classics. Includes: Egmonts Leben und Tod, Die Belagerung von Antwerpen
	Maria Stuart	Oxford University Press/Buchheim, Carl Adolf	260	.50	German Classics
	Poems	Holt/Nollen, John S.	381	.80	
	Wallensteins Lager	Macmillan/Cotterill, Henry B.	113		
	Wilhelm Tell	Maynard and Merrill/Minckwitz, Richard A. von	355	.65	Foreign School Classics
	Wilhelm Tell	American Book/Roedder, Edwin C.	352	.70	
	Wilhelm Tell	Heath/Deering, Robert W.	333	.75	Modern Language Series
Sealsfield, Charles (Postl, Karl)	Die Prärie am Jacinto	Holt/Nichols, Alfred Bull	131	.35	
Seidel, Heinrich	Leberecht Hühnchen und andere Sonderlinge	American Book/Bernhardt, Wilhelm	75		
Stifter, Adalbert	Das Heidedorf	Heath/Heller, Otto	50		Modern Language Series
Stökl, Helene	Alle fünf In: Aus Herz und Welt	Heath/Bernhardt, Wilhelm	92	.25	Modern Language Series
Storm, Theodor	Geschichten aus der Tonne	Heath/Vogel, Frank	156	.40	Modern Language Series

Sudermann, Hermann	Frau Sorge	Holt/Gruener, Gustav	268	Modern Language Series
	Johannes	Heath/Schmidt, Friedrich G.	126	
	Teja	Holt/Sanborn, Herbert C.	110	.75
Wildenbruch, Ernst von	Das edle Blut	Heath/Schmidt, Friedrich G.	84	Modern Language Series
	Kindertränen. Zwei Erzählungen: Der Letzte and Die Landpartie	Silver, Burdette/Truscott, Fred W.	91	.40 Silver Series of Modern Language Textbooks
Wilhelmi, Alexander (Zechmeister, Alexander Viktor)	Einer muß heiraten and Benedix's Eigensinn	Holt/Hervey, William A.	124	.25
Zschokke, Heinrich	Das Abenteuer der Neujahrsnacht	Heath/Handschin, Charles H.	130	.35 Modern Language Series
	Der tote Gast and Goethe's Die neue Melusine In: Two German Tales	Holt/Nichols, Alfred Bull	256	.40
	Der zerbrochene Krug	Holt/Faust, Albert B.		
	Der zerbrochene Krug	Heath/Joynes, Edward S.	76	.25 Modern Language Series

1906

Andersen, H. C.	Märchen	Heath/Super, Ovando B.	187	.90 Modern Language Series
Baumbach, Rudolf	Der Schwiegersohn	Heath/Bernhardt, Wilhelm		.40 Modern Language Series
Benedix, Roderich	Die Hochzeitsreise	Heath/Schiefferdecker, Natalie		.25 Modern Language Series
Chamisso, Adelbert von	Peter Schlemihls wundersame Geschichte	Heath/Primer, Sylvester	96	.25 Modern Language Series

333

APPENDIX F (Continued)

Author	Title	Publisher/Editor	Pages	Price	Series and Contents
Ebner, Theodor	Herr Walther von der Vogelweide	Macmillan/North, E. G.	115	.50	Siepmann's German Series
Eichendorff, Joseph von	Aus dem Leben eines Taugenichts	Holt/Howe, George M.	227		
Frenssen, Gustav	Gravelotte. Chapter Fourteen of Jörn Uhl	Ginn/Heller, Otto	67	.25	International Modern Language Series
Freytag, Gustav	Aus dem Staat Friedrichs des Großen	Heath/Hager, Hermann	115	.30	Modern Language Series
	Die Journalisten	Heath/Toy, Walter Dallam	191	.30	Modern Language Series
	Die Journalisten	Scott, Foresman/Wilson, Charles B.	218	.50	Lake German Classics
Fulda, Ludwig	Das verlorene Paradies	Ginn/Grumman, Paul H.	194	.45	International Modern Language Series
Gerstäcker, Friedrich	Irrfahrten	Heath/Sturm, Frederick B.	203	.45	Modern Language Series
Goethe, J. W. von	Goethe's Sesenheim	Heath/Huss, Hermann Carl O.	83	.25	Modern Language Series
	Götz von Berlichingen	Holt/Goodrich, Frank P.	170	.70	
	Iphigenie auf Tauris	Ginn/Allen, Phillip S.	218	.60	International Modern Language Series
	Iphigenie auf Tauris	Macmillan/Eggert, Charles A.	178	.60	German Classics
	Iphigenie auf Tauris	Holt/Winkler, Max	211	.60	
Hauptmann, Gerhart	Die versunkene Glocke	Holt/Baker, Thomas S.	206		
Heine, Heinrich	Poems	Ginn/Eggert, Carl Edgar	233		International Modern Language Series
	Prose	Macmillan/Faust, Albert B.	341		German Series

334

Heyse, Paul	Das Mädchen von Treppi	Heath/Joynes, Edward S.	124		Modern Language Series
	L'Arrabbiata	Allyn and Bacon/Bacon, Paul Valentine	116	.50	Allyn and Bacon's German Texts
Hillern, Wilhelmine von	Höher als die Kirche	Heath/Clary, Stedman W.	105	.25	Modern Language Series
	Höher als die Kirche	Ginn/Eastman, Clarence W.	107	.30	International Modern Language Series
Jensen, Wilhelm	Die braune Erika	Heath/Joynes, Edward S.	101	.35	Modern Language Series
Keller, Gottfried	Kleider machen Leute	Heath/Lambert, Marcus B.	140		Modern Language Series
Lessing, G. E.	Hamburgische Dramaturgie	Holt/Harris, Charles	356		
	Minna von Barnhelm	Holt/Nichols, Alfred Bull	212		
	Minna von Barnhelm	Macmillan/Cutting, Starr Willard	224		German Classics
Ludwig, Otto	Zwischen Himmel und Erde	Heath/Meyer, Edward S.	240		Modern Language Series
Moser, Gustav von	Ein amerikanisches Duell, with Müller's Im Wartesalon erster Klasse, Pohl's Die Schulreiterin and Rosen's Ein Knopf In: Four German Comedies	Ginn/Allen, Phillip S., and Edward Manley	210	.45	International Modern Language Series
Müller, Hugo	Im Wartesalon erster Klasse, with Moser's Ein amerikanisches Duell, Pohl's Die Schulreiterin and Rosen's Ein Knopf In: Four German Comedies	Ginn/Allen, Phillip S., and Edward Manley	210	.45	International Modern Language Series

APPENDIX F (Continued)

Author	Title	Publisher/Editor	Pages	Price	Series and Contents
Müller, Max	Deutsche Liebe	Ginn/Johnston, James C.	185	.45	International Modern Language Series
Pohl, Emil	Die Schulreiterin, with Moser's Ein amerikanisches Duell, Müller's Im Wartesalon erster Klasse, and Rosen's Ein Knopf In: Four German Comedies	Ginn/Allen, Phillip S., and Edward Manley	210	.45	International Modern Language Series
Raspe, Rudolf E.	Münchhausen: Reisen und Abenteuer	Heath/Schmidt, Friedrich G.	123	.30	Modern Language Series
Riehl, Wilhelm H.	Der Fluch der Schönheit	Heath/Thomas, Calvin	116	.30	Modern Language Series
	Die vierzehn Nothelfer	Ginn/Raschen, Frederick L.	79	.25	International Modern Language Series
Rosen, Julius	Ein Knopf, with Moser's Ein amerikanisches Duell, Müller's Im Wartesalon erster Klasse and Pohl's Die Schulreiterin In: Four German Comedies	Ginn/Allen, Phillip S., and Edward Manley	210	.45	International Modern Language Series
Saar, Ferdinand	Die Steinklopfer	Holt/Handschin, Charles H., and Edwin C. Roedder	117	.35	
Scheffel, Joseph Viktor von	Der Trompeter von Säkkingen	Ginn/Sanborn, Herbert C.	590	.90	International Modern Language Series
	Ekkehard. Geschichte aus dem zehnten Jahrhundert	Heath/Wenckebach, Carla	235		Modern Language Series
Schiller, J. C. F. von	Der Neffe als Onkel	Maynard and Merrill/Sanborn, Herbert C.	199	.45	

	Die Jungfrau von Orleans	Heath/Wells, Benjamin W.	292		Modern Language Series
	Maria Stuart	Macmillan/Schoenfeld, Hermann	322		German Classics
	Wilhelm Tell	American Book/ Roedder, Edwin C.	352	.70	
	Wilhelm Tell	Heath/Deering, Robert W.			Modern Language Series
Seidel, Heinrich	Aus goldenen Tagen	Heath/Bernhardt, Wilhelm	144	.35	Modern Language Series. Includes: Der Lindenbaum, Die alte Gouvernante, Daniel Siebenstern
Spyri, Johanna	Moni der Geißbub	Heath/Guerber, Helene A.	74	.25	Modern Language Series
	Rosenresli	Heath/Boll, Helene H.	62	.25	Modern Language Series
Storm, Theodor	Im Sonnenschein and Ein grünes Blatt	American Book/ Swiggett, Glen L.	78		
	Immensee	Heath/Bernhardt, Wilhelm	120		Modern Language Series
Sudermann, Hermann	Teja	Heath/Ford, Richard Clyde	69	.25	Modern Language Series
Wildenbruch, Ernst von	Das edle Blut	Heath/Schmidt, Friedrich G.	52		Modern Language Series
	Das edle Blut	Holt/Hardy, Ashley K.	112		
	Der Letzte	Heath/Schmidt, Friedrich G.	73	.35	Modern Language Series

1907

Baumbach, Rudolf	Das Habichtsfräulein	Heath/Bernhardt, Wilhelm	191	.40	Modern Language Series
	Der Schwiegersohn	Heath/Bernhardt, Wilhelm	187	.40	Modern Language Series
	Die Nonna. Blaustrumpfgeschichte	Heath/Bernhardt, Wilhelm	97	.30	Modern Language Series

APPENDIX F (*Continued*)

Author	Title	Publisher/Editor	Pages	Price	Series and Contents
Benedix, Roderich	Waldnovellen	Heath/Bernhardt, Wilhelm	155	.35	Modern Language Series. Includes: Das stählerne Schloß, Warum die Großmutter nicht schreiben kann, Sankt Huberti Wunder, Schleierweiß, Der Kobold im Keller, Die gefangene Drude
	Eigensinn and Wilhelmi's Einer muß heiraten	Holt/Hervey, William A.	124	.25	Modern Language Series
Blüthgen, Viktor	Das Peterle von Nürnberg	Heath/Bernhardt, Wilhelm	144	.35	Modern Language Series
Chamisso, Adelbert von	Peter Schlemihls wundersame Geschichte	Heath/Primer, Sylvester	96	.25	Modern Language Series
Freytag, Gustav	Aus dem Staat Friedrichs des Großen	Heath/Hager, Hermann	115	.30	Modern Language Series
	Die Ahnen. Erster Teil: Die Ingo	Macmillan/Siepmann, Otto	263	.90	Siepmann's German Series
	Die Journalisten	Heath/Toy, Walter Dallam	191	.30	Modern Language Series
Frommel, Emil	Eingeschneit. Studentengeschichte	Heath/Bernhardt, Wilhelm	114	.30	Modern Language Series
Fulda, Ludwig	Das verlorene Paradies	Ginn/Grumman, Paul H.	194	.45	International Modern Language Series
	Der Talisman	Heath/Prettyman, Cornelius	125	.35	Modern Language Series
Gerstäcker, Friedrich	Germelshausen	Heath/Lewis, Orlando F.	100	.25	Modern Language Series
Goethe, J. W. von	Faust. Erster Teil	Holt/Goebel, Julius	384	1.12	Modern Language Series
	Hermann und Dorothea	Heath/Adams, Warren A.	189	.65	Modern Language Series
	Herman und Dorothea	Macmillan/Hatfield, James Taft	187	.60	German Classics

338

	Iphigenie auf Tauris	Ginn/Allen, Phillip S.	218	.60	International Modern Language Series
	Torquato Tasso	Heath/Thomas, Calvin	181	.75	Heath's German Series
Grillparzer, Franz	Der arme Spielmann	Heath/Howard, William G.	143	.35	Modern Language Series
	Die Ahnfrau	Holt/Heuser, Frederick W. J., and George H. Danton	257	.80	
Grimm, Jakob and Wilhelm	German Stories Retold	American Book/Kern, James R., and Minna M. Kern	95	.30	
	Kinder- und Hausmärchen	Heath/Smissen, W. H. van der			Modern Language Series
Hauff, Wilhelm	Lichtenstein	Heath/Vogel, Frank	274		Modern Language Series
Heine, Heinrich	Die Harzreise	Heath/Vos, Bert John	196	.45	Modern Language Series
	Lieder und Gedichte	Macmillan/Buchheim, Carl Adolf	376		
	Poems	Heath/White, Horatio S.			Modern Language Series
Heyse, Paul	Das Mädchen von Treppi	Holt/Brusie, Charles F.	111	.25	
Hillern, Wilhelmine von	Höher als die Kirche	Heath/Clary, Stedman W.	121	.30	Modern Language Series
Hoffmann, E. T. A.	Das Fräulein von Scuderi	Holt/Gruener, Gustav	105	.35	
	Meister Martin der Küfner	Holt/Fife, Robert H.	132	.35	
Keller, Gottfried	Das Fähnlein der sieben Aufrechten	Heath/Howard, William G., and Albert M. Sturtevant	170	.40	Modern Language Series
	Romeo und Julia auf dem Dorfe	Heath/Adams, Warren A.	120	.30	Modern Language Series
Leander, Richard (Volkmann, Richard von)	Träumereien an französischen Kaminen	Holt/Watson, Idelle B.	170		

APPENDIX F (Continued)

Author	Title	Publisher/Editor	Pages	Price	Series and Contents
	Träumereien an französischen Kaminen	Heath/Smissen, W. H. van der	185		Modern Language Series. Includes: Der kleine Vogel, Das kleine bucklige Mädchen, Die himmlische Musik, Die künstliche Orgel, Der Wunschring, Die drei Schwestern mit den gläsernen Herzen, Von der Königin, die keine Pfeffernüsse backen, und dem König, der nicht das Brummeisen spielen konnte, Vom unsichtbaren Königreiche, Pechvogel und Glückskind, Die Traumbuche, Der kleine Mohr und die Goldprinzessin
Lessing, G. E.	Emilia Galotti	Heath/Winkler, Max	128		Modern Language Series
	Minna von Barnhelm	Holt/Whitney, William D.	191		Whitney's German Texts
	Minna von Barnhelm	Appleton/Wilson, Charles B.	196	.60	Twentieth Century Textbooks
	Minna von Barnhelm	Merrill/Allen, Phillip S.	285		Merrill's German Texts
Liliencron, Detlev von	Anno 1870. Kriegsbilder	Heath/Bernhardt, Wilhelm	138		Modern Language Series
Meyer, Conrad F.	Der Heilige	Holt/Eggert, Carl Edgar	215	.80	
Moltke, H. K. B. von	Die beiden Freunde	Holt/Jessen, Karl Detlef	140	.35	
Moser, Gustav von	Der Bibliothekar	Heath/Wells, Benjamin W.	138		Modern Language Series
Riehl, Wilhelm H.	Burg Neideck	Heath/Jonas, Johannes B. E.	139	.35	Modern Language Series
	Das Spielmannskind and Der stumme Ratsherr	Heath/Eaton, Abbie Fiske	167		Modern Language Series

Author	Title	Editor	No.	Price	Series
Scheffel, Joseph Viktor von	Der Trompeter von Säkkingen	Ginn/Sanborn, Herbert C.	590	.90	International Modern Language Series
Schiller, J. C. F. von	Das Lied von der Glocke	Heath/Chamberlin, Willis A.	43		Modern Language Series
	Der Neffe als Onkel	Maynard and Merrill/Sanborn, Herbert C.	199	.45	
	Die Jungfrau von Orleans	Heath/Wells, Benjamin W.	226		Modern Language Series
	Die Jungfrau von Orleans	Appleton/Rhoades, Lewis A.	276		Twentieth Century Textbooks
	Die Jungfrau von Orleans	Macmillan/Humphreys, Willard C.	259		German Classics
	Wallensteins Tod	Heath/Eggert, Charles A.	189		Modern Language Series
	Wilhelm Tell	Macmillan/Carruth, William H.	317		German Classics
Seidel, Heinrich	Aus goldenen Tagen	Heath/Bernhardt, Wilhelm	144	.35	Modern Language Series. Includes: Der Lindenbaum, Die alte Gouvernante, Daniel Siebenstern
Storm, Theodor	In St. Jürgen	Heath/Wright, Arthur S.	129		Modern Language Series
Sudermann, Hermann	Johannes	Heath/Schmidt, Friedrich G.	126		Modern Language Series
	Teja	Heath/Ford, Richard Clyde	69	.25	Modern Language Series
Uhland, Ludwig	Poems	Macmillan/Hewett, Waterman T.	352		German Classics
Wilhelmi, Alexander (Zechmeister, Alexander Viktor)	Einer muß heiraten and Benedix's Eigensinn	Holt/Hervey, William A.	124	.25	
Zschokke, Heinrich	Das Abenteuer der Neujahrsnacht	Heath/Handschin, Charles H.	130	.35	Modern Language Series
	Der zerbrochene Krug	Heath/Joynes, Edward S.	80	.25	Modern Language Series

APPENDIX F *(Continued)*

1908

Author	Title	Publisher/Editor	Pages	Price	Series and Contents
Arnold, Hans (Bülow, Babette von)	Fritz auf Ferien	American Book/Thomas, May		.25	
Auerbach, Berthold	Brigitta	Ginn/Gore, J. Howard		.55	International Modern Language Series
Baumbach, Rudolf	Der Schwiegersohn	Holt/Heller, Otto	235	.40	
Benedix, Roderich	Die Hochzeitsreise	Heath/Schiefferdecker, Natalie	94	.25	Modern Language Series
	Nein	Heath/Werner-Spanhoofd, Arnold	69	.25	Modern Language Series
Biedermann, Friedrich Karl	Deutsche Bildungszustände	Holt/Walz, John A.	205	.70	
Blüthgen, Viktor	Der Rügenfahrer In: Der Weg zum Glück	Heath/Bernhardt, Wilhelm	177	.40	Modern Language Series
Böhlau, Helene	Ratsmädelgeschichten	Heath/Haevernick, Emma	50	.40	Modern Language Series
Campe, Joachim H.	Robinson der Jüngere	Heath/Ibershoff, Carl Henry	201	.40	Modern Language Series
Ebner-Eschenbach, Marie von	Lotti die Uhrmacherin	Holt/Needler, George Henry	162	.35	
Eckstein, Ernst	Der Besuch im Carcer and Wildenbruch's Das edle Blut	Ginn/Sanborn, Herbert C.	239	.50	International Modern Language Series
Elz, Alexander	Er ist nicht eifersüchtig	Heath/Wells, Benjamin W.	57	.20	Modern Language Series
Ernst, Otto (Schmidt, Otto Ernst)	Überwunden	Holt/Hatfield, James Taft	66	.30	

342

Author	Title	Editor	Pages	Price	Series
Eschstruth, Nataly von	Ihr Ideal and Eine Plauderstunde auf der "Seehalde" In: Auf der Sonnenseite	Heath/Bernhardt, Wilhelm	146	.35	Modern Language Series
Freytag, Gustav	Aus dem Staat Friedrichs des Großen	Heath/Hager, Hermann	115	.30	Modern Language Series
	Die Journalisten	Heath/Toy, Walter Dallam	191	.30	Modern Language Series
	Soll und Haben	Heath/Files, George Taylor	255	.65	Modern Language Series
Frommel, Emil	Das eiserne Kreuz In: Auf der Sonnenseite	Heath/Bernhardt, Wilhelm	146	.35	Modern Language Series
	Eingeschneit. Studentengeschichte	Heath/Bernhardt, Wilhelm	114	.30	Modern Language Series
Gerstäcker, Friedrich	Irrfahrten	Heath/Sturm, Frederick B.	203	.45	Modern Language Series
Goethe, J. W. von	Hermann und Dorothea	Merrill/Minckwitz, Richard A. von	268	.60	Merrill's German Texts
	Hermann und Dorothea	Heath/Hewett, Waterman T.	243	1.00	Modern Language Series
	Hermann und Dorothea	American Book/Hewett, Waterman T.	328	.60	
	Iphigenie auf Tauris	Heath/Rhoades, Lewis A.	139	.70	Modern Language Series
	Iphigenie auf Tauris	Holt/Winkler, Max	211	.60	
	The Vicar of Sesenheim	Holt/Nichols, Alfred Bull	164	.35	
	Torquato Tasso	Ginn/Coar, John Firman	327	.80	International Modern Language Series
Grillparzer, Franz	Der Traum ein Leben	Heath/Meyer, Edward S.	128	.60	Modern Language Series
Grimm, Jakob and Wilhelm	German Stories Retold	American Book/Kern, James R., and Minna M. Kern	95	.30	

APPENDIX F (*Continued*)

Author	Title	Publisher/Editor	Pages	Price	Series and Contents
Hauff, Wilhelm	Der Zwerg Nase	Heath	38		
Heine, Heinrich	Die Harzreise	Heath/Vos, Bert John	196	.45	Modern Language Series
	Die Harzreise	American Book/Kolbe, Parke R.	272	.50	
Heyse, Paul	Die Blinden	Holt/Carruth, William H.	131	.35	
	Er soll dein Herr sein	American Book/Haertel, Martin H.	106	.30	
	Hochzeit auf Capri	Heath/Bernhardt, Wilhelm	128	.30	Modern Language Series
	L'Arrabbiata	Heath/Bernhardt, Wilhelm	86	.25	Modern Language Series
Hillern, Wilhelmine von	Höher als die Kirche	Heath/Clary, Stedman W.	121		Modern Language Series
Hoffmann, E. T. A.	Meister Martin der Küfner	Holt/Fife, Robert Herndon	132	.35	
Jensen, Wilhelm	Die braune Erika	Heath/Joynes, Edward S.	142	.35	Modern Language Series
Leander, Richard (Volkmann, Richard von)	Träumereien an französischen Kaminen	Ginn/Jonas, Johannes B. E., and Anne T. Weeden	243	.40	International Modern Language Series. Includes: Der kleine Vogel, Das kleine bucklige Mädchen, Die himmlische Musik, Die künstliche Orgel, Der Wunschring, Die drei Schwestern mit den gläsernen Herzen, Von der Königin, die keine Pfeffernüsse backen, und dem König, der nicht das Brummeisen spielen konnte, Vom unsichtbaren Königreiche, Pechvogel und Glückskind, Die Traumbuche, Der kleine Mohr und die Goldprinzessin

344

Author	Title	Editor	Pages	Price	Series
Lessing, G. E.	Minna von Barnhelm	Holt/Nichols, Alfred Bull	212		Modern Language Series
	Minna von Barnhelm	Heath/Primer, Sylvester	218		Modern Language Series
	Nathan der Weise	Macmillan/Curme, George O.	300		German Classics
Lohmeyer, Julius	Tot oder Lebendig In: Der Weg zum Glück	Heath/Bernhardt, Wilhelm	177	.40	Modern Language Series
Moltke, H. K. B. von	Die beiden Freunde	Holt/Jessen, Karl Detlef	140	.35	
Moser, Gustav von	Der Bibliothekar Ultimo	Holt/Farr, Hollon A. Holt/Crow, Charles L.	176 213	.40 .35	
Riehl, Wilhelm H.	Das Spielmannskind and Der stumme Ratsherr	Heath/Eaton, Abbie Fiske	167		Modern Language Series
	Der Fluch der Schönheit	Heath/Thomas, Calvin	116		Modern Language Series
	Der Fluch der Schönheit	Ginn/Leonard, Arthur N.	137	.40	International Modern Language Series
Schiller, J. C. F. von	Ballads and Lyrics	American Book/ Rhoades, Lewis A.	264	.60	
	Der Geisterseher. Erstes Buch	Heath/Joynes, Edward S.	126		Modern Language Series
	Der Neffe als Onkel	Holt/Sturm, Frederick B.	112	.35	
	Der Neffe als Onkel	Heath/Beredsford-Webb, H. S.	121		Modern Language Series
	Die Jungfrau von Orleans	Heath/Wells, Benjamin W.	292		Modern Language Series
	Wilhelm Tell	Macmillan/Carruth, William H.	317		German Classics
	Wilhelm Tell	Heath/Deering, Robert W.	333	.75	Modern Language Series
Seidel, Heinrich	Der ruhige Mieter and Wie man einen Weinreisenden los wird In: Auf der Sonnenseite	Heath/Bernhardt, Wilhelm	146	.35	Modern Language Series

APPENDIX F (Continued)

Author	Title	Publisher/Editor	Pages	Price	Series and Contents
Spyri, Johanna	Moni der Geißbub	Heath/Guerber, Helene A.	74	.25	Modern Language Series
Storm, Theodor	Der Schimmelreiter	Ginn/MacGillivray, John, and Edward J. Williamson	331	.70	International Modern Language Series
Sudermann, Hermann	Der Gänsehirt In: Auf der Sonnenseite	Heath/Bernhardt, Wilhelm	146	.35	Modern Language Series
	Frau Sorge	Holt/Gruener, Gustav	268		
Wildenbruch, Ernst von	Das edle Blut	Heath/Schmidt, Friedrich G.	52		Modern Language Series
	Das edle Blut and Eckstein's Der Besuch im Carcer	Ginn/Sanborn, Herbert C.	239	.50	International Modern Language Series
	Der Letzte	Heath/Schmidt, Friedrich G.			Modern Language Series
	Neid	Heath/Prettyman, Cornelius	128	.35	Modern Language Series

1909

Arndt, Ernst M.	Deutsche Patrioten in Rußland	Heath/Colwell, William A.		.30	Modern Language Series
Auerbach, Berthold	Die Kriegspfeife In: Baker's German Stories	Holt/Baker, George Merrick	228	.40	
Baumbach, Rudolf	Das Habichtsfräulein	Holt/Stewart, Morton C.	224	.40	
	Der Schwiegersohn	Ginn/Hulme, Hedwig	186	.40	International Modern Language Series
	Nicotiana und andere Erzählungen	Heath/Bernhardt, Wilhelm	106	.30	Modern Language Series
Benedix, Roderich	Eigensinn	Oxford University Press		.15	

Blüthgen, Viktor	Der Rügenfahrer In: Der Weg zum Glück	Heath/Bernhardt, Wilhelm	177	.40	Modern Language Series
Chamisso, Adelbert von	Peter Schlemihls wundersame Geschichte	Heath/Primer, Sylvester	96	.25	Modern Language Series
Eichendorff, Joseph von	Aus dem Leben eines Taugenichts	Heath/Osthaus, Carl Wilhelm	235		Modern Language Series
Ernst, Otto (Schmidt, Otto Ernst)	Wie man sich bildet	Oxford University Press		.15	
Freytag, Gustav	Die Journalisten	Heath/Toy, Walter Dallam	191	.30	Modern Language Series
Frommel, Emil	Die Journalisten	Holt/Thomas, Calvin	224	.35	College Series of German Plays
	Eingeschneit. Studentengeschichte	Heath/Bernhardt, Wilhelm	114	.30	Modern Language Series
	Mit Ränzel und Wanderstab	Heath/Bernhardt, Wilhelm	144	.35	Modern Language Series
Gerstäcker, Friedrich	Germelshausen, with Seidel's Der Lindenbaum and Storm's Immensee	Scott, Foresman/ Manley, Edward	197	.50	Lake German Series
	Germelshausen	Heath/Lewis, Orlando F.	100	.25	Modern Language Series
Goethe, J. W. von	Goethe in Italy. Extracts from the Italienische Reise	Holt/Nichols, Alfred Bull	125	.40	
	Hermann und Dorothea	Heath/Adams, Warren A.	189	.65	Modern Language Series
	Poems	Holt/Goebel, Julius	244	.80	
	Torquato Tasso	Holt/Thomas, Calvin	181	.75	Heath's German Series
	Eine Hochzeitsnacht In: Baker's German Stories	Holt/Baker, George Merrick	228	.40	
Goldhammer, Leo	Märchen and Schiller's Der Taucher	Heath/Smissen, W. H. van der	214	.65	Modern Language Series
Grimm, Jakob and Wilhelm	Lichtenstein	Heath/Vogel, Frank	274		Modern Language Series
Hauff, Wilhelm	Das Mädchen von Treppi	Heath/Joynes, Edward S.	124		Modern Language Series
Heyse, Paul	L'Arrabbiata	Heath/Bernhardt, Wilhelm	91	.25	Modern Language Series

347

APPENDIX F (*Continued*)

Author	Title	Publisher/Editor	Pages	Price	Series and Contents
Hillern, Wilhelmine von	Höher als die Kirche	Heath/Clary, Stedman W.	121		Modern Language Series
Jensen, Wilhelm	Die braune Erika	Heath/Joynes, Edward S.	142	.35	Modern Language Series
La Roche, Max von	Ein Todesritt In: Baker's German Stories	Holt/Baker, George Merrick	228	.40	
Leander, Richard (Volkmann, Richard von)	Träumereien an französischen Kaminen	Heath/Smissen, W. H. van der	185		Modern Language Series. Includes: Der kleine Vogel, Das kleine bucklige Mädchen, Die himmlische Musik, Die künstliche Orgel, Der Wunschring, Die drei Schwestern mit den gläsernen Herzen, Von der Königin, die keine Pfeffernüsse backen, und dem König, der nicht das Brummeisen spielen konnte, Vom unsichtbaren Königreiche, Pechvogel und Glückskind, Die Traumbuche, Der kleine Mohr und die Goldprinzessin
	Von Himmel und Hölle In: Baker's German Stories	Holt/Baker, George Merrick	228	.40	
Lessing, G. E.	Emilia Galotti	Heath/Winkler, Max	128		Modern Language Series
	Minna von Barnhelm	Heath/Primer, Sylvester	218		Modern Language Series
	Minna von Barnhelm	Scott, Foresman/Heller, Otto	293	.50	Lake German Classics
Lohmeyer, Julius	Tot oder lebendig In: Der Weg zum Glück	Heath/Bernhardt, Wilhem	177	.40	Modern Language Series
Ludwig, Otto	Zwischen Himmel und Erde	Heath/Meyer, Edward S.	240		Modern Language Series
Niese, Charlotte	Tante Federsen In: Baker's German Stories	Holt/Baker, George Merrick	228	.40	

Polenz, Wilhelm	Der arme Grule In: Baker's German Stories	Holt/Baker, George Merrick	228	.40	International Modern Language Series
Riehl, Wilhelm H.	Der Fluch der Schönheit	Ginn/Leonard, Arthur N.	137	.40	
Scheffel, Joseph Viktor von	Hugideo In: Baker's German Stories	Holt/Baker, George Merrick	228	.40	Modern Language Series
Schiller, J. C. F. von	Der Taucher and the Grimms' Märchen	Heath/Smissen, W. H. van der	214	.65	Modern Language Series
	Die Jungfrau von Orleans	Heath/Wells, Benjamin W.	292	.70	Modern Language Series
	Die Jungfrau von Orleans	American Book/Florer, Warren W.	375		
	Maria Stuart	Heath/Rhoades, Lewis A.	314		Modern Language Series
	Maria Stuart	Ginn/Nollen, John Scholte	361	.75	International Modern Language Series
	Wallenstein Trilogie	Macmillan/Winkler, Max	446		
	Wallensteins Tod	Heath/Eggert, Charles A.	189		Modern Language Series
	Wilhelm Tell	Macmillan/Carruth, William H.	317		German Classics
	Wilhelm Tell	Heath/Deering, Robert W.	333	.75	Modern Language Series
Seidel, Heinrich	Der Lindenbaum, with Gerstäcker's Germelshausen and Storm's Immensee	Scott, Foresman/Manley, Edward	197	.50	Lake German Series
Stökl, Helene	Alle fünf	Heath/Bernhardt, Wilhelm	101	.30	Modern Language Series
	Unter dem Christbaum	Heath/Bernhardt, Wilhelm	168	.60	Modern Language Series. Includes: Vom Bübchen vor der Himmelsthür, Der vergessene Koffer, Eingeschneit, In der Weihnachtszeit, Am Heiligen Abend

APPENDIX F *(Continued)*

Author	Title	Publisher/Editor	Pages	Price	Series and Contents
Storm, Theodor	Immensee	Heath/Bernhardt, Wilhelm	120		Modern Language Series
	Immensee, with Gerstäcker's Germelshausen and Seidel's Der Lindenbaum	Scott, Foresman/ Manley, Edward	197	.50	Lake German Series
Sudermann, Hermann	Der Katzensteg	Heath/Wells, Benjamin W.	203		Modern Language Series
	Heimat	Heath/Schmidt, Friedrich G.	129	.35	Modern Language Series
	Teja	Heath/Ford, Richard Clyde	69	.25	Modern Language Series
Viebig, Clara	Jaschu In: Baker's German Stories	Holt/Baker, George Merrick	228	.40	
Wildenbruch, Ernst von	Das edle Blut	Heath/Schmidt, Friedrich G.	84		Modern Language Series
Zschokke, Heinrich	Das Abenteuer der Neujahrsnacht	Heath/Handschin, Charles H.	130		Modern Language Series
	Der zerbrochene Krug and Das Wirtshaus zu Cransac	Allyn and Bacon/ Manley, Edward	160	.50	Allyn and Bacon's German Texts

191-

| Benedix, Roderich | Der Weiberfeind, with Elz's Er ist nicht eifersüchtig and Müllers Im Wartesalon erster Klasse | Holt | 82 | .50 | |

Elz, Alexander	Er ist nicht eifersüchtig, with Benedix's Der Weiberfeind and Müller's Im Wartesalon erster Klasse	Holt	82	.50
Müller, Hugo	Er ist nicht eifersüchtig Im Wartesalon erster Klasse, with Benedix's Der Weiberfeind and Elz's Er ist nicht eifersüchtig	Holt Holt	32 82	.50	College Series of German Plays
Pohl, Emil	Die Schulreiterin	Steiger/Ahn	47		Ahn's Series of German Comedies

1910

Arnold, Hans (Bülow, Babette von)	Fritz auf Ferien	Heath/Werner-Spanhoofd, Arnold	99	.20	Modern Language Series
Baumbach, Rudolf	Das Habichtsfräulein	Heath/Bernhardt, Wilhelm	191	.40	Modern Language Series
	Das Habichtsfräulein	Holt/Stewart, Morton C.	224	.40	Modern Language Series
	Der Schwiegersohn	Allyn and Bacon/Florer, Warren W., and Edward H. Lauer	260	.60	Allyn and Bacon's German Texts
	Märchen und Gedichte	Ginn/Manley, Edward	209	.45	International Modern Language Series
Benedix, Roderich	Der Prozeß	Heath/Wells, Benjamin W.	61	.20	Modern Language Series
Blüthgen, Viktor	Der Rügenfahrer In: Der Weg zum Glück	Heath/Bernhardt, Wilhelm	177	.40	Modern Language Series
Bruneck, Otto von (Elster, Otto)	Zwischen den Schlachten	Macmillan/Hirsch, Ludwig	254	.75	Siepmann's German Series
Droste-Hülshoff, Annette von	Die Judenbuche	Oxford University Press/Eckelmann, Ernst O.	161	.60	Oxford German Series

APPENDIX F *(Continued)*

Author	Title	Publisher/Editor	Pages	Price	Series and Contents
Freytag, Gustav	Die Journalisten	Appleton/Bronson, Thomas B.	194	.45	Twentieth Century Textbooks
Fulda, Ludwig	Der Dummkopf	Holt/Stewart, William K.	179	.35	
	Der Talisman	Heath/Prettyman, Cornelius	125	.35	Modern Language Series
Gerstäcker, Friedrich	Germelshausen	American Book/Busse, Adolf	121	.30	
	Irrfahrten	Heath/Sturm, Frederick B.	203	.45	Modern Language Series
Goebel, Ferdinand	Rübezahl	Macmillan/Hurley, Daniel B.	173	.35	Siepmann's German Series
Goethe, J. W. von	Einführung in Goethe's [sic]Meisterwerke	Heath/Bernhardt, Wilhelm	275	1.50	Modern Language Series
	Götz von Berlichingen and Zu Shakespeares Namenstag	Ginn/Hildner, Karl August	225	.80	International Modern Language Series
	Hermann und Dorothea	Heath/Adams, Warren A.	189	.65	Modern Language Series
	Iphigenie auf Tauris	Macmillan/Cotterill, Henry B.	183	.70	Siepmann's German Series
	Selections, with selections by Herder and Lessing's Laokoon	Holt/Howard, William Guild	470	1.50	
Grillparzer, Franz	König Ottokars Glück und Ende	Holt/Eggert, Carl Edgar	184	.60	
Gutzkow, Karl F.	Uriel Acosta	Holt/Cutting, Starr W., and Adolf Carl von Noé	105	.35	
	Zopf und Schwert	Holt/Lange, Franz	163		College Series of German Plays
Hauff, Wilhelm	Lichtenstein	Heath/Vogel, Frank	274		Modern Language Series
	Lichtenstein	Holt/King, James P.	363	.80	

352

Author	Title	Editor/Publisher	Pages	Price	Series
Heine, Heinrich	Prose	Macmillan/Faust, Albert B.	341		German Series
Herder, J. G.	Selections, with selections by Goethe and Lessing's Laokoon	Holt/Howard, William Guild	470	1.50	
Heyse, Paul	Anfang und Ende	Ginn/Busse, Adolf	119	.35	International Modern Language Series
	Anfang und Ende	Holt/McLouth, Lawrence A.	165	.40	
Hillern, Wilhelmine von	Niels mit der offenen Hand	Heath/Joynes, Edward S.	105		Modern Language Series
	Höher als die Kirche	Heath/Clary, Stedman W.	121		Modern Language Series
	Höher als die Kirche	Merrill/Heuser, Frederick W. J.	184	.50	Merrill's German Texts
Hoffmann, Hans F.	Der faule Beppo In: Stille Wasser	Heath/Bernhardt, Wilhelm	149	.35	Modern Language Series
Jensen, Wilhelm	Die braune Erika	Heath/Joynes, Edward S.	142	.35	Modern Language Series
Keller, Gottfried	Romeo und Julia auf dem Dorfe	Heath/Adams, Warren A.		.30	Modern Language Series
Krane, Anna von	Solitaria In: Stille Wasser	Heath/Bernhardt, Wilhelm	149	.35	Modern Language Series
Kurz, Isolde	Die Humanisten	Macmillan/Voegelin, Ada	141	.35	Siepmann's German Series
Lessing, G. E.	Emilia Galotti	Heath/Winkler, Max	128		Modern Language Series
	Laokoon, with selections by Goethe and Herder	Holt/Howard, William Guild	470	1.50	
	Minna von Barnhelm	Oxford University Press/Wiehr, Josef	239	.60	Oxford German Series
	Nathan der Weise	Heath/Primer, Sylvester	300		Modern Language Series
Lohmeyer, Julius	Tot oder lebendig In: Der Weg zum Glück	Heath/Bernhardt, Wilhelm	177	.40	Modern Language Series

353

APPENDIX F *(Continued)*

Author	Title	Publisher/Editor	Pages	Price	Series and Contents
Ludwig, Otto	Der Erbförster	Holt/Stewart, Morton C.	159	.35	
Mügge, Theodor	Riukan-Voss	Holt	55		
Ries, Clara E.	Easy German Stories	American Book/Bierman, Ernest H.	183	.35	
Schiller, J. C. F. von	Die Jungfrau von Orleans	Ginn/Allen, Phillip S., and Steven T. Byington	334	.70	International Modern Language Series
	Geschichte des Dreißigjährigen Kriegs	Heath/Prettyman, Cornelius	170		Modern Language Series
	Maria Stuart	Heath/Rhoades, Lewis A.	314		Modern Language Series
	Wilhelm Tell	Heath/Deering, Robert W.	333	.75	Modern Language Series
Schönberg, Hans	Die Schildbürger	Heath/Betz, Frederick	126	.35	Modern Language Series
Schrader, Friedrich	Friedrich der Große und der Siebenjährige Krieg	Macmillan/Allpress, Robert H.	161	.35	Siepmann's German Series
Spyri, Johanna	Was der Großmutter Lehre bewirkt	Heath/Barrows, Sarah T.	73	.30	Modern Language Series
Storm, Theodor	Auf der Universität	Holt/Corwin, Robert N.	198	.35	
	Immensee	Heath/Bernhardt, Wilhelm	120		Modern Language Series
	In St. Jürgen	Heath/Wright, Arthur Silas	129		Modern Language Series
Sudermann, Hermann	Der Katzensteg	Heath/Wells, Benjamin W.	203		Modern Language Series
Wachenhusen, Hans	Vom ersten bis zum letzten Schuß	Macmillan/Bayley, Thomas H.	169	.35	Siepmann's German Series
Wildenbruch, Ernst von	Das edle Blut	Macmillan/Siepmann, Otto	135	.35	Siepmann's German Series

	Das Orakel In: Stille Wasser	Heath/Bernhardt, Wilhelm	149	.35	Modern Language Series
	Der Letzte	Heath/Schmidt, Friedrich G.	115	.35	Modern Language Series
Zastrow, Karl	Wilhelm der Siegreiche	Macmillan/Ash, E. P.	192	.35	Siepmann's German Series

1911

Andersen, H. C.	Märchen	Heath/Super, Ovando B.		.90	Modern Language Series
Baumbach, Rudolf	Der Schwiegersohn und andere Erzählungen	Scott, Foresman/Manley, Edward	224	.50	Lake German Classics. Includes: Die Siebenmeilenstiefel, Der Eselsbrunnen, Der Schwiegersohn
	Die Nonna. Blaustrumpfgeschichte	Heath/Bernhardt, Wilhelm	97	.30	Modern Language Series
Benedix, Roderich	Der Prozeß and Günstige Vorzeichen, with Wilhemi's Einer muß heiraten In: Drei kleine Lustspiele Nein	Heath/Wells, Benjamin W.			Modern Language Series
		Heath/Werner-Spanhoofd, Arnold	69	.25	Modern Language Series
Blüthgen, Viktor	Mama kommt and Schanz's Die Alte	Scott, Foresman/Betz, Frederick	168	.50	Lake German Classics
Böhlau, Helene	Ratsmädelgeschichten	Heath/Haevernick, Emma	50	.40	Modern Language Series
Chamisso, Adelbert von	Peter Schlemihls wundersame Geschichte	Heath/Primer, Sylvester	96	.25	Modern Language Series
Eichendorff, Joseph von	Aus dem Leben eines Taugenichts	Heath/Osthaus, Carl Wilhelm	235		Modern Language Series
	Grete Minde	Holt/Hewett-Thayer, Harvey	184		
Fontane, Theodor	Vor dem Sturm	Macmillan/Weiss, Aloys	268	.75	

355

APPENDIX F (*Continued*)

Author	Title	Publisher/Editor	Pages	Price	Series and Contents
Freytag, Gustav	Aus dem Staat Friedrichs des Großen	Heath/Hager, Hermann	115	.30	Modern Language Series
	Die Journalisten	Merrill/Potter, Henry A.	264	.60	Merrill's German Texts
	Karl der Große/Aus dem Klosterleben/Aus den Kreuzzügen	Holt/Nichols, Alfred Bull	200	.75	
	Soll und Haben	Heath/Files, George Taylor	255	.65	Modern Language Series
Fulda, Ludwig	Der Talisman	Ginn/Manthey-Zorn, Otto	239	.45	International Modern Language Series
Gerstäcker, Friedrich	Germelshausen	Heath/Lewis, Orlando F.	100	.25	Modern Language Series
Goethe, J. W. von	Hermann und Dorothea	Heath/Adams, Warren A.	189	.65	Modern Language Series
Hauff, Wilhelm	Lichtenstein	Heath/Vogel, Frank	274		Modern Language Series
Hebbel, Friedrich	Agnes Bernauer	Oxford University Press/Klenze, Camillo von	178	.60	Oxford German Series
Heine, Heinrich	Die Harzreise	Heath/Vos, Bert John	196	.45	Modern Language Series
Heyse, Paul	Das Mädchen von Treppi	Heath/Joynes, Edward S.	124		Modern Language Series
	Hochzeit auf Capri	Merrill/Robson, Charles W.	135	.40	Merrill's German Texts
	L'Arrabbiata	Ginn/Byington, Steven T.	82	.30	International Modern Language Series
	Vetter Gabriel	Holt/Corwin, Robert N.	216	.35	
Hoffmann, Hans F.	Das Gymnasium zu Stolpenburg	Heath/Buehner, Valentin	145	.35	Modern Language Series
	Iwan der Schreckliche und sein Hund	Oxford University Press/Poor, Charles M.	344	.60	Oxford German Series

356

Keller, Gottfried	Kleider machen Leute	Heath/Lambert, Marcus B.	140		Modern Language Series
	Zwei Novellen: Die drei gerechten Kammacher, Frau Regel Amrain und ihr Jüngster	Oxford University Press/Kip, Herbert Z.	268	.60	Oxford German Series
Kurz, Isolde	Die Humanisten	Macmillan/Voegelin, Ada	141	.35	Siepmann's German Series
Lessing, G. E.	Minna von Barnhelm	Heath/Primer, Sylvester	218		Modern Language Series
	Nathan der Weise	Macmillan/Curme, George O.	300		German Classics
Lohmeyer, Julius	Geißbub von Engelberg	Heath/Bernhardt, Wilhelm	182		Modern Language Series
Meyer, Conrad F.	Jürg Jenatsch	Heath/Kenngott, Allen	220	.60	Modern Language Series
Moser, Gustav von	Der Bibliothekar	Heath/Wells, Benjamin W.	178		Modern Language Series
Raabe, Wilhelm	Else von der Tanne	Oxford University Press/Pease, Samuel J.	111	.50	
Rosegger, Peter	Der Lex von Gutenhag	Heath/Morgan, Bayard Q.	148	.40	Modern Language Series
Salomon, Ludwig	Die Geschichte einer Geige	Heath/Tombo, Rudolf, and Rudolf Tombo, Jr.	88	.25	Modern Language Series
Schanz, Frida (Soyaux, Frida Schanz)	Die Alte and Blüthgen's Mama kommt	Scott, Foresman/Betz, Frederick	168	.50	Lake German Classics
Scheffel, Joseph Viktor von	Der Trompeter von Säkkingen	Heath/Wenckebach, Carla	181		Modern Language Series
	Ekkehard and Audifax und Hadumoth	American Book/Handschin, Charles H., and William F. Luebke	251	.60	
Schiller, J. C. F. von	Ballads	Heath/Johnson, Henry	165		Modern Language Series
	Der Neffe als Onkel	Heath/Beredsford-Webb, H. S.	109		Modern Language Series

APPENDIX F (Continued)

Author	Title	Publisher/Editor	Pages	Price	Series and Contents
	Die Jungfrau von Orleans	Macmillan/Humphreys, Willard C.	259		German Classics
	Wilhelm Tell	Ginn/Vos, Bert John	387	.70	International Modern Language Series
	Wilhelm Tell (without vocabulary)	Ginn/Vos, Bert John	300	.60	International Modern Language Series
Spyri, Johanna	Moni der Geißbub	Heath/Guerber, Helene A.	74	.25	Modern Language Series
Sudermann, Hermann	Frau Sorge	Holt/Gruener, Gustav	408		
	Frau Sorge	Heath/Leser, Eugene, and Carl Osthaus	353	.90	Modern Language Series
Wichert, Ernst A.	Die verlorene Tochter	Holt/Babbit, Eugene H.	117	.35	
Wildenbruch, Ernst von	Der Letzte	American Book/Beckmann, John H.	139	.30	
	Kindertränen. Zwei Erzählungen: Der Letzte and Die Landpartie	Holt/Vestling, Axel E.	179	.35	
Wilhelmi, Alexander (Zechmeister, Alexander Viktor)	Einer muß heiraten, with Benedix's Der Prozeß and Günstige Vorzeichen In: Drei kleine Lustspiele	Heath/Wells, Benjamin W.			Modern Language Series
Zschokke, Heinrich	Der zerbrochene Krug	Heath/Joynes, Edward S.	80		Modern Language Series

1912

Author	Title	Publisher/Editor	Pages	Price	Series and Contents
Arnold, Hans (Bülow, Babette von)	Einst im Mai	Holt/Lovell, George B.	142	.35	
Baumbach, Rudolf	Das Habichtsfräulein	Heath/Bernhardt, Wilhelm	191	.40	Modern Language Series

	Der Schwiegersohn	Heath/Bernhardt, Wilhelm	187	.40	Modern Language Series
Benedix, Roderich	Es war einmal (stories by Baumbach and Wildenbruch)	American Book/ Bernhardt, Wilhelm	174	.65	
	Im Zwielicht	American Book/ Bernhardt, Wilhelm			
	Doktor Treuwald	Longmans, Green/ Beredsford-Webb, H. S.	188	.60	
Bruneck, Otto von (Elster, Otto)	Doktor Wespe	Holt	116	.25	College Series of German Plays
	Zwischen den Schlachten	Macmillan/Hirsch, Ludwig	254	.75	Siepmann's German Series
Ebner, Theodor	Herr Walther von der Vogelweide	Macmillan/North, E. G.	115	.35	Siepmann's German Series
Eckstein, Ernst	Der Besuch im Carcer	Merrill/Stephens, T. A.	86	.25	
Fouqué, Friedrich de la Motte	Undine	Holt/Jagemann, Hans Carl G.	229	.50	
Fischer, Wilhelm	Die wandelnde Glocke	Maynard and Merrill/ Allpress, Robert H.	96	.25	Mayndard's German Texts
Freytag, Gustav	Aus dem Jahrhundert des großen Krieges	Maynard and Merrill/ Morich, R. J.	126	.40	Maynard's German Texts
	Das Nest der Zaunkönige	Heath/Roedder, Edwin C., and Charles H. Handschin	281	.65	Modern Language Series
Goebel, Ferdinand	Hermann der Cherusker	Macmillan/Esser, G. J.	163	.35	Siepmann's German Series
	Rübezahl	Macmillan/Hurley, Daniel B.	173	.35	Siepmann's German Series
Görner, Karl August	Englisch	Holt/Edgren, August H.	61	.25	
Goethe, J. W. von	Faust. Erster und zweiter Teil	Heath/Thomas, Calvin			Modern Language Series
	Hermann und Dorothea	Putnam		1.00	German Classics for American Students

APPENDIX F *(Continued)*

Author	Title	Publisher/Editor	Pages	Price	Series and Contents
Grillparzer, Franz	Italienische Reise	Merrill/Beredsford-Webb, H. S.	146	.50	
	Des Meeres und der Liebe Wellen	Holt/Schütze, Martin	156	.70	
Grube, August W.	Bilder aus der Turkei	Merrill/Lyon, W. S.	92		
Hauff, Wilhelm	Das kalte Herz	American Book/Holzwarth, Franklin J., and William J. Gorse	168	.35	
	Das kalte Herz	Holt/Beck, George A. D.	87		
	Das kalte Herz	Holt/Brooks, Neil C.	158	.35	
Hebbel, Friedrich	Agnes Bernauer	Heath/Evans, Marshall B.	163	.50	Modern Language Series
Heine, Heinrich	Die Harzreise	Heath/Vos, Bert John	196	.45	Modern Language Series
	Die Harzreise	Holt/Fife, Robert Herndon	342	.50	
	Die Harzreise	Holt/Burnett, A. W.	97	.30	
	Die Harzreise and Das Buch Le Grand	Holt/Fife, Robert Herndon	310	.90	Unterhaltungs-Bibliothek
Heyse, Paul	Anfang und Ende	American Book/Lentz, Max Carl G.	105		
	L'Arrabbiata	Wahr/Florer, Warren W.	85	.35	
Jung-Stilling, Heinrich	Lebensgeschichte	Holt/Stern, Sigmon Martin	285		
Keller, Gottfried	Romeo und Julia auf dem Dorfe	Holt/Corwin, Robert N.	249	.35	
Königswinter, W. M. von	Sie hat ihr Herz entdeckt	Holt/Stern, Sigmon Martin			Selected German Comedies

Author	Title	Editor	Pages	Price	Series
Kotzebue, A. F. F. von	Die deutschen Kleinstädter	Merrill/Matthews, J. H. O., and W. H. Witherby		.40	
Mörike, Eduard	Mozart auf der Reise nach Prag	Ginn/Glascock, Clyde C.	195	.45	International Modern Language Series
Pauli, Reinhold	Zwei ausgewählte Aufsätze: Robert Blake, ein Seestück; Cromwell	Merrill/Corser, Charles W. S.		.40	Merrill's German Texts
Raabe, Wilhelm	Eulenpfingsten	Heath/Lambert, Marcus B.	189	.45	Modern Language Series
Riehl, Wilhelm H.	Die Lehrjahre eines Humanisten	Merrill/Morich, R. J.	102	.40	Merrill's German Texts
	Meister Martin Hildebrand	Merrill/Beredsford-Webb, H. S.	88	.40	Merrill's German Texts
Rosegger, Peter	Waldheimat. Selections	Ginn/Fossler, Laurence	165		International Modern Language Series
Roth, Richard	Ein nordischer Held (Gustav I of Sweden)	American Book/Boll, Helene H.	175	.35	
Scheffel, Joseph Viktor von	Der Trompeter von Säkkingen	Macmillan/Milner-Barry, E. L.		.80	Siepmann's German Series
Schiller, J. C. F. von	Die Jungfrau von Orleans	Appleton/Rhoades, Lewis A.	276		Twentieth Century Textbooks
	Die Jungfrau von Orleans	Hinds and Noble/Hervey, William A.	268		Hinds and Noble's German Classics
	Don Carlos	Oxford University Press/Lieder, Frederick W. C.	585	1.25	Oxford German Series
	Historische Skizzen	Oxford University Press/Buchheim, Emma S.			German Classics. Includes: Egmonts Leben und Tod, Die Belagerung von Antwerpen
	Kabale und Liebe	Holt/Hervey, William A.	279	1.25	
	Wilhelm Tell	Holt/Sachtleben, Augustus		.50	Whitney's German Texts
	Wilhelm Tell	Languages Publishing	265	.25	Ideophonic Texts

APPENDIX F *(Continued)*

Author	Title	Publisher/Editor	Pages	Price	Series and Contents
	Wilhelm Tell	Heath/Deering, Robert W.	333	.75	Modern Language Series
Schrammen, Johannes	Legends of German Heroes	Merrill/Lechner, A. R.	158	.40	
Seidel, Heinrich	Leberecht Hühnchen	Steiger/Ahn	94	.20	Ahn's Series of German Novels
	Weihnachten bei Leberecht Hühnchen	Merrill/Morich, R. J.		.25	
Simrock, Karl	Wieland der Schmied	Oxford University Press/Wilson, A. E.	72	.40	
	Wieland der Schmied	Frowde/Wilson, A. E.	72	.40	
Stökl, Helene	Alle fünf	Heath/Bernhardt, Wilhelm	101	.30	Modern Language Series
Storm, Theodor	Immensee	Holt/Burnett, Arthur W.		.25	
	Immensee	Merrill/Beresford-Webb, H. S.	133	.40	Merrill's German Texts
Tieck, Ludwig	Zwei Märchennovellen: Die Elfen, Das Rothkäppchen	Holt/Simonson, Leopold			
Treitschke, Heinrich von	Das deutsche Ordensland Preußen	Maynard and Merrill/Lyon, Walter S.	139		Maynard's German Texts
Uhland, Ludwig	Poems	Macmillan/Hewett, Waterman T.	352		German Classics
Wildenbruch, Ernst von	Das edle Blut	Heath/Schmidt, Friedrich G.	90	.30	Modern Language Series
	Das edle Blut	Macmillan/Siepmann, Otto	135		Siepmann's German Series
	Das edle Blut and Der Letzte	Allyn and Bacon/Florer, Warren W., and M. R. Shelly	232	.60	Allyn and Bacon's German Texts
	Die Rabensteinerin	Heath/Ford, Richard Clyde	120	.35	
	Es war einmal (stories by Wildenbruch and Baumbach)	American Book/Bernhardt, Wilhelm	174	.65	Modern Language Series

		1913			
Zschokke, Heinrich	Der zerbrochene Krug	Heath/Joynes, Edward S.	80		Modern Language Series
Auerbach, Berthold	Brigitta	Ginn/Gore, J. Howard		.55	International Modern Language Series
Bolt, Niklaus	Peterli am Lift	Heath/Betz, Frederick	142	.40	Modern Language Series
Budde, Ernst	Mannuckerle und Mannickerle In: Aus der Jugendzeit	Heath/Betz, Frederick	159	.40	Modern Language Series
Freytag, Gustav	Die Journalisten	Wahr/Hildner, Karl A. J., and Tobias J. C. Diekhoff	174		
Gerstäcker, Friedrich	Germelshausen	Merrill/Haller, Ralph W.	123	.40	Merrill's German Texts
Grillparzer, Franz	Libussa	Oxford University Press/Curme, George O.	186	.50	Oxford German Series
Hansjakob, Heinrich	Die Heimat, Der Ristehansele und der Hansjörgle, and Wie der Hermesbur gestorben ist In: Schwarzwaldleut'	Holt/Roedder, Edwin Carl	173		
Hauff, Wilhelm	Der Zwerg Nase	Heath/Patzwald, Otto R., and Charles W. Robson	107	.30	Modern Language Series
Hebel, Johann Peter	Schatzkästlein des rheinischen Hausfreundes	American Book/Stern, Menco	179	.40	
Heyse, Paul	L'Arrabbiata	Heath/Bernhardt, Wilhelm; revised by Robert W. Deering	79	.30	Modern Language Series
	L'Arrabbiata	Allyn and Bacon/Bacon, Paul Valentine	116		Allyn and Bacon's German Texts

363

APPENDIX F (Continued)

Author	Title	Publisher/Editor	Pages	Price	Series and Contents
Leander, Richard (Volkmann, Richard von)	Träumereien an französischen Kaminen	American Book/Hanstein, Amalie	172	.35	Includes: Der kleine Vogel, Das kleine bucklige Mädchen, Die himmlische Musik, Die künstliche Orgel, Der Wunschring, Die drei Schwestern mit den gläsernen Herzen, Von der Königin, die keinePfeffernüsse backen, und dem König, der nicht das Brummeisen spielen konnte, Vom unsichtbaren Königreiche, Pechvogel und Glückskind, Die Traumbuche, Der kleine Mohr und die Goldprinzessin
Lienhard, Friedrich	Der Pandurenstein In: Aus der Jugendzeit	Heath/Betz, Frederick	159	.40	Modern Language Series
Meyr, Melchior	Ludwig und Annemarie	Oxford University Press/Schmidt, Friedrich	295	.60	Oxford German Series
Moser, Gustav von	Der Bibliothekar	Ginn/Lieder, Frederick W. C.	218	.45	International Modern Language Series
Niese, Charlotte	Die Seeräuberburg In: Aus der Jugendzeit	Heath/Betz, Frederick	159	.40	Modern Language Series
Perfall, Anton	Tejada-Spring	Jenkins/Lentz, Max Carl G.	106	.50	
Raabe, Wilhelm	Die schwarze Galeere	Oxford University Press/Williams, Charles A.	154	.60	Oxford German Series
	Else von der Tanne	Oxford University Press/Pease, Samuel J.	111	.60	
Schiller, J. C. F. von	Wilhelm Tell	Merril/Minckwitz, Richard A. von	355		Merrill's German Texts

Schmitthenner, Adolf	Wilhelm Tell	Allyn and Bacon/ Schlenker, Carl	443	.90	
	Der Dickkopf und das Peterlein In: Aus der Jugendzeit	Heath/Betz, Frederick	159	.40	Modern Language Series
Schurz, Carl	Lebenserinnerungen bis 1850	Allyn and Bacon/ Manley, Edward	223	1.00	
Seidel, Heinrich	Die Monate	American Book/ Arrowsmith, Robert			
	Die Versetzung In: Aus der Jugendzeit	Heath/Betz, Frederick	159	.40	Modern Language Series
Spielhagen, Friedrich	Das Skelett im Hause	Heath/Skinner, M. M.	217	.45	Modern Language Series
Stern, Adolf E.	Die Wiedertäufer	Heath/Sturm, Frederick B.	173	.40	Modern Language Series
Storm, Theodor	Pole Poppenspäler	Holt/Leser, Eugene	186	.44	
	Psyche	Oxford University Press/Eisterhardt, Ewald	111	.40	Oxford German Series
Supper, Auguste	Sein System In: Schwarzwaldleut'	Holt/Roedder, Edwin Carl	173	.35	
Villinger, Hermine	Der Töpfer von Kandern In: Schwarzwaldleut'	Holt/Roedder, Edwin Carl	173	.35	
Wildenbruch, Ernst von	Die Landpartie In: Aus der Jugendzeit	Heath/Betz, Frederick	159	.40	Modern Language Series
	Das edle Blut	Macmillan/Siepmann, Otto	135		Siepmann's German Series
	Der Letzte	Heath/Schmidt, Friedrich G.		.35	Modern Language Series
	Kindertränen. Zwei Erzählungen: Der Letzte and Die Landpartie	Merrill/Kreykenbohn, Caroline	192	.50	Merrill's German Texts

APPENDIX F *(Continued)*

1914

Author	Title	Publisher/Editor	Pages	Price	Series and Contents
Arnold, Hans (Bülow, Babette von)	Fritz auf Ferien	Ginn/Eastman, Clarence W.	112	.30	International Modern Language Series
Frenssen, Gustav	Jörn Uhl	Heath/Florer, Warren W.	317	.90	Modern Language Series
	Peter Moors Fahrt nach Südwest	Holt/Babson, Herman	207	.40	
Freytag, Gustav	Aus dem Staat Friedrichs des Großen	Heath/Hager, Hermann	115	.30	Modern Language Series
Goethe, J. W. von	Die Leiden des jungen Werthers	Oxford University Press/Feise, Ernst	294	.60	Oxford German Series
	Poems	Ginn/Schütze, Martin			International Modern Language Series
Hauff, Wilhelm	Lichtenstein	Ginn/Thompson, Garrett W.	556	.90	International Modern Language Series
Heine, Heinrich	Prose	Macmillan/Faust, Albert B.	341		Macmillan German Series
Keller, Gottfried	Die drei gerechten Kammacher	Heath/Collings, Harry T.	149	.35	Modern Language Series
	Romeo und Julia auf dem Dorfe	Heath/Adams, Warren A.	185	.35	Modern Language Series
Kleist, Heinrich von	Prinz Friedrich von Homburg	St. Martin's Press/Bridge, G. F.	157		Siepmann's German Series
	Prinz Friedrich von Homburg	Oxford University Press/Baker, George Merrick	248	.60	Oxford German Series
Kurz, Isolde	Zwei Märchen: Die goldenen Träume, König Filz	Oxford University Press/Poor, Charles M.	194	.40	Oxford German Series
Lessing, G. E.	Minna von Barnhelm	Macmillan/Cutting, Starr W.	224		German Classics

	Minna von Barnhelm	Oxford University Press/Wiehr, Josef	263		Oxford German Series
	Nathan der Weise	Ginn/Capen, Samuel P.	336	.80	International Modern Language Series
	Nathan der Weise	Macmillan/Curme, George O.	300		German Classics
Rogge, Bernhard	Der große Preußenkönig	Heath/Adams, Warren A.	160	.45	Modern Language Series
Rosegger, Peter	Das Holzknechthaus	Oxford University Press/Goebel, Marie	65	.35	Oxford German Series
Schiller, J. C. F. von	Wallenstein Trilogie	Macmillan/Winkler, Max	446		
	Wilhelm Tell	Oxford University Press/Schoenfeld, Hermann			Clarendon Press
Stifter, Adalbert	Brigitta	Oxford University Press/Crowell, Robert W.	178	.40	Oxford German Series
Storm, Theodor	Geschichten aus der Tonne	Paetel [sic]/Vogel, Frank	156		Modern Language Series
	Immensee	Holt/Burnett, Arthur W.	160	.30	
	Pole Poppenspäler	Scribner/Busse, Adolf	195	.50	Walter-Krause German Series
Wildenbruch, Ernst von	Das edle Blut	Holt/Hardy, Ashley K.	112	.30	
	Das edle Blut	Merrill/Heinig, William T.	129	.40	Merrill's German Texts

1915

Arnold, Hans (Bülow, Babette von)	Fritz auf Ferien	Scribner/Applemann, Anton H.	135	.50	Walter-Krause German Series
	Menne im Seebad	Heath/Thomas, May	102	.30	
Baumbach, Rudolf	Die Nonna. Blaustrumpfgeschichte	Holt/Leonard, Arthur N.	150	.35	Modern Language Series

APPENDIX F (Continued)

Author	Title	Publisher/Editor	Pages	Price	Series and Contents
Bruneck, Otto von (Elster, Otto)	Zwischen den Schlachten	Macmillan/Hirsch, Ludwig	254	.75	Siepmann's German Series
Fulda, Ludwig	Der Talisman	Heath/Prettyman, Cornelius	125	.45	Modern Language Series
Gerstäcker, Friedrich	Der Wilddieb	Heath/Myers, Walter R.	186	.40	Modern Language Series
Goethe, J. W. von	Hermann und Dorothea	Holt/Thomas, Calvin	167	.60	Classic German Plays
Grillparzer, Franz	Des Meeres und der Liebe Wellen	Holt/Schütze, Martin	156	.70	
Heine, Heinrich	Die Harzreise	Ginn/Gregor, Leigh R.	263	.50	International Modern Language Series
Leander, Richard (Volkmann, Richard von)	Träumereien an französischen Kaminen	American Book/Arrowsmith, Robert	224	.40	Includes: Der kleine Vogel, Das kleine bucklige Mädchen, Die himmlische Musik, Der künstliche Orgel, Der Wunschring, Die drei Schwestern mit den gläsernen Herzen, Von der Königin, die keine Pfeffernüsse backen, und dem König, der nicht das Brummeisen spielen konnte, Vom unsichtbaren Königreiche, Pechvogel und Glückskind, Die Traumbuche, Der kleine Mohr und die Goldprinzessin
Leskien, Ilse	Schuld and Other Stories	Oxford University Press/Morgan, Bayard Q.	154	.40	Oxford German Series. Includes: Schuld, Der Herr Maler, Hansen, Die Kleine
Lessing, G. E.	Nathan der Weise	American Book/Diekhoff, Tobias J. C.	368	.80	
Raabe, Wilhelm	Else von der Tanne	Oxford University Press/Pease, Samuel J.	111		

Author	Title	Publisher/Editor	Price	Pages	Series
Rosegger, Peter	Vom Kichel, der eingesperrt gewesen ist, with Seidel's Leberecht Hühnchen and Weinlese bei Leberecht Hühnchen In: Edle Herzen	Merrill/Kracher, Francis W.	.50	169	Merrill's German Texts
Schiller, J. C. F. von	Kabale und Liebe	Holt/Hervey, William A.	1.25	279	
	Wilhelm Tell	Heath/Deering, Robert W.	.75	358	Modern Language Series
Seidel, Heinrich	Leberecht Hühnchen and Weinlese bei Leberecht Hühnchen, with Roseger's Vom Kichel, der eingesperrt gewesen ist In: Edle Herzen	Merrill/Kracher, Francis W.	.50	169	Merrill's German Texts
	Leberecht Hühnchen	Scribner/Luebke, William F.	.50	145	Walter-Krause German Series
Storm, Theodor	Immensee	Scribner/Purin, Charles M.	.50	150	Walter-Krause German Series
	Karsten Kurator	Holt/Grummann, Paul H.	.35	147	
Wildenbruch, Ernst von	Lachendes Land	Oxford University Press/Price, Lawrence M.	.50	212	Oxford German Series. Includes: Das Märchen von den zwei Rosen, Mein Onkel aus Pommern, Ein Opfer des Berufs

1916

Author	Title	Publisher/Editor	Price	Pages	Series
Benedix, Roderich Blüthgen, Viktor	Die Phrenologen Das Peterle von Nürnberg	Steiger/Ahn American Book/Menger, Frederick J.	.25 .48	52 207	Ahn's Series of German Comedies
Ernst, Otto (Schmidt, Otto Ernst)	Asmus Sempers Jugendland	Heath/Osthaus, Carl Wilhelm	.60	305	Modern Language Series
Freytag, Gustav	Die Journalisten	Heath/Toy, Walter Dallam	.45	202	Modern Language Series

APPENDIX F *(Continued)*

Author	Title	Publisher/Editor	Pages	Price	Series and Contents
Gerstäcker, Friedrich	Germelshausen	Heath/Lewis, Orlando F.	113	.35	Modern Language Series
	Irrfahrten	Scribner/Price, William R.	245	.50	Walter-Krause German Series
Goethe, J. W. von	Poems	Ginn/Schütze, Martin	277	.75	International Modern Language Series
Grillparzer, Franz	Des Meeres und der Liebe Wellen	Oxford University Press/Kind, John L.	208	.70	Oxford German Series
	Sappho	Oxford University Press/Kind, John L.	231	.75	Oxford German Series
Heine, Heinrich	Die Harzreise	Allyn and Bacon/Keep, Robert P.	95	.75	
Hillern, Wilhelmine von	Höher als die Kirche	Heath/Clary, Stedman W.	129	.35	Modern Language Series
Keller, Gottfried	Zwei Novellen: Die drei gerechten Kammacher, Frau Regel Amrain und ihr jüngster	Oxford University Press/Kip, Herbert Z.	268		Oxford German Series
Riehl, Wilhelm H.	Burg Neideck	American Book/Thompson, Garrett W.	224	.48	
Storm, Theodor	Immensee	Heath/Bernhardt, Wilhelm	136	.35	Modern Language Series
	Immensee	American Book/Dirks, Louis H.	163	.40	
Wildenbruch, Ernst von	Das edle Blut	Scribner/Holzwarth, Charles H.	129	.50	Walter-Krause German Series

1917

| Auerbach, Berthold | Brigitta | Allyn and Bacon/Whitenack, Erasmus A. | 181 | .65 | |

Author	Title	Publisher/Editor	Pages	Price	Series
Baumbach, Rudolf	Der Schwiegersohn	Scribner/Lensner, Hermann J.	274	.60	Walter-Krause German Series
Benedix, Roderich	Die Lügnerin	Steiger/Ahn	45	.25	Ahn's Series of German Comedies
	Günstige Vorzeichen	Steiger/Ahn		.25	Ahn's Series of German Comedies
Blumenthal, Oscar	Paulas Geheimnis	Steiger/Ahn	45	.25	Ahn's Series of German Comedies
Goethe, J. W. von	Hermann und Dorothea	Allyn and Bacon/Roller, Julianne A.	302	.75	
	Hermann und Dorothea	Oxford University Press/Lieder, Frederick W.	315	1.00	Oxford German Series
Herzog, Rudolf	Hermann und Dorothea	Scribner/Feise, Ernst	173	.65	Walter-Krause German Series
	Die Burgkinder	Heath/Boetzkes, Ottilie G.	295	.65	Modern Language Series
Heyse, Paul	Die Blinden	Steiger/Ahn	105	.20	Ahn's Series of German Novels
	L'Arrabbiata	Holt/McLouth, Lawrence A., and Kurt E. Richter		.40	
Hillern, Wilhelmine von	Höher als die Kirche	Macmillan/Pitcher, Stephen L.	228	.40	Macmillan German Series
	Höher als die Kirche	Scribner/Kenngott, Alfred	162	.50	Walter-Krause German Series
Ibsen, Henrik	Ein Volksfeind	Oxford University Press/Boysen, J. Lassen	193	.90	Oxford German Series
Lessing, G. E.	Nathan der Weise	Macmillan/Curme, George O.	300	.45	German Classics
Meyer, Conrad F.	Gustav Adolfs Page	Holt/Roulston, Robert B.	160	.45	
Meyr, Melchior	Zwei Freier	Steiger/Ahn	38	.20	Ahn's Series of German Novels
Moser, Gustav von	Er soll dein Herr sein	Steiger/Ahn	41		Ahn's Series of German Comedies
Rosegger, Peter	Das Holzknechthaus	Oxford University Press/Goebel, Marie	65	.35	Oxford German Series
	Der Lex von Gutenhag	Heath/Morgan, Bayard Q.	148		Modern Language Series
Storm, Theodor	Immensee	Macmillan/Fick, Alma S.	177	.40	Macmillan German Series

APPENDIX F *(Continued)*

Author	Title	Publisher/Editor	Pages	Price	Series and Contents
Wildenbruch, Ernst von	In St. Jürgen Das edle Blut	Holt/Heller, Otto Macmillan/Weigel, John C.	147 145	.45 .40	Macmillan German Series
1918					
Auerbach, Berthold	Brigitta	Allyn and Bacon/Whitenack, Erasmus A.	181	.65	
Baumbach, Rudolf	Der Schwiegersohn	Merrill/Perrin, Marshall L., and Joel Hatheway	272	.60	Merrill's German Texts
	Die befreiten Seelen and Bruder Klaus und die treuen Tiere In: Ährenlese	Heath/Bierwirth, Heinrich C., and Asbury H. Herrick	284		
Bechstein, L.	Der Fuchs und der Krebs, Gevatter Tod and Der Schmied von Jüterbog In: Ährenlese	Heath/Bierwirth, Heinrich C., and Asbury H. Herrick	284		
Blüthgen Viktor	Das Peterle von Nürnberg	Macmillan/Doniat, Josephine C.	183	.40	Macmillan German Series
Frommel, Emil	Wie man Diebe fängt In: Ährenlese	Heath/Bierwirth, Heinrich C., and Asbury H. Herrick	284		
Goebel, F.	Der starke Drescher In: Ährenlese	Heath/Bierwirth, Heinrich C., and Asbury H. Herrick	284		
Goethe, J. W. von	Torquato Tasso	Longmans, Green/Robertson, John G.	191	1.50	Modern Language Texts
Hansjakob, Heinrich	Wie der alte Hermesbauer gestorben ist In: Ährenlese	Heath/Bierwirth, Heinrich C., and Asbury H. Herrick	284		

Horn, W. O. von	Der arme Musikant und sein Kollege In: Ährenlese	Heath/Bierwirth, Heinrich C., and Asbury H. Herrick		284
Kerkhoff, I.	Ein Traum In: Ährenlese	Heath/Bierwirth, Heinrich C., and Asbury H. Herrick		284
Rosegger, Peter	Die Wunderlampe In: Ährenlese	Heath/Bierwirth, Heinrich C., and Asbury H. Herrick		284
Schiller, J. C. F. von Schlicht, J.	Wilhelm Tell Die Grenzfichte In: Ährenlese	Languages Publishing Heath/Bierwirth, Heinrich C., and Asbury H. Herrick	.25 Ideophonic Texts	265 284
Seidel, Heinrich	Der Zwerg und die Gerstenähre and Der Lindenbaum In: Ährenlese	Heath/Bierwirth, Heinrich C., and Asbury H. Herrick		284
Simrock K.	Die teuren Eier and Das Gegengeschenk In: Ährenlese	Heath/Bierwirth, Heinrich C., and Asbury H. Herrick		284
Spyri, Johanna	Zwei Geschichten: Beim Weiden-Josef, Moni der Geißbub	Scott, Foresman/ Balduf, Emery W.	.50 Lake German Classics	189
Stöber, K.	Kurze Reise nach Amerika In: Ährenlese	Heath/Bierwirth, Heinrich C., and Asbury H. Herrick		284
Sturm, J.	Der bekehrte Stiefelknecht In: Ährenlese	Heath/Bierwirth, Heinrich C., and Asbury H. Herrick		284
Trojan, J.	Das Abenteuer im Walde In: Ährenlese	Heath/Bierwirth, Heinrich C., and Asbury H. Herrick		284
Vogel, R.	Wie die Wodansmühle entstand In: Ährenlese	Heath/Bierwirth, Heinrich C., and Asbury H. Herrick		284

APPENDIX G

Appendix G is a list of those texts consulted or listed which provided no main author listing and do not appear in Appendix F. These books are listed chronologically by editor, or by title when no editor is given. Further information includes publisher, number of pages, and name of series.

APPENDIX G

Editor	Title	Publisher	Pages	Price	Series
		1865			
Simonson, Leopold	Deutsches Balladenbuch	DeVries, Ibarra	304	1.75	
	Deutsches Balladenbuch	Christern	304	1.75	
		1868			
Simonson, Leopold	Deutsches Balladenbuch	Leypoldt and Holt	304	1.75	
		1875			
Buchheim, Carl Adolf	Deutsche Lyrik	Macmillan	415	1.50	Golden Treasury Series
		1879			
Klemm, Louis Richard	Poesie für Haus und Schule	Putnam	314	1.25	
		1881			
Klemm, Louis Richard	Poesie für Haus und Schule	Putnam	314	1.25	
		1885			
Knortz, Karl	Representative German Poems (German and English)	Holt	352	3.50	
	Representative German Poems (German and English)	Schoenhof	352	3.50	
Wenckebach, Carla, and Helene Wenckebach	Schönste deutsche Lieder	Schoenhof	70		
	Schönste deutsche Lieder	Christern	70		

		1886		
Wenckebach, Carla, and Helene Wenckebach	Schönste deutsche Lieder	Holt	363	
		1888		
[no editor listed]	Ali Baba and the Forty Thieves (Gustav Weil translation)	Kilborn		.15 Selected German Texts
Schrakamp, Josepha	Erzählungen aus der deutschen Geschichte	Holt	286	.90
Wenckebach, Carla, and Helene Wenckebach	Schönste deutsche Lieder	Holt	363	1.20
		1889		
Buchheim, Emma S.	German Poetry for Beginners	Macmillan	150	.50
Grandgent, C. H.	Ali Baba and the Forty Thieves (Gustav Weil translation)	Heath	53	.20 Heath's German Series
Knortz, Karl	Representative German Poems (German and English)	Holt	352	3.50
		1891		
Buchheim, Carl Adolf	Balladen und Romanzen	Macmillan		1.00 Golden Treasury Series
		1893		
Klemm, Louis Richard	Poesie für Haus und Schule	Putnam	314	
Schrakamp, Josepha	Sagen und Mythen	Dyrsen and Pfeiffer	163	.75

APPENDIX F (Continued)

Author	Title	Publisher	Pages	Price	Series and Contents
Wenckebach, Carla	Sagen und Mythen	Schoenhof	163	.75	
	Sagen und Mythen	Holt	163		
	Ausgewählte Meisterwerke	Heath	276		Modern Language Series
1894					
Schrakamp, Josepha	Berühmte Deutsche	Dyrsen and Pfeiffer	207	.85	
	Berühmte Deutsche	Holt	207	.85	
	Berühmte Deutsche	Schoenhof	207	.85	
	Sagen und Mythen	Dyrsen and Pfeiffer	163	.75	
1895					
Klenze, Camillo von	Deutsche Gedichte	Holt	331	.90	
[no editor listed]	German and French Poems for Memorizing	Holt		.20	
Schoenfeld, Hermann	German Historical Prose	Holt	213	.80	
Simonson, Leopold	Deutsches Balladenbuch	Holt	304		
1896					
Grandgent, C. H.	Ali Baba and the Forty Thieves (Gustav Weil translation)	Heath	53	.20	Heath's German Series
Wenckebach, Carla	Ausgewählte Meisterwerke	Heath	276		Modern Language Series
1898					
Grandgent, C. H.	Ali Baba and the Forty Thieves (Gustav Weil translation)	Heath	53	.20	Heath's German Series

Müller, Hermann	Deutsche Gedichte	Ginn	71	.45	International Modern Language Series
		1899			
Stern, Sigmon Martin	Aus deutschen Meisterwerken	Holt	225	1.20	
		1900			
[no editor listed]	German and French Poems for Memorizing	Holt		.20	
Hatfield, James Taft	German Lyrics and Ballads	Heath	224	.75	Modern Language Series
Wenckebach, Carla	Ausgewählte Meisterwerke	Heath	276		Modern Language Series
		1901			
Florer, Warren Washburn	Biblische Geschichten	Wahr	99	.40	
[no editor listed]	German and French Poems for Memorizing	Holt		.20	
Schoenfeld, Hermann	German Historical Prose	Holt	213	.80	
		1902			
Bacon, Edwin Faxon	Hermannia Liederkranz	Bardeen	128	.35	
Parry, C., and G. Robinson	German Poetry for Schools	Longmans, Green		.50	
		1903			
Dillard, James H.	Aus dem deutschen Dichterwald	American Book		.60	

APPENDIX G (Continued)

Editor	Title	Publisher	Pages	Price	Series
Hatfield, James Taft	German Lyrics and Ballads	Heath	224		
Smissen, W. H. van der	Shorter Poems in Chronological Order	Appleton	291	.60	Twentieth Century Textbooks
Wenckebach, Carla	Ausgewählte Meisterwerke	Heath	276		Modern Language Series
1904					
[no editor listed]	German and French Poems for Memorizing	Holt		.20	
1905					
Buchheim, Emma S.	Short German Plays	Oxford University Press	91	.60	
Tombo, R., and R. Tombo, Jr.	Deutsche Reden	Heath	290	.90	Modern Language Series
Wenckebach, Carla	Ausgewählte Meisterwerke	Heath			Modern Language Series
1906					
Hatfield, James Taft	German Lyrics and Ballads	Heath	224		Modern Language Series
[no editor listed]	Hundred Best German Poems	Jacobs		.50	
1907					
[no editor listed]	German and French Poems for Memorizing	Holt	35	.25	

Hatfield, James Taft	German Lyrics and Ballads	Heath	224	Modern Language Series
Jürgensen, Hans, and Carl Schlenker	Deutsche Gedichte	Wilson	82	.50
Wenckebach, Carla	Ausgewählte Meisterwerke	Heath		

1908

Grandgent, C. H.	Ali Baba and the Forty Thieves (Gustav Weil translation)	Heath	53	.20	Heath's German Series

1909

Betz, Frederick	Till Eulenspiegels lustige Streiche	Heath	92	.30	Modern Language Series
Chalmers, William P.	Deutsche Gedichte zum Auswendiglernen	Crowell	127	.40

1910

Betz, Frederick	Till Eulenspiegels lustige Streiche	Heath	92	.30	Modern Language Series
Collitz, Klara H.	Early German Literature	American Book	285	1.00
Klenze, Camillo von	Deutsche Gedichte	Holt	332	.90
Schrakamp, Josepha	Ernstes und Heiteres	American Book	202	.35
Wenckebach, Carla	Ausgewählte Meisterwerke	Heath			Modern Language Series

1911

Betz, Frederick	Till Eulenspiegels lustige Streiche	Heath	92	.30	Modern Language Series
Hatfield, James Taft	German Lyrics and Ballads	Heath			Modern Language Series

APPENDIX G (Continued)

Editor	Title	Publisher	Pages	Price	Series
		1912			
Chalmers, William P.	Deutsche Gedichte zum Auswendiglernen	Crowell	127	.40	
Collmann, Chester W.	Easy German Poetry for Beginners	Ginn	140		International Modern Language Series
Purin, Charles M., and Edwin C. Roedder	Deutsche Gedichte und Lieder	Heath	154	.60	Modern Language Series
Schrakamp, Josepha	Sagen und Mythen	Holt			
[no editor listed]	University Regents' Selections	Bardeen	163	.10	
		1913			
Collmann, Chester W.	Easy German Poetry for Beginners (revised edition)	Ginn	176	.40	International Modern Language Series
Drechsel, K. C. H.	Die sieben Reisen Sinbads (Albert Ludwig Grimm revision)	American Book	188	.40	
		1915			
Hatfield, James Taft	Shorter German Poems	Heath	110	.35	Modern Language Series
		1917			
Burkhard, Oscar Carl	German Poems for Memorizing	Holt	129	.40	
		1918			
Straube, Bernhard C.	Märchen und Sagen	Macmillan	220	.40	Macmillan German Series

382

Index

Adams Warren Austin, 40–41, 128
Alcott, Louisa May, 164
Alexis, Willibald, 137
Alkmar, Heinrich von, 13, 14, 15, 38
Andersch, Alfred, 2
Andersen, Hans Christian, 64, 117, 147, 191
Ariosto, Lodovico, 16
Aristotle, 17
Arndt, Ernst Moritz, 59–61, 62, 195
Arnold, Hans (Babette von Bülow), 162–163, 166, 185, 194
Auerbach, Berthold, 118–120, 152, 193
Auerbach, Doris, 1, 11

Babbitt, Eugene H., 9, 16
Babson, Herman, 181–182
Baker, George Merrick, 174, 186, 188
Bathke, Edith, 142
Baumbach, Rudolf, 54, 99, 143–146, 147, 162, 182, 189, 192, 197
Bechstein, Ludwig, 67
Beitter, Ursula, 1, 2
Benedix, Roderich, 81–83, 87, 89, 113, 121, 147, 156, 189, 191
Bentley, Eric, 2
Bernhardt, Wilhelm, 11, 14, 19–20, 21, 28, 29, 32, 33, 35, 38, 40, 42, 44, 45, 46, 48, 49, 51, 53–54, 55–56, 60, 62, 63, 64, 65, 67, 68, 70, 71, 73, 74, 76, 77, 78, 83, 84, 86, 87, 88, 92, 94, 95, 100, 105, 118, 119, 122, 124, 125–126, 131, 138, 140, 141, 143, 145–146, 154–155, 158–159, 160, 163, 164, 165–166, 173, 174, 196
Betz, Frederick, 15, 176, 188
Bichsel, Peter, 197
Bierwirth, Heinrich C., 67
Blüthgen, Viktor, 157–158, 185, 195
Blumenthal, Oskar, 106, 108, 111, 118, 193
Boccaccio, Giovanni, 77
Böhlau, Helene (Helene al Raschid Bey), 183–185, 195–196
Böll, Heinrich, 2, 100
Börne, Ludwig, 90, 92
Boetzkes, Ottilie, 179–180
Books in Print, 3–4
Borchert, Wolfgang, 2, 174
Brandt, Hermann C. G., 9
Brant, Sebastian, 63
Brecht, Bertolt, 2, 31, 174
Brett-Evans, David, 125
Breul, Karl Hermann, 15
Brooks, Neil C., 72
Buchheim, Carl Adolf, 7
Buehner, Valentin, 183
Bülow, Babette von. *See* Arnold, Hans
Bürger, Gottfried, 21, 22, 193
Bürstenbinder, Elizabeth. *See* Werner, Ernst
Byron, George Gordon, Lord, 32

Campe, Joachim Heinrich, 15–16, 195
Cannon, Lee E., 187
Carruth, William Herbert, 9, 13,

Carruth (*continued*)
  15, 50
Carse, Alice, 1, 9
Chamisso, Adelbert von, 8, 75–76, 192
Christern, F. W., 4
Clauren, H. (Karl Gottlob Samuel Heun), 71
Clodius, Christian August Heinrich, 59
Committee of Twelve, Report of, 9–10, 15, 16, 23, 29–30, 64, 67, 85, 92, 96, 102, 108–109, 112, 113, 117, 121, 123, 124, 141, 142, 149, 152, 154, 161, 163–164, 173, 189
Corneille, Pierre, 17, 20, 32
Crowell, Robert Warner, 89
Cutting, Starr Willard, 9, 42, 93

Dahn, Felix Ludwig Sophus, 99, 138–139, 140, 153, 154, 194
Debs, Eugene V., 179
Defoe, Daniel, 15
Doniat, Josephine, 158
Droste-Hülshoff, Annette von, 85–86, 89, 94, 187, 195
Dürrenmatt, Friedrich, 100
Durzak, Manfred, 1–2

Ebers, Georg, 138, 139–140, 144, 152, 153, 154, 189, 193
Ebner-Eschenbach, Marie von, 158–160, 194
Eckstein, Ernst, 99, 152–154, 194
Ehlert, K., 2
Eichendorff, Joseph von, 74–75, 113, 191
Elisabeth of Rumania. *See* Sylva, Carmen
Elz, Alexander, 10, 108–110, 113, 118, 121, 134, 146, 192
Ernst, Otto (Otto Ernst Schmidt), 177–179, 182, 195
Eschstruth, Nataly von, 156, 165–166, 194

Eucken, Rudolf, 133
Euripides, 77
Evans, Edward Payson, 147

Feise, Ernst, 26, 40
Fiedler, Leonhard, 46, 147, 177
Fife, Robert Herndon, 74
Fischart, Johann, 63
Flom, George T., 111, 112
Fontane, Theodor, 99, 137–138, 159, 194
Ford, Richard Clyde, 171
Fouqué, Friedrich de la Motte, 8, 69–71, 72, 75, 157, 191
François, Louise von, 99, 163
Freiligrath, Ferdinand, 113
Frenssen, Gustav, 7, 181–182, 195
Frenzel, Herbert A., and Elisabeth Frenzel, 11, 13, 16, 83, 88–89, 94, 101
Frey, Friedrich Hermann, *See* Greif, Martin
Freytag, Gustav, 99, 104–106, 118, 135, 183, 192–193
Friedrich, Werner P., 15, 26, 182, 185–186
Frisch, Max, 100
Frommel, Emil, 154–156, 176, 194
Fulda, Ludwig, 99, 116–118, 138, 195

Gaiser, Gerd, 2
Geffcken, F. H., 139, 168, 178
Gellert, Christian Fürchtegott, 13, 14, 15, 192
Gerstäcker, Friedrich, 8, 140–143, 156, 157, 194
Goebel, Julius, 30, 42–43
Goethe, Johann Wolfgang von, 2, 16, 21, 22–23, 24, 34, 37, 57, 58, 69, 73, 122, 127, 143, 154, 184, 185, 189, 190, 191, 192; *Die Campagne in Frankreich*, 44; *Dichtung und Wahrheit*, 16, 24, 29, 43–44; *Egmont*, 24, 25, 26–27;

Faust, 24, 25, 26, 29, 39, 41–43; *Götz von Berlichingen*, 24–25, 26, 37, 38, 41, 43, 61, 86, 179, 190; *Hermann und Dorothea*, 24, 25, 29, 37, 39–41, 57, 85, 152, 190; *Iphigenie*, 23, 24, 25, 29, 37–38, 41, 77, 79; *Die italienische Reise*, 44; *Die Leiden des jungen Werthers*, 24, 25–26, 29, 38, 41, 43, 48, 149; lyric poetry and ballads, 27–30, 31, 32, 33, 43, 91; *Das Märchen*, 39; *Reineke Fuchs*, 14, 15, 24, 26, 38–39; *Torquato Tasso*, 24, 25, 38, 79, 86: *Die Wahlverwandtschaften*, 24; *Wilhelm Meister*, 24, 26, 54; *Zu Shakespeares Namenstag*, 25
Goeze, Johann Melchior, 17
Gordon, John, 1
Gotthelf, Jeremias, 119
Gottsched, Johann Christoph, 16
Grandgent, Charles Hall, 9
Grass, Günter, 2, 100
Grillparzer, Franz, 10, 27, 53, 78–79, 80, 81, 175, 193
Greif, Martin (Friedrich Hermann Frey), 102
Grimm, Hermann, 7, 154, 191
Grimm, Jakob, 66–67, 191, 192
Grimm, Wilhelm, 66–67, 191, 192
Gutzkow, Karl, 92–94, 192, 195

Haertel, Martin, 136
Haevernick, Emma, 184
Halm, Friedrich (Eligius Franz Joseph, Freiherr von Münch-Bellinghausen), 79–81
Handschin, Charles H., 133
Hansjakob, Heinrich, 175–176, 195
Harris, Charles, 30
Hartmann, Moritz, 94, 192
Hatfield, Henry, 2
Hauff, Wilhelm, 15, 71–72, 192
Hauptmann, Gerhard, 7, 99, 116, 171–173, 190, 195
Hebbel, Friedrich, 100–102, 104, 105, 106, 118, 122, 195
Hebel, Johann Peter, 76–77, 196
Heine, Heinrich, 2, 29, 73, 85, 89–92, 113, 154, 192
Heinsohn, Wolfgang, 1, 3, 7, 8, 11, 139, 140, 144, 189
Hench, G. A., 9
Henckels, Théodor, 114
Herder, Johann Gottfried, 21, 24, 38
Herrick, Asbury H., 67
Herwegh, Georg, 94
Herzog, Rudolf, 179–180, 196
Heun, Karl Gottlob Samuel. *See* Clauren, H.
Heuser, Frederick W. J., 10, 160
Heyse, Paul, 8, 99, 116, 121–124, 153, 156, 157, 162, 183, 185, 187, 191, 195
Hildner, Karl August, 25
Hillern, Wilhelmine von, 158, 160–162, 163, 187, 192
Hitler, Adolf, 42
Hoffacker, H., 2
Hoffmann, E. T. A., 72–74, 75, 76, 191, 195
Hoffmann, Hans, 182–183, 195
Hohlfeld, Alexander R., 159
Holberg, Ludvig, 16
Holt, Henry, 5
Hosmer, James K., 17–18, 19, 26, 31–32, 33, 39, 41, 44, 46, 48, 55, 60, 62–63, 66–67, 68, 69, 70, 74, 90, 100, 104–105, 118, 122, 130, 154
Howard, William Guild, 24, 87
Howe, George M., 75

Ibershoff, Carl Henry, 16
Ide, H., 2
Iffland, August Wilhelm, 35, 57, 82

Immermann, Karl Leberecht, 27, 134

Jean Paul (Johann Paul Friedrich Richter), 62–64, 70, 72, 73, 134, 193
Jensen, Wilhelm, 99, 146–147, 153, 191
Johnson, Uwe, 2
Joynes, Edward Southey, 23, 123, 147
Jung-Stilling, Heinrich, 21, 22–23

Kant, Immanuel, 58
Keep, Robert Porter, 90, 91
Keller, Gottfried, 99, 122, 126–128, 153, 154, 181–182, 193
Kenngott, Alfred, 136
Khull, Ferdinand, 5
Kleist, Heinrich von, 64–66, 81, 101, 149, 193
Klinger, Maximilian, 54
Klopsch, O. P., 178
Körner, Theodor, 61, 62, 191
Kolbe, Parke Rexford, 90
Kopp, W. LaMarr, 1
Kotzebue, August von, 8, 37, 57–58, 121, 195
Krell, Leo, 46, 147, 177
Krumpelmann, John T., 142
Kummer, Friedrich, 8, 31, 59, 60, 61, 62, 63, 64, 65, 68, 71, 74–75, 76, 77, 78, 79, 82, 83, 84, 86–87, 88, 91, 93, 96, 97, 101, 103, 104, 105, 107, 108, 114, 115, 116, 119, 120–121, 122, 125, 127, 128–129, 131, 134, 135, 137, 138–139, 140, 141, 143, 146, 147–148, 149, 153, 154, 156, 159, 160, 163, 165, 166, 167, 169, 170, 172, 173, 177, 181, 182, 184, 185, 186
Kurian, George Thomas, 4
Kurz, Heinrich, 11, 13, 14, 15, 16, 20, 23, 27–28, 29, 33, 37, 38, 39–40, 45, 46, 47, 49, 51, 53, 55, 56, 58, 65, 66, 68, 69–70, 73, 74, 75–76, 77, 80, 81, 83, 84, 86, 87–88, 92–93, 94–95, 96–97, 100–101, 102, 104, 105, 113, 119, 120, 122, 124, 126, 128, 140–141, 147, 151, 122, 124, 126, 128, 140–141, 147, 151
Kurz, Isolde, 185–186, 195

Lambert, Marcus, 135
L'Arronge, Adolf, 106
Laube, Heinrich, 92
Leander, Richard (Richard von Volkmann), 156–157, 193
Lentz, Max, 124
Lenz, Siegfried, 197
Leonard, Arthur N., 130
Lerner, Alan Jay, 142
Leskien, Ilse, 187, 196
Lessing, Gotthold Ephraim, 17, 24, 77, 143, 154, 189, 192; *Emilia Galotti*, 18, 19, 190; *Die Erziehung des Menschengeschlechts*, 17–18, 20, 116, 191; fables, 13, 14–15; *Hamburgische Dramaturgie*, 20, 21; *Laokoon*, 20–21; *Minna von Barnhelm*, 18–19, 21, 147, 190, 191; *Nathan der Weise*, 18, 19–20, 23, 117
Library of Congress Catalogue, 4
Lienhard, Friedrich, 176–177, 196
Liliencron, Detlev von, 173–174, 195
Lindau, Paul, 106
Ludwig, Otto, 100, 102–104, 105, 106, 118, 122, 195
Luebke, William F., 151
Luther, Martin, 13, 15

Marlitt, E. (Eugenie John), 164
Merrick, Joan, 2
Mews, Siegfried, 106

Meyer, Conrad Ferdinand, 99, 127, 135–137, 185, 194, 195
Meyer, Edward, 144
Meyer-Förster, Wilhelm, 156
Meyr, Melchior, 151–152, 193
Modern Language Journal, 10, 30, 40, 90, 129–130, 141, 151, 178, 187
Mörike, Eduard, 86–87, 89, 195
Morgan, Bayard Quincy, 1, 7, 148
Moser, Gustav von, 8, 100, 106–108, 111, 118, 146, 193
Mügge, Theodor, 97, 191
Müller, Hugo, 192
Müller von Königswinter, Wolfgang, 113, 118
Müllner, Adolf, 53
Münch-Bellinghausen, Eligius Franz Joseph, Freiherr von. *See* Halm, Friedrich
Myers, Walter, 141

Napoleon I, 55, 56, 60
Nathusius, Marie, 89, 192
National Union Catalog, 4
New York Herald Tribune, 1
New York Times, 1, 2, 3, 6–8, 24, 30, 32, 139, 140, 144, 189, 196
Niebuhr, Barthold Georg, 8
Niese, Charlotte, 188, 196
Nietzsche, Friedrich, 31
Nollen, John Scholte, 30
Novalis (Friedrich von Hardenberg), 157

Osthaus, Carl Wilhelm F., 142, 178

Patzwald, Otto R., 72
Picard, Louis Benoît, 48–49
Platen, August Graf von, 27
Pochmann, Henry A., 1, 7, 8, 24, 26, 30
Polenz, Wilhelm von, 174–175
Poll, Max, 19

Postl, Karl. *See* Sealsfield, Charles
Prettyman, Cornelius W., 117
Priest, George Madison, 11, 54, 56, 58–59, 62, 65–66, 67, 68, 70, 73, 75, 76, 77, 78, 79, 80, 83, 84, 86, 87, 88, 93, 96, 101, 102, 103, 104, 105, 107, 108, 116, 119, 122–123, 125, 127, 129, 132, 134, 135, 137, 139, 140, 143, 147, 149, 154, 159, 167, 169, 172, 173, 174, 175, 177–178, 179, 181, 182, 183, 185, 186
Primer, Sylvester, 18–19
Publishers Trade List Annual, 4
Publishers Weekly, 4
Putlitz, Gustav zu, 15, 120–121, 191

Raabe, Wilhelm, 133–135, 153, 154, 181–182, 196
Raspe, Rudolf Erich, 21–22, 195
Reimarus, Hermann Samuel, 17
Report of the Committee of Twelve. *See* Committee of Twelve, Report of
Robson, Charles W., 72
Richter, Johann Paul Friedrich. *See* Jean Paul
Riehl, Wilhelm Heinrich, 128–130, 135, 192–193
Roedder, Edwin Carl, 175–176
Roquette, Otto, 83, 137, 189, 192
Rosegger, Peter Kettenfeier, 100, 147–149, 194
Rosen, Julius, 193

Saar, Ferdinand von, 100, 147
Sachs, Julius, 129–130, 190
Sander, Volkmar, 1, 189
Schanz, Frieda (Frieda Schanz Soyaux), 163, 196
Scheffel, Joseph Viktor von, 5, 31, 83–85, 89, 122, 143, 183, 193, 194, 197
Schiller, Johann Christoph

Schiller (continued)
Friedrich von, 2, 7, 8, 21, 23, 29, 37, 61, 69, 73, 79, 128, 143, 154, 166, 184, 185, 191, 192; *Der Abfall der Niederlande*, 46–47; *Die Braut von Messina*, 52, 53–54, 55, 57; *Don Carlos*, 45–46, 52; *Der Geisterseher*, 46; *Die Geschichte des Dreißigjährigen Kriegs*, 46–47; *Die Jungfrau von Orleans*, 50–53, 55, 61; *Kabale und Liebe*, 34–35, 46, 48, 52, 179, 190; lyric poetry and ballads, 30–33, 91; *Maria Stuart*, 23, 49–50, 52; *Der Neffe als Onkel* 48–49; *Die Räuber*, 34, 35, 86, 101, 190; *Über Anmut und Würde*, 45; *Über naive und sentimentalische Dichtung*, 44–45; *Die Verschwörung des Fiesco zu Genua*, 34, 35; *Wallenstein*, 46, 47–48, 50, 55, 56, 57, 61; *Wilhelm Tell*, 52, 55–57, 61, 190–191
Schlegel, August Wilhelm, 58
Schlegel, Friedrich, 58
Schlegel, Johann Elias, 16
Schlenker, Carl, 57
Schmid, Christoph, 8
Schmidt, Friedrich Georg Gottlob, 152, 168
Schmidt, Otto Ernst. *See* Ernst, Otto
Schönberg, Hans Friedrich von, 15
Schücking, Levin (friend of Droste-Hülshoff), 94–95
Schücking, Levin, 9, 197
Schütze, Martin, 30
Schultz, Arthur R., 1
Schulz-Behrend, George, 125, 126
Schurz, Carl, 5, 196
Scott, Sir Walter, 70, 72
Scribe, Eugène, 81, 105, 121
Sealsfield, Charles (Karl Postl), 8, 95–97, 140, 141, 195

Seidel, Heinrich, 64, 100, 146, 149–151, 155, 177, 182, 193
Senger, Joachim Henry, 70–71
Seume, Gottfried, 37, 58–59
Shakespeare, William, 17, 25, 28, 56, 65
Simrock, Karl, 69, 113
Skinner, M. M., 132
Smissen, William Henry van der, 156
Soyaux, Frida Schanz. *See* Schanz, Frida
Spenser, Edmund, 32, 157
Spielhagen, Friedrich, 130–133, 138, 195, 196
Spyri, Johanna, 194
Steiger, Emil, 4
Stein, Heinrich Friedrich Karl, Freiherr vom und zum, 60
Stern, Menco von, 76
Stern, Sigmon Martin, 23
Stewart, Morton C., 103–104
Stifter, Adalbert, 87–89, 193
Stökl, Helene, 146, 163–164, 165, 166
Storm, Theodor, 100, 124–126, 156–157, 162, 191
Stroebe, Lilian, 78–79, 81, 82, 93–94, 101, 103, 104, 105–106, 107, 114, 116–117, 119, 123, 125, 127, 132, 134, 135–136, 137, 139, 140, 142, 143, 147, 159, 164, 167, 170, 172, 173, 177, 179, 181, 184, 185, 186
Sudermann, Hermann, 7, 100, 116, 168–171, 194
Supper, Auguste, 196
Sylva, Carmen (Elisabeth of Rumania), 165, 166, 196

Tanselle, Thomas, 4
Tasso, Torquato, 32
Tebbel, John William, 3, 4

Index

The American Catalogue, 3, 5
The United States Catalog, 3
Thomas, Calvin, 9, 11, 20–21, 22, 24–26, 27, 28–29, 32, 33, 34, 35, 37–38, 39, 40, 42–43, 45, 47, 48, 50, 52, 54, 57, 61, 63–64, 65, 66, 67, 68, 70, 72, 73–74, 75, 76, 78, 79, 84–85, 86, 87, 91, 93, 102, 104, 105, 114, 119, 123, 125, 127, 129, 131–132, 134, 135–136, 137, 139, 140, 143, 147, 167, 169, 171–172, 173
Thompson, Garret W., 129, 130
Tieck, Ludwig, 67–69, 80, 157, 191
Timme, Marie. *See* Villamaria
Toy, Walter Dallam, 106
Twain, Mark (Samuel L. Clemens), 114–115

Uhland, Ludwig, 29, 61–62, 192

Vergil (Publius Vergilius Maro), 19, 21, 32, 152
Viebig, Clara, 186–187, 188, 195
Villinger, Hermine, 196
Vilmar, August Friedrich Christian, 11, 14, 17, 18, 21, 22, 27, 28, 29, 31, 34, 39, 41, 43–44, 45, 47, 49, 51, 52, 53, 54–55, 57–58, 59–60, 61, 62, 63, 64–65, 68, 69, 72–73, 74, 76–77, 78, 79–80, 85–86, 89, 92
Volkmann, Richard von. *See* Leander, Richard
Vos, Bert John, 40, 141, 151

Wagner, Richard, 7, 27, 30, 100, 104, 106, 118, 195
Weil, Gustav, 5
Weisstein, Ulrich, 11
Wells, Benjamin Willis, 9, 11, 32, 33, 42, 48, 49–50, 51–52, 52–53, 56, 80, 81–82, 83, 84, 93, 95, 104, 105, 106–107, 107–108, 108–109, 110, 111, 113–114, 115, 116, 119, 120, 121, 122, 125, 126–127, 128, 131, 133–134, 135, 137, 138, 139, 141, 143, 146, 147, 152–153, 154, 159, 160, 164, 166–167, 168–169, 171, 172, 173
Wenckebach, Carla, 85
Werner, Ernst (Elizabeth Bürstenbinder), 146, 164, 165, 166, 189
Werner, Zacharias, 53
Werner-Spanhoofd, Arnold, 13, 15, 16, 22, 149–150, 162–163
White, Horatio S., 15
Whitney, Marian P., 78–79, 81, 82, 93–94, 101, 103, 104, 105–106, 107, 114, 116–117, 119, 123, 125, 127, 132, 134, 135–136, 137, 139, 140, 142, 143, 147, 159, 164, 167, 170, 172, 173, 177, 179, 181, 184, 185, 186
Wichert, Ernst, 111–113, 118, 121, 162, 189, 194
Wieland, Christoph Martin, 16
Wilbrandt, Adolf, 43, 100, 113–116, 118, 195
Wildenbruch, Ernst von, 100, 138, 158, 166–168, 171, 194
Wildermuth, Ottilie von, 8, 165
Wilhelmi, Alexander (Alexander Viktor Zechmeister), 54, 110–111, 113, 118, 121, 134, 146, 189, 191
Wilson, A. E., 69
Winkler, Max, 19
Wittke, Carl, 4, 5

Zechmeister, Alexander Viktor. *See* Wilhelmi, Alexander
Zeydel, Edwin H., 3, 196–197
Zschokke, Heinrich, 21, 23–24, 138, 152, 154, 156, 176, 189, 192

ECHOES AND INFLUENCES OF GERMAN ROMANTICISM
Essays in Honour of Hans Eichner
Edited by Michael S. Batts, Anthony W. Riley and Heinz Wetzel

ISBN 0-8204-0511-6   291 pages   paperback US $ 35.00*

*Recommended price – alterations reserved

The rich legacy of German Romanticism is the focus of the sixteen essays by North American and European scholars written expressly for this volume. Although most of the essays are concerned with the echoes of Romanticism in literature and especially in the works of individual writers (e.g. Büchner, Mörike, Nietzsche, Thomas Mann, Hesse, Musil, and Christa Wolf), the political and philosophical implications of Romantic thought and ideas as well as their influence on the fine arts are examined. The book is a tribute to Hans Eichner, one of the most outstanding scholars in the field of Romanticism.

Contents: Romanticism in the works of Nietzsche, Mörike, Büchner, Thomas Mann, Musil, Hesse, Christa Wolf – The Romantic Künstlernovelle – A. W. Schlegel's *Sommernachtstraum* – Romantic Nationalism at the turn of the century, *inter alia*.

PETER LANG PUBLISHING, INC.
62 West 45th Street
USA – New York, NY 10036

Roger Hillman

«ZEITROMAN»
The Novel and Society in Germany 1830–1900

Australian and New Zealand Studies in German Language and Literature.
Vol. 12
ISBN 0-8204-0010-6   186 pages   paperback US $ 19.45*

*Recommended price – alterations reserved

The development of the «Zeitroman» is traced through detailed analysis of five examples of the genre, beginning with Immermann's «Die Epigonen» and concluding with H. Mann's «Im Schlaraffenland». Marking a new direction in German literature of the 19th century, the «Zeitroman» was frequently concerned with locating the changing relationship between social classes in the broad social conditions of the age portrayed. Approaches ranged in formal terms from the panoramic novels of Immermann, Spielhagen and Gutzkow to less ambitious, but artistically more satisfying works later in the century. Tensions typifying the «Zeitroman» include those between universal and ephemeral concerns, between historical documentation and a fictional rendering of reality, and between characterizing individuals and depicting an age in more abstract terms. Through examination of these varying balances, plus reference to the German «Bildungsroman» and social novels in England and France of the same period, a closer understanding is reached of the much abused term «Zeitroman».

Contents: Chapter 1: The «Zeitroman» as a form – Chapter 2: Karl Immermann: Die Epigonen – Chapter 3: Friedrich Spielhagen: Problematische Naturen – Chapter 4: Gottfried Keller: Martin Salander – Chapter 5: Theodor Fontane: Der Stechlin – Chapter 6: Heinrich Mann: Im Schlaraffenland – Chapter 7: Conclusion.

PETER LANG PUBLISHING, INC.
62 West 45th Street
USA – New York, NY 10036

Nancy A. Kaiser

SOCIAL INTEGRATION AND NARRATIVE STRUCTURE
Patterns of Realism in Auerbach, Freytag, Fontane and Raabe

New York University Ottendorfer Series. Vol. 23
ISBN 0-8204-0327-X   229 pages   paperback US $ 27.25*

*Recommended price – alterations reserved

Defining realism as a category of literary communication, this study delineates three distinct patterns of reader experience within 19th-century German Realism. In considering the interaction of text and reader as constructing the world which a «realistic» novel is often said to reflect or describe, the author coordinates an analysis of the social systems constituted within the texts with a consideration of the narrative structure. The first pattern connects village tales by Auerbach with Freytag's *Soll und Haben*. A second pattern of reader experience, demonstrated in three novels by Fontane, exposes and manipulates the mechanisms of social integration. The final pattern, two works from Raabe's Braunschweig Trilogy, undermines the middle-class reality it evokes.

Contents: Readers, Realities and Narrative Structure – Reading as Reaffirmation: Auerbach und Freytag – Social Convention and Narrative Refraction: Fontane – Narration as Disorientation: Raabe.

PETER LANG PUBLISHING, INC.
62 West 45th Street
USA – New York, NY 10036